WORDSWORTH'S POETRY

1787–1814

# WORDSWORTH'S POETRY

## 1787–1814

### BY GEOFFREY H. HARTMAN

NEW HAVEN AND LONDON

YALE UNIVERSITY PRESS

Designed by John O. C. McCrillis
and set in Linotype Baskerville type.
Printed in the United States of America by
The Carl Purington Rollins Printing-Office of the
Yale University Press.

Distributed in Great Britain, Europe, and Africa by
Yale University Press, Ltd., London; in Canada by
McGill-Queen's University Press, Montreal; in Latin America by Kaiman
& Polon, Inc., New York City; in Australasia by
Australia and New Zealand Book Co., Pty., Ltd.,
Artarmon, New South Wales; in India by UBS Publishers'
Distributors Pvt., Ltd., Delhi; in Japan by John
Weatherhill, Inc., Tokyo.

*In memoriam*

ERICH AUERBACH

And he said, Go forth, and stand upon the
mount before the Lord. And, behold, the Lord
passed by, and a great and strong wind rent
the mountains, and brake in pieces the rocks
before the Lord; but the Lord was not in the
wind: and after the wind an earthquake; but
the Lord was not in the earthquake: And
after the earthquake a fire; but the Lord was
not in the fire: and after the fire a still
small voice.

I KINGS 19:11–12

# Contents

# Retrospect 1971

It is seven years since this book appeared; and as books have their own fate, this one too has been interpreted in ways its author could not foresee. There have been many generous comments, also some misunderstandings. One critic, quite upset, reduced the book to the interesting if bloody-minded argument that Wordsworth needed to kill or violate nature in order to achieve his moments of visionary poetry. I must admit that poetry can exact a price, but I would not put it so high. Indeed, I thought my book had argued almost the reverse: that Wordsworth, deeply wary of visionary poetry of Milton's kind, foresaw a new type of consciousness, satisfied with nature, or at least not obliged to violate it in imagination. Wordsworth was haunted, certainly, by the fear that coming-to-consciousness was connected with the sense of violation or trespass: so Oswald, in *The Borderers,* "raises the consciousness" of Marmaduke by having him commit a murder. Yet the poet's utopian or saner view is that we do not have to pay a blood price for consciousness. A similar confusion underlies the argument that I was "too preoccupied with self-consciousness to give much thought to the creative or social aspects of imagination." Yet the difficult humanizing of imagination is what I chiefly followed in Wordsworth. I would not have needed to follow it if it were not a problem. Just as the first critic had little appreciation of dialectical thinking, so the second saw the counterbalanced and ideal vision rather than the labor necessary to achieve it.

I could discuss other misunderstandings but that might become an exercise in self-justification. I hope, however, that a brief summary of the book's central purposes will be helpful to old as well as new readers. It will also allow me to restate some of my themes

in terms which reflect what has interested me since the completion
of this study.

What I did, basically, was to describe Wordsworth's "conscious-
ness of consciousness." Everything else—psychology, epistemology,
religious ideas, politics—was subordinated. If that is phenomenolo-
gical procedure, so be it. I did not, however, support any special
(Hegelian, Jungian, etc.) theory of personal identity or human and
historical development. Though sometimes adducing analogies
from other writers, I tried to describe "things" strictly as they ap-
peared to the poet, while raising the question as to why he so care-
fully respected their modes of appearance. The answer given by
Wordsworth was that he had made when young a providential
error: then it was already consciousness that was appearing, not
simply things; and the blindness which caused the growing spirit
to feel not its own burden but that of natural objects (they lay upon
his mind "like substances" and "perplexed the bodily sense")
initiated a quest-romance in pursuit of the creation, one which gave
the boy's imagination time to naturalize itself, to direct its great
but uncertain powers toward the things of this world.

In short, I followed Wordsworth's self-interpretations as closely
as possible. I saw him trace certain sensory fixations, especially an
obsession with place. Haunted by the idea of a secret or sacred
"spot" on which nature seemed to converge, he rediscovered the
religious (and romance) motif of numinous places. My analysis of
how, and with what difficulty, Wordsworth's "spirit" detached
itself from "place" and raised itself to the larger, more generous
idea of "nature" showed that the notion of "spots of time" was still
indebted to that of "spirit of place." Poetic genius, in Wordsworth,
never quite freed itself of the genius loci, and in attempting to
respect these nature-involved epiphanies, he relived on the very
ground of his senses the religious struggle between Hellenic (fixed
and definite) and Hebraic (indefinite, anti-anthropomorphic) rep-
resentations of the divine.

This, too, was one of the few occasions when terms from outside
poetry seemed useful. I called the haunting-and-haunted spot an
*omphalos* (after Mircea Eliade's studies of myth) and the movement
of the mind toward it "centroversion" (after Jung's studies of the

process of individuation). Other terms could have been suggested: the power-place, though in nature (or at least sub specie naturae), could have been associated with Freud's "primal scene." I did not want to overdefine, however, and for the same reason, later in the book, did not develop the implications of calling the contrary of apocalypse an *akedah,* after the "binding" of Isaac by Abraham in Genesis 22.

The poet's development, I argued, was essentially a matter of converting apocalypse into akedah, or binding to nature, as a preparatory humanizing, an otherworldly power of imagination. "Otherworldly," in that the imagination tended to seek a separate reality and that the everyday world was often so inadequate that the imagination preferred withdrawal or ecstasy: the illusion of a life beyond life. Wordsworth rarely expressed this flight in "visionary" terms because vision was a symptom of the disease he wanted to cure. The difficulty of adjusting his reality-hunger to reality—a hunger which could paradoxically turn into an "appetite for death"— is pursued in its many changeable forms as an important, even intrinsic factor in the growth of the individual mind. Nature, fearful and beautiful, succeeds at first in attaching the child's thoughts to itself and becomes a foster home to this alien from the sphere of celestial light. But as he grows aware of what is within and separates imagination more clearly from nature (redeeming his emanation, Blake would say) the child passes from unselfconsciousness to selfconsciousness and faces all the dangers of that complex passage. He realizes both his inner strength and his vulnerability: he fears isolation yet rejoices in autonomy. In retrospect, nature is seen to have played an essential though self-transcending role in the growth of the mind. It drew the poet's fantasies toward life yet left them room; it gave him the basis for his faith that imagination was an "excursive power" able to find satisfaction in man as it had in nature.

This barest summary does not suggest the "broken windings" of the theme: Wordsworth's doubts, revisions, and vacillations—in short, the *temporalization* of insight as he moves from poem to poem or year to year. But it can suggest how complex a fate, for Wordsworth, being a poet was. How is he to interpret what he foresees, the time when nature is dumb to human imagination? Does it forebode apocalypse or simply the transition from love of nature to love of man as we mature? Since the mind is (or is to be) "lord and master," should he not write without waiting to be moved by accidents of sense, by peculiar encounters that heighten his consciousness—in other words, should he not turn from occasional and nature poetry to epic?

The self-reflections on this matter that launch *The Prelude* are well known. But Wordsworth's uncertainty reaches also into the lyrics. He refuses to classify "I wandered lonely as a cloud" as a Poem of the Imagination because "the subject of these Stanzas is rather an elementary feeling and simple impression (approaching to the nature of an ocular spectrum) upon the imaginative faculty, than an *exertion* of it." That is, the factor of accident was too strong or the inner initiative too weak. Nature had forced itself on him. This tendency to calculation, this increasingly fussy scrutiny of what moved his mind, surely hastened his decline; yet it was joined from the outset to an unusual sense of vocation. He alone stood between us and the death of nature to imagination. His subtlest feelings had a larger destiny. He was at a turning point in history which would see either a real marriage of the mind of man with nature or their apocalyptic severance.

Most of the time, of course, Wordsworth remained in conflict, unable to accept or yet to reject this extreme vocation. One part of him said, leave nature and cleave to imagination. The other part, fearing that imagination could not be cleaved to, indeed that it would take him beyond human-heartedness even out of this world, answered, cleave to nature and leave vision and romance, those errors of the childhood of poetry. Two powers, as I said somewhat dramatically, fought for his soul—Nature and Milton. His earliest verses depict a poet-figure blending spectrally features of Milton and Ossian: the reconciling ideal was both at once, imagination wedded to familiar nature rather than flying the alien air of Icarus. Milton was omnipresent not only because he was a great *native* visionary, but also because his inner conflict was similar to that in Wordsworth, and led to an exemplary re-vision of Romance. Milton's evolution from "L'Allegro" and "Il Penseroso" to *Paradise*

*Lost* transformed puerile into heroic. Milton broke through, said Keats, "the clouds which envelop so deliciously the Elysian fields of verse and committed himself to the Extreme." I tried to describe the part that Extreme played in the achievement of a poetry that so scrupulously bypassed or subsumed visionariness.

I respected, therefore, Wordsworth's great counter-myth to Milton: that Nature itself led him beyond nature and to the borders of vision. It is also, indirectly, a counter-myth to Dante; for Nature, like Virgil, is empowered to lead the poet to the upper reaches of Purgatory (to the earthly paradise he celebrated in the famous "Recluse" fragment), yet not beyond. The poet remains a "limit-our," licensed to haunt only the borders of the country from which imagination comes and to which it seeks to return. Traveling along a *via naturaliter negativa* he finds that the senses have a life of their own, an anagogical dialectic which emancipates him from them, above all from the tyranny of visuality. The euphrasy and rue which purged his eyes were Nature's own, not Vision's. To stay with nature became, therefore, a moral act: a fidelity beyond what nature itself seemed to urge. The poet's "return" was a self-covenanting on the part of imagination or will, a heroic curriculum that enlisted memory and duty in order to temper skylarking desire. By 1805 the myth was complete and Wordsworth had achieved a style (which diffused rather than densely imaged ideas of power) to go with it. He never wavered in future years from the project of marrying mind to nature.

It was mainly through style that the poet's development could be traced. The self-thwarting of sight was indicated by the poet's rigid use of the heroic couplet, the antithetical grid imposed on perception, the static or picturesque personifications, and an absurd emphasis on "spots," or spirit of place. These crude contrasts, in which sight thwarts sight, in which "the line where being ends" is constantly posited and annulled, are replaced in his blank verse by blendings, and a finer purgation of fixities. Wordsworth's mature style is characterized by an interaction of visual and visionary, perception and recollection, eye and ear, continuity and discontinuity. It scales down sublime to subtle and disperses blocking terms in a way similar to modern philosophical or psychological analysis.

Hence its organic touch, its natural mind-time. It is not, of course, without its moments of sublimity where we seem to look directly into "the life of things." Yet even when "things are lost in each other, and limits vanish, and aspirations are raised" (as he writes to Landor in 1824), Wordsworth carefully retains the genetic, matter-of-fact, earth-bound context. Things may be lost in each other but they are not lost to each other.

What moved me most, perhaps, was the poet's exceptional openness to both visionary feelings and an anxious self-scrutiny of Puritan proportions. They go together and are difficult to separate. His distrust of pure imagination—of ecstasy—is not unlike Dr. Johnson's. Margaret and the Solitary's wife (in *The Excursion*) unbind themselves from earth; and Emily in "The White Doe of Rylstone" is also in danger of losing contact when the "divine animal" brings her back. A soul has to renaturalize itself. What other poet has such honest, awkward reflections on the difficulty of binding imagination to nature or world—such husbanding of the "curious links" that weld self, or self and world, together— conjoined with great, as if contrary, passages of visionary poetry old-style in which excess of imagination triumphs and renews the poet's fear of apocalyptic dissolution? This exposedness of a mind, together with its search for "garments" *(Prelude* V. 24)—for mediations drawn from self-experience—was the burden of my book.

I did not neglect the historical milieu, but neither did I offer it as an explanation. In a strange way the violence in France as well as the slower trauma of industrialization coincided with Wordsworth's inner sense of irreparable change: they foreboded a cosmic wounding of Nature—of natural rhythms, of organic growth— which reinforced his fear of an apocalyptic rate of change and nature-loss. The last ten years have made us more sensitive to Wordsworth's anxiety for nature. Apocalypse is not habitable. Yet I did not achieve, or seek, a single transvaluing insight that might derive from Wordsworth a systematic view of human development. I remained more interested in "error"—in the process and particulars of what the evolving mind thinks of as an emergence from error—than in the poet's anticipation of modern findings. In some sense *emergence* itself, our unsteady growth into self-consciousness, became the subject.

Perhaps Wordsworth never did emerge to an assured sense of self or a decisive poetry. There is something peculiar in the way his text corrupts itself: the freshness of earlier versions is dimmed by scruples and qualifications, by revisions that usually overlay rather than deepen insight. I should have paid some attention to this problem but was more interested, I now see, in the integrity of the mind than in that of the single poem. I wanted to identify the forces ranged against emergence, against the achievement of a humane imagination, and I did not count among these forces intellectual confusion or a Coleridgean metaphysical hangover. The situation seemed more complex than that. It seemed, indeed, as perplexing as the one glimpsed by Freud when he surmised that the death instinct was in the midst of life and embraced the libido. The *antithetical* forces to development had no single discernible locus or identity: Wordsworth insisted on the creativeness of the mind and foretold its wedding to nature, yet what I saw mainly was the solipsism inherent in a great imagination, the despair tracking apocalyptic hope, the disabling shadow of ecstatic memories, and passion betrayed into compulsive empathy. All that could be said with certainty was that the antithetical resided inside life, that strength somehow obstructed itself, and that to heighten consciousness was to intensify rather than assuage the sense of isolation.

At several points in the book I approached a general theory linking verbal figures and structures of consciousness. But I managed to evade my own insight and to remain with Wordsworth instead of translating him into decisive modernisms. There is, surely, a relation between the overdetermined or centroverted character of the omphalos and that of the symbol. The flight from these charged places of discourse or imagination—through doublings, circlings, the generation of personae, metaphorical transference, and syntactical distribution—suggests a vital schizophrenia or decentering expressive of so much in personal growth. It is like moving away from parental or idolatrous fixation toward the cultivation of a love that is more than pointedly sexual, or like the overcoming of eye concepts that block sense experience. There is a line of descent to be established between lyrical narratives like "The Thorn," which converge so strongly and frustratingly on an ocular center we are never sure of (has a crime been committed there, or is the crime an illusion to stimulate crude imaginations?), and lyrical movies like Antonioni's *Blow-up* and Resnais's *Last Year at Marienbad*. The center they converge on is an absence; the darkness they illumine has no heart.

Take Wordsworth's lightest mystery story, "Strange fits of passion." Can we discern its poetics?

> Strange fits of passion have I known:
> And I will dare to tell,
> But in the Lover's ear alone,
> What once to me befel.
>
> When she I loved looked every day
> Fresh as a rose in June,
> I to her cottage bent my way,
> Beneath an evening moon,
>
> Upon the moon I fixed my eye,
> All over the wide lea;
> With quickening pace my horse drew nigh
> Those paths so dear to me.
>
> And now we reached the orchard-plot;
> And, as we climbed the hill,
> The sinking moon to Lucy's cot
> Came near, and nearer still.
>
> In one of those sweet dreams I slept,
> Kind Nature's gentlest boon!
> And all the while my eyes I kept
> On the descending moon.
>
> My horse moved on; hoof after hoof
> He raised, and never stopped:
> When down behind the cottage roof,
> At once, the bright moon dropped.
>
> What fond and wayward thoughts will slide
> Into a Lover's head!
> "O mercy!" to myself I cried,
> "If Lucy should be dead!"

The lyric has more *error* (anticlimax, illusion, mismatching of event and meaning) than *center*. The action is now too slow and now too fast, now overstated (first stanza) and now understated (last stanza). A "wayward" comment on wayfaring, it opens on a ballad note of high adventure yet from that perspective the almost plotless story is an anticlimax. A word like "fits" is equally unsettled, not quite at home in its vernacular sense nor quite referable to its archaic provenance (faict → fact = act = section of a ballad or romance). The rider too is strangely displaced. Is he man plus horse, or a becalmed knight from Romance? He is certainly not the conventional hotspur of ballad tradition, and his night ride has a touch of parody. Instead of sparking hooves and a charged message, a gentle distractable trot. All is "error" in this poem: the lover's mind wanders.

Or does it? It is not over-anticipating, taking the moon as its mark, so that it is already where it wishes to be—with the beloved, and beyond a changeable, sublunar world? So that it is, after all, haste ridden like a ballad hero's?

Such strong anticipation or omening—call it *futuring*—is both expressed and limited by Wordsworth's poetics of error. In mood, style, and subject, his poems are a defense against ecstasy of this kind. Ecstasy, in which the soul goes out of the body, becomes ordinary and almost funny (a "fit"). We sense the psychopathology of everyday life as the rider approaches an invisible boundary, the point at which he will go through into another world. He never does; when he wakes from his trance or dream he is very much in this world, and we do not know where his mind has been. The crash—the moment proper of discovery—is leaped or avoided. The poem swerves from this "center" or hovers between natural events and the intimation of an ecstatic sphere—just as the moon itself is a borderer, separating starry and mortal worlds.

The poets, we know, anticipated Freud, but depth analysis will not explain this poem any more than romance does. It is with both and with neither. Its figurative life is not a displaced life but the very movement of imagination's eccentric path. Because imagination leaps over time, because a star almost halts the traveler (his consciousness of the way), the narrative movement stalls and tends to collapse almost as soon as begun. This means, structurally, that the poem's middle—the narrative proper—barely keeps beginning and end apart as they converge. In "A slumber did my spirit seal" (where the slumber corresponds to the trance of "Strange fits") this convergence has already taken place, leaving only two stanzas as poles of the vanished narrative, and the center a blank.

Can we at least identify the poles? They are related, clearly, to "imagination" and "nature," to "romance" and "realism." Yet they veer, converge, or cross. You fall, in Wordsworth, from the abyss of ideality (stanza one of "A slumber") to the abyss of temporality (stanza two), or vice versa. You never remain *in* nature or *in* imagination. Let us say, then, that the lover of "Strange fits" rides into the poem out of Romance. He is still appareled, like the child of the Great Ode, with an aura not purely of this world. And let us admit that were he to ride out of the poem it would be into trauma. But losing his way he remains in a poem that mediates the poles.

*New Haven, Conn.*

# Preface

The view of Wordsworth presented in this book covers three things: the individual poem, the sequence of the poems, and the generic relation of poetry to the mind. Since Wordsworth is directly concerned with the growth of the individual mind, a study of the first two subjects connects easily and fruitfully with the last.

I state a thesis in the first part and support it by an analysis of four poems. The second part expands the implications of the thesis and applies it to three episodes of *The Prelude*. The third part studies the thesis in its most dynamic form: as it illumines the development of Wordsworth's poetry from 1787 to 1814. There might have been a further chapter dealing with Romantic poetry in general, but I have restricted myself to hints on this.*

Minute stylistic or structural analysis has been avoided, except for a few "close-ups," notably pp. 61–67 and 203 ff., and technical terms have been held to a minimum. Some are inevitable: just as the terms of seventeenth-century rhetoric are now familiar to us— one of the really fruitful endeavors of modern scholarship has been to describe older poets by means of the rhetoric or poetics which they helped to evolve—so perhaps the terms suggested by Words-worth himself, or carefully extrapolated from his practice, may in time become familiar and serve larger, synoptic purposes. Yet there is, here, a methodological problem. The Romantics have not yet completely succeeded in creating either the taste by which they might be enjoyed or the terms which best describe their practice. There are many reasons for this; I will mention only one, that

---

* In "Romanticism and Anti-Self-Consciousness," *Centennial Review* (Autumn 1962), I do, however, express some tentative generalizations.

they are not often read in a context that is large enough. Spenser, Donne, Jonson, Crashaw, and Milton are seen *through* the very traditions they continued or reformed; they are nobly supported by that largest international movement, the Renaissance; and when we study the relation of Donne to meditational techniques or of Jonson to the plain style or of Spenser and Milton to Epic, we are put in touch with currents larger than English, and from which, indeed, the specifically English quality of these writers was often to be generated. It is not surprising, therefore, that the Romantic poets must also be placed in a larger context, either by considering them parts of an international and modern movement, or by linking them to their native sources in the Renaissance. When I talk of the humanizing of imagination, the reader will be reminded of a great theme initiated in the Renaissance, exacerbated by the Enlightenment, and brought to its crucial modern form in Wordsworth. When I talk of self-consciousness, the reader will be reminded of a contemporary European (but also American) phenomenon.

One term, not technical, requires special comment. By "apocalyptic," as in "apocalyptic imagination," I intend the Apocalypse of St. John (the Book of Revelation), and, more generally, the kind of imagination that is concerned with the supernatural and especially the Last Things. The term may also describe a mind which actively desires the inauguration of a totally new epoch, whether preceding or following the end of days.* And since what stands between us and the end of the (old) world is the world, I sometimes use "apocalyptic" to characterize any strong desire to cast out nature and to achieve an unmediated contact with the principle of things.

The critical bibliographies for each chapter should rightly be called personal bibliographies: they indicate what I have found

* A distinction might be made between millennial and apocalyptic thinking, but they are crucially and often ambiguously joined in both the Book of Revelation and the history of its exegesis. See E. L. Tuveson, *Millennium and Utopia* (Berkeley and Los Angeles, 1949), and M. H. Abrams, "English Romanticism: The Spirit of the Age," in *Romanticism Reconsidered,* ed. Northrop Frye (New York and London, 1963), esp. pp. 30–60.

useful and best and do not seek to be exhaustive. They can be taken
to suggest the limits of my reading. Yet I have tried to review what
is central in modern interpretations of Wordsworth. To offer a
mere listing would be redundant at a time when there are excellent
annual and specialized bibliographies, and when the *MLA* volume
on the English Romantic Poets and such useful pamphlets as that
of Henley and Stam can bring earlier gatherings up to date. I did
not wish, at the same time, to omit all reference to alternative or
parallel points of view. I do not consider my approach exclusive,
but sustaining a thesis required a certain purity in the matter of
exposition. The notes and bibliographies reintroduce perspectives
that might be additionally considered.

My approach is comprehensive, but I regret that it is not com-
prehensive enough. *Peter Bell* should have found a niche; it is typi-
cal and curious and has an important polemical history. "Laoda-
mia" is omitted and the sonnets are slighted. The important issue
of Wordsworth's relation to words as such is treated only in pass-
ing. Wordsworth's theory of words, except for the significant at-
tack on poetic diction, took the form of poetry rather than prose,
and is more reticent than in Coleridge, Hopkins, or the modern
poet. But his unique style, in which metaphor (transference) is
a generalized structure rather than a special verbal figure, though
I have tried to describe it, remains unexplored in its larger impli-
cations.

I have not dwelt on, or schematized, an emerging Phenomenology
of Mind. The drama of consciousness and maturation, being faced
directly, with Adamite vision—a "Power like one of Nature's"—
and communicated more hesitantly, though with a strange and in-
novative plainness, is what I attempted to follow. "The matter of
the greatest interest," said Ortega y Gasset in an essay on Goethe, "is
not the man's struggle . . . with his external destiny, but his struggle
with his vocation." This is a book about Wordsworth's vocation, his
struggle with it, and the authenticity of that struggle.

It is a pleasure to acknowledge many obligations. To Yale Uni-
versity and the University of Iowa for free time and financial aid.
To the editors of *PMLA,* the *Journal of English and Germanic
Philology,* and *Modern Philology* (© University of Chicago Press)

for permission to reprint articles which first appeared in their journals. To John C. Gerber and J. C. Weaver for their encouragement; to the trustees and librarian of Dove Cottage, Grasmere, and to George Healey, curator of the Wordsworth Collection at Cornell, for indispensable help. I have benefited greatly from the advice of Alvin Feinman, Lila and Ralph Freedman, Liliane and Thomas Greene, E. D. Hirsch, Cecil Y. Lang, Henri Peyre, Martin Price, and Amélie and Richard Rorty. I want above all to express my gratitude to those who advised me on the completed manuscript: Harold Bloom, F. A. Pottle, J. C. Stillinger, and René Wellek. René Wellek and Frederick Pottle have taken a generous interest in this book from its inception; Jack Stillinger's eyes saved me from error; and from Harold Bloom I have received criticism, comfort, and conversation during the whole time of its writing. My wife, Renée, has helped me at every stage, fulfilling Genesis 2:18. I dedicate this book to a scholar whom I knew too short a time but whose example was as strong as his work was great-hearted.

*Iowa City, Iowa*
*November 1963*

Geoffrey Hartman


A few corrections, too minor to be specified, have been made in this reissue. The Critical Bibliographies are not brought up to date except for articles of exceptional importance: it would need a supplementary essay to do justice to the work of the last years. I would like to mention, however, two older items slighted by me. I appreciate more now the final pages of F. W. Bateson's *Wordsworth*. The poet, says Bateson, achieved greatness "because his private struggles toward psychic integration have a representative quality." We differ in our description of this "integration," and of Wordsworth's "sickness," but agree on the presence of a "daimon" and the exemplary character of the poet's struggle with it. Like Bateson, Joseph Texte stressed Wordsworth's "daimon" in an essay indebted to Legouis (see Texte's *Études de Littérature Européenne,* 1898). France, he says, reduced the author of *The Prelude* "to the modest rank of poet of childhood and family-life. It has contemptuously neglected the thinker. . . ." After correcting the French image of the poet, Texte wonders whether Wordsworth might achieve in the next century his proper place in European letters. Seventy years after that query, and almost a hundred years after Arnold placed him among the principal poets of the modern period, Wordsworth's affinity to the great European Romantics—to Rousseau, Hölderlin, Hegel, and others—is still not fully appreciated. It is my hope that the present book, though it abstains from explicit literary comparisons, can clarify that affinity.

*March 1967*

G. H.

# I. THESIS: THE HALTED TRAVELER

*Siste, viator*

# I. "The Solitary Reaper"

Wordsworth records in "The Solitary Reaper" his reaction to an ordinary incident. What others might have passed by produces a strong emotional response in him, therefore the imperatives: Behold, Stop here, O listen! His response rather than the image causing it is his subject, yet he keeps the latter in mind and returns to it, especially in the last stanza, so that our attention is drawn to a continuous yet indefinite relationship between mind and image, each of which retains a certain autonomy.

To value Wordsworth's emotions is sometimes hard. Coleridge, his most sympathetic critic, is surely right in saying that they may be "disproportionate to such knowledge and value of objects described, as can be fairly anticipated of men in general, even of the most cultivated classes."[1] Wordsworth quite consciously distinguished his "lyrical" ballads from the popular poetry of the day by allowing feeling to "give importance to the action and the situation, and not the action and situation to the feeling."[2] Now this problem of the appropriateness or decorum of the poet's feelings may seem to be a rather simple one, to be resolved not a priori but by individual critical decision, or by these decisions insofar as they indicate a consensus. One might agree, for instance, that the feelings developed in "The Solitary Reaper" are appropriate and that the poem as a whole is a success, while those expressed in the stanzas on the daisy (already mocked by *The Simpliciad*) are too big for their subject. Wordsworth criticism, however, does not provide a consensus that effectively separates his mental or emotional bombast from appropriate lyrical effusion.

Today, for example, no objection is made to Wordsworth's lyric on the daffodils ("I wandered lonely as a cloud"). It seems as fine a poem as "The Solitary Reaper." Yet Coleridge thought its last stanza excessive in its stated emotion,[3] and Anna Seward, a not un-romantic bluestocking, waxes almost hysterical about it. "Surely Wordsworth must be as mad as was ever the poet Lee," she writes in her only extended comment on his poetry.[4] "Those volumes of his* . . . have excited, by turns, my tenderness and warm admiration, my contemptuous astonishment and disgust. The two latter rose to their utmost height while I read about his dancing daffodils, ten thousand, as he says, in high dance in the breeze beside the river, whose waves dance with them, and the poet's heart, we are told, danced too. Then he proceeds to say, that in the hours of pensive or of pained contemplation, these same capering flowers flash on his memory, and his heart, losing its cares, dances with them again." After dismissing the poem with the irony of paraphrase, she rises to the final thunder of invective: "Surely if his worst foe had chosen to caricature this egotistic manufacturer of metaphysic importance upon trivial themes, he could not have done it more effectually!" This is the same poem A. C. Bradley called "a pretty thing" that "could scarcely excite derision"; and which F. A. Pottle considers at length in *Wordsworth Centenary Studies* because of the very feature which so disturbed Anna Seward, the strange crescendo of those "capering flowers."[5]

Although there is no consensus, it is clear that a crux in Words-worth criticism was established early. Anna Seward is not alone in her opinions. Contemporary opposition to Wordsworth and the Lake School, whether based on a principle of decorum, the doc-trine of general nature, or deeply ingrained social and religious dif-fidence, tended to center on what Keats termed the "egotistical sublime." Keats' comment on this fault in Wordsworth[6] is signifi-cant in that it should repeat (in a finer tone, as it were) Anna Sew-ard's objection and that Coleridge and Jeffrey should ally them-selves in reprehending a new species of bombast that is laid to the poet's excessive involvement in random, personal experience.[7]

Wordsworth's egotism, however, would have been beneath notice had it not contained something precariously "spiritual" which was

---

* *Poems in Two Volumes* (1807).

not exhausted by his overt choice of scenes from low or rural life. Those who objected to Wordsworth often commended Burns, Crabbe, and even Robert Bloomfield, and the magazine poetry of the 1790's is full of compassionate subjects, rural themes, and personal reflections.[8] Modest Christian sentiment was welcome, and to "suck Divinity" (or even metaphysics) from daffodils[9] was too common a poetic indulgence to have roused the contemptuous disgust of a literary lady. What is so precariously spiritual about Wordsworth, and so difficult to separate from egotism, is the minute attention he gives to his own most casual responses, a finer attention than is given to the nature he responds to. He rarely counts the streaks of the tulip, but he constantly details the state of his mind. When Wordsworth depicts an object he is also depicting himself or, rather, a truth about himself, a self-acquired revelation. There is very little "energetic" picture-making in him.[10]

I call this aspect of Wordsworth's poetry spiritual because its only real justification (which few of his contemporaries were willing to entertain) was that it carried the Puritan quest for evidences of election into the most ordinary emotional contexts. Wordsworth did not himself talk of election or salvation but, as we shall see, of renovation (regeneration), and he did not seem to be directly aware of his Puritan heritage, although the *Poems* of 1807, which includes both "I wandered lonely as a cloud" and "The Solitary Reaper," shows a heightened intimacy with seventeenth-century traditions.[11] Failure or access of emotion (inspiration) vis-à-vis nature was the basis of his spiritual life: his soul either kindled in contact with nature or it died. There was no such thing as a casual joy or disappointment. Such 'justification by nature' was not, however, a simple matter, to be determined by one experience—Wordsworth's response is often delayed for a considerable time. His spirit may be "shy," or stirrings may rise from almost forgotten depths. It was on reading a sentence in a friend's manuscript (Wilkinson's "Tour in Scotland") that the two-year-old memory of the solitary reaper returned to him;[12] and though the poem does not record this directly, it reflects an analogous fact, that the imagination was revived from an unsuspected source.

Anna Seward might have reached new heights of indignation

had she known the religious and metaphysical effusion in Book VI of *The Prelude,* drawn from the poet when he remembers and interprets a mood fourteen years old.[13] Religion cannot wait on such freaks of the heart. The heart's response, moreover, is always too great or too small; and since without this disproportion there is no such thing as man conscious of himself, we see how precarious Wordsworth's condition is, how inevitably linked to a self-consciousness that may seem egotistical. Yet I confess I am moved by a poet so faithful to his condition, so totally "spiritual" that the most insignificant mood is weighed because it should be significant of something beyond itself, of some actual or hidden relation to the possibilities of self-renewal.

It is a dangerous half-truth, however, to connect Wordsworth's spirituality with habits of introspection spread abroad by such different movements as Protestantism, Rationalism, and Rousseauism. No doubt, as Mme. de Staël said, with her inexhaustible talent for charming vulgarization, while "the ancients had, so to say, a corporeal soul whose motions were strong, direct, and efficacious . . . the soul of the moderns, nourished by Christian repentance, has fallen into the habit of continually returning on itself."[14] As important, however, as the shared fact of self-consciousness is the way each poet faces it. "The Solitary Reaper" is not a brooding analytic inquiry into the source of an emotion. The poet does not explain why he responded so strongly to the Highland girl but takes advantage of the strength of his response. After expressing the fact that he is moved, he allows the emotion its own life and delights in new accesses of thought and feeling. A poet, we read in the preface to *Lyrical Ballads,* "rejoices more than other men in the spirit of life that is in him."

Neither is this the whole truth, for the poet's spirit, tinged by melancholy, is not completely free-moving. Some burden of mystery is present, linked to his initial mood. To take this mood as expressing nothing more than surprise is to dispel the mystery too quickly. Though the poem begins in surprise—an ordinary sight is modified by an unusual circumstance: the harvester is alone and her song heightens the solitude where communal and joyful activity was expected—surprise turns into something pensive, even elegiac. There is an inward sinking, as if the mind, having been moved by the Highland girl, is now moved by itself. The mystery lies in that sudden deepening, or doubled shock.

I put this in the form of an impression but the text supports it. If the first imperative, "Behold her, single in the field," is addressed to the reader, the second, "Stop here, or gently pass," is certainly said also by the poet to himself. The inward sinking or turning—the reflexive consciousness—is quite clear. The poet himself is made to stop, reflect, and listen, like a traveler who has come on the scene by chance. An image has "singled" him out.[15]

At the end of the first stanza, moreover, we are still in the shadow of the mystery and uncertain why the poet is moved. His third imperative, "O listen!," again addressed either to an auditor or to himself, is followed by an explanation ("for the Vale profound / Is overflowing with the sound") which explains nothing. It would be inane if "listen" did not suggest an activity more intense than hearing, and if "overflowing" did not heighten the idea of strong emotional participation. Even the vale seems to be moved: and should not a passerby, therefore, stop and respond? It would be ungenerous not to enter into communion.

The question why the poet is moved is subordinated to the fact *that* he is moved, that his mind overflows under the influence of song. While the poem begins with a girl who is alone in her work and in her song, which is not expressly for others but which she sings to herself, she and her song reach across the valley to halt the traveler, who then resumes his journey with music in his heart. The last lines of the poem,

> The music in my heart I bore,
> Long after it was heard no more,

have a literal and an extended meaning, which collaborate to express response, repercussion, overflow. The poet heard the girl inwardly after he had passed out of actual range of hearing (the literal import), yet the "long after" may be taken to reach to the moment of composition two years later. "The Solitary Reaper" is evidence that the song has survived in his heart.

The overflow of the poet's feelings, and the pleasure he takes in

each new mood or thought, can be traced stage by stage. In the
second stanza he has already traveled, as through a magic casement,
beyond the immediate scene, and though he returns to the present
in stanza three, it is only to begin a new 'dallying with surmise.'*
Even the question on which he returns is significant. "Will no one
tell me what she sings?" is a sociable gesture revealing how the song
has spread beyond itself to cause this appeal he whimsically makes.
His new address to the reader blends outward-directed feeling and
inward-going thought.

The third stanza, composed of two surmises, continues to ad-
vance *through* the solitary to the social.[16] Does the song, it is asked,
"flow" for sufferings associated with a historical or mythical past, or
does it treat of familiar things, past, present, and future? This re-
turn to the familiar, and from the fixed past to the more open "has
been, and may be again," is characteristically Wordsworthian and
anticipates the "something evermore about to be" toward which the
poem tends. For in the final stanza, though Wordsworth gives up
surmise and reverts to the indicative, his variations of the central
word (sang, song, singing), his circling back to the figure of the
girl at work (is she in a laboring or a thoughtful attitude?), and his
first use of feminine rhyme ("ending" / "bending") modify the
matter-of-factness of the event. As the poet returns in thought from
one solitary, the girl, to another, himself, and therefore uses the "I"
more overtly than before, the power for communion in so random
an image, and its indefinite echo, are acknowledged. A finitude is
removed from the verbs as from the action.

Thus Wordsworth, under the impress of a powerful feeling,
turns round both it and its apparent cause, respecting both and
never reducing the one to the other. By surmise he multiplies his
moods, if not the phenomenon. His surmises have a pattern, which
is to proceed through the solitary to the social and from stasis to
motion, or to make these interchangeable. Yet everything stays in
the realm of surmise, which approves, in any case, of such fluidity.
Surmise is fluid in nature; it likes "whether . . . or" formulations,
alternatives rather than exclusions, echoing conjecture (Keats' "Do

---

* Milton, "Lycidas," line 153.

I wake or sleep?") rather than blunt determinateness. The actual is in some way the potential, and in "The Solitary Reaper" surmise has unobtrusively influenced even the rhythm and certain verbal figures. Such a line as "Stop here, *or* gently pass" (my italics) is directed in theme and format against the purely determinate. The line contains, in fact, one of the many 'fluidifying' doublings of this poem ("Reaping and singing," "cuts and binds," "Things, and battles," "Perhaps . . . or"). Because the second phrase of each doubling is expanded thematically or in the number of syllables or by an equally subtle increment, the effect is that of expansion: "cuts and binds" flows into "and sings," and a parallel lengthening occurs in each stanza, whose symmetry is beautifully disturbed by the fourth line of six syllables, which expands into regular tetrameter at the end.

An exhaustive analysis of verbal effects is not necessary and may even distract us. The essential fact is that Wordsworth allows the sudden emotion (or, in the daffodil poem, sudden optical impression) to invade and renew his mind instead of reducing the emotion by an act of mind. Knowing that his relation to nature is as unpredictable as a relation of Grace—that whether or not he originally responded, and whether or not he responded fully, the encounter has a secret life that may later flash out and renew his feelings—Wordsworth adopts the stance of surmise which points to liberty and expansiveness of spirit. In "The Solitary Reaper" it is impossible to distinguish what originally happened from what happened to the mental traveler in the field of Wilkinson's prose. But however we construe the situation, Wordsworth's response reflects the importance of surmise both in his own and in Romantic lyricism.

I would like to deal briefly with the enlarged role of surmise in Romantic poetry by comparing Milton at his most Romantic with Wordsworth and Keats. Milton resorts to surmise when he wishes to "interpose a little ease" during his lament for Lycidas. To make death seem less deadly he turns first to the old pastoral myth of sympathetic Nature and calls on the Sicilian Muse (the Muse of Bion, Theocritus, and others who originally used the myth) to bid all flowers mourn his friend. A gorgeous *anthology* follows, in which each flower is evocatively invoked (lines 133–51), but Chris-

tian honesty then compels Milton to dismiss this consoling picture
as a dallying with "false surmise" (line 153) and to proceed to a
more painful conjecture that culminates in the truer "ease" of Res-
urrection:

> Ay me! Whilst thee the shores, and sounding Seas
> Wash far away, where'er thy bones are hurl'd,
> Whether beyond the stormy *Hebrides,*
> Where thou perhaps under the whelming tide
> Visit'st the bottom of the monstrous world;
> Or whether thou to our moist vows denied,
> Sleep'st by the fable of *Bellerus* old,
> Where the great vision of the guarded Mount
> Looks toward *Namancos* and *Bayona's* hold;
> Look homeward Angel now, and melt with ruth:
> And, O ye *Dolphins,* waft the hapless youth.
>     Weep no more, woeful Shepherds weep no more,
> For *Lycidas* your sorrow is not dead.

The "surmise" might be thought an ad hoc invention of Mil-
ton's, but it is actually a specific rhetorical figure developed by him
from Classical sources.[17] My purpose being prospective rather than
retrospective, it is sufficient to indicate that he did use the surmise
as a conscious and distinct figure of thought. His most striking use
of it outside "Lycidas" comes in *Paradise Lost* (I.740–46), where
another "false surmise" interrupts the narrative and tempts us with
a charming pagan fable. Milton's pastoral evocation of Mulciber's
fall from heaven, sheer mythopoeic embroidery of a hint from *The
Iliad,* is immediately followed by the harsh disclaimer: "thus they
[the Pagans] relate / Erring. . . ." Yet while the fable is being told,
our mind is released from the harsh pressure of a higher truth, and
a meditative pause, not irreconcilable with Christian inwardness,
calms the poem.[18]

If "Lycidas" is compared with "The Solitary Reaper" and Keats'
odes, it is apparent that surmise is no longer an exceptional figure
of thought but an inalienable part of the poetry. The poem itself is
now largely surmise, a false surmise perhaps, but the poet has
nothing else to dally with, and the distinction is less between false

and true than between surmise and surmise. This too is an unsatis-
factory formulation of the difference, for the single projections add
up to more than their sum: they revive in us the capacity for the
virtual, a trembling of the imagined on the brink of the real, a sus-
tained inner freedom in the face of death, disbelief, and fact.[19]

All is surmise in "The Solitary Reaper" except the startled open-
ing: the poet's mind swings far from the present to which it keeps
returning until raised to the virtue of the song it hears, apposing to
the song the mind's own flowingness. In Keats' odes, however, there
is from the outset a strong attempt to transcend surmise, to turn it
into real vision, and his poems are this flight and faltering. Words-
worth's more leisurely procedure can lead to a dangerous prolixity
rarely felt in Keats; through Keats' sharper vacillations, moreover,
we once again feel "the surmise" as a separate movement, although
this separateness is not intellectual, as in Milton, but based on lev-
els of imaginative intensity. Surmise, for Keats, is the middle-
ground of imaginative activity, not reaching to vision, not falling
into blankness. Stanza five of "Ode to a Nightingale," which owes
a specific debt to Milton's flower passage in "Lycidas," and which
by its profuse tenderness, and this reminiscence, anticipates an ease-
ful death, is a perfect expression of the mood of surmise as such:[20]

> I cannot see what flowers are at my feet,
> Nor what soft incense hangs upon the boughs,
> But, in embalmed darkness, guess each sweet
> Wherewith the seasonable month endows
> The grass, the thicket, and the fruit-tree wild. . . .

It might be useful to consider the Romantic lyric as a develop-
ment of the surmise. We have no proper definition, formal or his-
torical, of this kind of lyric, which disconcertingly turns all terms
descriptive of mode into terms descriptive of mood. When we say,
for example, that "The Solitary Reaper" is a blend of idyll and
elegy we refer more to states of mind expressed by it than to formal
genres. Though the surmise is not a genre originally, it is a specific
rhetorical form whose rise and modifications one can trace and
which significantly becomes a genre in the Romantic period.

Yet the designation "a lyric of surmise" would be too simple and

artificial. In "The Solitary Reaper," as in Keats' ode ("Darkling I
listen . . ."), surmise is tinged by a *penseroso* element that sinks
toward melancholy. Romantic lyricism, pensiveness, and melan-
choly are interrelated, even if the exact nature of the relation has
remained obscure. We know that surmise expresses the freedom of
a mind aware of itself, aware and not afraid of its moods or poten-
tialities—what darker burden, then, is expressed by this "dewy"
melancholy?[21]

These questions of mood, and the relation of mood to mode, are
clarified by a strange line in Wordsworth's poem. "Stop here, or
gently pass" is a variant of apostrophes to the passing traveler found
on gravestones or commemorative statues. "Look well upon this
statue, stranger," is the opening of one of Theocritus' *Inscriptions*.
Again: "Stand and look at Archilochus, the old maker of iambic
verse." This is sometimes coupled with the wish that soil or tomb
lie lightly on the dead man: "Blessed be this tomb for lying so
light above the sacred head of Eurymedon."[22] Wordsworth's poem
is linked to the epitaph, though we do not know immediately what
valor or virtue it mourns, and though it is strange that a harvest
scene should suggest this memento mori to the poet. The traveler—
man, the secular pilgrim—is halted by an affecting image. And
something peculiar in the image, or the suspension itself of habit-
ual motion, or an ensuing, meditative consciousness, brings him
into the shadow of death. That shadow is lightened or subsumed as
the poem proceeds, and the unusual image pointing like an epitaph
to the passerby is transformed into a more internal inscription testi-
fying of continuance rather than death: "The music in my heart I
bore, / Long after it was heard no more."

The reflective stopping of the poet, which is like the shock of
self-consciousness and may express it in a mild and already dis-
tanced form, is a general feature of Romantic lyricism and related
to its penseroso or "white" melancholy. The halted traveler, of
course, does not always appear so clearly and dramatically. But a
meditative slowing of time—a real deepening of mind-time or self-
consciousness—is always present and often sharply announced, as in
the first strong beats of "My heart aches" (Keats) or the absolute-
ness of "A sudden blow . . ." (Yeats). In Wordsworth's poetry local

traditions of genre are still felt, and many of his poems are recognizably cognate with the Epitaph, or at least the Inscription: the latter is the most contemporary way of being Classical about Spirit of Place. One of Wordsworth's first genuinely lyrical poems is such an epitaph-inscription, namely the "Lines left upon a Seat in a Yew-tree which stands near the Lake of Esthwaite"; and even the "Lines composed a few miles above Tintern Abbey," with their specific registry of place and date and a distinctly elegiac and memorializing strain, carry some marks of the genre they transcend.[23]

Is there a more archetypal situation for the self-conscious mind than this figure of the halted traveler confronting an inscription, confronting the knowledge of death and startled by it into feeling "the burden of the mystery"? Two problems remain, however, one of which is peculiar to Wordsworth and the other more general, touching on the Romantic as such. The first broaches again the mystery of the poet's initial response. That strangely intense response, never directly explained within the poem, is part of the frame or donnée of a situation now identified as an access—a new birth—of self-consciousness. "No one," says Willard Sperry, "has come to the heart of Wordsworth's verse unless he is fully aware of the poet's quickened subjectivity in the presence of one or another of his chosen subjects from the outer world."[24] But why should *this* scene have renewed or intensified his self-awareness?

Biography can enter here in a limited way. The original incident stems from a tour made in 1803; this tour elicited a number of poems gathered later under the title of "Memorials," most of which are elegiac in mood, memorials in more than one sense. They include verses written at the grave of Burns, of Rob Roy, and of "Ossian." Others are ballads, and there are also commemorative sonnets and inscriptions.[25] The North Country, it appears, associated with Burns and the bards and ballad singers of old, was to Wordsworth a poetic ground as sacred as the "South Country" (the Mediterranean) to other Romantics. The song of the Highland girl is probably an Erse ballad, whether composed long ago or contemporaneous with Burns. It should also be noted that "The Solitary Reaper" was not written till 1805, the year Wordsworth lost his brother, and the year preceding the "Elegiac Stanzas" on Peele

Castle, with the darkest lines, perhaps, that Wordsworth ever wrote: "A power is gone, which nothing can restore; / A deep distress hath humaniz'd my soul."

Though this context should be respected in some way, it cannot explain the poet's reaction to the solitary reaper unless his poem is melancholy simply by association and he has transferred to it his sadness on his brother's death, or his thoughts on dead poets, or even on the death of communal poetry in touch with "nature." All this may well be present, but unless we feel that the relation of mood to incident is incongruous, we must suppose these personal facts are subsumed like the genre of the epitaph itself, and that the true way to relate them to the poem is via the poem, which is their center rather than vice versa.

Allowing, then, the poem to integrate the biography of the poet, we come on the following reason for its intense opening. The unusual solitariness and melancholy of the harvester may have suggested that the link between harvesting and joy—"they that sow in tears shall reap in joy"*—is broken; that a natural order is reversed. The idea of reversal could have deepened under the pressure of the context already detailed. Wordsworth forebodes a betrayal, a harvest of death rather than life. "In nature there is nothing melancholy," Coleridge had argued in a poem addressed to William and Dorothy[26] and which denies that the nightingale is, as Milton had said, "most musical, most melancholy." (Milton's description, says Coleridge, has only a dramatic propriety, being spoken in the character of "il penseroso.") Yet the human nightingale Wordsworth hears in the Highlands is of this melancholy species: an alien note has entered her song, she is no "skylark warbling in the sky," no "happy Child of earth."[27] She reminds the poet that there is no harvest except death or through death. This thought is almost explicit, some years before John Wordsworth drowned, in a poem already haunted by the apparent defeat or reversal of the promise of Nature. Wordsworth again reflects on a passage from scripture and implicitly compares his faith to that of the lilies of the field (Matthew 6):

* Psalm 126:5, one of the psalms of exile.

My whole life I have lived in pleasant thought,
As if life's business were a summer mood;
As if all needful things would come unsought
To genial faith, still rich in genial good;
But how can He expect that others should
Build for him, sow for him, and at his call
Love him, who for himself will take no heed at all?

I thought of Chatterton, the marvellous Boy,
The sleepless Soul that perished in his pride;
Of Him who walked in glory and in joy
Following his plough, along the mountain-side;
By our own spirits are we deified:
We Poets in our youth begin in gladness;
But thereof come in the end despondency and madness.[28]

The poet's elegiac response to the Highland girl is, of course, converted into a consolation, an "eternity structure"[29] of a kind. The song he hears spreads sociably from one person to another over great spaces of fantasy and solitude. It flows and overflows; it transcends the finitude of self and the fixity of self-consciousness. It continues secretly in the poet's heart, and its idea later revives the image that inspires the poem.

The larger question to be answered is whether self-consciousness and Wordsworth's lyricism are connected in an intrinsic and more than occasional way. May self-consciousness, as well as having a bearing on the subject or form of a particular poem, be related also to the very nature of poetry, at least of Wordsworth's poetry?

The startled, yet subdued, opening of "The Solitary Reaper" is, as we have seen, not fortuitous. In fact, the more typical a Wordsworth poem the more it arises "from some incident which, for him, had a novel and arresting character and came on his mind with a certain shock; and if we do not get back to this through the poem, we remain outside it."[30] This shock, though consonant with the ordinary mechanism of heightened awareness, may also be, as some poems indicate explicitly, a "conversion" or "turning" of the mind. "My mind turned round," Wordsworth can say, "As with the might of waters."[31] In the Lucy poem, "Strange fits of passion," the moon dropping suddenly behind the cottage roof engenders as suddenly a thought of death, and if the poet mutes its implication (it is called "fond and wayward") the thought has some truth, as the ensuing poems telling of Lucy's death suggest. Is Wordsworth aggrandizing the prophetic character of ordinary perception or subduing an extraordinary perception? In "The Solitary Reaper," likewise, ordinary attention blends with a stronger awareness (call it imagination or revelation) as if the poet were afraid of distinguishing them too precisely.

We can understand the blending best if we suppose that the "Behold" by which Wordsworth's attention is engaged or redirected signals the influx of an unusual state of consciousness which is quickly normalized. A Wordsworth poem is then seen to be a *reaction* to this consciousness as well as its *expression*. "The Solitary Reaper" may be viewed as the product of two kinds of consciousness, old and new, ordinary and supervening, which gather in tension around the precipitating image. This view introduces a dialectical factor and considers the poem as the synthesis of a mind in conflict with itself.

There is an episode, perhaps the most significant in *The Prelude,* which shows the poet in the actual grip of the special consciousness we are positing. There, too, a halted traveler appears. In 1804, describing how he and a friend crossed the Alps some fourteen years earlier, Wordsworth is usurped by something in his mind which is both a new interpretation of the episode and a new state of consciousness, and he records the fact in place:

> Imagination—here the Power so called
> Through sad incompetence of human speech,
> That awful Power rose from the mind's abyss
> Like an unfathered vapour that enwraps,
> At once, some lonely traveller. I was lost;
> Halted without an effort to break through.[32]

To this episode, considered in its context, we shall return in the second part of this book. An ecstatic passage follows (ending with line 616) in which Wordsworth does break through to resolve partially the stasis, for the usurping consciousness produces its own rush of verses, becomes its own subject as it were, and so retains momentarily a separate existence. Wordsworth calls this separate consciousness "Imagination."

It is a strange name to give it. Imagination, we are usually told, vitalizes and animates. Especially the Romantic Imagination. Yet here it stands closer to death than life, at least in its immediate effect. The poet is isolated and immobilized by it; it obscures rather than reveals nature; the light of the senses goes out. Only in its secondary action does it vitalize and animate, and even then not nature but a soul that realizes its individual greatness, a greatness independent of sense and circumstance. A tertiary effect does finally reach nature, when the soul assured of inner or independent sources of strength goes out from and of itself.

However removed this episode is from "The Solitary Reaper," the halting of the traveler in that poem is also more than part of the random context. It expresses a sudden consciousness and is quietly linked to a memento mori. The great difference, indeed, is that this consciousness blends at once and imperceptibly with a new state or rather motion of mind, stasis being replaced by an evolving sense of continuity, till the traveler proceeds on his journey. The supervening consciousness does not have an abrupt and strongly separate existence as in *Prelude* VI. There is a pause, the mind sinks toward an intimation of death, but the vital rhythm is restored almost at once, and only an echo of that pause remains, as in the desert image and Hebrides-silence of stanza two. The initial halting, so quickly countervailed, is at the source of many Wordsworth poems, and it is time to identify its character precisely. Together with the poem that is at once its overflow and masking, it will tell us something significant about the relation of poetry to the mind.

A definition can now be offered. The supervening consciousness, which Wordsworth names Imagination in *Prelude* VI, and which also halts the mental traveler in the Highlands, is *consciousness of self raised to apocalyptic pitch*. The effects of "Imagination" are always the same: a moment of arrest, the ordinary vital continuum being interrupted; a separation of the traveler-poet from familiar nature; a thought of death or judgment or of the reversal of what is

taken to be the order of nature; a feeling of solitude or loss or sepa-
ration. Not all of these need be present at the same time, and some
are obliquely present. But the most important consequence is the
poem itself, whose developing structure is an expressive reaction
to this consciousness. The poem transforms static into continuous
by a gradual crescendo which is the obverse of the fixating initial
shock. The Highland girl, a single, lonely figure, startles Words-
worth into an exceptionally strong self-consciousness, yet no stark
feelings enter a poem which mellows them from the beginning.
The poem here is on the side of "nature"* and against the "imagi-
nation" which fathered it; it hides the intense and even apocalyptic
self-consciousness from which it took its rise; it is generically a veil-
ing of its source.

It may be objected that Wordsworth rarely associates imagina-
tion and apocalypse. His tendency, indeed, is to deny any intrinsic
link between imagination and the supernatural. "Peter Bell," he
writes, "was composed under a belief that the Imagination not
only does not require for its exercise the intervention of supernat-
ural agency, but that, though such agency be excluded, the faculty
may be called forth as imperiously, and for kindred results of
pleasure, by incidents within the compass of poetic probability, in
the humblest departments of daily life."[33] Yet here, as always, it is
the evidence of the poems which is decisive; the prose, in fact, de-
pends for its sense on the poetry. Wordsworth, in his comment on
*Peter Bell,* is talking of the *already naturalized* imagination. His
hope is that the imagination can be domesticated, that nature can
satisfy a mind which seeks, or used to seek, the supernatural. Imagi-
nation is consciousness of self at its highest pitch (or an immediate
imaginal reaction to this), but Wordsworth writes in the faith that
Nature will suffice the energies of consciousness. The full story of
how he arrived at that faith is given in *The Prelude,* from which I
now choose one of the earliest passages to be composed, the story of
the Boy of Winander. It shows Nature both fostering and modify-
ing the growing self-consciousness of the child.

---

* The poem begins in a disturbance of the idea of nature or natural order,
which is then subsumed.

## 2. The Boy of Winander

The tumultuous mimicry of the Boy of Winander is interrupted by a pause which parallels the other haltings. The pause affects the youngster by gently foretelling, and already fashioning, a later state of mind. His relation to nature must change from glad animal movements to a calmer and more conscious love. The episode went originally with others from the poet's childhood found in Books I and II, and illustrated how the child is moved gently and unhurt toward the consciousness of nature's separate life, this being an early step in the growth of the mind.

In *Prelude* V there is a slight displacement from this theme to accommodate it to the book's argument: as well as suggesting the gradualism of this process, Wordsworth supports the more general idea of how resourcefully nature educates a boy entrusted to her rather than to a human agency. She is not held to single expedients, to an unvarying course of generative or regenerative action. Her infinite resources mock the presumptuous followers of Rousseau, educators who treat children like engines, confining them by a timetable scheme of development and seeking to eliminate idleness and fruitful accidents.

In both versions of the episode, however, the idea that nature leads the child into consciousness of nature is accompanied by the idea that she forms the child the more deeply as her action is less consciously present to him. Wordsworth knows that there must be "shock," but his doublings qualify the notion that shock is nature's only or primary means. By a beautiful diminuendo the awareness (of nature as Nature) seeded in that pause between the hootings becomes "a gentle shock of mild surprise" and is followed by the further qualification, "or . . . unawares." The suggestion of "Severer interventions, ministry / More palpable" (*Prelude* I.355–56) is minimized.

By this mild guidance the Boy of Winander reaches a sense of nature's, and perhaps his own, separate life. But he dies before self-consciousness can fully emerge. The boy's death (no cause given) is related in a second paragraph, though the first indicates the fulfillment of a scheme that would lead him via consciousness of nature to consciousness of Self. A later comment of Wordsworth's shows that his theme was growth and immortality, not death: the binding of imagination by nature for the mutual benefit of both. "Guided by one of my own primary consciousnesses," he writes, "I have represented [in this sketch] a commutation and transfer of internal feelings, co-operating with external accidents to plant, for immortality, images of sound and sight, in the celestial soil of the Imagination."[1] In one of the early manuscripts, moreover, the Boy of Winander is identified as Wordsworth himself ("And when it chanced / That pauses of deep silence mocked *my* skill," etc.),[2] so that the death of the Boy may have been an afterthought, strangely self-referring, and perhaps contrary to the episode's first intent. The episode is, in any case, contemporaneous with the Lucy poems, which also tell of a mysterious death and were composed in Germany during the early winter of 1798–99.[3]

As in "The Solitary Reaper," therefore, we encounter a mysterious and supervening thought of death. The simplest explanation for it is that Wordsworth, sensitive to audience reaction, may have felt "There was a Boy" needed a literal context. To publish it as it stood might crudely puzzle his readers: There was a Boy, and —what happened to him? For the original sketch is a lyrical ballad in that it emphasizes "character" rather than "incident," psychology rather than plot. As to its rhetorical form, it is merely an elaborate sentence. The completed sketch, however, nicely rounded by converting a figurative death into an actual, yields to the prevalent taste and becomes a beautifully extended epitaph (There was a Boy, and—he died).

Yet Wordsworth cannot squelch his own genius. The conventionalizing incident becomes a new shock to popular taste, as Jeffrey's reaction showed. Jeffrey did not see the point of Wordsworth standing dumbly, a full half-hour, at the boy's grave.[4] (Many, like-wise, would not see the point of "Simon Lee," as the poet antici-pated by humorously self-conscious interpolations.) Though rounding off his sketch and making an incident out of an inward action, Wordsworth injects a new emphasis on inwardness. The strange half-hour pause suggests that he looks not only at some-thing external, a grave, but also at something within, his former heart. Thus the original meaning of "There was a Boy" is retained (if we agree to weigh the elegiac implication of "was"): the poet is mourning the loss of a prior mode of being but meditates on the necessity of a loss which leads into matured awareness. "Other gifts have followed."

This interpretation of the second paragraph accords with other considerations. The timing of the boy's death and the tone in which it is narrated remind us strongly of the Lucy poems. Both Lucy and the Boy of Winander die before consciousness of self can emerge wholly from consciousness of nature. (Of the Lucy poems it would be more exact to say before the poet's conscious-ness of Lucy's individuated and mortal nature can emerge.) It is as if the Boy of Winander were fated to reach a developmental im-passe. Growing further into consciousness means a simultaneous development into death (i.e. the loss of a previous, joyfully unself-conscious mode of being), and not growing further also means death (animal tranquillity, absorption by nature). The space or ellipsis between paragraphs one and two, which should be com-pared to that between stanzas one and two of "A slumber did my spirit seal," points to that impasse, or precarious transition. Now, in one sense, every mature human being does bridge it, and Words-worth indicates as much by replacing the boy with himself: he *was* a boy like that, but has now become self-conscious and aware of mortality. In another sense, however, no one crosses that gulf, at least not intact: the survivor contemplates his own buried child-hood.

The Boy of Winander, then, dies at a crossroads in human life. Instead of waking from consciousness of nature into consciousness of self, he falls like Sleeping Beauty into the gentler continuum and quasi immortality of nature. He will experience no discontinuity, no uprooting; the places of his birth and death could not be closer: "Fair is the spot, most beautiful the vale / Where he was born; the grassy churchyard hangs / Upon a slope above the village school."[5] Perhaps it is better thus to die into nature than to survive one's former self. The poet who stands at the child's grave knows that consciousness is always *of* death, a confrontation of the self with a buried self.

The poet at the grave is, in fact, a type of the halted traveler. Yet the crisis of recognition—the shock of self-consciousness—is once more elided. A forgetful gaze, a downward and inward look (the very emblem of surmise or meditation) displaces a naked peripety. Though the link between consciousness and discontinuity is established by an insidious lapse from tumult to silence to death, while the poet's "full half-hour" gaze, by a similar crescendo-diminution, seems to lengthen the "lengthened pause" that baffled the child, encompassing presences soon make themselves felt:* the churchyard in which Wordsworth stands overhangs the village school; the "throned Lady" of the church sits atop her green hill forgetful of the grave at her feet, listening only to the rising sounds of children at play. The poet's ideal, stated clearly in *Prelude* V.425, is "Knowledge not purchased by the loss of power"; and it is because the wages of knowledge are death that the other death, by which Nature takes the child to herself, appears merciful.

* In the first paragraph the implication of a discontinuity intrinsic to human development yet possibly fatal to it is practically submerged by the depiction of the beauties of nature enveloping the child. The paragraph starts with a broken phrase, "There was a Boy," an elegiac opening accentuated by the syntactical break: on this short phrase the whole description hinges, like a countermovement dispelling a tragic thought almost before the words are out. We think not of death but of the continuous natural presences, of stars rising and setting, of the responsive owls, of the generous circle of influences. The version here discussed is that of the 1805 *Prelude* V.423 ff.; the version printed in the 1800 *Lyrical Ballads* ends with the poet gazing mutely at the boy's grave.

# 3.   "Strange Fits of Passion . . ."

We turn again to a traveler. The first stanza of this Lucy poem differs in tone from the others: its "fits" and "dare" contrast with the understatement that follows and show that the poem is a "lyrical" ballad, preferring mood to the ballad-mongers' stock-in-trade of supernatural or extraordinary incidents. "To freeze the blood I have no ready arts."[1] The poem ironically evades the broadside crudity announced in its prologue.

Yet Wordsworth's innovations are always more than rhetorical. We can say of him that he grounded rhetoric in the heart, as Yeats grounded (or felt he did) mythology in the earth. By its understatement and rhetoric of implication, the poem again rejects a naked rendering of the moment of self-consciousness (or of the peripety that could bring it on), though expressing a mind moving ever closer to it. The *point* of the experience is displaced, appearing as "fond and wayward."

The thought of death intervenes here in explicit form. It is no less mysterious, however, for being explicit: the relationship between it and the omen is not transpicuous. To take the moon's drop as the direct cause of the thought assumes that the lover has identified his beloved with the moon. This is exactly what he has done, but why he has been psychically able to establish a link between Lucy and the moon, and, again, between the moon's drop and Lucy's death (no thought of Lucy's dying haunts the poet consciously during that ride; "When she I loved looked every day / Fresh as a rose in June"[2]) is not easily explained.

The moon is not a static symbol but part of an action. Its sudden drop punctuates a hypnotic progress. As the rider draws near the cottage, his eyes fixed on the moon, the moon also draws near the cottage. Lucy seems to be their common center. The hypnotic ride lasts from the second stanza to the fifth, in which the lines:

> My horse moved on; hoof after hoof
> He raised, and never stopped,

suggest a monotone and supernatural slowing,* motion approaching yet never quite attaining its end, and the horse advancing, as it were, apart from the rider, who is somewhere else. At this point the moon's drop breaks the hypnosis, stops the action, and releases a presage of death.

At the climax, there is no consciousness intervening between horse and moon: a horse climbs on by itself toward a bright moon. The only way to interpret this ghostliness (or depersonalization) is to suppose that the sense of self has been elided, that rider and moon approaching the cottage in the infinity of a slowed moment express powerfully an obscure resistance: resistance to a concentering action that draws them together to one point, the 'point' of self. The dropping of the moon then snaps the poet into self-awareness and an oblique ("wayward") thought of death. As long as his movement toward the 'center' is gentle, a continuous motion rather than an abruptly achieved stasis, the poet dwells in a dream state in which the mortal self—that vulnerable point at the center of being—is forgotten and the illusion of deathlessness takes over. But when the dream ("Kind Nature's gentlest boon") is broken, self-consciousness returns, and with it the thought of death.

This interpretation should not destroy the poem as a love poem. Its subject remains a going out of the self toward the beloved, but the "ek-stasis" is linked to a more general need of which love and poetry are the strongest results: "a going out of our own nature," as Shelley says, "and an identification of ourselves with the beautiful which exists in thought, action, or person, not our own."[3] This identification is inherently incomplete: Lucy, by the very fact of

---

* The lines come after the word "moon" in a rhyme position: moon . . . moon, my horse "moved on"; "hoof after hoof"; notice also the accumulation of spirants (h) not quite elided, just articulate enough to force a slowing division (helped by the monosyllables) between the words.

being loved, is something more than herself, becomes a landscape even (the moon, "those paths so dear to me"), and may not appear as only a person. The unconscious yet natural transfer from Lucy to the moon (also a single figure, cf. "Fair as a star, when only one / Is shining in the sky")[4] already denotes the power of love to draw the self out of itself, though still toward an image which is incipiently a new fixation.

## 4. "Tintern Abbey"

The halting of the traveler in "Tintern Abbey" is felt more in the slowed rhythm and meditative elaboration of its first lines than as part of the casual frame. We begin with "Five years have past," a phrase as quietly elegiac as "There was a Boy," and again a countervailing movement is felt at once. It is expressed by a peculiar type of redundance and indicates resistance to abrupt progression. The feminine caesurae (winters, waters, murmur) plus echoing sound enrich our sense of inwardness and continuity. It is no single means that produces the lingering or "lengthening" effect also present in The Boy of Winander passage, and which a metrical scholar might wish to analyze as an intensification of quantitative values. As in all blank verse it is the pace (or breathing) which most immediately affects us, and this depends in good part on the distribution of pauses, on subtle organic or meditative haltings. However precarious an amateur rhythmical analysis may be, I am tempted to say that in the opening verses of "Tintern Abbey," as well as in other sections, there is a *wave effect* of rhythm whose characteristic is that while there is internal acceleration, the feeling of climax is avoided. For example, as the rhythm reaches toward a peak, the resistance of the verse becomes more pronounced, and we find heavier overflow lines, either early breaking (3 and 7 syllable) or late subsiding (7 and 3 syllable), while an already loose sentence may be loosened still more (lines 19 ff.). Even when many eddies of a loose sentence seem to build up to a quasi-climactic point, a further statement, sometimes an understatement, comes to relax them once more. We can rarely tell, in fact, whether the "wave" is rising or falling:

> For I have learned
> To look on nature, not as in the hour
> Of thoughtless youth; but hearing oftentimes
> The still, sad music of humanity,
> Nor harsh nor grating, though of ample power
> To chasten and subdue.

Carried by a strong explicative particle and a negative, the first lines lead the reader to anticipate a forceful "but": yet Wordsworth breaks the rhythm by a semicolon (a favorite check), and instead of introducing a second main verb, he lets the construction trail into the form of a loose sentence. "Hearing" depends, despite the semicolon, on "to look on nature" and introduces one long unbroken verse, immediately qualified by several phrases having the effect of eddies.

I connect this rhythm with the shying from peripety or abrupt illumination, here as in other poems. On the thematic level, however, it is linked in "Tintern Abbey" to a vacillating calculus of gain and loss, of hope and doubt: Wordsworth remarks in a note to the 1800 edition of *Lyrical Ballads* that though he did not venture to call his poem an ode, "it was written with a hope that in the transitions, and impassioned music of the versification, would be found the principal requisites of that species of composition." This note I have never seen entirely explained; it must mean that Wordsworth is distilling from the versification itself, and probably from the informal transitions of one verse paragraph to another, an emotional analogue to the *turn* and *counterturn* of the traditional Sublime Ode.

By this wavering rhythm the halted consciousness flows precariously into the continuousness of meditation. Wordsworth, though sensing his mortality—that nature can no longer renew his genial spirits—continues to go out of himself and toward nature. His sight gradually expands into communion. A sentence from "Tintern Abbey" may start with the first person yet end on "all things"; and that which has moved the poet sometimes, somewhere, as a personal feeling, becomes a principle animating the world.

And I have felt
A presence that disturbs me with the joy
Of elevated thoughts; a sense sublime
Of something far more deeply interfused,
Whose dwelling is the light of setting suns,
And the round ocean and the living air,
And the blue sky, and in the mind of man:
A motion and a spirit, that impels
All thinking things, all objects of all thought,
And rolls through all things.

Thus the "I hear," "I see," and "I have felt," these simple personal acts, open a sustained movement of surmise ranging through present, past, and future, and raising the indicative mood of the first paragraph to the freer optative of the last.

The individual mind, its shadowy self-exploration, is always felt in "Tintern Abbey." Wordsworth journeys, by a typical descent, into landscape and mental landscape, to find at mutual depth an image of the "sole self" (the Hermit). This *descensus,* or deepening of the mind, is prophetic in purpose. The living mind questions nature to find an omen of its destiny. The contrary of hope, for the religious man, is fear for his salvation; and for the man whose sense of separate and mortal being is especially strong, as with Donne and his "sin of fear" (the last and greatest of these), or with Wordsworth and his subtler doubts, the labor of faith is to overcome that fear of an absolute death, of a final separation from the sources of renewal. In the last paragraph of "Tintern Abbey" the halted traveler faces once more these fears and tries to overcome them. Wordsworth turns from nature to Dorothy, and what could have been an inscription poem, written not far from a ruined abbey and addressed implicitly to the passing Stranger, is now directed to the person at his side, "Thou my dearest Friend, My dear, dear Friend." It becomes a vow, a prayer, an inscription for Dorothy's heart, an intimation of how this moment can survive the speaker's death. Binding the landscape, his memory of the landscape and of his sister, and even his sister's future mind, into a single skein of

life, Wordsworth foresees the survival of his kind ot fidelity to
nature:

> Nor, perchance—
> If I should be where I no more can hear
> Thy voice, nor catch from thy wild eyes these gleams
> Of past existence—wilt thou then forget
> That on the banks of this delightful stream
> We stood together; and that I, so long
> A worshipper of Nature, hither came
> Unwearied in that service: rather say
> With warmer love—oh! with far deeper zeal
> Of holier love. Nor wilt thou then forget,
> That after many wanderings, many years
> Of absence, these steep woods and lofty cliffs,
> And this green pastoral landscape, were to me
> More dear, both for themselves and for thy sake!

Death in the shape of a god-sent plague; a voice from the whirl-
wind; a still small voice; the inscription on a grave; a sudden calm;
an image that waylays; such interpositions, mild or terrible, make
a man stop, consider, remember his end and his beginning:

> Here must thou be, O Man!
> Strength to thyself; no Helper hast thou here;
> Here keepest thou thy individual state.[1]

Wordsworth is as "self-haunting" a spirit as Coleridge. Yet his
imagination flowed with nature's aid back into nature. To join
imagination to what both Wordsworth and Spinoza call Intellec-
tual Love is the solitary work, the solitude-redeeming labor, of
which the poet speaks at the end of *The Prelude*.

The summons to self-consciousness is rarely presented by Words-
worth as violent and supernatural.[2] Anything in nature stirs him
and renews in turn his sense for nature. But this is already the
perspective of hope and salvation. It is sometimes forgotten that
Wordsworth's poetry looks back in order to look forward the bet-

ter. The poet's great hope lies in unviolent regeneration and nature appears to him in the light of a hope which nature itself
originally kindled. The story of how nature came to be associated
so strongly with this anti-apocalyptic view of regeneration, and
poetry with nature, is told in the following pages. It is first considered synoptically, via several crucial episodes in *The Prelude,*
then studied chronologically, to do fuller justice to the growth of
a notion and the development of a poet.

# II. SYNOPSIS: THE VIA NATURALITER NEGATIVA

*I do not know the man so bold*
*He dare in lonely place*
*That awful stranger Consciousness*
*Deliberately face—*
　　　　　—EMILY DICKINSON

*Beguiled . . . to the very heart of loss.*
　　—ANTONY AND CLEOPATRA IV.12.29

Many readers have felt that Wordsworth's poetry honors and even worships nature. In this they have the support of Blake, a man so sensitive to any trace of "Natural Religion" that he is said to have blamed some verses of Wordsworth's for a bowel complaint which almost killed him.[1] Scholarship, luckily, tempers the affections, and the majority of readers have emphasized the poet's progression from nature worship or even pantheism to a highly qualified form of natural religion, with increasing awareness of the "ennobling interchange" between mind and nature and a late yielding of primacy to the activity of the mind or the idealizing power of imagination. A very small group, finally, has pointed to the deeply paradoxical character of Wordsworth's dealings with nature and suggested that what he calls imagination may be *intrinsically* opposed to nature.[2] This last and rarest position seems to me closest to the truth, yet I do not feel it conflicts totally with more traditional readings stressing the poet's adherence to nature. It can be shown, via several important episodes of *The Prelude*, that Wordsworth thought nature itself led him beyond nature; and, since this movement of transcendence, related to what mystics have called the negative way, is inherent in life and achieved without violent or ascetic discipline, one can think of it as the progress of a soul which is *naturaliter negativa*.

1.

*The Prelude* opens with a success immediately followed by a failure. Released from the "vast city" and anticipating a new freedom, the poet pours out a rush of fifty lines: "poetic numbers came / Spontaneously to clothe in priestly robe / A renovated spirit" (I.51–53).[3] Here is the consecration, the promise of poetry as a sacrament, a gift efficacious beyond the moment. Why should a chance inspiration assume such significance? The reason is that Wordsworth was not used to make "A present joy the matter of a song"; yet here, apparently, is evidence that he may soon become self-creative, or need no more than a "gentle breeze" (the untraditional muse of the epic's opening) to produce a tempest of poetry. "Matins and vespers of harmonious verse!" is the hope held out to him, and having punctually performed matins the poet is content to slacken, to be gradually calmed by the clear autumn afternoon.

He meditates beneath a tree on a great poetic work soon to be begun. The sun sets, and city smoke is "ruralised" by distance. He starts to continue his journey, but now it is clearly time for vespers:

> It was a splendid evening, and my soul
> Once more made trial of her strength, nor lacked
> Aeolian visitations. (I.94–96)

An outside splendor challenges the creative mind. Is the poet strong enough to answer it spontaneously, as if he needed only a suggestion, the first chord?

> but the harp
> Was soon defrauded, and the banded host
> Of harmony dispersed in straggling sounds,
> And lastly utter silence! "Be it so;
> Why think of any thing but present good?" (I.96–100)

Wordsworth once again sees present good, like present joy, strangely opposed to the quickening of verse. The poetic outburst which he had considered a religious thing ("punctual service high . . . holy services") is now disdained as profane and *servile:*

> So, like a home-bound labourer I pursued
> My way beneath the mellowing sun, that shed
> Mild influence; nor left in me one wish
> Again to bend the Sabbath of that time
> To a servile yoke. (I.101–05)

His reversal of mood is surprisingly complete. One who, at the
impassioned outset of his reflections, had been so sure of the freely
creative, autonomous nature of his poetic soul that famous pas-
sages on the emancipated spirit—from *Paradise Lost* and Exodus[4]
—swell the current of his verse, while he thinks to possess total free-
dom of choice,

> now free,
> Free as a bird to settle where I will (I.8–9)

that same person now writes of himself, with a slight echo of Gray's
*Elegy:*

> So, like a home-bound labourer I pursued
> My way.

The meaning of the reversal is not immediately clear. It does
not deject the poet; it endows him, on the contrary, with a Chauce-
rian kind of cheer and leisure:

> What need of many words?
> A pleasant loitering journey, through three days
> Continued, brought me to my hermitage.
> I spare to tell of what ensued, the life
> In common things—the endless store of things. (I.105–09)

The form of the reversal is that of a return to nature, at least to its
rhythm. For the moment no haste remains, no tempest, no impa-
tience of spirit. It is the mood of the hawthorn shade, of a portion
of Wordsworth's Cambridge days, when he laughed with Chaucer
and heard him, while birds sang, tell tales of love (III.278–81).

In the exultant first lines of *The Prelude,* Wordsworth had fore-
seen the spirit's power to become self-creative. Though fostered by
nature it eventually outgrows its dependence, sings and storms at
will (I.33–38). The poet's anticipation of autonomy is probably
less a matter of pride than of necessity: he will steal the initiative
from nature so as to freely serve or sustain the natural world should
its hold on the affections slacken. His poetic power, though admit-
tedly in nature's gift, must perpetuate, like consecration, vital if

transitory feelings. Without poetry the supreme moment is nothing.

> Dear Liberty! Yet what would it avail
> But for a gift that consecrates the joy? (I.31–32)

But he is taught that the desire for immediate consecrations is a wrong form of worship. The world demands a devotion less external and willful, a wise passiveness which the creative will may profane. The tempest "vexing its own creation" is replaced by a "mellowing sun, that shed / Mild influence." Nature keeps the initiative. The mind at its most free is still part of a deep mood of weathers.

Wordsworth's failure to consecrate, through verse, the splendid evening is only the last event in this reversal. It begins with the poet placing (so to say) the cart before the horse, Poetry before Nature: "To the open fields I told / A prophecy: poetic numbers came . . ." (I.50 ff.). He never, of course, forgets the double agency of inward and outward which informs every act of poetry. So his heart's frost is said to be broken by both outer and inner winds (I.38 ff.).[5] Such reciprocity is at the heart of all his poems. Yet he continually anticipates a movement of transcendence: Nature proposes but the Poet disposes. Just as the breeze engendered in the mind a self-quickening tempest, so poetry, the voice from that tempest, re-echoing in the mind whence it came, seems to increase there its perfection (I.55 ff.). The origin of the whole moves farther from its starting point in the external world. A *personal* agent replaces that of nature: "I paced on . . . down I sate . . . slackening my thoughts by choice" (I.60 ff.). There is a world of difference between this subtle bravado and the ascendancy of *impersonal* constructions in the final episode: "Be it so; / Why think of any thing but . . . What need of many words? . . . I pursued / My way . . . A pleasant loitering journey . . . brought me to my hermitage."

This change, admittedly, is almost too fine for common language. Syntax becomes a major device but not a consistent one. In the 1850 text, while the poet muses in the green, shady place, certain neoclassical patterns, such as the noble passive combined with synecdoche, create an atmosphere in which personal and impersonal, active and passive, blend strongly:

> Many were the thoughts
> Encouraged and dismissed, till choice was made
> Of a known Vale, whither my feet should turn. (I.70–72)

Devices still more subtle come into play. In the passage immediately preceding, Wordsworth describes the quiet autumn afternoon:

> a day
> With silver clouds, and sunshine on the grass,
> And in the sheltered and the sheltering grove
> A perfect stillness. (I.67–70)

"Sheltered and sheltering"—typical Wordsworthian verbosity? The redundance, however, does suggest that whatever is happening here happens in more than one place; compare "silver clouds, and sunshine on the grass." The locus doubles, redoubles: that two-fold agency which seems to center on the poet is active all around to the same incremental effect. The grove, sheltered, shelters in turn, and makes "A perfect stillness." The poet, in a sense, is only a single focus to something universally active. He muses on this intensifying stillness, and within him rises a picture, gazing on which with *growing* love "a higher power / Than Fancy" enters to affirm his musings. The reciprocal and incremental movement, mentioned explicitly in I.31 ff., occurs this time quite unself-consciously, clearly within the setting and through the general influences of Nature.

No wonder, then, that the city, which the poet still strove to shake off in the first lines, appears now not only distant but also "ruralised," taking on the colors of nature, as inclosed by it as the poet's own thought. The last act of the reversal is the episode of the splendid sunset. Wordsworth not only cannot, he *need* not steal the initiative from nature. Her locus is universal, not individual; she acts by expedients deeper than will or thought. Wordsworth's failure intensifies his sense of a principle of generosity in nature. That initial cry of faith, "I cannot miss my way" (I.18), becomes true, but not because of his own power. The song loses its way.

Wordsworth's first experience is symptomatic of his creative difficulties. One impulse vexes the creative spirit into self-depend-

ence, the other exhibits nature as that spirit's highest object. The
poet is driven at the same time from and toward the external
world. No sooner has he begun to enjoy his Chaucerian leisure
than restiveness breaks in. The "pilgrim," despite "the life / In
common things—the endless store of things," cannot rest content
with his hermitage's sabbath. Higher hopes, "airy phantasies,"
clamor for life (I.114 ff.). The poet's account of his creative diffi-
culties (I.146–269) documents in full his vacillation between a
natural and a more than natural theme, between a Romantic tale
and one of "natural heroes," or "a tale from my own heart" and
"some philosophic song"—but he adds, swinging back to the more
humble, "Of Truth that cherishes our daily life." Is this inde-
terminacy the end at which nature aims, this curious and never
fully clarified restlessness the ultimate confession of his poetry?

It would be hard, in that case, to think of *The Prelude* as de-
scribing the "growth of a poet's mind"; for what the first part of
Book I records is, primarily, Wordsworth's failure to be a visionary
or epic poet in the tradition of Spenser and Milton. No poem of
epic length or ambition ever started like his. The epic poet begins
confidently by stating his subject, boasts a little about the valor of
his attempt, and calls on the Muse to help him. Yet Wordsworth's
confident opening is deceptive. He starts indeed with a rush of
verses which are in fact a kind of self-quotation, because his sub-
ject is poetry or the mind which has separated from nature and
here celebrates its coming-of-age by generously returning to it.
After this one moment of confidence, all is problematic. The song
loses its way, the proud opening is followed by an experience of
aphasia, and Wordsworth begins the story of the growth of his
mind to prove, at least to himself, that nature had intended him to
be a poet. Was it for this, he asks, for this timidity or indecision,
that nature spent all her care (I.269 ff.)? Did not nature, by a
process of both accommodation and weaning, foster the spirit's
autonomy from childhood on? Yet when the spirit tries to seize the
initiative, to quicken of itself like Ezekiel's chariot, either nature
humbles it or Wordsworth humbles himself before her. "Thus
my days," says Wordsworth sadly, "are past / In contradiction; with
no skill to part / Vague longing, haply bred by want of power, /

From paramount impulse not to be withstood, / A timorous capacity from prudence, / From circumspection, infinite delay" (I.237–42).

Wordsworth never achieved his philosophic song. *Prelude* and *Excursion* are no more than "ante-chapels" to the "gothic church" of his unfinished work. An unresolved opposition between Imagination and Nature prevents him from becoming a visionary poet. It is a paradox, though not an unfruitful one, that he should scrupulously record nature's workmanship, which prepares the soul for its independence from sense-experience, yet refrain to use that independence out of respect of nature. His greatest verse *still takes its origin* in the memory of given experiences to which he is often pedantically faithful. He adheres, apparently against nature, to natural fact.

### 2.

There are many who feel that Wordsworth could have been as great a poet as Milton but for this return to nature, this shrinking from visionary subjects. Is Wordsworth afraid of his own imagination? Now we have, in *The Prelude,* an exceptional incident in which the poet comes, as it were, face to face with his imagination. This incident has many points in common with the opening event of *The Prelude;* it also, for example, tells the story of a failure of the mind vis-à-vis the external world. I refer to the poet's crossing of the Alps, in which his adventurous spirit is again rebuffed by nature, though by its strong absence rather than presence. His mind, desperately and unself-knowingly in search of a nature adequate to deep childhood impressions, finds instead *itself,* and has to acknowledge that nature is no longer its proper subject or home. Despite this recognition, Wordsworth continues to bend back the energy of his mind and of his poem to nature, but not before we have learned the secret behind his fidelity.

Having finished his third year of studies at Cambridge, Wordsworth goes on a walking tour of France and Switzerland. It is the summer of 1790, the French Revolution has achieved its greatest success and acts as a subtle, though, in the following books, increasingly human background to his concern with nature. Setting out to cross the Alps by way of the Simplon Pass, he and a friend are separated from their companions and try to ascend by themselves. After climbing some time and not overtaking anyone, they meet a peasant who tells them they must return to their starting point and follow a stream down instead of further ascending, i.e. they had already, and without knowing it, crossed the Alps. Disappointed, "For still we had hopes that pointed to the clouds," they start downward beset by a "melancholy slackening," which, however, is soon dislodged (VI.557–91, 616 ff.).

This naive event stands, however, within a larger, interdependent series of happenings: an unexpected revelation comes almost immediately (624–40), and the sequence is preceded by a parallel disappointment with the natural world followed by a compensatory vision (523 ff.). In addition to this pattern of blankness and revelation, of the soulless image and the sudden renewed immediacy of nature, we find a strange instance of the past flowing into the present. Wordsworth, after telling the story of his disappointment, is suddenly, in the very moment of composition, overpowered by a feeling of glory to which he gives expression in rapturous, almost self-obscuring lines (VI.592 ff.). Not until the moment of composition, some fourteen years after the event,[6] does the real reason behind his upward climb and subsequent melancholy slackening strike home; and it strikes so hard that he gives to the power in him, revealed by the extinction of the immediate external motive (his desire to cross the Alps) and by the abyss of intervening years, the explicit name Imagination:

> Imagination—here the Power so called
> Through sad incompetence of human speech,
> That awful Power rose from the mind's abyss
> Like an unfathered vapour that enwraps,
> At once, some lonely traveller. I was lost;
> Halted without an effort to break through;
> But to my conscious soul I now can say—
> "I recognise thy glory." (VI.592–99)

Thus Wordsworth's failure vis-à-vis nature (or its failure vis-à-vis him) is doubly redeemed. After descending, and passing through a gloomy strait (621 ff.), he encounters a magnificent view. And crossing, one might say, the gloomy gulf of time, his disappointment becomes retrospectively a prophetic instance of that blindness to the external world which is the tragic, pervasive, and necessary condition of the mature poet. His failure of 1790 taught him gently what now (1804) literally *blinds* him: the independence of imagination from nature.

I cannot miss my way, the poet exults in the opening verses of *The Prelude*. And he cannot, as long as he respects the guidance of nature, which leads him along a gradual via negativa to make his soul more than "a mere pensioner / On outward forms" (VI. 737 f.). It is not easy, however, to "follow Nature." The path, in fact, becomes so circuitous that a poet follows least when he thinks he follows most. For he must cross a strait where the external image is lost yet suddenly revived with more than original immediacy. Thus a gentle breeze, in the first book, calls forth a tempest of verse, but a splendid evening wanes into silence. A magnificent hope, in the sixth book, dies for lack of sensuous food, but fourteen years later the simple memory of failure calls up that hope in a magnificent tempest of verse. When the external stimulus is too clearly present the poet falls mute and corroborates Blake's strongest objection: "Natural Objects always did and now do weaken, deaden, and obliterate Imagination in Me."[7] The poet is forced to discover the autonomy of his imagination, its independence from present joy, from strong outward stimuli—but this discovery, which means a passing of the initiative from nature to imagination, is brought on gradually, mercifully.

Wordsworth does not sustain the encounter with Imagination. His direct cry is broken off, replaced by an impersonal construction—"here the Power." It is not Imagination but his "conscious soul" he addresses directly in the lines that follow. What, in any case, is the soul to do with its extreme recognition? It has glimpsed the height of its freedom. At the end of his apostrophe to Imagination, Wordsworth repeats the idea that the soul is halted by its discovery, as a traveler by a sudden bank of mist. But the simile this time suggests not only a divorce from but also (proleptically) a return to nature on the part of the soul,

Strong in herself and in beatitude
That hides her, like the mighty flood of Nile
Poured from his fount of Abyssinian clouds
To fertilise the whole Egyptian plain. (VI.613–16)

3.

It follows that nature, for Wordsworth, is not an "object" but a
presence and a power; a motion and a spirit; not something to be
worshiped and consumed, but always a guide leading beyond itself.
This guidance starts in earliest childhood. The boy of *Prelude* I is
fostered alike by beauty and by fear. Through beauty, nature often
makes the boy feel at home, for, as in the Great Ode, his soul is
alien to this world. But through fear, nature reminds the boy from
where he came, and prepares him, having lost heaven, also to lose
nature. The boy of *Prelude* I, who does not yet know he must suf-
fer this loss as well, is warned by nature itself of the solitude to
come.

I have suggested elsewhere how the fine skating scene of the first
book (425–63), though painted for its own sake, to capture the
animal spirits of children spurred by a clear and frosty night,
moves from vivid images of immediate life to an absolute calm
which foreshadows a deeper and more hidden life.[8] The Negative
Way is a gradual one, and the child is weaned by a premonitory
game of hide-and-seek in which nature changes its shape from fa-
miliar to unfamiliar, or even fails the child. There is a great fear,
either in Wordsworth or in nature, of traumatic breaks: *Natura
non facit saltus*.

If the child is led by nature to a more deeply meditated under-
standing of nature, the mature singer who composes *The Prelude*
begins with that understanding or even beyond it—with the spon-
taneously creative spirit. Wordsworth plunges into *medias res*,
where the *res* is Poetry, or Nature only insofar as it has guided
him to a height whence he must find his own way. But Book VI,
with which we are immediately concerned, records what is chron-
ologically an intermediate period, in which the first term is
neither Nature nor Poetry. It is Imagination in embryo: the mind
muted yet also strengthened by the external world's opacities.
Though imagination is with Wordsworth on the journey of 1790,

nature seems particularly elusive. He goes out to a nature which seems to hide as in the crossing of the Alps:

The first part of this episode is told to illustrate a curious melancholy related to the "presence" of imagination and the "absence" of nature. Like the young Apollo in Keats' *Hyperion*, Wordsworth is strangely dissatisfied with the riches before him, and compelled to seek some other region:

> Where is power?
> Whose hand, whose essence, what divinity
> Makes this alarum in the elements,
> While I here idle listen on the shores
> In fearless yet in aching ignorance?[9]

To this soft or "luxurious" sadness, a more masculine kind is added, which results from a "stern mood" or "underthirst of vigor"; and it is in order to throw light on this further melancholy that Wordsworth tells the incident of his crossing the Alps.

The stern mood to which Wordsworth refers can only be his premonition of spiritual autonomy, of an independence from sense-experience foreshadowed by nature since earliest childhood. It is the 'underground' form of imagination, and *Prelude* II.315 ff. describes it as "an obscure sense / Of possible sublimity," for which the soul, remembering *how* it felt in exalted moments, but no longer *what* it felt, continually strives to find a new content. The element of obscurity, related to nature's self-concealment, is necessary to the soul's capacity for growth, for it vexes the latter toward self-dependence. Childhood pastures become viewless; the soul cannot easily find the source from which it used to drink the visionary power; and while dim memories of a passionate commerce with external things drive it more than ever to the world, this world makes itself more than ever inscrutable.[10] The travelers' separation from their guides, then that of the road from the stream (VI.568), and finally their trouble with the peasant's words that have to be "translated," express subtly the soul's desire for a *beyond*. Yet only when poet, brook, and road are once again "fellow-travellers" (VI.622), and Wordsworth holds to Nature, does that reveal—a Proteus in the grasp of the hero—its prophecy.

This prophecy was originally the second part of the adventure, the delayed vision which compensates for his disappointment (the "Characters of the great Apocalypse," VI.617–40). In its original sequence, therefore, the episode has only two parts: the first term or moment of natural immediacy is omitted, and we go straight to the second term, the inscrutability of an external image, which leads via the gloomy strait to its renewal. Yet, as if this pattern demanded a substitute third term, Wordsworth's tribute to "Imagination" severs the original temporal sequence, and forestalls nature's renewal of the bodily eye with ecstatic praise of the inner eye.

The apocalypse of the gloomy strait loses by this the character of a *terminal* experience. Nature is again surpassed, for the poet's imagination is called forth, at the time of writing, by the barely scrutable, not by the splendid emotion; by the disappointment, not the fulfillment. This (momentary) displacement of emphasis is the more effective in that the style of VI.617 ff., and the very characters of the apocalypse, suggest that the hiding places of power cannot be localized in nature.[11] Though the apostrophe to Imagination—the special insight that comes to Wordsworth in 1804—is a real peripety, reversing a meaning already established, it is not unprepared. But it takes the poet many years to realize that nature's "end" is to lead to something "without end," to teach the travelers to transcend nature.

The three parts of this episode, therefore, can help us understand the mind's growth toward independence of immediate external stimuli. The measure of that independence is Imagination, and carries with it a precarious self-consciousness. We see that the mind must pass through a stage where it experiences Imagination as a power separate from Nature, that the poet must come to think and feel as if by his own choice, or from the structure of his mind.[12]

VI-a (557–91) shows the young poet still dependent on the immediacy of the external world. Imagination frustrates that dependence secretly, yet its blindness toward nature is accompanied by a blindness toward itself. It is only a "mute Influence of the soul, / An Element of nature's inner self" (1805, VIII.512–13).

VI-b (592–616) gives an example of thought or feeling that came from the poet's mind without immediate external excitement. There remains, of course, the memory of VI-a (the disappointment), but this is an internal feeling, not an external image. The poet recognizes at last that the power he has looked for in the outside world is really within and frustrating his search. A shock of recognition then feeds the very blindness toward the external world which helped to produce that shock.

In VI-c (617–40) the landscape is again an immediate external object of experience. The mind cannot separate in it what it desires to know and what it actually knows. It is a moment of revelation, in which the poet sees not as in a glass, darkly, but face to face. VI-c clarifies, therefore, certain details of VI-a and *seems* to actualize figurative details of VI-b.* The matter-of-fact interplay of quick and lingering movement, of up-and-down perplexities in the ascent (VI.567 ff.), reappears in larger letters; while the interchanges of light and darkness, of cloud and cloudlessness, of rising like a vapor from the abyss and pouring like a flood from heaven have entered the landscape bodily. The gloomy strait also participates in this actualization. It is revealed as the secret middle term which leads from the barely scrutable presence of nature to its resurrected image. The travelers who move freely with or against the terrain, hurrying upward, pacing downward, perplexed at crossings, are now led narrowly by the pass as if it were their rediscovered guide.

4.

*The Prelude,* as history of a poet's mind, foresees the time when the "Characters of the great Apocalypse" will be intuited without the medium of nature. The time approaches even as the poet writes, and occasionally cuts across his narrative, the imagination rising up, as in Book VI, "Before the eye and progress of my Song" (version of 1805). This phrase, at once conventional and exact, suggests that imagination waylaid the poet on his mental journey. The "eye" of his song, trained on a temporal sequence with the vision in the strait as its final term, is suddenly obscured. He is momentarily forced to deny nature that magnificence it had shown in the gloomy strait, and to attribute the glory to imagination,

* VI-c was composed before VI-b, so that while the transference of images goes structurally from VI-b to VI-c, *chronologically* the order is reversed.

whose interposition in the very moment of writing proves it to be a power more independent than nature of time and place, and so a better type "Of first, and last, and midst, and without end" (VI. 640).

We know that VI-b records something that happened during composition, and which enters the poem as a new biographical event. Wordsworth has just described his disappointment (VI-a) and turns in anticipation to nature's compensatory finale (VI-c). He is about to respect the original temporal sequence, "the eye and progress" of his song. But as he looks forward, in the moment of composition, from blankness toward revelation, a new insight cuts him off from the latter. The original disappointment is seen not as a test, or as a prelude to magnificence, but as a revelation in itself. It suddenly reveals a power—imagination—that could not be satisfied by anything in nature, however sublime. The song's progress comes to a halt because the poet is led beyond nature. Unless he can respect the natural (which includes the temporal) order, his song, at least as narrative, must cease. Here Imagination, not Nature (as in I.96 ff.), defeats Poetry.

This conclusion may be verified by comparing the versions of 1805 and 1850. The latter replaces "Before the eye and progress of my Song" with a more direct metaphorical transposition. Imagination is said to rise from the mind's abyss "Like an unfathered vapour that enwraps, / At once, some lonely traveller." The (literal) traveler of 1790 becomes the (mental) traveler at the moment of composition. And though one Shakespearean doublet has disappeared,* another implicitly takes its place: does not imagination rise from "the dark backward and abysm of time" (*The Tempest*, I.2.50)? The result, in any case, is a disorientation of time added to that of way; an apocalyptic moment in which past and future overtake the present; and the poet, cut off from nature by imagination, is, in an absolute sense, lonely.

The last stage in the poet's "progress" has been reached. The

---

* De Selincourt, *William Wordsworth, The Prelude* (1959), p. 559, calls "Before the eye and progress of my Song" a Shakespearean doublet, which is right except that the text he refers us to should be *Much Ado about Nothing*, IV.1.238, rather than *King John*, II.1.224.

travelers of VI-a had already left behind their native land, the pub-
lic rejoicing of France, rivers, hills, and spires; they have separated
from their guides, and finally from the unbridged mountain
stream. Now, in 1804, imagination separates the poet from all else:
human companionship, the immediate scene, the remembered
scene. The end of the via negativa is near. There is no more "eye
and progress"; the invisible progress of VI-a (Wordsworth cross-
ing the Alps unknowingly) has revealed itself as a progress inde-
pendent of visible ends,[13] or engendered by the desire for an "in-
visible world"—the substance of things hoped for, the evidence of
things not seen. Wordsworth descants on the Pauline definition
of faith:

> in such strength
> Of usurpation, when the light of sense
> Goes out, but with a flash that has revealed
> The invisible world, doth greatness make abode,
> There harbours; whether we be young or old,
> Our destiny, our being's heart and home,
> Is with infinitude, and only there;
> With hope it is, hope that can never die,
> Effort, and expectation, and desire,
> And something evermore about to be. (VI.599–608)

Any further possibility of progress for the poet would be that of
song itself, of poetry no longer subordinate to the mimetic func-
tion, the experience faithfully traced to this height. The poet is a
traveler insofar as he must respect nature's past guidance and re-
trace his route. He did come, after all, to an important instance of
bodily vision. The way is the song. But the song often strives to be-
come the way. And when this happens, when the song seems to
capture the initiative, in such supreme moments of poetry as VI-b
or even VI-c, the way is lost. Nature in VI-c shows "Winds thwart-
ing winds, bewildered and forlorn," as if they too had lost their
way. The apocalypse in the gloomy strait depicts a self-thwarting
march and counter-march of elements, a divine mockery of the
concept of the Single Way.
    But in VI-c, nature still stands over and against the poet; he is

still the observer, the eighteenth-century gentleman admiring a new manifestation of the sublime, even if the lo! or mark! is suppressed. He moves haltingly but he moves; and the style of the passage emphasizes continuities. Yet with the imagination athwart there is no movement, no looking before and after. The song itself must be the way, though that of a blinded man, who admits, "I was lost." Imagination, as it shrouds the poet's eye, also shrouds the eye of his song, whose tenor is nature guiding and fostering the power of song.

It is not, therefore, till 1804 that Wordsworth discovers the identity of his hidden guide. VI-c was probably composed in 1799, and it implies that Wordsworth, at that time, still thought nature his guide. But now he sees that it was imagination moving him by means of nature, just as Beatrice guided Dante by means of Virgil. It is not nature as such but nature indistinguishably blended with imagination that compels the poet along his Negative Way. Yet, if VI-b prophesies against the world of sense-experience, Wordsworth's affection and point of view remain unchanged. Though his discovery shakes the foundation of his poem, he returns after a cloudburst of verses to the pedestrian attitude of 1790, when the external world and not imagination seemed to be his guide ("Our journey we renewed, / Led by the stream," etc.).[14] Moreover, with the exception of VI-b, imagination does not move the poet directly, but always through the agency of nature. The childhood "Visitings of imaginative power" depicted in Books I and XII also appeared in the guise or disguise of nature. Wordsworth's journey as a poet can only continue with eyes, but the imagination experienced as a power distinct from nature opens his eyes by putting them out. Wordsworth, therefore, does not adhere to nature because of natural fact, but despite it and because of human and poetic fact. Imagination is indeed an *awe-full* power.

5.

"And men go about to wonder at the heights of the mountains, and the mighty waves of the sea, and the wide sweep of rivers, and the circuit of the ocean, and the revolution of the stars, but themselves they consider not." Petrarch, opening on the top of Mt. Ventoux his copy of Augustine's *Confessions,* and falling by chance on this passage, is brought back forcefully to self-consciousness: "I closed the book, angry with myself that I should still be admiring earthly things, who might long ago have learned from even the pagan philosophers that nothing is wonderful but the soul, which, when great itself, finds nothing great outside itself."[15]

Wordsworth's experience, like Petrarch's or Augustine's, is a conversion: a turning about of the mind as from one belief to its opposite, and a turning *ad se ipsum.* It is linked to the birth of a sharper self-awareness, and accompanied by apocalyptic feelings. By "apocalyptic" I mean that there is an inner necessity to cast out nature, to extirpate everything apparently external to salvation, everything that might stand between the naked self and God, whatever risk in this to the self.

It is often the "secret top" of a mountain which turns the man about. Mountains, according to the general testimony of the imagination, are fallen heroes: they have giants in or below them. Atlas stares mutely out of Mt. Atlas. The Titans groan under Mt. Aetna. "What can have more the Figure and Mien of a Ruin," asks Burnet, for whom the hills are noble relics of the Flood, "than Crags, and Rocks, and Cliffs?"[16] An old world, a former self, is passed over; a new consciousness is born. Wordsworth's mountains also tell of the passing of an order—their own order, for nature there prophesies its doom. An eternal witness amid eternal decay, it reveals the "Characters of the great Apocalypse." The poet's earliest sketch of Mt. Blanc condenses in one couplet this monitory and prophetic role:

> Six thousand years amid his lonely bounds
> The voice of Ruin, day and night, resounds.[17]

Many years later, after a further visit to the Alps, ancient myth joins personal intuition to give the idea its most explicit form:

> Where mortal never breathed I dare to sit
> Among the interior Alps, gigantic crew,
> Who triumphed o'er diluvian power!—and yet
> What are they but a wreck and residue,
> Whose only business is to perish?—true

To which sad course, these wrinkled Sons of Time
Labour their proper greatness to subdue;
Speaking of death alone, beneath a clime
Where life and rapture flow in plenitude sublime.[18]

It is as if the mountains exhibited, on a monster-scale, the
Christian virtue of self-abnegation. Yet all concepts of transcend-
ence imply some such necessity. The revolutionary or apocalyptic
mind sees a future so different from the past that the transition
must involve violence. The Titans, in Keats' *Hyperion*, are weighed
down by the mystery as well as the fact of change. In Christian es-
chatology the new heaven and earth are separated from our fa-
miliar world by a second Deluge: the flood of fire and terror de-
scribed in the Book of Revelation. There is a necessary violation
of nature or of a previous state of being. Yet Wordsworth keeps
his faith in the possibility of an unviolent passage from childhood
to maturity or even from nature to eternity. He converts nature
into a paraclete, *the* paraclete. Perhaps he remembers that though
according to Paul "we shall be changed," and in a twinkling, a rape
of time, there is the counter-balancing promise that "All shall sur-
vive."[19] The divine hiatus, the revolutionary severance of new
from old, is never total: the previous order, as if nothing could die
absolutely, remains latent, waiting to return.

Wordsworth's explicit subject, however, is not cosmic or societal
except in implication. His subject is the growth of the mind, and
the question of apocalypse arises therefore in a limited though spe-
cific way. The special nature of his theme, his focus on the individ-
ual mind, is already a sign of a "general and gregarious advance"
in human self-consciousness. Keats says that Wordsworth thinks
into the human heart more than Milton does, not because he is
the greater poet, but because he is a great poet coming at a later
time.[20]

On the matter of apocalypse, there was a bridge between Milton
and Wordsworth via the theological concept of the Light of Na-
ture. Wordsworth never refers specifically to it, but we need a join-
ing concept from the area linking nature and personal conscious-
ness. Although I am not primarily concerned with drawing a
parallel between the two poets, it might clarify Wordsworth's non-

apocalyptic view of how the mind grows. He always, of course, looks at growth from within, and this provides a rather rigid limit to comparison. Wordsworth is still part of the experience he narrates, as many subtle and some startling changes of consciousness reveal; while Milton has divided his subject in advance, and is truly *spectator ab extra,* except where the desire to subsume Classical myth allows his imagination an autonomous vigor. But some episodes are directly comparable, and I propose to bring together Adam's personal story of how he woke to his first thoughts, and beyond them to God *(Paradise Lost,* VIII.253 ff.), and the account, already partially covered, of how nature during the Alpine journey woke in the young poet the sense of his own, separate consciousness. In both episodes the human mind is led from nature to beyond nature.[21]

Milton divides the growth of Adam's mind into clear and easily separated phases. The most significant of these is what is attained by the light of nature and what by supernatural illumination. Adam's apostrophe to the sun,

> Thou Sun, said I, fair Light,
> And thou enlight'n'd Earth, so fresh and gay,
> Ye Hills and Dales, ye Rivers, Woods, and Plains
> And ye that live and move, fair Creatures, tell,
> Tell, if ye saw, how came I thus, how here?
> Not of myself; by some great Maker then,
> In goodness and in power preëminent . . .[22]

shows him instinctively seeking knowledge, recognizing ascending order and reciprocity, recognizing also that there are creatures participating like himself in life and movement. By the light coming from nature and by the light of nature in him he then deduces the existence of an invisible Maker:

> For the invisible things of him from the creation of the world are clearly seen, being understood by the things that are made, even his eternal power and Godhead.[23]

So far, and no farther, does natural light extend. There is a Maker, he is preeminently good and powerful. Man, without further illumination, thirsts for knowledge and is unrequited:

While thus I call'd, and stray'd I knew not whither,
From where I first drew Air, and first beheld
This happy Light, when answer none return'd,
On a green shady Bank profuse of Flow'rs
Pensive I sat me down; there gentle sleep
First found me.[24]

In that sleep, which separates Adam clearly yet gently from his previous state, God dream-walks him to Eden, and natural light begins to be complemented by supernatural revelation.

But if Milton distinguishes categorically between natural and supernatural, he still allows the former a generous domain. That is why a comparison between him and Wordsworth is fruitful. His respect for the mind's natural powers anticipates that of Wordsworth. Supernatural guidance enters as late as possible, and even then is not inevitably overpowering. It cooperates with natural light in a most gentle way, though it must indeed occasionally extinguish that light, as before Eve's birth, when the *tardemah,* the deep sleep of Genesis 2:21, falls on Adam (a somewhat ominous occurrence which foreshadows the first wounding of man and the later wounding of creation by the Fall). Even the *tardemah,* however, is not presented by Milton as total loss of sight, for the "Cell of Fancy," the internal sight, survives, and Adam is allowed to see the operation that must at once complete and deplete him.

In fact, each internal as well as external "generation" of Adam is preceded by a merciful sleep allowing the natural being to persist or even strengthen during influx of divine power. There is first the "soundest sleep" from which he wakes into being. He is bathed in a balmy sweat, the birth-dew of existence. That nature willingly cooperates in his birth is shown by the grotesque image of a Sun feeding on the amniotic or generative moisture.[25] This image is, of course, a conceit on evaporation; but the natural view and the visionary exploitation of it coexist and suggest from the outset the more general coexistence (in the unfallen world at least) of natural and supernatural. Instead of waking, moreover, to revelation and in Eden, Adam's reason is allowed to unfold more gradually.

Only at its limit, thirsting for what it cannot find, does it call on God, "call'd by thee I come thy Guide." The supernatural does not intervene before the natural is perfected, and responds rather than intervenes.

When it finally appears it is superbly gentle, a "soft oppression." For the sleep by which it comes has its own charitable, paracletic function. Before Adam is allowed to see Eden in actual sight, as before he is allowed to look at Eve, both are anticipated in dream, because the reality is too great to bear without the adumbration of a dream, or because Adam's spirit must be gently raised toward the truth that is to meet him. By these repeated dream-awakenings divine light kindles rather than darkens the natural light in man.

But for a further sleep, and awakening into the darkness of the Fall, Adam's eyes might have been permanently tempered to the divine. Within the limits of sacred story, and the explicit framework of natural and supernatural, Milton approaches Wordsworth's view of a mind led from stage to transcendent stage by a similar monitory gentleness. No rape of the mind is necessary; no wounding of nature or of a previous mode of being. Milton's delicacy, in this matter, is absolute. When Raphael, divine historian, has finished his relation of the first things, Adam is impelled to tell of his own beginning: grateful, excited into reciprocity, desiring to converse longer with the Angel, "now hear mee relate / My story." The response of his mind to the Angel has by contagion some of the charm and energy of the Angel's own—Adam is already "ascending winged."

But Wordsworth cannot, like Milton, go back to a fixed beginning, to prehistory. "How shall I seek the origin?" he asks, knowing that the beginning is already the middle (and muddle) of things. Though deprived of both first term and last, of *arche* and *eschaton*, he still undertakes to trace the history of his mind. To what end? To justify the faith he has in the possibility of his renovation through daily and natural means, or to settle that wavering faith. Nature restored him unapocalyptically in the past; it surely can do so again. The restoration he talks of is identical with being renewed as a poet: it is not dryness of heart that plagues him, but the fear that nature is not enough, that his imagination is essentially apocalyptic and must violate the middle world of common things and loves.

The Alpine journey, as we have seen, contains three distinct reversals. The structure of each is that a disappointment is followed by a compensation. The imagination does not find, and strays like Adam, and is then seemingly completed. Two of the reversals, though having in them an element of surprise, are not violent; and the third, which is violent, and supplants nature as the poet's muse, still somehow returns to nature. For nature remains in Wordsworth's view the best and gentlest guide in the development surpassing her. It is part of the poet's strength that he faithfully records an experience he did not at the time of writing and still does not control. The greatest event of his journey is not VI-c (the "Characters of the great Apocalypse"), or the parallel bewilderment of time and way near Gravedona (VI.688–726), but the spectral figure of Imagination cutting him off, fulfilling Nature's prophecy, and revealing the end of his Negative Way.

Besides these reversals there is the tempo of the whole journey. This is often neglected for the striking events that detach themselves only partially from it. Wordsworth generally avoids making his epiphanies into epocha: into decisive turns of personal fate or history. A mythic structure would allow him to do that; Milton even overuses his "firsts" when it comes to a psychological matter: "Then Satan first knew pain" (cf. "there gentle sleep / First found me"). Though Wordsworth must pattern his story and life, he is as apologetic about this as Raphael is for having to relate divine matters in terms intelligible to human sense—whenever possible he assumes a mazy motion which makes *The Prelude* a difficult poem to follow.

The reason for Wordsworth's avoidance of epochal structure is complex and linked probably to his avoidance of myth. For though he is compelled to seek beginnings, the unfolding causes of things, nature itself resists this kind of exactness, as if it diminished her generosities, her power to make anything a new beginning. To excerpt the various epiphanies from Wordsworth's narrative is, in any case, to neglect the pull of the underlying verse that refuses

them too great a distinctity of self. Much of the drama, as I now
hope to show, is played out on a quietly continuing level; the or-
dinary events swelling into and absorbing the special insights; the
peripeties threatening but finally sustaining the light of nature.
The young travelers of Book VI instinctively associate nature
with freedom. They believe it has the strength to waken or re-
awaken man. By glorious chance their destination is a land where
human nature seemed born again on account of revolution (339
ff.). Man is again as open as nature itself:

> once, and more than once,
> Unhoused beneath the evening star we saw
> Dances of liberty, and, in late hours
> Of darkness, dances in the open air
> Deftly prolonged. (369–73)

They are not sidetracked, however, by these public rejoicings. "We
held our way" (350), "We glided forward with the flowing stream"
(377), "We sailed along" (385), "We pursued our journey" (416)
—various clichés and fillers abundant in the topographical litera-
ture of the eighteenth century, including Wordsworth's own earlier
work, recover life and literal significance. Nature is their principal
guide and even the energy which bears them on:

> Swift Rhone! thou wert the *wings* on which we cut
> A winding passage with majestic ease
> Between thy lofty rocks. (378–80)

Along this southerly route marked out by nature, they are
caught up in a crowd of delegates returning home from the "great
spousals"* in Paris. Though Wordsworth and his friend are also
"emancipated" (387), they remain among them like "a lonely
pair of strangers" (384). We glimpse here the encounter of two
different types of human freedom. The encounter always keeps be-
low the level of allegory: it is accidental and unpredictable as all
incidents in *The Prelude*. It has, nevertheless, the force of provi-
dence peering through chance, or idea through matter-of-fact.

* VI. 389. The marriage of the People and the King, or of the Estates and
the King, in the Constitution of July 1790.

The first type is the revolutionary. Wordsworth and he are traveling along the same road and have much in common. Both delight in freedom and believe man may be regenerated by human or natural power. Their eye is on this world: the "great spousals" are a political fact, just as the marriage of heaven and earth, which first emboldened Wordsworth to think he could be a poet (IV.323–38; VI.42–57), is a daily fact. But there are also important differences. The revolutionaries are journeying home, merry and sociable: they receive the poet and his friend as Abraham of old the angels (394 ff.). This world is their home, they have no other. The poet and his friend, on the other hand, are lonely men, "strangers" or "angels" whose freedom has connotation of exile. They are obscurely looking for another home: this-worldly perhaps, yet more awe-full, more sublime than what they have seen.

In this respect they do not resemble revolutionaries but pilgrims. The pilgrim is the second type of human freedom. He travels through this world as a free man, pushing toward the place nearest heaven. He has no home properly speaking, no company, only an obscure burden which drives him from one spot to another. Although there is a "home" toward which he strives, the way is important and becomes an essential worship. Wordsworth shares his homelessness, his solitude, his respect for the way. He has already compared himself to a pilgrim in Book I. His travels here are also a "pilgrimage" (763); the Alpine region is a "temple" (741); he aspires, guided by nature, to reach "the point marked out by Heaven" (753). His use of religious terms seems very sparse, a kind of poetic seasoning. Yet when the lonely traveler, many years removed from the young adventurer of 1790, obtains a sudden glimpse of the soul's home, he bursts into that descant on the Pauline definition of faith:

> our being's heart and home,
> Is with infinitude, and only there;
> With hope it is, hope that can never die. (604–06)

Wordsworth cannot be identified with either of these mutually exclusive types. He holds a precarious middle position as a new, emergent type, not unknown by the end of the eighteenth century, but as unstable as the Bedouin-Quixote figure ("Of these was neither, and was both at once") of which he dreams in *Prelude* V. This radically ambivalent type takes many forms, appearing as Cain, Ahasuerus, Childe Harold, or simply poet-errant. In Book VI he is no more than "wanderer," "traveller." Yet we recognize him by the fact that fugitive and pilgrim, pursuer and pursued are unified in his person.

The Chartreuse, the first significant stop in the Alpine journey, will act as catalyst to divide clearly pilgrim from revolutionary, and to show that Wordsworth is both and neither, that he typifies a new vision, or perhaps by-pass, of the relation between natural and supernatural. Pursuing nature, the poet is actually pursued by nature beyond it. But it seems, for a moment, as if he might be swept along by the revolutionaries: he travels their road and occasionally becomes one of them. This foreshadows *Prelude* IX to XI, where Wordsworth is almost swept away. Yet nature with its intimations of a more private peace and a less ostensive freedom gradually separates the two strangers from the "merry crowd" (386), "blithe host" (387), "bees . . . gaudy and gay as bees" (391), "proud company" (394), "boisterous crew" (413):

> The monastery bells
> Made a sweet jingling in our youthful ears;
> The rapid river flowing without noise,
> And each uprising or receding spire
> Spake with a sense of peace, at intervals
> Touching the heart amid the boisterous crew
> By whom we were encompassed. Taking leave
> Of this glad throng, foot-travellers side by side,
> Measuring our steps in quiet, we pursued
> Our journey. (408–17)

And, as Wordsworth approaches the Chartreuse, the revolutionaries change proleptically into "riotous men" (425) who expel its religious community and desecrate the spirit of the place. Wordsworth, "by conflicting passions pressed," adopts two voices to argue for the preservation of the Chartreuse without condemning revolutionary zeal.[26]

His view of the monastery is, however, quite unambiguous. He sees it as a stronghold of nature's paracletic function rather than as a Catholic institution. The conquest of nature is here aided by an impulse from nature herself. The monastery's sublime natural setting *bodies forth* the ghostliness of things. But it also *clothes* it, mediating between the "bodily eye" and the "blank abyss" (470), between man's power of vision and his utter nakedness before the apocalyptic vision.[27] There is paradox here, but not ambiguity.

After the Chartreuse a new landscape begins. The positive and privative aspects of nature intermingle more obviously. Every step of the travelers attends on swift interchanges:

> Abroad, how cheeringly the sunshine lay
> Upon the open lawns! Vallombre's groves
> Entering, we fed the soul with darkness; thence
> Issued, and with uplifted eyes beheld,
> In different quarters of the bending sky,
> The cross of Jesus stand erect, as if
> Hands of angelic powers had fixed it there,
> Memorial reverenced by a thousand storms;
> Yet then, from the undiscriminating sweep
> And rage of one State-whirlwind, insecure. (479–88)

The travelers' pace seems to speed up; the earth changes its images and forms as fast as clouds are changed in heaven (492); and the uphill-downhill motion which culminates in VI-a to VI-c becomes prominent. The friends not only wing or sail along but are birds of prey, a ship on the stretch (498). We feel something of their joy in movement, in variety, and hardly suspect that nature is eluding their expectations. Then she clearly fails them for the first time just before their blind crossing of the Alps.

The failure is quickly redeemed, but it has come and prepares for VI.592 ff. The very day they look with bounding heart on an "aboriginal vale" they also see Mt. Blanc and grieve:

> To have a soulless image on the eye
> That had usurped upon a living thought
> That never more could be. (526–28)

When Wordsworth discovers that the mind has no home except
with

> ... something evermore about to be (VI-b, 608)

he sounds the depth of the disparity between Nature and Imagi-
nation.

VI-b, of course, is the peripety of a traveler many years ad-
vanced. His actual progress, to judge by the two epiphanies or
compensations given by nature, the first for the blank of Mt. Blanc,
the second for his blind crossing of the Alps, is as propaedeutic as
Adam's dreams. The first, the poet's sight of the valley of Cha-
monix (VI.528–40), still serves to reconcile imagination and na-
ture: it carefully veils the naked vision of transcendent forces.
Man is still the measure of this view.. The streams of ice are bal-
anced by five rivers broad and vast; small birds and leafy trees
flourish in the same atmosphere as soaring eagle; yellow sheaf and
haycock, reaper and maiden, live easily among the wilder forces
of nature. Winter sports like a lion, but one well-tamed. In the
second, as if penultimate view (VI-c), the balance breaks. Now the
"dumb cataracts" (530) find voice, become "stationary blasts"
(626); there is no well-tamed descent but torrents shooting from
the clear blue sky; no warbling but muttering and ravings; no
broad, spacious living but winds thwarting winds in the narrow
rent; no leisurely, seasonal occupation but giddy interchanges of
opposite powers. All this is still "food" (the metaphor occurs in
line 723 at the end of another fantastic bewilderment, a vacillation
from "fairest, softest, happiest influence" to a night ensnared by
witchcraft), but one is no longer certain whence it comes or what
in man it feeds. An impassioned envoi to the book finally cautions
us not to think the poet a passive recipient here or anywhere in
*The Prelude:*

> Not rich one moment to be poor for ever;
> Not prostrate, overborne, as if the mind
> Herself were nothing, a mere pensioner
> On outward forms. (735–38)

To be more emphatic, the poet then returns to an image found in
the opening episode of his poem: that of the external breeze wak-
ing an internal tempest, an acceleration which propels the trav-
elers along, as if nature were discovering to them their own powers.
Their mind is being raised to nature as at least equal in dignity
to it:

> whate'er
> I saw, or heard, or felt, was but a stream
> That flowed into a kindred stream; a gale,
> Confederate with the current of the soul,
> To speed my voyage. (742–46)

It is clear that in 1790 Wordsworth's soul was already making a
"trial of its strength," with poetic numbers as the "banded host"
and nature as the objective to be gained. Only in 1804 does
Wordsworth realize he mistook his objective. The soul, in VI-b, is
its own objective. It is so sure of its home *away from* nature that
it has no need to snatch a "trophy of the sun."[28] But Wordsworth,
in truth, is never able to look complacently at the sun. He can
never say with Petrarch that "nothing is wonderful but the soul,
which, when great itself, finds nothing great outside itself." Even
the verse of his decline, however placid in sentiment, is a trial of
strength: the failing endeavor to meet with his own light the light
once emanating from nature.

### 6.

The ascent of Snowdon, a great moment in poetry, stands in a
place of honor: Wordsworth chooses it as his coda episode for *The
Prelude*. Not only is it, as poetry, a true "mounting of the mind";
it is also a culminating evidence that imagination and the light of
nature are one. The certainty that there is an imagination in na-
ture analogous to that in man opened to him a "new world." The
incident is a difficult one to interpret, not only for us, but for the
poet himself; yet he insists that though nature on Snowdon points
to imagination, and even thrusts the vision of it on him, what he
sees is still a Power like nature's (XIII.312, XIV.86 ff.). This time

his recognition of imagination *sub specie naturae* does not (as in VI-b) give a mortal shock to nature. The episode is Wordsworth's most astonishing avoidance of apocalypse.

We must not forget, however, that the peripety described in VI-b followed all others studied in this chapter, if we can trust the extant manuscripts. It is the last of a series of evaded recognitions, a magnificent yet inexorable after-birth. From late January to April 1804, Wordsworth was intensely engaged in work on *The Prelude;* and, under that pressure of composition, came once, and only once, face to face with his imagination. Comparing the mountain experience of Book VI with that of Book XIV, we obtain a clear picture of a mind finally forced to meet and to recognize its inherently apocalyptic vigor.

The experience again falls into three parts. The travelers ascend and are soon surrounded by mist (XIV-a, 11–39). There follows the vision proper (XIV-b, 39–62), and a meditation arising immediately after it (XIV-c, 63 ff.). The first part, as in the ascent of the Alps, is akin to inscrutability, while the second, a moment of strong bodily sight, could be compared to the "Characters of the great Apocalypse" (VI-c), delayed by the tribute to imagination. This tribute is itself comparable to the last section, a moment of insight which understands the external events as revealing expressly (i.e. in open sight) a power similar to the human imagination. The sequence of events in *Prelude* XIV might therefore be an unscrambling of the order of events in VI: inscrutability, followed by the immediacy of an external image, then by the interpretation (immediate here, delayed in VI) of that image as the resemblance of an inner power.

But since VI-b is *hors de série* we cannot properly talk of unscrambling: the sequence of XIV existed before that of VI was complete. It is here that we meet a problem peculiar to *The Prelude.* In most poems we need only respect the structural sequence, according to which XIV does indeed come after VI. But in a poem also autobiography, and in which the act of composition may itself produce a further biographical event, two other sequences may have to be kept in mind. They are the biographical and the compositional order of events.

The Crossing of the Alps, for example, may be read in three ways, all essential to meaning:

| | | | | |
|---|---|---|---|---|
| structurally | VI | a | b | c |
| biographically | VI | a | c | b |
| compositionally | VI | c | a | b |

The ascent of Snowdon, on the other hand, seems to have been composed in sequence, and is not interrupted by an insight incorporated as a new event, so that the three patterns coincide. But if we take VI (abc) and XIV (abc) together, a new problem of ordering arises.

The biographical and compositional contiguity of the two ascents is masked by their final (structural) place in the poem. Both describe mountain trips perhaps not more than a year apart; and it is therefore significant that from the biographical point of view the clearest difference between them is that in XIV full understanding comes immediately after the event, and nonviolently, while in VI the final illumination takes fourteen years to be born, and then comes abruptly. But this fact is, in turn, modified by our knowledge of the compositional sequence, which suggests that the birth of VI-b was induced by the poet's prior composition of or reflection on XIV, which is mediately present when VI-ab comes to be written, just as VI-c (composed in 1799) may have been in the poet's mind when XIV was written. The single event has a life in memory that cannot be isolated to point or meaning of origin.

We begin by looking at the biographical sequence:

1. VI-ac      1790
2. XIV-abc    1791 (1793)[29]
3. VI-b       1804

This ordering does not prove to be particularly significant. The first two experiences are rather similar in form, and could be made even more symmetrical by equating XIV-c with the last lines of VI-c (636 ff.), for both are interpretative moments closely joined to the sight they interpret. In VI-c there is a slight formal gap between sight and interpretation, but the latter is linked to the former as part of the same breath, the exhaling as it were; in XIV-c the gap is both temporal and formal, but also not large or abrupt. What really distinguishes the two episodes from each other is the sudden arrival of VI-b: the nearest to that reversal is, in XIV, the "flash" which heralds the vision and leads from XIV-a to XIV-b.

The compositional sequence will prove to be more interesting:

1. VI-c        1799
2. XIV-abc     1804: February-March
3. VI-ab       1804; April

This suggests a progressive mounting of the mind toward self-consciousness. In VI-c the style avoids conveying the feeling of abrupt illumination. XIV-b, the visionary part of the ascent of Snowdon, strikes more suddenly—like a flash—yet remains a physical illumination fused with the immediate landscape. Then VI-a, starting as matter-of-factly as XIV, is broken across by an abrupt illumination which cannot blend with the remembered landscape, and must finally create its own. It usurps the poet and for the first time shows Imagination as a power radically separate from Nature. Thus:

1. VI-c        circumvents abrupt illumination; interpretative moment dissociable from vision yet grammatically and temporally linked

2. XIV-ab      abrupt illumination fused with landscape vision and to that extent still subdued;
   XIV-c       interpretative moment formally and temporally separate but time gap minimal

3. VI-ab       abrupt illumination not fused with landscape, obscuring it even; the interpretative moment constructing its own landscape for the illumination to blend with

The compositional sequence confirms Wordsworth's tendency to avoid an apocalyptic self-consciousness. It confirms also that VI (abc) and XIV (abc) are two rival highpoints of *The Prelude*. In one, imagination breaks through to obscure the light of nature; in the other, the poet sees imagination directly via the light of nature.

The meaning of Snowdon is not changed in the retelling by a sudden, reflexive consciousness.

This consciousness occurs, however, in a displaced form: it merges with the very structure of the episode. We glimpse VI-b flickering as a middle-term, and when it finally leaps out it is the product not only of the Alps but also of Snowdon. Yet writing of Snowdon Wordsworth still escapes the speech-blindness which ensues on coming face to face with a power that disowns nature. He never sees more than the back of the imagination, as Moses saw the back of God. The main attributes that define imagination *figuratively* in VI-b are still a *literal* part of the landscape.

The Snowdon travelers, for example, mount directly into the mist, as if already in imagination's landscape. The mist does not appear suddenly and as from an abyss to halt them; yet later they are shown to have climbed not only a mountain but also an abyss similar to that from which imagination springs. At least something springs also from it. Just as the mountain is seen to be an abyss, the silent mist, which had covered the sky and now lies at their feet, discloses the upward roar of torrent voices. This reversal of perspectives or natures is anticipated by Wordsworth's description of the climb as also a descent into the mind, and vice-versa. The almost emblematic

> With forehead bent
> Earthward, as if in opposition set
> Against an enemy, I panted up
> With eager pace, and no less eager thoughts . . . (XIV.28–31)

hints at this up-and-down. As they climb higher, or sink deeper into thought, each person becomes a "lonely traveller"; and the "unearthing" of the hedgehog, which emphasizes by contrast the persistent coil of silence and concentration, prefigures casually the later twofold unearthing: the flash of the moon still hiding a second revelation, the upward "flash" of sound. It is as if the poet, in passing through the mist, had passed his own imagination unawares: not only because the voices from below are like imagination unveiling as the power he has blindly crossed, but also because the first revelation proves to be incomplete, which suggests that instead of apocalypse there is only developing and self-displacing vision.

Thus reflection, in Wordsworth, becomes reflexive. It is not passive recall but a precarious mental journey. If the poet's descent into the "deep backward and abysm of time" appears here like a few dream-like moments, it is because imagination, independent of time, nihilates the latter, and does not yet impose itself as the more awesome burden. In a sense it nihilates even itself, for it enters the picture only as an infinitely shifty middle-term. The energy which is imagination does not substantialize as a single specter, an awful power rising from the mind's abyss. It blends with the semblance of a realm, a landscape of the colors of nature through which the poet moves as in a wakeful dream. He moves toward a self-recognition, which will halt the traveler, erase the landscape, break the dream. But though he comes as close to this point as in the scene to the "fixed, abysmal, gloomy breathing-place," the fixating shock of self-consciousness is avoided.

The escape from fixity, in the vision, is extended beyond the doubling of the central recognition to inform even the properties of things and the relationship between thing and symbol. The mist is like a sea yet also "solid" like the mountains; it seems to mimic other elements. The poet says the mist "hung" low; yet later it is the moon that "hung naked" in the firmament. Such displacement also interferes with the stabilizing of thing as symbol. We have seen that we cannot fully associate the mist with imagination even by calling in VI-b. It is the sudden light of the moon and the voices rising from below the mist which really startle the traveler. Yet Wordsworth is also unable to make a sharp "symbolic" identification of the imagination with moon or sounding abyss.[30] Neither of these *is* the imagination, which cannot be localized in mind or nature or any part of nature. The difficulty of identification is apparent when we ask where or what in the vision the imagination may be? Snowdon, as even the syntax occasionally suggests,[31] does not project the image of an agent but at most the image of an action. Wordsworth tries to define this action when he says that the imagination imparts to one life the functions of another: shifts, creates, "trafficking with immeasurable thoughts."

When a poet approaches the ineffable, a critic is inclined to fall back on the nearest steadying commonplace. It would suffice to say that the imagination and the sense of infinity are related, if the vision itself were not minutely particular. Some of its strangely effective shifts, transfers, and "mutations" (XIV.94) have been detailed. Wordsworth's greatest poetry is such a web of transfers, which are not showy or patently metaphorical and are rarely felt as unusual turns of speech. Even at climactic points—

> the sick sight
> And giddy prospect of the raving stream,

—we must try to take the 'merely' transferred epithets as literally as possible. They indicate, in the presence of other signs, a dizzy openness of relation between the human mind and nature. Such to-and-fros ("traffickings") between inner and outer, literal and figurative, or present and past, often span entire episodes and even cross them. The relation of the mist of XIV to that of VI-b and to the inscrutability of nature in VI-a is an example of a cross-episode transfer. For a sustained series of intra-episode transfers we could return to Wordsworth's account of the Simplon Pass (curiously enough a "crossing" on the thematic level), where many qualities migrate from the external scene of VI-a to VI-b, then reappear in the landscape of VI-c.*

It is impossible to determine whether these transfers show the poet's imagination participating in or striving to break with na-

---

* For example, the movement from having crossed the Alps "blindly" to being suddenly "blinded" by imagination, to the implicit destruction of the very concept of Way in "Winds thwarting winds, bewildered and forlorn." Or the progress from upward motion to up-and-down (VI.594, 614–16), and to the continuous reversal, though with a distinct downward pull, expressed in the features of the apocalypse. Or—an especially subtle case—the transition from the indirectness of the peasant's words reported in oblique though italicized speech, to the direct cry "Imagination . . . " immediately broken off and ending with an impersonal construction (yet reverting to a formalized directness in "I recognize thy glory"), to "Black drizzling crags that spake by the wayside," and the whole prospect's speaking oracular face, too close to be understood.

ture. The to-and-fro they depict is still a fluctuation and bounded by some cyclical or dialectical pattern. But could we feel more strongly that nature is open to man and man to nature? Here there is no one beginning or one end but an infinite capacity for sight, insight, regeneration. We have already pointed out how the apocalypse of 1790 loses the character of a terminal experience. The poet is suddenly renewed from an unexpected and casual source. The Simplon Pass and Snowdon bring a twofold revelation that could have been sevenfold as in John the Divine. But they differ from traditional apocalypses by being purely natural and by not inevitably associating rebirth and violent purgation. The Book of Revelation that is Nature sees life dying into eternal life with or without those apocalyptic labors. Even in a vision Wordsworth does not limit the ways of God.

### 7.

At the beginning of *The Prelude* a poet returns to nature, yet the poem he writes is about the difficulties of that return. He cannot always sustain his quest to link what makes a poet, the energy of imagination, to the energy of nature. In its purity the imagination is "unfathered"—a self-begotten, potentially apocalyptic force. But poetry, like the world, can only house an imagination which is a borderer, which will not disdain earthly things. Whatever the imagination's source, its end as poetry is the nature all recognize, and still a nature that leads beyond itself.

Snowdon is a magic mountain. It is a place of enchantment and danger as Spenser and many Romantics have pictured. Everything that happens on this mountain is deceptive because everything leads beyond (though not away from) itself. It is easy to overlook the fact that Wordsworth sets out to see the dawn and encounters a rising-up of the powers in darkness. "Night unto night showeth knowledge."

Reduced to its simplest structure the experience of the poet on Snowdon shows a doubling of the idea of the inscrutable breaking into revelation. Mist into flash of light, mist into stream of sound —the same element bears two surprises. The Inscrutable, one might

say, brings forth Immediacy (the isolate moon) which seeks out—
is sustained by—the Inscrutable breaking into Immediacy (the real
behind the misty ocean, the evidence of the voices in XIV-b).

This is the perfect instance of the ternary pattern we have found
in the chief incidents of Books I, VI, and XIV. It provides a clear
case where immediacy acts as a medium, which is as good a descrip-
tion of poetry's effect as any. Poetry leads from pleasure to pleas-
ure; and, enjoying each as it engages the mind, we are surprised
by the next. This is what Coleridge may have meant when he re-
newed an old dictum and said that a poem has both pleasure and
truth in it, but that the pleasures of the way are as important as the
truth of the destination.[32]

Nature and Poetry matter only as they quicken regeneration.
The most enthralling impression should still be a middle-term, a
thoroughfare to a new birth of power and liberty. The vision re-
acts on the man, leads his senses beyond themselves, from moon
to sounding abyss and finally back to his own creative powers. But
the clearest sign of a truly creative, self-renewing mind is to build
up greatest things from least suggestions. As at the beginning of
*The Prelude,* anything may guide, even a "trackless field." Words-
worth's rhapsodic opening, muted too soon, does not express faith
in nature but rather in the quickening relation of imagination to
nature. Nature, however, is real and important enough. Spreading
light and life in subtle, not catastrophic ways, it has brought the
poet to his present faith that self-renewal is possible without a
violence of apocalypse.

"Visionary power," Wordsworth writes at one point, "Attends
the motions of the viewless winds, / Embodied in the mystery of
words" (V.595–97). The contrast of visionary and viewless is like
that of greatest things built up from smallest. Only in this respect
is Poetry a second Nature. It learns from nature the "wondrous in-
fluence of power gently used" (XII.15). We start with something
viewless or inscrutable like the source of the Nile, still given in
Wordsworth's day either a natural or supernatural explanation.[33]
When Wordsworth comes face to face with his own creative power,
with imagination rising "like an unfathered vapour," i.e. hiding its
natural source, he glimpses the supernatural fountains of his

genius. But in the lines that follow, the hiding that bespeaks mystery and apocalypse opens once more into nature. The imagination hides itself by overflowing as poetry, and is compared to the Nile which overflows its banks and the Egyptian plain. Wordsworth the traveler now alludes to the natural explanation for the rise of the Nile. The energy of imagination enters into a natural cycle though apart from it; while the lines describing his soul as

> Strong in herself and in beatitude
> That hides her, like the mighty flood of Nile
> Poured from her fount of Abyssinian clouds
> To fertilise the whole Egyptian plain . . . (VI.613–16)

renew the connection between the waters above and the waters below,[34] between heaven and earth.

Toward this marriage of heaven and earth the poet proceeds despite apocalypse. He is the matchmaker, his song the spousal verse. His dedication to poetry is a dedication to this myth become sense. An awful power rises from the mind's abyss, disowning nature; another descends fertile from Abyssinian clouds. He seeks his earthly paradise not "beyond the Indian mount" but in the real Abyssinia[35]—any mountain-valley where poetry is made.

# III.  THE CHRONOLOGICAL PATTERN

*the mind in the act of finding / What will suffice*
—WALLACE STEVENS

*. . . the story of the mind, greatly conscious of its own enigma, gradually establishing its secure relationship with a world equally enigmatic. The two enigmas indeed, remain; but we understand that they are bound together in one inevitable destiny of companionship. . . . This is the modern epic; this is the heroic strain today, the grand theme of man's latter experience.*
—LASCELLES ABERCROMBIE

# The Argument

It was once the custom to attach to one's book a summarizing emblem, a kind of pictorial machine disposing the argument into an easily intuitable form. What device can help us follow Wordsworth's growth so that its pattern is not lost in the details? The image of a Mutilated Bower comes to mind.

I take it from "Nutting," a sketch written in the winter of 1798–99, and published in the *Lyrical Ballads* of 1800, though originally intended for Wordsworth's poem on the growth of his mind. Close to a turning-point in English poetry, "Nutting" recalls the Romance tradition at the same time as it foreshadows its loss. The Romantic poets certainly step back—over the Enlightenment—into Romance: they honor in Spenser and others their own primal sympathies. But their recovery of an earlier mode is a new beginning rather than an end in itself. Poetry cannot exist without Romance, yet modern poetry cannot subsist on Romance. Wordsworth allows us to trace, in his very growth as a poet, the emergence of a modern imagination from the toils and temptations of the old.

Few before him would have been inspired by the event recorded in "Nutting." That Wordsworth is so inspired argues a new phase in the development of the sympathetic imagination—but this is to anticipate matters. In "Nutting," a youngster sallies forth, ritually decked for his exploit with nutting-crook, wallet, and old clothes. He comes to a beautiful nook (a "virgin scene," says the poet, still using a Latin elegance), and there the hazels rise temptingly with their clusters. After a moment of sensuous restraint, after allowing himself to be soothed and distracted by the beauty of the spot, the boy ravages the sheltered trees, though not unconscious of pain when he beholds the mutilated bower.

The action here is almost purely psychological. The boy's initial restraint, and the very quietness of nature, feed his sense of power, which then overflows as a desecration clearly due to *strength* of spirit. His later apprehensiveness, that the wood is suffering and alive, is also understandable as a psychological reaction. Yet, though all is handled lightly, with only an overtone of sexuality and hunter's lust, and though the animism in "shades," "silent trees," "intruding sky," is subdued to the purpose of objective description, we are continually reminded of a more heroic pattern of quest, ravage, spirit-vengeance. The youngster is not unlike "the Orlando of Ariosto, the Cardenio of Cervantes, who lays waste the groves that would shelter him": * his act, like that of a hero in Romance, is both interesting and reprehensible, heroic and against nature. The scene, however, remains English, the hero a boy, the wood a wood.

Wordsworth has clearly passed *through* the realm of "Flora and Old Pan" on the way to becoming a poet of the human heart. His psychology is prompted by images from Romance. The bower, emblematically speaking, may be the bower of Romance itself, which Keats also sought to transcend. It is as if the poetic spirit had to become conscious of its autonomy and transcend its archaic modes in order to engage human nature. Wordsworth, said Keats, "martyred" himself to the human heart, meaning by this that literary progress lay in an abnegation of Miltonic and Spenserian modes, in a completer humanization of the themes and agents of poetry. Yet the great imaginations of the past, far from being bounded by the human, had dealt with both men and gods, with the cosmos as a whole. The dilemma confronting the Romantics was that to humanize the spirit of man, or to exile the gods, might actually mean an abandonment of poetical thought. To restrict imagination to a middle flight, as the Enlightenment had done, was tantamount to putting imagination in question.

The following chapters show that Wordsworth came under the

* From Wordsworth's prefatory essay to *The Borderers*. The play and essay date from the years 1796–97.

joint imperative of English Protestantism and the Enlightenment, both of which urged him to humanize (at least in poetry) his imagination, and so to abandon the older mythical and cosmological imaginings. It seems to me that though he tried to obey their injunction he found no way to humanize his spirit without renouncing it, and that his problem became his subject. According to Wordsworth, the imagination of a child is, like a Romance hero, in nature but not of it, and "Nutting" anticipates the larger story of how that imagination moves precariously closer to nature and perhaps extinction. The youngster's consciousness is being bound to this world, partly in fear, but mostly in understanding. An element of fear is present, for the boy's mind senses "unknown modes of being"—perhaps the all-pervading moral order of "The Ancient Mariner" with its dangers of trespass and avenging tutelary spirits. Yet the Romance notion of a sympathetic universe, one which participates in the feelings and destiny of man, survives only in a muted or sophisticated form. The subject of "Nutting" is not the life in nature, or its secret manifestation, but how the child's willful consciousness matures into the sympathetic imagination. Nature's activity or pedagogy is related primarily to this end. It seems to the boy that the bower has suffered him in patience and gentleness; and it seems to the poet that this appearance of suffering nature was essential in the growth of his mind. The supernatural intimation in this appearance is never entirely removed, yet one who has been taught to feel for "mute, insensate things" will surely come to participate in the joy and pain of fellow creatures. Wordsworth's point may be disputed, but it is unmistakable. By this violation of the bower (a familiar theme of Romance), the child is joined to rather than separated from nature. His feelings begin to be humanized, and the marriage of imagination and nature, of which "The Recluse" speaks, is anticipated.

# 1. "The Vale of Esthwaite"

Wordsworth's first sustained original poem, "The Vale of Esthwaite," was finished at the age of seventeen, and prior to his departure for Cambridge. Its measure, octosyllabic couplets, is that of Milton's "L'Allegro" and "Il Penseroso"; from these poems Wordsworth also borrowed the opening exorcism and perhaps the ambulatory scheme. But he is the melancholy and cheerful man in one, and his poem expresses a precarious interplay of opposing moods.[1] De Selincourt's text is a composite of several manuscripts, and the editor indicates that we have to do with a fragmentary work, originally of greater length than the text he prints, and which may have been pillaged for *An Evening Walk*.[2]

The almost six hundred lines reproduced are of some interest in any continuous exposition of the poet's work. They are the relics of a poem that intermingles gothic passages with "loco-descriptive" images directly from nature. Because of the poem's fragmentary state it is not possible to say whether the gothic scenes are to be taken as literal adventures, which would make the poem a Romance, or whether they are, as in Beattie's *Minstrel*, the fantasies of a "lone enthusiast" whose progress from the first dawning of imagination Beattie traced.

Wordsworth's verbal echoes of *The Minstrel* and his interest in the growth of the mind favor the latter supposition. Beattie, moreover, inspired by Percy's essay on ancient minstrelsy, and perhaps by eighteenth-century Progress poems, anticipates the Wordsworthian theme of how difficult it is to humanize imagination.[3] His work is divided into two books, of which the first describes the young genius roaming at large with wild and natural fancies; the second begins the woeful tale of imagination's humanizing.

But Wordsworth as poet is far more problematic than Beattie's minstrel. He is desperately unsure not only of whether his imagination can pass from nature to man but also of whether it can stay with nature itself. His doubts do not come (as yet) from any broad conceptual scheme concerning the origin of the poetic impulse. But having lost father and mother, and deprived of sister and everything that used to be home, he is in danger of being detached from the "social chain." His dilemma is increased by the fact that nature itself is not—or no longer—sufficient for a mind awakened, by these separations, to its independence. Though he insists that nothing "from the social chain can tear / This bosom link'd forever there," his imagination is unable to stay with the only society (Esthwaite Valley) he knows. This gentlest of valleys, his home for the last eight years, begins to haunt him—or rather, it is his mind which haunts supernaturally through nature, as the gothic and "terrific" scenes of the poem reveal.

Should his imagination be inherently opposed to the social principle, Wordsworth might have to choose between society and minstrelsy. He knows, of course, that the opposition has always been recognized in a traditional if mitigated form. The poet, at least since the Renaissance, where the so-called Romantic commonplace of the lonely poet first began, is conceived to follow Virgil's model and only gradually to raise himself from the subject of man in nature to that of man conscious of his social or cosmic destiny. The nature-notes of Pastoral swell into the sterner music of Epic. When Wordsworth puts at the head of some extracts from his poem the following verses from the end of *The Minstrel,*

> Adieu ye lays that fancy's flowers adorn
> The soft amusement of the vacant mind

he is echoing, like Beattie himself, the traditional farewell by which the poet turns to a higher theme.[4] Wordsworth, who is about to leave for Cambridge, is indicating his intention to put off childish things: either all poetry, because imagination and the social principle are at odds, or fantasy in favor of a poetry dealing with social man.

But in "The Vale of Esthwaite" itself, Wordsworth composes an adieu of his own, and complicates an already complicated situation. It is impossible to tell whether his valedictory is aimed at poetry as such or only at the "gothic lyre," his present obsession with gloomy, solipsistic, supernatural fancies:

> Adieu, ye forms of Fear that float
> Wild on the shipwreck of the thought,
> While fancy in a Demon's form
> Rides through the clouds and swells the storm,
> To thee, sweet Melancholy, blind,
> The moonlight of the Poet's mind. (546–51)

I doubt that Wordsworth knew very precisely what he was saying farewell to in his poem. Almost twenty years later, in *The Prelude* (which is his own Progress poem), his imagination is still uncertain of its true subject; and almost thirty years later, he prefaces the first edition of *The Excursion* with his most famous renunciation of "gothic" projections and myths:

> Not Chaos, not
> The darkest pit of lowest Erebus,
> Nor aught of blinder vacancy, scooped out
> By help of dreams—can breed such fear and awe
> As fall upon us often when we look
> Into our Minds, into the Mind of Man—
> My haunt, and the main region of my song.[5]

Wordsworth's uncertainties, despite that bold preface, are not resolved even in *The Excursion*. The apocalyptic tendency of his imagination remains in conflict with the social or socializing principle[6] in human life. Nature is at the center of this conflict because it both binds and liberates imagination—binds it to forms that are not reducible to human meanings or purposes. "The Vale of Esthwaite" anticipates Wordsworth's later hope that the imagination can be married to this world, a hope often belied by the very imagination at work in his poems. It is quite clear that he is on the side of the Milton who praises Christianity for expelling from nature the obscene deities, and on the side of the Beattie who goes much further and (in the fashion of the Enlightenment) commends the

"Philosophick Spirit" for humanizing or, as we would say, demy-thologizing the mind.[7] Yet the very things Beattie and Milton purge—

> In the deep windings of the grove, no more
> The hag obscene, and griesly phantom dwell;
> Nor in the fall of mountain-stream, or roar
> Of winds, is heard the angry spirit's yell,[8]

—force their way back into Wordsworth's mind:

> But he, the stream's loud genius [yelling spectre[9]], seen
> The black arch'd boughs and rocks between
> That brood o'er one eternal night,
> Shoots from the cliff in robe of white. (35–38)

He cannot see nature straight. Nor man; except in the confessional passage at the end of his poem Wordsworth's human figures are not separable from a gothic machinery of shrieking phantoms, ghostly tapers, and haunted castles.

Enough survives of "The Vale of Esthwaite" to let us glimpse its rudimentary plot, and to determine that its subject is indeed the mind of Wordsworth, understood generically as the Mind of a Poet. The partly illegible lines with which De Selincourt's text opens imply that Wordsworth is exorcizing something that hides "the landskip's various treasure." Out of a mist that steals away there appears a lovely green valley. But the poet's feelings are raised quickly to a curious pitch: he marks a shepherd's dog jumping about, and the shepherd himself, "Who knows his transport while he sees / His cottage smoking from the trees." Transport is too strong a word, and "knows his transport" an awkward hint at Virgil's "Too happy if they knew their happiness."[10] Both point to the reversal of mood which ensues: the mind that knows its joy is unable to go further, and plummets to a peculiar dejection. The homely scene, emerging from the veils of mist and night, is suddenly dropped:

> At noon I hied to gloomy glades,
> Religious woods and midnight shades,

> Where brooding Superstition frown'd
> A cold and awful horror round. (25–28)

In this gloomy wood the poet has a vision of human sacrifice. "Superstition," as the Hawkshead school exercise suggests,[11] means heathenish practices (by extension, Catholicism) which a milder *religio loci* settling in the Britannic isle expelled:

> And hark! the ringing harp I hear
> And lo! her druid sons appear.
> Why roll on me your glaring eyes?
> Why fix on me for sacrifice? (31–34)

If this is puerile, it must be recalled that a similar fancy recurs to the poet wandering solitary over Salisbury plain six years later.[12] Next comes a puzzling transition to the apparently welcome yet not less terrible sight of a waterfall ("But he, the stream's loud genius . . ."; see above p. 79). This image, mused upon, dies into a "faint rill tinkling softly sweet," after which an obscure fragment lets us glimpse a gothic mansion "in the black centre of a wood" (43–50).

Wordsworth has described an experience of alternation. A landscape emerges from darkness and returns to it.[13] Or there are two equally disturbing types of landscape, sterner and milder. Though the poet seems to be exorcizing "*that* beauty, which, as Milton sings, / Hath terror in it,"[14] the milder landscape he turns to cannot hold him. In Wordsworth's maturer work, emotion, when contemplated, increases like the expanding ripples in a lake, then settles to all-embracing stillness. Here (though the fragmentary nature of the poem must be remembered) the swift step-up of emotion is followed by catastrophe rather than expansion. "At noon I hied to gloomy glades." The spirit has turned once more to sterner beauty.

If we look at the first mild imagery closely, we find this reversal foreshadowed in the ambivalent delight with which the poet regards valley and mist:

> And see, the mist, as warms the day,
> From the green vale steals away;

> And ah! yon lingering fleecy streak,
> As breaks the rainbow, soon shall break. (5–8)

Such moralizing is a masked sentimental adhesion which indicates that Wordsworth is unwilling to relinquish the least object that might feed imagination, perhaps for fear that what is to come will satisfy still less. But nothing can tame his mood. His mind is quickly vexed to paroxysm; calls on darkness; and is then whelmed by the vision called up. The imagination falls victim to its own intuitions of power:

> Why roll on me your glaring eyes?
> Why fix on me for sacrifice?

From this curious self-fixation (antecedent to later and starker moments of self-consciousness) the sound of the waterfall, visually interpreted, saves the poet. But the spell is not entirely broken till he hears the water's sound as sound, and what seemed a yelling specter dies into an intimation of mild and natural being. The supernatural is exorcized; the apocalyptic directness evaded.

The pattern of this alternation is repeated in many parts of "The Vale of Esthwaite." The landscape having been depicted at dawn and noon, lines 75 to 136 describe nightfall. Wordsworth wanders along Lake Esthwaite wrapt in soft mystic feelings. Images of envelopment are multiplied in the Miltonic fashion of redundance:

> Twilight, wrapp'd in dusky s[hroud],
> Slow journey'd from her cave of cloud;
> Where, as she sleeps the livelong day
> And dreams of Philomela's lay,
> Her Elfins round her feebly sing,
> Or fan her face with silken wing. (77–82)

Though this scene is compared to the approach of night in Eden, images of envelopment are gradually replaced by a stark simplification of the spectrum to black and white:

> While in the west the robe of day
> Fades, slowly fades, from gold to gray,

> The oak its boughs and foliage twines
> Mark'd to the view in stronger lines,
> Appears with foliage marked to view,
> In lines of stronger browner hue,
> While, every darkening leaf between,
> The sky distinct and clear is seen. (95–102)

The preternatural face in nature begins to reveal itself; a synchronism in the landscape shows imagination stripped of mildness and envelope, growing in strength through its secret dissatisfaction with external objects, and inciting the catastrophic turn to terrible beauty. Only an idea of compensation, that as some things darken others are seen more clearly, retards night's blackout, which arrives swiftly enough:

> But now a thicker blacker veil
> Is thrown o'er all the wavering dale . . . (103–04)

A rock or a church steeple momentarily resists by rearing its head against the gloom, but the valley graced with woods, hills, and hamlets, is flattened into a level waste, the black fir mingles with the plain, and hills over hills

> From the blunt baffled Vision pass
> And melt into the gloomy mass. (115–16)

This time, however, no complete reversal ensues. The next twenty lines, after which the manuscript breaks off, although they skirt the vision of terrible beauty, tell of a different deployment of the baffled senses:

> And on its bosom all around
> No softly sunken vale is found,
> Save those seen faintly [that] combine
> To form the Horizon's broken line.
> Now holy Melancholy throws
> Soft o'er the soul a still repose,
> Save where we start as from a sleep
> Recoiling from a gloom too deep.
> Now too, while o'er the heart we feel

> A tender twilight softly steal,
> Sweet Pity gives her forms array'd
> In tenderer tints and softer shade. (117–28)

The plunge to terrible beauty is avoided by a reversion to twilight feelings of dilation and diffusion, to broken, dying, streaking, blending, lengthening, and dissolving lines.

Yet melancholy, offspring of the eighteenth-century elegiac tradition, is a precarious remedy. It rarely succeeds in calming imagination. Many a time the poet starts to evoke his sad-cheerful scene:

> Yon hamlet far across the vale
> Is deck'd in lustre soft and pale;
> Hope, like this moon, emerging fair
> On the dark night of sad despair,
> Till higher mounted cannot chear
> The sable mountains frowning near
> Yet does she still all fondly play
> On scenes remote with smiling ray. (163–70)

In vain; the scene slips into darker mood, till the style reveals the poet's mind stuttering in the grove of gloom:

> 'Tis thus the dawning queen of Night
> While ineffectual is her light
> To gild the mountains near array'd
> In gloomy blank impervious shade
> Bounds o'er the gloom. (171–75)

The poet starts once more, evokes a "tear-glistering morn" in Eden vale, but is soon caught by proleptic despair, which he tries to expel by another circling, this time round a pyre:

> To mark the white smoke rising slow
> From the wood-built pile below,
> Hang like a Spirit on its way,
> Hang lingering round with fond delay
> Round the dear Spot where late it[15] fell,
> And it had lov'd so long and well.

> Methinks my rising soul would smile
> With joy, to linger here awhile. (186–93)

Later in the poem the idea of a "spot" pursues him. It is involved with thoughts of sacrifice and loss, with memory, fixity and fixation. He imagines a haunted castle in which an ashy-hued female appears holding a blue taper. She leads him through ghastly echoing passages to an iron coffer marked with blood:

> The taper turn'd from blue to red
> Flash'd out—and with a shriek she fled.
> With arms in horror spread around
> I mov'd—a form unseen I found
> Twist round my hand an icy chain
> And drag me to the spot again. (262–67)

Though such adventures are self-derided as "poor and puny joys / Fond sickly Fancy's idle toys," Wordsworth goes on to enumerate still more hair-raising things. His soul seems to be hypnotized by powers lodged in the external world. He yearns for calmer pleasures, yet a terrible landscape draws him on compulsively. He is made to haunt giddy heights accompanied by a hellish music:

> her dark cheek all ghastly bright,
> Like a chain'd Madman laugh'd the Night.
> Again! the deep tones strike mine ear,
> My soul will melt away with fear,
> Or swell'd to madness bid me leap
> Down, headlong down, the hideous steep. (282–87)

A picture of Grasmere's dreamy vale suggests itself, but is quickly replaced by an image of flowers sleeping at peace while the tempest prepares their destruction.

Having described these alternations, we must interpret them more explicitly. Their significant feature is that the turn to sterner beauty coincides with seeing nature in supernatural terms. Nature's familiar aspect is eroded; quasi-apocalyptic creatures and visions emerge. This, we know, is a sign that imagination is begin-

ning to reveal itself as a power separate from or even opposed to
nature; yet it seems to Wordsworth as if nature, not imagination,
were rising up against him. It is nature that is demonic, and the
leisurely peripatetics of the Miltonic or eighteenth-century rambler
become a nightmare straying through regions in which the poet is
no longer in control of his imagination. The harp assaults the min-
strel.[16]

> And oft as ceased the owl his song
> That screamed the roofless walls among,
> Spirits yelling from their pains
> And lashes loud, and clanking chains,
> Were heard by minstrel led astray
> Cold wandering thro' the swampy way,
> Who, as he flies the mingled moan,
> Deep sighs his harp with hollow groan.
> He starts the dismal sound to hear,
> Nor dares revert his eyes for fear:
> Again his harp with grating thrill
> Shrieks at his shoulder sharp and shrill;
> Aghast he views, with eyes of fire,
> A grisly Phantom smite the wire.
> Then fancy, like the lightning gleam,
> Shot from wondrous dream to dream. (51–66)

As poetry this is already acerb and aglow: the imagination, both
as theme and in fact, is taking over, and the harshness of its energy
shows something of apocalyptic character. Such visions, moreover,
guide or rather compel the poet to a dangerous "spot." What that
spot signifies, what memory or deed it hides, is impossible to de-
termine. It is more the *idea* of a spot that haunts Wordsworth: the
idea of a point of powerful stasis, a concentration and fixation of
power. The poet, to speak colloquially, is in danger of being "fixed
to the spot":

> I mov'd—a form unseen I found
> Twist round my hand an icy chain
> And drag me to the spot again.

Another instance, not yet mentioned, involves a carelessly destructive act:

> The ploughboy by his gingling wain
> Whistles along the ringing lane,
> And, as he strikes with sportive lash
> The leaves of thick o'erhanging ash,
> Wavering they fall; while at the sound
> The blinking bats flit round and round. (194–99)

In the last verse the thing the mind wished to hide is stirred up: a fixation, together with the blind attempt to escape it. The turn to sterner beauty always leads to such "spots"; and it is clear that the poem is their exorcism, an attempt to avoid them without voiding imagination.

Each type of avoidance will reappear in Wordsworth's later poems. Were we to give them a collective name it would coincide with what the mature poet calls Nature. His Nature is in opposition to the idea of a single or fixed or intransitive place of power. The alternations themselves are already a doubling and diversifying of experience, though their hypnotic pattern prevents Nature's variety from being felt. But the poem starts with an attempt to exorcize whatever hides the "landskip's various treasure." Perhaps Wordsworth turned to Milton's twin poems in the hope of learning their ambidextrousness of mood. Where contrary moods are so lightly and richly managed there is little danger of sinking into a "gloom too deep" or of the hurtling pain of recoil. The recoil or catastrophe itself is also avoided by glimpses of a symbolic (especially twilight) landscape, marked by dilation and diffusion, an emphasis of sound over sight, and the intuition of powerful motion in fixity or of life in darkness. Sometimes we can actually trace the poet's mind converting from its sudden or sinking gloom to a gradual crescendo encompassing both mild and terrific, picking up compensatory hints of life, and envisioning the presence at any moment of a symphony of powers:

> How sweet at Eve's still hour the song
> Of streams, the hills and vales among!
> Wide as the schoolboy's step the rill

> Drops from the near rock tinkling shrill;
> The Brook, scarce worth a bridge of stone,
> Soothes the lull'd ear with softer moan;
> A deep majestic murmur shews
> Where the slow solemn River flows;
> The torrent like the raving shore
> Swells the full choir['s] sullen roar. (153–62)

And lastly, the crisis point of the poet's struggle against fixation is discerned by a verbal mannerism. In the first episode:

> And ah! yon lingering fleecy streak,
> As breaks the rainbow, soon shall break . . .

in the second:

> While in the west the robe of day
> Fades, slowly fades, from gold to gray.

These are the beginnings of the Wordsworthian turn (incremental redundance).[17] The poet purges a too static or adhesive mood by means of gradually progressive repetition.

In "The Vale of Esthwaite," then, Wordsworth's imagination is turned strongly, too strongly, toward nature. There is a danger of his imagination being 'alienated' by the valley and as if buried in it. The spot he seeks and avoids is the place of his own imagination which hides in the valley the consciousness of its separateness. He strays, willing unwilling as in a dream, toward a center which is his separated yet therefore vulnerable self. In that centric spot an apocalyptic wounding takes place: it is associated with sacrifice, with druids, an iron coffer marked with blood, the putting out of eyes, suicide, murder, the black center of a wood, a deep dungeon.

Why did the Vale of Esthwaite become the scene of this drama? Wordsworth came to the valley shortly after the death of his mother, and he stayed from 1779 to his removal to Cambridge in 1787. His poem began in some form not long after his father's death in 1784 (mentioned in the confessional part, lines 418 ff.). We know that in these years he increasingly loved nature for its own sake. This is the time which must bind imagination, if bound it is

to be. But it is also the time when "social" links are loosened
through the death of father and mother and the forced separation
from Dorothy. Now Wordsworth is about to leave for Cambridge.
Should he lose this valley also, the reality principle itself might be
lost. The boy needs something truly external, some belief in the
reality of a larger body of which he is a part; his soul must be linked
to or rooted inalienably in something, and this eight-year associa-
tion with Esthwaite, the place of his strongest dreams and deepest
imaginings, becomes for him a needful spiritual fact. Lines 416 to
543 in De Selincourt's edition, a long sentimental review of the
loss of his parents, envision Esthwaite as that place which cannot
be taken from him, so charged is it with personal and imaginative
history. Every rock there might tell a tale, every memory find its
niche. Rising and setting in its confines, the imagination can never
be homeless.[18]

The demonic aspect of nature is therefore also its daimonic as-
pect and shows what danger the soul runs in seeking a natural
home. For its intense effort not to know its own separateness re-
sults in so forceful an attribution of its own energy to parts of na-
ture that these appear endowed with independent life and vex the
very power that has given them this life. The imagination *sub spe-
cie naturae* may fail to recognize itself and rise up as nature against
itself.[19] Huge and mighty forms "that do not live / Like living
men"[20] move slowly through the boy's mind by day and by night.
To overcome this new otherness, to redeem it by sympathetic ap-
propriation, the imagination may alienate itself still further, till
the repulsive is vanquished by becoming the compulsive, and leads
to a deepening estrangement.

Despite this danger, was it possible for Wordsworth to choose
the alternative—homelessness of mind? Apparently not, for the po-
em's maturest verses are those in which Wordsworth vows to keep
the valley always in his heart. The alternative seems to him too
dreadful. He shudders at a future day in which his power of
thought might be

> Sick, trembling at the world unknown
> And doubting what to call her own. (502–03)

He is afraid, in other words, of two things between which the distinction is not clearly drawn: madness and visionary blindness (blindness to nature), his senses covered by a "vast blank impervious cloud."

At one point, in fact, the poem exhibits that blind visionary: a kind of Tiresias figure or, to anglicize him, the specter of Milton. A tall thin figure appears whose eyes are "like two wan withered leaves,"[21] and who bears on his branded arm "the poet's harp of yore." This grisly guide leads Wordsworth to Helvellyn's inmost womb (a culmination of the "spot" theme),[22] and the obscure and terrible sight which follows ends with:

> I saw the ghosts and heard the yell
> Of every Briton [ ] who fell
> When Edmund deaf to horror's cries
> Trod out the cruel Brother's eyes
> With [ ] heel and savage scowl,
> While terror shapeless rides my soul,
> [ ] together we are hurled
> Far, far amid the shadowy world.
> And since that hour, the world unknown,
> The world of shades is all my own. (369–78)[23]

This 'blinding' initiation could express the condition of the visionary who feeds on darkness, having acknowledged the power of the spirit in him, and relinquished the inspiration from nature. He has tasted vision, as Persephone in the underworld tasted the pomegranate of Hades, and now belongs at least partially to that world, or it to him. Yet "The Vale of Esthwaite" is also devoted to the other Milton, whose "Il Penseroso" and "L'Allegro" show an unsurpassed English richness of nature imagery, with the chosen mood discovering its pleasures and the pleasures varying according to mood. That Wordsworth's first original poem reverts so often to a gothic and visionary gloom reveals the strength of the conflict in him between the homeless and the naturalized imagination, a conflict never to be quieted.

## 2. *An Evening Walk*

*An Evening Walk* was published at the same time as *Descriptive Sketches* in 1793, although its composition may have begun as early as 1787, shortly after "The Vale of Esthwaite" was concluded.[1] It borrows many images from the latter and continues the same concerns. Again a topographical poem, it serves to provide a frame for a multitude of images and sensations culled from nature, either by direct observation or via the eyes of unusually exact observers whose travel books Wordsworth had read.[2] In plan it is the history of a poet's evening, though admittedly a composite of evening walks through several places. The embryonic structure of "The Vale of Esthwaite" is modified; the poet omits morning and height of day and begins with noon in abatement. An introduction suggests that morning is equated with delights already past,

> Return Delights! with whom my road begun,
> When Life rear'd laughing up her morning sun . . . (27–28)

while the evening is evidently where the poet stands now "in the dial's moral round":

> the sport of some malignant Pow'r,
> He knows but from its shade the present hour. (41–42)

That we are not told very much about the time when "Most cool and pleasant is the tender blade," or when "breathless pale and still / The sultry noontide broods on every hill / . . . A deep religious gloom—a dread repose," suggests that the poet is seeking an ideal or symbolic landscape: one fitted to the soul, immune to the moods and vacillations depicted in his first poem. *An Evening*

*Walk* abounds even so in intimations of sterner beauty and deadly stasis. It begins as

> the wan noon brooding still,
> Breath'd a pale steam around the glaring hill . . . (53–54)

which could serve to characterize a veiling of sterner beauty. "Glaring" describes a fixed visual intensity, but "breathed" is a more organic sign of relaxed motion, of freedom from savage emotions:

> Oh! ye Rocks and Streams,
> And that still Spirit of the evening air!
> Even in this joyous time I sometimes felt
> Your presence, when with slacken'd step we breath'd
> Along the sides of the steep hills.[3]

The opening pictures, similarly, which give a general view of the districts to be visited, strive to attain a balance between sterner and milder, or sublime and picturesque:

> Far from my dearest Friend,* 'tis mine to rove
> Thro' bare grey dell, high wood, and pastoral cove;
> His wizard course where hoary Derwent takes
> Thro' craggs, and forest glooms, and opening lakes,
> Staying his silent waves, to hear the roar
> That stuns the tremulous cliffs of high Lodore:
> Where silver rocks the savage prospect chear
> Of giant yews that frown on Rydale's mere;
> Where peace to Grasmere's lonely island leads. (1–9)

Yet to consider this passage closely would mean to change constantly the terms that are to be balanced. Sterner and milder nature are one pair but no single set will do. This variability in contrasts is not insignificant. Contrast becomes the basis of variety though always in danger of falling back into contrast. Thus "Bare grey dell" stands against "high wood," while "pastoral cove" is both verbally and semantically an intermediate notion; the quietly

---

* Dorothy Wordsworth, from whom the poet is still separated. The genre of the poem is, as the full title makes clear, that of a verse epistle to her.

meandering Derwent is set against the vertical and stilling roar of
the waterfall; the juxtaposition of "silver" and "savage" tells its
own story; "shy Winander," a solo figure, peeps from among the
sociable milieu of "clust'ring isles"; and "bosom'd deep" pairs
easily with "holly-sprinkl'd steeps." This variety (the "ever-vary-
ing charm" of line 18) is not due to the synoptical technique
alone: such minglings are elsewhere too:

> Bright'ning with water-breaks the sombrous gill . . . (72)

> Sole light admitted here, a small cascade,
> Illumes with sparkling foam the twilight shade . . . (79–80)

> And with long rays and shades the landscape shines . . . (98)[4]

> Blue pomp of lakes, high cliffs, and falling floods . . . (126)

> Deep yellow beams the scatter'd boles illume,
> Far in the level forest's central gloom . . . (163–64)

> from three paly loopholes mild and small,
> Slow lights upon the lake's still bosom fall,
> Beyond the mountain's giant reach that hides
> In deep determin'd gloom his subject tides . . . (335–38)

> silver'd wreaths of quiet charcoal smoke. (430)

This chequered nature, of almost Hopkinsian density, is easier
to appreciate in the segment than in the mass. An incredible visual
appetite is at play: the poet relies mainly on sight (the impor-
tance of sound will, however, become apparent) or on a strong re-
duction of the visual to alternations of high and low, stasis and
motion, and, above all, light and shade. He even anticipates at
times the visionary oxymoron of *Descriptive Sketches*.[5] Yet his
intent is again anything but visionary in the Miltonic sense of the
word. Commenting later on his couplet

> And, fronting the bright west in stronger lines,
> The oak its dark'ning boughs and foliage twines . . . (193–94)

Wordsworth supports the idea that *An Evening Walk* is an an-
thology of purely natural images. I date from this image, he says,

"my consciousness of the infinite variety of natural appearances which had been unnoticed by the poets of any age or country . . . and I made a resolution to supply, in some degree, the deficiency."[6] In the revision of the poem that began probably in 1794, a similar statement of purpose is found. Addressing his sister as directly as in "Tintern Abbey," Wordsworth commends her for being tremblingly awake to nature, like a willow in a wind or a lake responding to the lightest gale.* There are favored souls, he goes on, who by imagination and patient thought "see common forms prolong the endless chain / Of joy and grief, of pleasure and of pain"[7]— which suggests, of course, not only the variety in nature but also its intertwining with the passions of men.

The anthology view of *An Evening Walk* is also supported by its often directly acknowledged borrowings—but Wordsworth borrows finely observed phenomena as well as finely expressed sentiments—and by an architecture typical of the eighteenth-century descriptive poem. The poem's plan, ultimately based on Virgil's *Georgics,* which proved country matters could be the substance of a sustained poetry, consists of the juxtaposition of pictures and topics: first the abating noon, next the picture of a retreat sheltering from the sun; then the eye is caught by a rill or cliff; after that a description of sunset, first as it affects the scenery, then the late laborers; this is interspersed with a picture of the farmyard cock, a relation of local superstitions touching on twilight, and so on.[8] *The Prelude* will modify this pattern of frames radically by blending several memories together.[9] But *An Evening Walk* is still a gallery of discrete pictures, and to consider it as an anthology of images from nature is therefore persuasive, or at least prudent.

I believe, however, that a greater theme is present, and that nature's variety is not depicted for its own sake. The theme is again the growth of a poet's mind, and Wordsworth's interest in nature's wealth is related to a spiritual development approaching its crisis.

* William's reunion with Dorothy in 1794 coincides with his first real change of style, shown by these revisions: the poetry begins to be more relaxed, that is to say, less aggressively mimetic, less under the oppression of sight and rich externals. See the tribute to Dorothy (or Mary) in *Prelude* XII.151 ff., and below, pp. 257 f.

Wordsworth says at the beginning of his poem that he is alienated, that he looks on nature "with other eyes" (17 ff.); and there is no reason to think this crisis merely a matter of fashion, of poetic vapors. The very plan of the poem springs from Wordsworth's desire to show that many joys remain, though they differ in some way from previous ones. They differ, of course, in being more thoughtful: the poet now walks with Memory at his side (43). Memory, however, is often opposed to joy; it reminds him of loss; and in the body of the poem itself no vivid and *Prelude*-like retrospects occur. The poet's new or maturer delight, to judge from this history of a poet's evening, is simply that of observing nature's multitudinous phenomena: their variety, and (as Coleridge might have said) distinctity. Like the "Dutch" painters, except that his gaze is kinetic, Wordsworth gives every trait of nature its due, building larger prospects out of minutiae, and never sacrificing the part to the picturesque.

This is not the entire story, however. The poem has a plot, 'natural' perhaps, but also quite ingenious. While Wordsworth is intently engaged in observing nature, day slopes into darkness, baffles his observations, and the question arises of whether he can adhere in the encroaching darkness to nature's "ever-varying charm." Having escaped the curious stillness of noon, will he now succumb to night-thoughts, to apocalyptic intimations of the world's loss? He has already lamented that the present is known only by its shade, and now as the literal shades deepen, a prophetic despair arises. We glimpse here the real, if submerged, drama: his mind faces the coming of a night in which that variegated nature is no more.

Such a night never falls on the poet. Though his poem opens with a flight from sterner beauty and proceeds to intimations of sternest beauty, Wordsworth's hold on phenomena proves strong enough to reveal the life that persists even in darkness. His imagination is never stripped to itself, or naked of natural charms. There are precarious moments, however, in which the richly changing individualities of nature—changing like the "devious" steps of the poet or Derwent's "wizard" stream—almost disappear, and create a void in which imagination rises or on which it broods. "On the dark earth the baffl'd vision fails" (364).

Wordsworth's energy of description is doubly vigorous because his love of nature is linked intimately to a rearguard action against apocalyptic fears:

> Their pannier'd train a groupe of potters goad,
> Winding from side to side up the steep road;
> The peasant from yon cliff of fearful edge
> Shot, down the headlong pathway darts his sledge;
> Bright beams the lonely mountain horse illume,
> Feeding 'mid purple heath, "green rings," and broom;
> While the sharp slope the slacken'd team confounds,
> Downward the pond'rous timber-wain resounds;
> Beside their sheltering cross of wall, the flock
> Feeds on in light, nor thinks of winter's shock;
> In foamy breaks the rill, with merry song,
> Dash'd down the rough rock, lightly leaps along;
> From lonesome chapel at the mountain's feet,
> Three humble bells their rustic chime repeat;
> Sounds from the water-side the hammer'd boat;
> And blasted quarry thunders heard remote. (109–24)

We are kept suspended, in this picture of a mountain at sunset, between a point of view which intuits powers that threaten man and one for which they seem lightly ("naturally") available to him. The image of the rill, dashed down the rock yet leaping along, repeats that of the peasant with his sledge: the actions are seen almost simultaneously from this dual point of view. There is, moreover, a crude if telling shift within each sentence from passive to active (grammatically from past participle to the present indicative tense) which points to a desired capacity of absorbing shock and turning it to personal energy. Strange contrasts, at the same time, between headlong motion and quiet pasturing, make one uncertain as to whether the powers in this magic mountain are ordinary, or whether they are near to overwhelming ordinary perception. Wordsworth's edgy point of view (on the edge between a natural

and a supernatural perspective)[10] is intensified by the visually dis-
crete enumerations that couplet after couplet nervously compose
the picture, and by verbs so placed as to assume something of
noun status, wavering between static and dynamic.[11] The final
images, by modulating from sight to sound, as well as by juxta-
posing light with laboring sounds, continue that wavering of
power between its two faces of mild and stern, or potential and
excessive. The passage challenges comparison with the fuller res-
olution at the end of the poem (433 ff.), where nature, perceived
purely under the latent species of sound, again attests the presence
of ominous energies.

In the structure of the poem as a whole we occasionally find the
same precariousness as in this passage and certainly the same res-
olution. There is often no real harmony between what one again
recognizes as sterner and milder nature. The idyll of the swans in
their sheltered home of rushes leads to a picture of the Female Va-
grant, her children exposed to the elements:

> —No more her breath can thaw their fingers cold,
> Their frozen arms her neck no more can fold;
> Scarce heard, their chattering lips her shoulder chill,
> And her cold back their colder bosoms thrill;
> All blind she wilders o'er the lightless heath,
> Led by Fear's cold wet hand, and dogg'd by Death. (281–86)

Yet no sooner has Wordsworth given his awkward tribute to Fear,
Death, Tempest, and Lightning, than the tenor of the evening
scene is reasserted:

> Sweet are the sounds that mingle from afar,
> Heard by calm lakes, as peeps the folding star. (301–02)

Though his picture of the Vagrant is as unduly empathic as his
panegyric on domestic swans, Wordsworth does progress haltingly
toward such soundscapes, with their peculiar distancings and
blendings. If we did not know Wordsworth for its author, *An Eve-
ning Walk* might still be preserved for its renderings of tranquil-
lity in which undercurrent sounds emerge. It is true that Thom-
son's muse condescends to the "little noisy summer race" and

delights in the shock and musical aftermath of storms; yet one continues to feel the baton of Man Superior leading the chorus of glad creation. Even Beattie's melodious catalogue (which demonstrably influenced Wordsworth and is itself the "realistic" equivalent of Spenser's florilegia) has the stylized quality of the ear being exerted to make its point once, each sound being duly registered.[12] Wordsworth's melodies of evening have a more covert eloquence of intent. Their diminuendos build up into a crescendo of secretly continuing life. He is sensitive to whistling swain, slow-winding wagon, the sugh of swallows, horses beating on the lake's edge while slaking thirst, the sweep of late mowers' scythes, a talking boat, the faint uproar (a fine oxymoron) of bathers, and one "restless piper wearying out the shore." Meanwhile, as if to continue these dyings into another realm,

> in sweet cadence rising small and still
> The far-off minstrels of the haunted hill,
> As the last bleating of the fold expires,
> Tune in the mountain dells their water lyres. (325–28)

The plan of the poem allows, of course, the increased emphasis on sounds as light fades and the narration draws to its close. As one thing disappears, another is born; each fading reveals a less apparent stratum of life; light ebbs, and the phenomena of darkness come forth. Wordsworth is already in quest of a natural principle of compensation, weighing the gain against the loss. The dominance of sound compensates for night's drowning of the visible scene. Yet an almost explicit moment of bewilderment does occur:

> Last evening sight, the cottage smoke no more,
> Lost in the deepen'd darkness, glimmers hoar;
> High towering from the sullen dark-brown mere,
> Like a black wall, the mountain steeps appear,
> Thence red from different heights with restless gleam
> Small cottage lights across the water stream,
> Nought else of man or life remains behind
> To call from other worlds the wilder'd mind,
> Till pours the wakeful bird her solemn strains
> Heard by the night-calm of the wat'ry plains. (369–78)

The "other worlds" is not an otiose reference; it suggests the needs of Imagination. Unsatisfied, threatened by an absence of familiar nature, it returns to itself and loses contact with life and man. Even the nightingale, whose timely if traditional strains break the bewilderment, is not effective, and the poet's gloom deepens. The spirit started toward prophetic despair is hard to arrest, and in a verse movement reminiscent of "The Vale of Esthwaite" Wordsworth asks the sadly-pleasing sights to stay—"Ah no! as fades the vale, they fade away" (386). But nightingale is reinforced by owl, and owl predicts moon; and with the rising moon an unsuspected world becomes visible, "The deepest dell the mountain's breast displays." This night vision then seems to him a more perfect thing than the daylight, since "the scene is waken'd, yet its peace unbroke." In the closing paragraph, containing the narrative's finest verse, Wordsworth is able to create a night-piece which intimates the persistence of vital powers in or despite profoundest stillness:

> Sound of clos'd gate, across the water born,
> Hurrying the feeding hare thro' rustling corn;
> The tremulous sob of the complaining owl;
> And at long intervals the mill-dog's howl;
> The distant forge's swinging thump profound;
> Or yell in the deep woods of lonely hound. (441–46)

If there is symbolic landscape in the poem, it is this moment of powerful tranquillity. It will be evoked more than once in Wordsworth's later poetry. "And all that mighty heart is lying still!" It indicates the possible coexistence of power and peace, of loss and power. *An Evening Walk* begins with an imperfect suggestion of it, when "hoary" Derwent is described as taking his "wizard course"

> Thro' craggs, and forest glooms, and opening lakes,
> Staying his silent waves,[13] to hear the roar
> That stuns the tremulous cliffs of high Lodore. (4–6)

The passage also contains a reminiscence from "Lycidas": "where *Deva* spreads her wizard stream." Milton deplores that the water nymphs could do nothing to save Lycidas from being whelmed by the remorseless deep. It is one of many reminiscences, direct or indirect, which Wordsworth includes, and the presence of Milton is not an abstract tribute. His style is associated for Wordsworth with the supreme objectification of personal loss in pastoral and epic form. Milton's privations, including loss of sight, served only to increase an inner brightness. The figure of the blind man, of the spirit feeding on darkness, already haunted through "The Vale of Esthwaite," and we know that Wordsworth's own loss, mentioned at the beginning of his poem, is the difficulty of taking joyous nourishment from visible nature, together with strange tidal movements of his increasingly self-aware, autonomous spirit. The paradox of loss in one direction and an added sense of power in another, is expressed in barbarously concentrated form when Wordsworth says, comparing childhood to his present changed state:

> Then did no ebb of chearfulness demand
> Sad tides of joy from Melancholy's hand. (21–22)

Though Miltonic blindness is not his ideal (Wordsworth fears the spirit left to itself and darkness) it remains the great example of a principle of compensation he seeks to find in nature but which may also live at nature's expense:

> In dangerous night so Milton worked alone
> Cheared by a secret lustre all his own
> That with the deepening darkness clearer shone.[14]

Milton is Vision, the might of a spirit separated from nature and therefore seeing nature's truly supernatural aspect. There is a theory that two powers fought for the soul of Keats: Milton and Shakespeare.[15] Two powers also fight for the soul of Wordsworth: let us call them Nature and Milton. This is unfair, of course; "Il Penseroso" and "L'Allegro" showed Wordsworth how romance could be combined with realism, vision with nature poetry. Yet he is never able to accept the more visionary poetry of *Paradise Lost,* which is based on the rejection of familiar nature or on some epochal loss in original human nature. Though his senses grow dim or dissatisfied he continues to look to nature as well as to himself; it is nature, in fact, or an incipient myth of it, that helps him to pass safely the still points of noon and of night. He advances from intimations of deadly stasis to the revelation of infinite hiding places of power. This revelation, moreover, is as "natural" in manner as in content: a simple, temporal unfolding, a gradual interchange of the powers of sight and sound, the one emerging more clearly as the other fails, but diversifying sense experience rather than substituting one sense for another.

As *poetry*, however, there is something decidedly strange about Wordsworth's first productions. How harsh they are! "Not musical as is Apollo's lute." When we think of any great poet, of Keats or Spenser or Milton himself, we realize that their juvenile verse is sensuous and indulgent. Disciplined, yes, but words are enjoyed for the sheer, neutral, self-justifying energy in them. The word is sound before it is sense; logos before logic; myth before meaning. If I may use a profane analogy: their poetry is like sexual desire unconscious of the one function that may later be imposed.[16] Even in the mature Wordsworth, who is much more relaxed, and who redeems blank verse from the lapidary style assigned to it,[17] there are practically no oases devoted to verbal pleasure, no such catalogues as fill one's mouth in Spenser, Milton, or Keats:

> Coole violets, and orpine growing still,
> Embathed balme, and chearfull galingale,
> Fresh costmarie, and breathful camomill.

And yet Wordsworth, we hear, is *the* poet of nature!

The contrary is as true. To follow nature meant, on his part, an extraordinary mimetic effort that reacts against the awakening or reawakening of apocalyptic thoughts. His realism, surely, is a kind of surrealism: it appropriates nature-facts with an energy which is spiritual rather than intellectual and tends to become a quality of the things appropriated. These mass upon us larger than life, and since we cannot explain their presence by any but the simplest plot idea ("he is telling us what he saw between noon and night") we think only of a virtuosity of the senses and link that easily to the poet's revolt against artificial eyes and ears. This revolt is certainly there; no genuine poem can be subdued to a single purpose. Yet

*An Evening Walk,* like "The Vale of Esthwaite," is always about to dissolve—to use the movie term—into apocalypse or fantasy, and that it does not is a considerable achievement. Wordsworth set out with less between himself and his imagination than perhaps any poet before him; he is somehow more vulnerable to apocalyptic starts and self-recognitions. When, therefore, he praises Nature, gratefully conscious of its role in his maturing, it is for interposing

> the covert of your shades,
> Even as a sleep, between the heart of man
> And outward troubles, between man himself
> Not seldom, and his own uneasy heart.[18]

*Descriptive Sketches* is as strenuous a poem as *An Evening Walk,* and its view of nature is even more problematic. Things get worse before they get better.

## 3.   *Descriptive Sketches*

Though drawing on several Wordsworthian rambles, *An Evening Walk* still preserves quasi unities of place and time, and depicts the poet walking at particular times of day, in one season, and with the imagery of the Lake District predominant. *Descriptive Sketches*, which really draws on a single sustained walk through the French and Swiss Alps, does not yield any such impression of unity. The reason, besides the long excursus on Liberty at the end,[1] is that the poet untiringly depicts a vacillation between mighty opposites that are far removed from the milder weathers and continuities of the English countryside. Fidelity to fact played a part in this, yet the focus on contrast is strongly and expressively schematic. Each "sketch" shows such swift variations of dark and light, or wintry and summery prospects, that time becomes a changeable function of place, until at Chamonix, as in Paradise, though with winter added, the seasons revel hand in hand.[2] Chamonix and Mt. Blanc are the last descriptive sketch given in the poem, and both exhibit single landscapes where seasons and times are juxtaposed:

> Last let us turn to where Chamouny shields,
> Bosom'd in gloomy woods, her golden fields . . . (680–81)[3]

> Alone ascends that mountain nam'd of white
> That dallies with the Sun the summer night . . . (690–91)

> Glad Day-light laughs upon his top of snow,
> Glitter the stars above, and all is black below. (700–01)

It is, however, less the destruction of a particular concept of time which concerns Wordsworth than the projection of his sense for a Power not diminished by time. The difference in this respect between *An Evening Walk* and *Descriptive Sketches* is interesting. The poet-traveler, in both poems, seeks the "hiding places" of power, and in *An Evening Walk* it is the natural lapse of time that reveals them. The poem's gradual course from noon to midnight shows that life hides in tranquillity and emerges in the day's dying. It foreshadows a principle of compensation expressed more clearly in "Tintern Abbey" and the Great Ode, where time is justified as the "mercy of eternity."[4] Yet in *Descriptive Sketches*, time plays no separate role; it is not a structural principle, hinting, like nature itself, that nothing dies absolutely. Instead, Wordsworth looks everywhere for a landscape which is all times at once, a Power in local form that interchanges seasons. The Journey has become a Quest.

That the poem *questions* nature has largely escaped its interpreters. Though Wordsworth is sure *that* Power abides, he is no longer sure *where* it abides. Almost every scene raises anew the question of the reality of the external world's power. Is it really nature that embodies or reveals "the life which cannot die"?[5] The last couplet quoted above recalls another of similar format in which the poet looks forward

> To where the Alps, ascending white in air,
> Toy with the Sun, and glitter from afar. (51–52)

In Pope, contrast is witty, or a means to pictorial emphasis; here it is less a rhetorical device than the awkward index of a mind uncertain as to what reality it should ascribe to nature. Augustan elegance of syntax,

> Toy with the Sun, and glitter from afar,

evokes, after slight change, a voice conscious of unfathomable contrast:

> Glitter the stars above, and all is black below.

There is no doubt that Wordsworth's sense for "powers and presences" has increased in *Descriptive Sketches*. But is this really linked to a further and distinct stage in his development? Is it not merely a reaction to the sublimer scenery now before him? The truth seems to be that the nature the poet hoped for and the nature he found were significantly different, and that his spiritual development turned on his interpretation of that difference. We know from both *Descriptive Sketches* and *The Prelude* that during the poet's trip through the Alps many scenes both impressed and vexed his sight: his sense for "powers and presences" is constantly roused, often deeply delighted, but still, somehow, unsatisfied. His quest, to localize his Idea of Nature in nature, fails. The one major exception to this, the Simplon episode,[6] is omitted from *Descriptive Sketches*. The poem shows only that his journey is a quest, and gives a first interpretation to the strong elusiveness of the nature he is seeking. The further and crucial interpretation is not fully achieved till he covers the same journey a second time in the sixth book of *The Prelude*.

His discovery during that second journey—this time as a mental traveler—is that the Alps brought him face to face with his imagination rather than with nature. The discovery is delayed some fourteen years, and comes over him during the actual process of composition.[7] The immediate result is his apostrophe to "Imagination . . . That awful Power." But in 1790–92 Wordsworth is still involved in intellectual (one could also say epistemological) crisis, and cannot separate his imagination from nature. *Descriptive Sketches* relates the story of an Idea of Nature in search of a nature adequate to it, and this quest, or its failure, constitutes the poem's peculiar authenticity.

Wordsworth's mature style is very different from that of *Descriptive Sketches*. The difference can be defined (perhaps too neatly) by saying that the "blendings" for which the later Wordsworth is famous are, despite anticipations already mentioned, remarkably absent in his early works. It is not possible to offer here a complete analysis of the poet's mature style, but its blendings or fusions are similar to what Coleridge termed Wordsworth's "original gift of spreading the tone, the atmosphere, and with it the depth and height of the ideal world around forms, incidents, and situations."[8] Although this comment is general rather than technical, it clearly could not apply to *Descriptive Sketches*, characterized by the strong contrasts and juxtapositions mentioned previously. *Descriptive Sketches*, in fact, gives the impression of being composed under the compulsion of stressing oscillation, bounding-line, contrast— anything but "blendings."

There are, again, two kinds of landscape in the poem. One is characterized by a mild, the other by a more fearful beauty, corresponding perhaps to the gentler and severer visitations of nature discriminated in *The Prelude*.[9] Both depict nature as a field of power, yet in only one is power dynamic, i.e. "revolving life."[10] For the vistas of sterner beauty suggest that life resides immutably in a few secret or sacred places: it is jealously self-contained, and reminds one of the Urizenic concept of power in Blake. The vistas of milder beauty, on the other hand, intimate a nature that benevolently multiplies the locus of power, being characterized by diversity of charm, by a *Tempe* aspect of pastoral and sublime. A forerunner of the landscape of "Tintern Abbey," it implies at least the possibility of natural blendings. The chill gloom of the Chartreuse, a region of "death-like peace," is nature in its sterner form, but we pass quickly to the milder solitude and varied pleasures of Como ("How bless'd, delicious Scene! the eye that greets / Thy open beauties, or thy lone retreats"). And in the last sketch the mingling beauties of Chamonix,

Five streams of ice amid her cots descend,
And with wild flowers and blooming orchards blend . . . (682–83)

are followed by the everlasting saturnine presence of Mt. Blanc:

Six thousand years[11] amid his lonely bounds
The voice of Ruin, day and night, resounds. (692–93)

The two types of landscape tend to alternate. Wordsworth even emphasizes their alternation beyond natural fact. The Chartreuse stands at the beginning, the region of Como toward the middle of the journey covered in *Descriptive Sketches*, yet he juxtaposes them. Elsewhere the poet evokes a "secret Power" that reigns in places of awful solitude, but a gentler picture soon emerges in the midst of the terrible sublime (283 ff. and 424 ff.). Or the two vistas become revolving features of one scene, and the reader must watch his step, so quick, occasionally, is the change:

> Now, passing Urseren's open vale serene,
> Her quiet streams, and hills of downy green,
> Plunge with the Russ embrown'd by Terror's breath,
> Where danger roofs the narrow walks of death;
> By floods, that, thundering from their dizzy height,
> Swell more gigantic on the stedfast sight. (243–48)

In addition to the abrupt change from one kind of landscape to another we have here a vertical oscillation (245–248) that can only point to a perplexity of the eyes. Nature, it seems, does not allow them to stay "stedfast." The interchange of stern and mild, therefore, is but a special case in a more general dynamism involving at once mind and nature. It is a dynamism of contrasts not of blendings, although the milder vistas, like Chamonix, anticipate a new concept emblematically. Yet even at Chamonix the passing of the poet's eye serially from one object to another will not allow any real meditative deepening of the tone.

It is true, certainly, that the strongest touches in the poem show nature as a quintessence of opposites. Sometimes a single verse is enough to suggest this:

> the chasmy torrent's foam-lit bed . . . (464)

> the mystic streams of Life and Death. (73)[12]

A couplet may show the same "power" in opposite manifestations:

> Where rocks and groves the power of waters shakes
> In cataracts, or sleeps in quiet lakes. (11–12)

Or it may suggest the same object throwing out obverse faces:

> Tower like a wall the naked rocks, or reach
> Far o'er the secret water dark with beach. (287–88)

Darkness and light, another important pair, keep their separate domains, yet set each other off:

> Here half a village shines, in gold array'd,
> Bright as the moon, half hides itself in shade. (106–07)

TO: MCLIBRARY - LIB MCLIBRARY

MESSAGE ID: 089622    DATE: 08/05/93    TIME: 1

*** SYSM INBASKET

*** REQUESTOR: MCLIBRARY - LIB MCLIBRARY

*** TERM=ME12; 08/05/93, M O

the poet wants contrast
e the idea of passive or

stless spire,
: springing fire,
sts throw
s below. (108–11)

nto opposites:

around,
s sound,
drown'd. (57–59)

has been said previously
s. We see now that the
The poet's contrasts re-
aclitan mind that breaks
Yet Wordsworth's mind
does not "murder to dis-
that its elements remain
ation and animism the
verything his glance en-
nse of life is misleading:
th half of the village has
is a multitude of objects
n blend. The poet's eye,

in the beautiful expression of *The Prelude,* seeks (but does not find) a surface where its power might sleep.[14]

*Descriptive Sketches,* therefore, is not a portrait of nature, or the projection on nature of an idea, but the portrayal of the *action* of a mind in search (primarily through the eye) of a nature adequate to its idea. It is already the "mind of man" which constitutes, however obscurely, the poet's 'haunt and main region.'[15] The eye, the most despotic of the bodily senses in Wordsworth, is thwarted in a peculiar manner. It seeks to localize in nature the mind's intuition of "powers and presences," yet nature itself seems opposed to this process, and leads the eye relentlessly from scene to scene.[16] Through this restless movement the poet always nears yet avoids total imaginative commitment. He often, of course, bogs down in static personification or absurd emphasis on "spirit of place," but he achieves in many passages a structure of dynamic effects quite different from the later technique of blending:

> 'Tis storm; and hid in mist from hour to hour
> All day the floods a deeper murmur pour,
> And mournful sounds, as of a Spirit lost,
> Pipe wild along the hollow-blustering coast. (332–35)

Floods, sounds, and coast are animized, yet how lightly! Though each thing or act is kept distinct and the passage crescendoes in overt personification (336–37), the dynamic emphasis of "deeper murmur," the concinnity of "murmur" and "mournful," the fine intransitive use of "pipe," and the illogically progressive "from hour to hour / All day" evoke successfully the presence of a more than local, of a multiplying energy. Yet when the poet

> stops the solemn mountain-shades to view
> Stretch, o'er their pictur'd mirror, broad and blue,
> Tracking the yellow sun from steep to steep,
> As up th' opposing hills, with tortoise foot, they creep . . . (102–05)

his multiplication of entities makes for a high poetic gibberish. Each power seems to thwart the other in the narrow space of the heroic couplet.

Thus Wordsworth's individual landscapes remain a tour de force or a conceit. The drama lies in the mind striving for them. The idea of power in Wordsworth is as perplexed by the external world to which it turns as the idea of power which haunts Shelley's encounter with Mt. Blanc.[17] It remains an idea, obscurely, confusedly. The sixth book of *The Prelude*, in which Wordsworth retraces his journey, confirms this. There he respects more clearly the hiatus between the idea that moves him and the external world it seeks out. Mt. Blanc is now an anticlimax soon passed over. The poet, on seeing it, "grieved / To have a soulless image on the eye / That had usurped upon a living thought / That never more could be" (*Prelude* VI.525–28). The clarification extends from plot to poetic method. In 1791–

92, no single "prospect" satisfying the idea in him, Wordsworth spreads the swift interchanges of seasons, times, and landscapes regularly over nature as a whole. But ten years later these moments of "grateful vicissitude" gather into a magnificent instance of visionary *contrasts*. The image produced by their consolidation expresses at last the idea of nature haunting the mind—of a place-bounded yet not time-bounded life that is the visible pledge of immortality:

> The immeasurable height
> Of woods decaying, never to be decayed,
> The stationary blasts of waterfalls,
> And in the narrow rent at every turn
> Winds thwarting winds, bewildered and forlorn,
> The torrents shooting from the clear blue sky,
> The rocks that muttered close upon our ears,
> Black drizzling crags that spake by the way-side
> As if a voice were in them, the sick sight
> And giddy prospect of the raving stream,
> The unfettered clouds and region of the Heavens,
> Tumult and peace, the darkness and the light—
> Were all like workings of one mind, the features
> Of the same face, blossoms upon one tree;
> Characters of the great Apocalypse,
> The types and symbols of Eternity,
> Of first, and last, and midst, and without end.[18]

Having determined 'what happens' in *Descriptive Sketches*, we still face the question of what this tells us about the growth of a mind, which is a *poet's* mind. The distance between Wordsworth's maturity and youth, between *The Prelude* and *Descriptive Sketches*, is enormous. One gets the impression of a radical break in style and thought. The truth, however, is more complex: *Descriptive Sketches* is a poem of crisis, essentially of a crisis tending to occur in every poet qua poet. The poem stands at such a distance from Wordsworth's maturer work because he records the crisis while still in its grip, and not, as in *The Prelude*, bent over a deepening insight.

The poet's crisis may be described as follows: In waking to his own power he passes through a curious moment of blindness to it, which forces him to go out (i.e. to nature) rather than in. Wordsworth later interprets this error as providential, but *Descriptive Sketches* no more than records it. A result of this inner blindness is, of course, too much sight: the eyes defeat themselves by looking everywhere, "Still craving combinations of new forms, / New pleasure, wider empire for the sight."[19] And by thus pitting the eye against itself, nature helps the poet eventually to confront his own "separate fantasy,"[20] the autonomous power in his mind that makes him a poet, though deeply, perhaps inextricably, involved with an idea of nature. Whether he really confronts it before his famous apostrophe to "Imagination . . . That awful Power" remains uncertain. But if we respect the style of *Descriptive Sketches*, especially verse-form and syntax,[21] we see how faithfully the poet records a defeat of the eye which eventually leads him *through* nature *beyond* it.

For his verse Wordsworth had three traditions to choose from. Heroic couplets were usual for loco-descriptive poems, but Thomson, Akenside, and Cowper used blank verse for their long descriptive works. There was also the possibility of octosyllables, used by Collins, Dyer, Warton, and Lady Winchilsea, and by Wordsworth himself in "The Vale of Esthwaite." It is difficult to say why Wordsworth chose the couplet. Legouis, who thinks he made an error in his choice of verse, has a good remark on the difficulties of the couplet for descriptive poetry: "Just as the couplet makes it difficult to sustain the breath throughout a narrative or an argument, so too it refuses to lend itself to description, and compels the writer to place everything, both the striking features and subordinate details of ,the picture, in the foreground; while it transforms description, to which the blending of tones is essential, into an enumeration of distinct and independent objects."[22]

Perhaps Wordsworth did make a mistake, but it is clear that the couplet helps him *not* to blend tones. Especially effective when expressing well-defined contrasts, it divides a scene—as Legouis suggests—into distinct and balanced objects (here . . . there), but also into distinct and balanced glances (now . . . now), and precise inclusions or exclusions (or . . . or). The things observed really express the observer's power of comparison. Frame after frame like glance after glance: the logic of the couplet expresses an eye laboring under the abstract consciousness of "too much" and very careful to retain its initiative. We are never, in *Descriptive Sketches*, allowed to forget that the poet is an outsider vis-à-vis nature: he "leads" the landscape as much as he is "led" by it. He *sees, marks, surveys, stops to view.* The form of the couplet provides an awkward yet rigid reminder that it is less nature than a certain idea of it that moves him. Almost every two lines, the mind performs a new act.

Yet if the couplet, in its received form, stresses what might be called the intellectual eye, in Wordsworth's hands it constantly knits the latter with the bodily eye, as if the two worked against each other to produce a single knot of strength. A passage like this—

> From the bright wave, in solemn gloom, retire
> The dull-red steeps, and darkening still, aspire,
> To where afar rich orange lustres glow
> Round undistinguish'd clouds, and rocks, and snow . . . (180–83)

shows the bodily eye in its restlessness, shuttling between light and darkness, and ascending, through a series of dynamic contrasts, from visible to invisible, from bright waves to undistinguished clouds. In following a purely sensuous line it seems, finally, to defeat itself. The intellectual eye is also there: its abstractly quick movement between opposites is abetted by the neoclassical form, which retards, through an external system of pauses, the full internal development of images, but cannot any longer compose contrasts into comparisons.

In *Descriptive Sketches*, therefore, transcendence is still mainly visual. It is the eye that both puts and restlessly exceeds the "line where being ends."[23] And for this tension the couplet is well suited. Blank verse allows meditative blending, but in the closed couplet feelings have little time to develop through one image before a second supervenes.[24] Wordsworth, in fact, destroys the meditative potential of the couplet by cramming it with visual data:

> —Thy lake, mid smoking woods, that blue and grey
> Gleams, streak'd or dappled, hid from morning's ray. (138–39)

This is counting the streaks of nature with a vengeance. No sooner has the eye fixed on one object or quality, than others jostle and extend. Yet if the eye continually goes beyond, it is only to fix a new line (to create a new visual entity), and to transcend that also. We expect the next verses to refer to the lake or to begin a new subject, but they draw out the adjectival phrase:

> hid from morning's ray
> Slow-travelling down the western hills, to fold
> It's green-ting'd margin in a blaze of gold. (139–41)

The ideal effect of the Wordsworthian couplet is, as here, to suggest a line where being ends, then to suggest how that line is surpassed. The eye departs from the lake only to return, yet its return brings a "blaze of gold" that extends the margin.[25]

Wordsworth's lapidary, quasi-Miltonic syntax, shows a correlative structure of effects. The syntax emphasizes as far as possible the self-contained rather than relational form of the words in a sentence. A whole line may, by syntax and word order, aspire to the condition of a noun:

> Where rocks and groves the power of waters shakes
> In cataracts.

Compare the absolute verb in

> Glitter the stars above, and all is black below.

Thus the poet minimizes not only scenic but also syntactical blendings. He uses an abnormally high proportion of intransitive verbs, of absolute constructions patterned on Latin or Milton, and substantival adjectives.[26] Visual fact, accumulating, presses against an even more static (substantive) syntax, and the final pattern reflects once more a mind haunted by the idea of fixed or intransitive powers, which goes unsatisfied from sight to sight, forced to transcend the bounded images it seeks.[27]

The thwarting of the eye is, from the later perspective of *The Prelude*, only a special case of nature's benevolence. Speaking, in Book XII, of the years of crisis, Wordsworth remarks:

> Nor only did the love
> Of sitting thus in judgment interrupt

My deeper feelings, but another cause,
More subtle and less easily explained,
That almost seems inherent in the creature,
A twofold frame of body and of mind.
I speak in recollection of a time
When the bodily eye, in every stage of life
The most despotic of our senses, gained
Such strength in *me* as often held my mind
In absolute dominion. Gladly here,
Entering upon abstruser argument,
Could I endeavour to unfold the means
Which Nature studiously employs to thwart
This tyranny, summons all the senses each
To counteract the other, and themselves,
And makes them all, and the objects with which all
Are conversant, subservient in their turn
To the great ends of Liberty and Power.
But leave we this: enough that my delights
(Such as they were) were sought insatiably.
Vivid the transport, vivid though not profound;
I roamed from hill to hill, from rock to rock,
Still craving combinations of new forms,
New pleasure, wider empire for the sight,
Proud of her own endowments, and rejoiced
To lay the inner faculties asleep.[28]

In 1805 (XI.185) Wordsworth anticipates "another Song" to describe how nature thwarted the tyranny of (in particular) the eye. That song was never written: but I think *Descriptive Sketches,* and to a lesser degree *An Evening Walk* with its major movement from sight to sound, are essential documents in this biography of the senses. They show the poet suffering from the power of a basilisk eye which nature seems to counter or subdue by examples of "revolving life, / And greatness still revolving; infinite." An essential dynamism of the soul is, in other words, reestablished.

Yet a second way of expressing this fact seems more complete, and is one of the "great arguments" of *The Prelude.* In early youth the external world satisfied the poet's senses unforgettably; now it seems to frustrate them; and the full understanding of the change leads to a discovery of the Imagination as a power separate from Nature. The loss of strength in one direction is really an excess of strength in another: Wordsworth sees his hope rather than what he hoped to see. Nature leads man to himself, to the transcendent power mutely at work in him.[29]

The call to "look home" (as Vaughan would have said) is not, however, nature's final message. It might have been had Wordsworth accepted Coleridge's point that the external world lives only from our own life. "The forms / Of Nature have a passion in themselves," he counters toward the end of *The Prelude*.[30] To become aware of imagination he also had to become aware of nature's role in this process, and even though nature's hold on the senses weakens, he cannot but trust and continue to *go out*. In this way the soul maintains what Wordsworth later calls its "excursive power," and avoids a solipsism inherent in the discovery of its independence from nature.

What the later "blendings" mean in terms of the growth of a poet's mind must be left to another chapter. That they also reflect the action of a mind in search of a nature adequate to its idea is made abundantly clear by the verse prospectus to "The Recluse," whose subject is the *blended might* of mind and external world.[31] Wordsworth's later thought is constantly busy with the fact that the eye is or should be subdued, and when he begins to experiment with blank verse circa 1797, i.e. toward the end of his period of crisis, he sees the whole structure of his experiences more clearly, and subordinates visual contacts. They are rendered as the first stage of a process that transcends them, albeit an inevitable stage.[32] He now sees into the life of things not by a defeat of the eye which drives it on, but rather "with an eye made quiet by the power / Of harmony, and the deep power of joy." The blendings exhibited by the landscape of "Tintern Abbey" are symptomatic of a new relation between visual and ideal.

The sunset storm of *Descriptive Sketches* shows how near the poet may come to this later and fuller conception of nature's anagogy. Wordsworth's picture of the storm is, at the same time, an image of nature's power to wake the mind to the "Characters of the great Apocalypse." The light of sense is extinguished, but

still through a blinding rather than (as in "Tintern Abbey") a
blending:

> 'Tis storm; and hid in mist from hour to hour
> All day the floods a deeper murmur pour,
> And mournful sounds, as of a Spirit lost,
> Pipe wild along the hollow-blustering coast,
> 'Till the Sun walking on his western field
> Shakes from behind the clouds his flashing shield.
> Triumphant on the bosom of the storm,
> Glances the fire-clad eagle's wheeling form;
> Eastward, in long perspective glittering, shine
> The wood-crown'd cliffs that o'er the lake recline;
> Wide o'er the Alps a hundred streams unfold,
> At once to pillars turn'd that flame with gold;
> Behind his sail the peasant strives to shun
> The west that burns like one dilated sun,
> Where in a mighty crucible expire
> The mountains, glowing hot, like coals of fire. (332–47)

In terms of style also it is contrast not blending that leads the eye to
suspect a progression beyond force of sight.[33] The first six lines de-
scribe a power—initially sound, then light—breaking from behind
darkness. The next six lines give three separate and distinct images
of light in crescendo, reflected as fire by eagle, cliffs, and streams.
In the last four lines it is not the sun alone or various reflectors but
the whole landscape that burns.

This general scheme is, however, strengthened by contrasts so
subtle that they can hardly be distinguished from the incremental
blendings of Wordsworth's later style. The streams, hidden from
sight, are "deeper" to the ears. The sun shakes its shield *behind*
the clouds, but the eagle wheels *on the bosom* of the storm. The
eagle *glances* in the light, but the cliffs are seen *in long perspective
glittering*. The discovered *streams* become flaming verticals, *pil-
lars*. The sun, at the end, no longer walks on *his* western field, the
latter is itself *one dilated sun*. Such revelation of power, multiplied
from hidden yet specific place, veiling itself finally with excess as
at first with loss, remains into the poet's maturity a fit image of
how life is planted in the mind "for immortality."[34]

## 4. From "Salisbury Plain" to "The Ruined Cottage"

Certain turns in a man's life seem to conspire with fate. History holds up a mirror to him, as if greatness were the capacity to recognize in it a *de te res agitur*. The opportunity for such self-recognition is not rare. Wordsworth by the beginning of 1793 had matured for shock; a birth was due and came:

> Amid the groves, under the shadowy hills,
> The generations are prepared; the pangs,
> The internal pangs, are ready.[1]

*Descriptive Sketches,* finished in the autumn of 1792, prefigures Wordsworth's inner preparedness for a break with nature: his imagination is increasingly forced back on itself, and beginning to recognize its autonomy or supernatural vigor. Then, in December 1792, the poet is obliged to return to England (and leave Annette, whose child is born that month); *Descriptive Sketches* is published in January 1793; and a month or so later history deals him a moral wound which opens perhaps many others and determines by action and reaction not only his individual character as a poet but also his understanding of what (generically) it is to be a poet.

In February 1793 England declares war on France.* It is this, and not as has occasionally been assumed, the failure of the Revolution to live up to its ideals, which presents the poet with his image of a Great Betrayal:

---

* So Wordsworth. Actually France declared war on England on the expulsion of the French ambassador.

> Not in my single self alone I found,
> But in the minds of all ingenuous youth,
> Change and subversion from that hour.²

To describe his shock Wordsworth recurs to images of schism, of violent rift, and uprooting. Their full significance will come to light on studying *The Prelude*. But it is already important to observe that they suggest a divorce from nature or natural process. More is betrayed than faith in England. What happens in 1793 seems to have opened to consciousness that break with nature which 'consciousness' as such implies, and the fruits of which are solitude and selfhood.

The prehistory of this break is of necessity obscure. Psychoanalysis has searched it back to the birth of the child and even the birth of the race. The breach in nature that consciousness is *felt* to be³ depends not on a single but rather on an intervolved series of happenings, and is certainly as complex as the metamorphosis of the butterfly, that ancient symbol for the soul. Yet it does strike into mind at one point: the idea of a single peripety persists, and Wordsworth says he has known no moral shock intense enough to be named a "revolution" before this betrayal. In myth, similarly, it is one irremediable act which strips man naked. The emphasis by this is shifted from prehistory to history proper: the wound, localized in memory or time, becomes a mark from which the individual projects as individual. The killing of the albatross in "The Ancient Mariner" is such a mark. The motive cannot be plumbed, and the act points to a mystery of separation which lies in the destiny of man. Nature is betrayed, an innocent creature slain, and it is the terrible consequence and the terrible beauty born of it which matter.

Wordsworth's development in the time under discussion is extremely complex. His separation from nature has almost too many resonances: psychological, ideological, apocalyptic. An inner reconstruction, moreover, of the idea of nature immediately begins. Like Paracelsus' balm which quietly seals all wounds of the earth, a surviving faith at once proceeds to heal his break with nature.

What is action (separation) and what reaction (sealing) becomes difficult to establish. But a synoptic view of the major poems of this period, "Salisbury Plain" (1793–95), *The Borderers* (1795–97), and "The Ruined Cottage" (1795?–98), will prepare us for the explicit if telescoped account of the growth of an "individual" mind given in *The Prelude*.

Viewed from the perspective of "The Vale of Esthwaite" and *Descriptive Sketches,* the major poems of 1793–98 are still haunted by a concern for specific place. Their humanitarian or political emphasis does not succeed in being central. We pity but are rarely angered by what is shown, and especially in "Salisbury Plain" the landscape is more intriguing than its people. The latter are almost aids to intensify our emotion for this landscape which sends a strange comfort of desolation into the heart:

> The troubled West was red with stormy fire
> O'er Sarum's plain a traveller wearily
> Measured his lonesome way the distant spire
> That fixed at every turn his backward eye
> Was lost tho' still he turned in the blank sky[.]
> By thirst and hunger pressed he gazed around
> And scarce could any trace of man descry
> Save wastes of corn that stretched without a bound
> But where the sower dwelt was nowhere to be found.
>
> No shade was there, no meads of pleasant green
> No brook to wet his lips or soothe his ear
> Long files of corn-stack here and there were seen
> But thence no smoke upwreathed his sight to cheer
> And see the homeward peasant dim appear[.]
> Far off, he sends a feeble shout—in vain
> No sound replies but winds that whistling near
> Sweep the thin grass and, passing, wildly plain,
> Or desert lark that pours on high a wasted strain[.][4]

Such stanzas express less a physical than a spiritual ordeal. The traveler, like one of Hardy's later figures, is an "exposed" person:

he moves solitary and shelterless, and neither the sights of nature nor thoughts of man bring him relief. He is literally an outsider, as if nature had ejected him. The changeable scenery, the up-and-down vacillation of *Descriptive Sketches*, is replaced by a horror of the horizontal which increases the sense of exposure. Later revisions stress still more the domain of the mental which is so beautifully mingled with physical need in "No brook to wet his lips or soothe his ear." Lines 24 to 26 become

> Perplexed and comfortless he gazed around,
> And scarce could any trace of man descry,
> Save cornfields stretched and stretching without bound.

The distinct sense of horizontal infinity is produced in part by Wordsworth's use of Spenserian features. Spenser's consonance, for example, which tends to be strongly initial (alliterative) and so to strengthen his line by a kind of vertical emphasis, is here retained in a subtler form (*scarce* . . . de*scr*y) but also extended in "stretched and stretching" to become almost a grammatical figure. Wordsworth renders the perplexity of a *glance* forced to go beyond finite place to linear infinity. He renders it by increasing the natural inertia of the Spenserian verse line which culminates appropriately in its final alexandrine. There is the sense of a tremblingly forward movement created in part by monotony of assonance ("Perplexed and comfortless he gazed around," "No sound replies but winds that whistling near / Sweep the thin grass"); but the most effective feature is the indefinite caesura. By a Spenserian multiplication of monosyllables as well as a generous use of inversion, Wordsworth fashions lines that have several possible pauses or no pause at all:

> And see the homeward peasant dim appear . . .
> But thence no smoke upwreathed his sight to cheer . . .
> No sound replies but winds that whistling near . . .

So marked is the faltering movement of this poetry that the horizontal appears as an expansion of the static. One could apply to such lines what Wordsworth says of the old Leech-gatherer, whom he compares to a cloud that "moveth all together, if it move at all." The same curious interaction of stasis and horizontal motion is felt in the poem's setting. Salisbury Plain undermines by its horizontality the very idea of place. It is a no-place, yet thereby rouses a nostalgia for specific place, for single or fixed points like spire, tree, "one dwelling." The starker the horizontal, the stronger this anticipation of a static point, and vice-versa. Neither extreme is free of horror. When in the poem a specific "spot" does appear, it is in the form of a clanging gibbet:

> He looked and saw on a bare gibbet nigh
> In clanking chains a human body hang
> A hovering raven oft did round it fly
> A grave the[re] was beneath which he could not descry.

> It was a spectacle which none might view
> In spot so savage but with shuddering pain
> Nor only did for him at once renew
> All he had feared from man but roused a train
> Of the mind's phantoms horrible as vain[.]
> The stones, as if to sweep him from the day
> Roll'd at his back along the living plain
> He fell, and without sense or motion lay
> And when the trance was gone again pursued his way[.]⁵

The circling raven emphasizes the enclosed, spot-like character of the sight; while the traveler's second encounter is with the "powerful circle" of Stonehenge. Both experiences, moreover, revive the past and therefore carry us back to the memory-vault image of "The Vale of Esthwaite." There is, of course, a character propriety to this, since the sailor (the traveler) is haunted by his conscience. Yet his fear or obsession in a sense precedes character: Wordsworth's poem is not a case study but deals with human nature in general. The Female Vagrant, whom the sailor meets in his third encounter, has analogous fears. The "Dead House" of the plain, in which both shelter, is said by her to have been the scene of a terrible discovery; a horse, so her story goes, had pawed so insistently on one stone that his master excavated it and found "the grim head of a late murdered corpse." The terror is gothic and ab-

surd enough, yet like the two previous episodes of the poem it
brings to demonic pitch the obsession with specific place. Every-
thing converges on one spot: sailor and woman, the horse pawing
again and again on the stone, the past rising from under it.

We remember imagination rising from the mind's abyss and
are tempted to understand such episodes as symbols for it. Such a
jump is too quick, and not meaningful enough. Basically, the link-
ing of past and place again expresses a fascination with the single
or fixed. Place, in "Salisbury Plain," is powerfully reduced to its
essence of spot. Powerfully: the centroversion[6] invests it with a
quality of fatedness, with demonic attraction or dark splendor:

> For oft, at dead of night, when dreadful fire
> Unfolds that powerful circle's reddening stones
> Mid priests and spectres grim and idols dire
> Far heard the great flame utters human moans
> Then all is hushed: again the desert groans
> A dismal light its farthest bounds illumes,
> While warrior spectres of gigantic bones
> Forth issuing from a thousand rifted tombs
> Wheel on their fiery steeds amid the infernal glooms.[7]

"Dead of night," that cliché, recovers here its sense of a "spot in
time" analogous to specific place and as charged with concentered
energy as totem or sacred idol. In *The Borderers,* Wordsworth has
Oswald relate a story which anticipates "The Thorn," and gives
the obsession with specific place its crudest yet also most vigorous
form. Every night, says Oswald, describing the first of Wordsworth's
many mad women:

> every night at the first stroke of twelve
> She quits her house, and, in the neighbouring Churchyard
> Upon the self-same spot, in rain or storm,
> She paces out the hour 'twixt twelve and one—
> She paces round and round an Infant's grave,
> And in the Churchyard sod her feet have worn
> A hollow ring; they say it is knee-deep.[8]

The spot syndrome (as I will now call it) is linked in *Descriptive Sketches* to the mind's search for a landscape adequate to its idea. The poet localized in nature his intuition of "Powers and Presences" but was forced to go from sight to sight and transcend the bounded image. His secret or sacred places alternate with "open beauties" and are resolved into a larger, dynamic landscape. They are not totally resolved, however; blocks of verse as of perception are juxtaposed with minimal blending. The eye is pitted against itself or confounded by anagogical contrast. In this way nature leads the senses beyond themselves, and imagination becomes aware of its autonomy.

"Salisbury Plain" shows a continuance of this process. But here, inspired as always by an actual landscape, Wordsworth projects a Power not only independent of time but also of place. He comes a step closer to the separation of his imagination from nature or to interpreting that apocalyptically as involving a *death* of nature. The spot syndrome—the obsession with specific place—is paradoxically stronger because imagination in its withdrawal from nature first withdraws to a single point. Its show-place is still nature but reduced to one center as dangerous as any holy site. This site is an *omphalos:*[9] the navel-point at which powers meet, the "one" place leading to a vision of the One. To describe it, the poet later resorts to the figure of an abyss (*Prelude* VI.594) which is a kind of verticalized point and a variant of the "narrow chasm" and "gloomy strait" (VI.621) he has actually crossed; while in another encounter he suddenly glimpses imagination in a "breach" or "dark deep thoroughfare" (1805 *Prelude* XIII.62 ff.).[10]

In its quality of omphalos, this place of places is at once breach and nexus, a breach in nature and a nexus for it and a different world. Like Porphyry's Cave of the Nymphs it leads perilously from one state of being to another. The image of a flood or sea— that "mighty gulph of separation" as the Female Vagrant calls it[11] —is often conjoined. In "Salisbury Plain," of course, stoniness not streaminess is dominant,[12] and even the horizontal infinite is seen to be an expansion of the fixed or static. Still, it is an *expansion*. Perplexing the eye, like the scenic contrasts of *Descriptive Sketches,* it can lead either to a near-apocalyptic horror of the boundless or to the vision of the mature Wordsworth who "sees not any line where being ends" and whose sense for blendings is anticipated by the milder vistas and occasional subtle crescendos of *Descriptive Sketches.* In the same way the spot syndrome anticipates the true omphalos. Stonehenge, full of a deadly *static,* charged with ghostly and whirlwind energies, will reappear in the "Winds thwarting winds, bewildered and forlorn" of the Ravine of Gondo. Even if the direction of the transference is from the Ravine of Gondo (crossed in 1790) to Stonehenge (visited 1793, versified 1793–95) and back again to the Ravine (versified 1799),[13] the crucial point is that both places approach the character of an omphalos, a strait between worlds.

Especially for the sailor, Salisbury Plain is exactly this: a purgatory, a strait between states of being. Perhaps the poem plays an analogous role in Wordsworth's own development. We know these are the critical years. As a man, Wordsworth is realizing what consciousness—or better, self-consciousness—implies. As a poet he is coming to know the autonomy of imagination. According to Jung, something very similar to the spot syndrome accompanies the process of self-discovery or individuation. True individuality, says Jung, is achieved when (conscious) ego and (unconscious) self are reconciled by means of *centroversion.*[14] The self is pictured by him as the center of the unconscious to which the ego turns in any effort of regeneration. The individual is whole when ego and self are one, or rather in communication and partnership (therefore more than 'one'); but during the process of individuation, which can be considered 'without end' just as unconsciousness is 'without beginning,' the ego runs the danger of being assimilated by the self, i.e. of returning to a preconscious wholeness which is an undifferentiated 'one.' Wordsworth is clearly fascinated by and fearful of a 'one' with magnetic force. The spot syndrome points to a centroversion as Jung describes it. The correlative sign of a katabasis or Night Journey is also present: the poem begins with such a journey on the part of the sailor, and the Female Vagrant is represented as having undergone a similar experience. She has passed through "a hollow deep" where "never clock was heard from steeple tower."[15]

Neither in "Salisbury Plain" nor in *Descriptive Sketches,* however, is the 'one' related to human form. The mind seeks it in nature or as an apocalyptic breach in nature. What human figures appear in "Salisbury Plain" actually put man in question: against him are ranged the powers in earth or of his own unrecognized imagination. Yet the active presence of human figures is interesting and constitutes an advance over *Descriptive Sketches.* Wordsworth invents for the first time a human machinery to express what is an essentially nonhuman landscape feeling. He uses a similar technique for "The Thorn" (March–April 1798), and anticipations of it are found in the figure of the Female Vagrant of *An Evening Walk.* The Vagrant of "Salisbury Plain" belongs to the earliest layer of the poem and goes back to at least 1791.[16]

Wordsworth still has to discover man as a subject for his imagination. He is not an anthropocentric artist and could never have said with Blake that "Imagination is the Body of Man." Nor will he ever attain that Christian or Blakean position. Christ is the 'one' related to human form, and the cross an omphalos. But Wordsworth's imagination, on separating from nature and self-consciously seeking its own sphere of action, enters the world of men only precariously. Can the poet, despite this, humanize imagination? Or does it intrinsically violate man as well as nature?

"Salisbury Plain" raises these questions. Yet it is more than a document revealing Wordsworth's passage from consciousness of nature to self-consciousness. It is also a poem participating in that movement. Wordsworth, first of all, gives an earnest of the mode of poetry he will adopt. Despite continued or even sharpened influxes of apocalyptic feeling, his realism strengthens, and it will issue in the beautiful story of the Female Vagrant in *Lyrical Ballads.* The simplicity and relative artlessness of this story Coleridge had already admired in a version preserved probably by MSS 1 and 2 of "Salisbury Plain."[17] Both poets are interested in effects analogous to the supernatural, but Wordsworth chooses to achieve them by a purely realistic method and content. We see now that this is an existential as well as technical matter: he is shying from an "apocalyptic" position. He does not want to find imagination in violation of man or nature.

But "Salisbury Plain" also provides an important clue concerning the generic role of poetry in the growth of the mind. It describes a purgatory, a precarious middle realm where man in exile seeks self-renovation. The use of the Spenserian stanza is here particularly apt: it reminds us not only of "all who in the wide deepe wandering arre" but also of the poet's freedom to interpose the image of another kind of world, and of Spenser's peculiar power to make this world a truly autonomous realm, mediating between the historical and the apocalyptic, yet somehow independent of either. Poetry itself is such a special realm of self-encounter, enabling the passage from one state of consciousness to another, and with the least damage. For, while to attain selfhood, or rather to accept it, one need simply break with nature by a criminal or ideological position, to achieve manhood more is required. To pass from selfhood to humanity the poet must recover in himself and perhaps for mankind those mediating symbols which destroy false separations or govern the flow of life between true ones. It is an open secret that he is the guardian of those symbols, and the dream-vision of *Prelude* V will confirm this.

In *The Borderers,* the second major work of this period, Wordsworth shows the insufficiency of a criminal or ideologically inspired separation from nature. Mediocre as drama, and written in a Shakespearean verse the poet had to purge before developing his own, it rises to a superb climax dominated by the confession of its Iago figure, Oswald. Oswald's individuality is determined by a single event. From this he dates his freedom and manhood. The event, significantly, is a betrayal. Yet Oswald has not received his fair share of attention: his very proximity to Iago has obscured the difference between them. Oswald is a *modern* villain who betrays the hero for the specific purpose of planting in him an irremediable self-awareness. A "lucifer," a light-bringer, he uses his intellect to betray others into enlightenment, as he himself was betrayed. He is probably the first explicit proponent in literature of intellectual murder: of a murder planned by the intellect for an ostensibly intellectual result.[18]

I should like to think that what remains a mystery in Iago is

clarified by the confession of Oswald. "What is done," he says to
Marmaduke, after tricking him into murder, "will save you from
the blank / Of living without knowledge that you live" (IV.
1870).[19] By this motive which he adds to others more similar to
those of Iago, Oswald becomes a metaphysical villain who forces
the hero to pass from a naive to a new and isolating consciousness.
The hero, Marmaduke, is made to realize the burden of solitary
and responsible thought weighing on individual man (III.1470 ff).
Faced with judging another person, his thoughts turn to self-judg-
ment (III.1516 ff.), and his later discovery that the supposed act
of justice is indeed a crime, and the murdered man an innocent,
only confirms his new and conscious selfhood.[20] At the end of the
play Marmaduke appears as a type of Wandering Jew, that strange
figure revived in the Romantic period because he is doomed to
eternal (i.e. generic) consciousness of self.

Like Oswald, who stands midway between Iago and the ideologi-
cal assassins depicted in modern fiction—Dostoevsky's Smerdyakov
or Malraux's Tchen—*The Borderers* as a whole stands irresolutely
between ancient tragedy and modern philosophical drama.[21] Writ-
ten between 1795 and 1797, it reflects the crucial role played by
ideas and ideologies in contemporary life—a role intensified by the
French Revolution. Matthew Arnold said that the French Revolu-
tion found its motive power in the intelligence of men and not in
their practical sense or conscience. "1789 asked of a thing, Is it ra-
tional? 1642 asked of a thing, Is it legal? . . . the French Revolu-
tion derives from the force, truth and universality of the ideas
which it took for its law, and from the passion with which it could
inspire a multitude for these ideas, a unique and still living
power."[22] *The Borderers,* though caught between two worlds, or at
least two genres, and therefore struggling with problems that often
have a provincial cast, such as Godwinism and sentimental moral-
ity, is one of the first plays to focus on the subject of an intellect
that has become fully conscious of its powers, including its po-
litical powers.[23] It projects, in fact, a myth of the birth of the mod-
ern intellectual consciousness, and explores the question of
whether that can ever have a moral function. If the intellect, fully
conscious of itself, is basically revolutionary or *contra naturam,*

how can it more than perpetuate the "crime against nature" from which it sprang? This difficult issue transforms the play from a pseudo-Shakespearean period piece, redeemed by genial flights of poetry, to philosophical drama.

The plot of *The Borderers* is simple: Oswald betrays his friend and chief Marmaduke in the same way he himself was once betrayed. He plots to have Marmaduke kill a pitiful old man, the blind and dispossessed Baron Herbert, whose daughter Idonea Marmaduke loves. Instead of killing Herbert, Marmaduke decides to submit him to a medieval "ordeal of the waste," yet unintentionally causes his death by forgetting to leave him his scrip of food. On Marmaduke's return from the waste, Oswald reveals that Herbert is innocent. He does this magnificently by first confessing how he had been betrayed into a similar crime (IV.1678). The crew of a ship had tricked him into marooning on a desert island a captain whom they hated but who was innocent of the crime imputed to him; and Oswald is left with the knowledge of their treachery and of his guilt. Yet after a period of crisis and remorse, throwing off the "soft chains" of the world, Oswald breaks with custom, opinion, and natural law—in short, with Nature in its strongest eighteenth-century connotations.[24] Allowing the crime to determine his individuality, he dates from it his freedom and manhood: "I seemed a Being who had passed alone / Into a region of futurity" (IV.1817).

In the case of Oswald, therefore, we see individuality springing from the unwitting commission of a crime and the discovery of a betrayal; Oswald, moreover, uses a consciousness born in betrayal to betray others. Treachery becomes for him an active ideological weapon, *ad majorem intellectus gloriam*. "I've joined us by a chain of adamant," he exults to Marmaduke, "Henceforth we are fellow labourers to enlarge / The intellectual empire of mankind."[25] Whether or not Oswald was conceived in revulsion, as a critique of Godwin's separation of head from heart, he fosters this imperialism of the intellect, this ruthless futurism of a revolutionary who would achieve autonomy at one blow and by a divorce from natural process. To this tempting philosophy Wordsworth himself once succumbed. Oswald's "I seemed a Being who

had passed alone / Into a region of futurity" finds its analogue in
*The Prelude,* when Wordsworth admits that in his crisis years
"wish was mine to see, / And hope that future times *would* surely
see, / The man to come, parted, as by a gulph, / From him who had
been." (*Prelude* XII.57–60).

What is great and strong in Oswald is certainly related to his
hatred of nature, of natural law and natural piety. He keeps his in-
tellect independent of all but present circumstance, and mocks
those healthy "prejudices" Burke defended against the revolution-
ary mentality. The only law Oswald respects is the "immediate
law, / From the clear light of circumstances, flashed / Upon an in-
dependent Intellect" (III.1494–96). These famous lines Words-
worth applies in *The Prelude* to describe his own error. And in a
further passage he reveals how deep a sin against nature he be-
lieved himself to have committed. "I took the knife in hand,"
says Wordsworth—and the image is not fortuitous—

> to probe
> The living body of society
> Even to the heart; I push'd without remorse
> My speculations forward; yea, set foot
> On Nature's holiest places. (1805 *Prelude* X.875–79)

In isolating Marmaduke from all beings, from Idonea, from his
loyal band of Borderers, and everything "that this earth can give"
(V.2317), Oswald is hastening a separation which might allow a
purely rational, autonomous mode of life. He acts on Marmaduke
as Mephistopheles, that necessary devil, acts on Faust. Whether
this separation from nature is a necessary stage in the development
of man or a historical error cannot here be examined; Wordsworth
remains ambivalent, though he may have ultimately thought of it
as a historical error connected with the French Revolution, one
which affected many contemporaries as well as himself.

Genuine consciousness of self, according to *The Borderers,* is
born of betrayal, is linked to the unwitting commission of a crime,
a crime essentially against nature; and is a stage (however dan-
gerous) in the growth of the mind. Yet every tragedy in which
awareness springs from betrayal could be said to express a similar

view. In *Oedipus* and *Othello* we also have a betrayal, whether by
man or by the gods; an unwitting crime against nature; and the
final isolation of the hero. However inferior in tragic power,
Wordsworth's play carries this pattern forward. Its real value is as
a drama revealing the perils of the soul in its passage toward in-
dividuation, or from a morality based on "nature" to one based
on the autonomous self.[26]

This brings us to the central issue of the play: can the intellect
yield true moral judgments? Is it not tainted by originating in a
crime against nature, however unwitting or inevitable this crime
may be?[27] The poet's question, obviously, is a tragic one, and in this
form can only be deepened, not answered. It supposes that growth
of mind, or into mind, involves a separation from nature which is
also, insofar as it is felt to be a crime, a separation from God. In
the light of this belief all moral action based on the intellect must
have seemed tainted or factitious to Wordsworth. *The Borderers*
has nothing positive except for vestiges of the old "nature" moral-
ity, active in the relationship between Idonea and her father, and
the Borderers and their chief. Marmaduke himself responds to Os-
wald's slanders only because the latter accuses Herbert of the most
*unnatural* of crimes: stealing someone else's daughter, keeping her
in ignorant captivity, and conspiring to sell her to a debauched
lord. But once Marmaduke has reached self-consciousness, he is of-
fered only impossible options. These are remorse, an essentially
Christian solution which Coleridge was exploring at about the
same time, both in his drama *Remorse* and in "The Ancient Mar-
iner"; complicity, which Oswald encourages by suggesting a mu-
tual association between him and Marmaduke, based on their com-
mon guilt and free of all but self-originated law; and a radical,
self-decreed exile from the common life of humanity.

That Wordsworth explored these choices and found them weak
the play makes very clear. Some of its strongest poetry is given to
Oswald's attack on remorse, and it is hard not to sympathize with
Oswald on this issue. Wordsworth may have been of his party
(and Nietzsche's) without knowing it. Remorse, says Oswald, fixes
the self to a past self, allows no growth, and dooms the mind to
"perish self-consumed" (IV.1813). But if the person can come to

accept self-consciousness, remorse is a weakling passion, that will
not stand up to thought: "Remorse— / It cannot live with thought;
think on, think on, / And it will die" (III.1560–62).[28] Complicity
fares no better than remorse. Oswald's idea of a new, guilt-based
association, which could then develop according to a purely
rational aim, is decisively criticized on two counts. The first is that
the independent intellect, as Oswald conceives it, is an illusion; for
while Oswald thinks he is independent, or has converted the past
into freedom, he is obviously its slave. One needs little psychology
to see how deeply compulsive Oswald is: the crime he instigates is
practically identical to his own, and in an unpublished preface to
the play Wordsworth came close to formulating the principle of
"repetition compulsion." Without Oswald's bondage to the past, a
past he recreates in his relationship to Marmaduke, the plot of *The
Borderers* would indeed be what the shocked Swinburne called it:
a "morbid and monstrous extravagance of horrible impossibility."[29]

Wordsworth's second criticism of the ethics of complicity is
more decisive still. He shows that Oswald does not suggest com-
plicity for the sake of the intellectual development of man, but,
obversely, awakens and isolates the hero for the sake of complicity.
Oswald seeks an accomplice because he is too weak to suffer the
liberty into which he was betrayed and needs Marmaduke to solace
his loneliness. Spurning what he calls the "slavery" of law and
opinion, he cannot himself live without enslaving others, without
"A shadow of myself—made by myself" (V.2009). The motive,
therefore, is satanic, and points to the mystery in all seduction.

As to the romantic exile which Marmaduke actually chooses, it is
a spiritual rather than moral position, and merely confirms the
stalemate. Both life and death are removed as possible solutions.
The man who not only thinks but is conscious of the origin of
thought knows that human life is a matter of death-in-life. "I will
wander on," says Marmaduke, "Living by mere intensity of
thought / A Being by pain and thought compelled to live / Yet
loathing life."[30] What seems for Marmaduke the exceptional, is
really the generic situation.

The choice of exile, moreover, is a defeat of the revolutionary
ideal embodied in the Borderers, that benevolent, self-justicing

band of outlaws whose chief Marmaduke is. For Marmaduke is not, like Oswald, the natural man who has to be alienated from nature in order to know himself, but the naive revolutionary who must be brought to the full consciousness of what his ideas imply. Yet on seeing what it means to judge another man Marmaduke yields the presumption of remaking justice and throws himself on the sole mercy of God.

At only one point in the play does Wordsworth suggest the possibility of an intellectual consciousness that is not *contra naturam*. The strength of Herbert, like that of the blind beggar in *Prelude* VII, is not based on a violation of nature—because it is invulnerably founded beyond nature. Herbert's blindness suggests a visionary faculty that cannot be mutilated. He is the most supernatural figure in the play (cf. I.108 ff.) and also, significantly, the major victim. Yet, insofar as he is above nature he is not in nature, so that the problem is by-passed rather than solved; and insofar as he is in nature Herbert remains too frail, too creaturely for his role. The analogy with Oedipus, moreover, when Herbert comes on stage led by Idonea (cf. the opening of *Oedipus at Colonus*), merely complicates his archetype, since the Greek hero's later stature as prophet was preceded by what the ancients considered as *the* crimes against nature (incest and patricide).[31]

*The Borderers* was completed in autumn 1797; less than a year later *Lyrical Ballads* appeared, the fruit of a collaboration between two very different poets. Coleridge's chief contribution, and his most famous poem, bears points of resemblance to *The Borderers* which have not been remarked. "The Ancient Mariner," according to Coleridge, came out of an abortive attempt of the two poets to compose a joint narrative on "The Wanderings of Cain." Wordsworth's play, completed as "The Ancient Mariner" began to be conceived, has been compared to it only in respect to the crime-punishment-remorse sequence which Coleridge had already labored in *Osorio*. There is, however, a more inclusive connection between the two; like *The Borderers,* but with an unparalleled purity of conception, Coleridge's poem traces the "dim and perilous way" of a soul that has broken with nature and feels the burdenous guilt of selfhood.

The *crime,* first of all, is purified of all extrinsic causes, even of possible motive. It is a founding gesture, or caesura dividing stages of being. It may anticipate the modern "acte gratuite" or reflect the willfulness in original sin, but only because both are epochal and determining acts of individuation. The *punishment,* moreover, is simply life itself under the condition of consciousness. Death or self-forgetfulness is not allowed: the Mariner becomes "A man by pain and thought compelled to live." Each man, to become a man, must pass through those straits of individuation, which Coleridge, like Wordsworth, could see as a summation of natural process rather than as an alienation from it:

> In Man the centripetal and individualizing tendency of all Nature is itself concentered and individualized—he is a revelation of Nature! Henceforward, he is referred to himself, delivered up to his own charge; and he who stands the most on himself, and stands the firmest, is the truest, because the most individual, Man. . . . Nor does the form of polarity, which has accompanied the law of individuation up its whole ascent, desert it here. . . . As the ideal genius and the originality, in the same proportion must be the resignation to the real world, the sympathy and the inter-communion with Nature. In the conciliating mid-point or equator, does the Man live, and only by its equal presence in both poles can that life be manifested![32]

The coincidence of theme is supported by certain details. In "The Ancient Mariner," as in *The Borderers,* the birth to self-consciousness is linked to the killing of an innocent being. Wordsworth himself suggested the form of the Mariner's crime. "Suppose, said I, you represent him as having killed one of these birds on entering the South Sea, and that the tutelary Spirits of those regions take upon them to avenge the crime."[33] It is Wordsworth, of course, who is haunted by spirit of place, and the "tutelary Spirits" are mythical representations of something he has wished to express in realistic fashion since "The Vale of Esthwaite." The archaic fear that the presence of man violates nature is probably related to the fact that consciousness *appears* as a breach or betrayal of nature.

A second detail, also connected with the imaginative-moral influence of place, is the becalming so vividly described in Coleridge's poem (section II) and anticipated by Oswald's experience:

The wind fell;
We lay becalmed week after week, until
The water of the vessel was exhausted;
I felt a double fever in my veins,
Yet rage suppressed itself;—to a deep stillness
Did my pride tame my pride;—for many days,
On a dead sea under a burning sky,
I brooded o'er my injuries, deserted
By man and nature;—if a breeze had blown,
It might have found its way into my heart,
And I had been—no matter—do you mark me? (IV.1692–1702)

A link is already made, here, between a stasis in nature and a stasis in the soul. Selfhood manifests its weight, and thought is fixed to a single thought. This constitutes one of the clearest perils of emergent self-consciousness. The beautiful formula, "to a deep stillness / Did my pride tame my pride," intimates not only inner conflict but also how energetically the divided self seeks recomposition. All the energy of the man goes inward; and, as in "The Ancient Mariner," an external deliverance—"a breeze," an action of grace or nature—is needed before the spell can be broken even in part.

Between 1791 and 1795 Wordsworth wrote a series of Spenserian stanzas which (like *The Borderers*) have the murder of a blind man for their subject.[34] These gothic stanzas, almost alchemical in their horrific imagination,[35] point to very basic and ordinary psychological processes. We are shown a young man at the point of maturity (a "stripling") who leads an old blind man into a cave to murder him. No motive is indicated, and the crime is made more incomprehensible by the obvious pitifulness of the old man and the pretense of compassion in the youth. Comparing these fragments to the poems under discussion will confirm the presence of a common theme.

The stripling of the tale in killing the old man would really be killing the principle of compassion in himself. He means to achieve by this his liberation from nature. Macbeth's murder of Duncan and Raskolnikov's of the pawnbroker have similar overtones. But here, as was pointed out, there is no visible motive, no sufficient dramatic frame, no feeling on the part of the narrator except a strong detachment. It is possible, therefore, that the blind man stands for the thing that is *necessarily* murdered in the process of passing from a prior, nature-involved and relatively blind state of consciousness to the enlightened pain of self-consciousness. Yet the cave the youth enters has already its ghostly inhabitants, as if he were doing again or once more what had already been done. Rather than depict the transition from consciousness to self-consciousness as a unique event, Wordsworth is showing the stripling *unconsciously* in the grip of that transition, and seeking to overcome totally a prior state (such as compassion) which is remembered but no longer vitally owned. The survival of the "old man," whether he has a real or only a psychic existence, is an affront to nature, which is held responsible for the movement toward individuation, or an affront to the liberated consciousness tormented by that vestigial dependence. In *The Borderers,* similarly, Oswald suggests that it is better to live not at all than in the death-in-life state which Herbert seems to evoke and which Marmaduke also shares if his consciousness is not entirely free. The murder suggested by Oswald implies the wish to have done with nature once and for all: it confirms one's (criminal) separation from it.

"A man goes into the world and is betrayed into a great crime."[36] This is in the nature of the world, and a story Wordsworth will hint at again; "going into the world" and "being betrayed into a great crime" are almost coterminous in the poetry of 1793–97. The political betrayal of 1793 is, in any case, traumatic in character and brings deeper, perhaps aboriginal emotions to the surface.[37] Wordsworth, at the time of *The Borderers,* fears that the mind and life of man are necessarily built up on murder, or based on a crime against nature. It is equally clear, however, that he is seeking a view which would not entail connecting individuality and violation. That view is attained, however precariously, in "The Ruined Cottage" and *The Prelude.* These two great poems are founded on the hope that man does not have to violate nature to become human. Perhaps there is no original innocence; perhaps human consciousness does necessarily imply a fall from nature, an irremediable division in the self. Yet the illusion of innocence survives, and poetry respects illusions. In sounding the dark passages that lead to consciousness of self *The Borderers* goes far deeper than *Osorio*. Then Coleridge, as if the two poets had collaborated, builds on what Wordsworth achieved, and attains the greater clarity and imaginative vigor of his "Mariner."

Since "The Ruined Cottage" (finished spring 1798) was later revised as *Excursion* I, a full discussion of it can be postponed. Only what it tells of the progress in Wordsworth's "consciousness about consciousness" need be considered. At last, consciousness is not a simple violation of nature. Though the poet realizes as strongly as before that imagination must separate from nature, he now sees the separation as part of a process providentially encouraged by nature itself. His description of the Pedlar, which includes his first portrait of the growth of a mind, makes Nature the governess of the entire individualizing movement from nature to self-consciousness. The child grows from a stage in which it walks *with* nature, to one in which it is in search *of* nature, and finally to a crisis when nature no longer suffices. This crisis is overcome when it is seen that Nature itself taught the mind to be free of nature and now teaches the mind to be free of mind and mingle with nature once more. The great Wordsworthian myth of Nature is about to be conceived.

For an exact description of this myth we must go to *The Prelude*. It is significant, however, that "The Ruined Cottage" gives us more than landscape pictures. Almost half the poem is directly about a man (the Pedlar) who without humanizing nature can perceive the human in nature; and the story told about the Pedlar is almost as important as the story he himself tells. This displacement from the tale to the teller (even during the Pedlar's tale we are mainly conscious of him) is a significant advance in the humanizing of Wordsworth's imagination. The MS history of "The Ruined Cottage," which probably extends from spring 1797 to spring 1798, reflects Wordsworth's entire progress between "Salisbury Plain" and *Lyrical Ballads* and can serve to conclude this chapter.

The idea of "The Ruined Cottage" is planted when the poet is stirred by spirit of place. Crossing a moor one night he comes on a ruined cottage: it is roofless and a broken pane glitters to the moon. His attitude toward this speck of glass expresses the spot syndrome in a form approaching the intensity of madness. "From this time / That speck of glass was dearer to my soul / Than was the moon in heaven." In another account of the incident he accuses himself of a "strange incontinence":

> my eye
> Did every evening measure the moon's height
> And forth I went before her yellow beams
> Could overtop the elmtrees o'er the heath,
> I went, I reach'd the cottage, and I found
> Still undisturb'd and glittering in its place
> That speck of glass.

He apparently visited the deserted spot often, for he tells how on a different occasion,

> The winds of Autumn drove me o'er the heath
> One gloomy evening: by the storm compell'd
> The poor man's horse that feeds along the lanes
> Had hither come among these fractur'd walls
> To weather out the night; and as I pass'd
> While restlessly he turn'd from the fierce wind
> And from the open sky, I heard, within,
> The iron links with which his feet were clogg'd
> Mix their dull clanking with the heavy noise
> Of falling rain—I started from the spot
> And heard the sound still following in the wind.

Something of the gibbet scene in "Salisbury Plain" seems to have entered into this: both express a similar obsession. He mentions further visits to this spot extending over at least two years; for he notices that a glow worm, a blackbird, and a linnet come here for a time and then disappear:

> I alone
> Remained: the winds of heaven remained: with them

My heart claimed fellowship and with the beams
Of dawn and of the setting sun that seemed
To live and linger on the mouldering walls.[38]

These fragments show Wordsworth as obsessed as in "Salisbury Plain" with singles and fixities. The process of individuation evokes both demonic and liberative images of the "one." At this pivotal point, equidistant from madness and vision, the "one" might become various things: the ego, the (pantheistic) divine, the independent intellect, the One of the philosophers. A fatality of the center persists and defies definition. But it remains bound up with nature, with the feeling of fated and specific place. "How dreadful is this place! This is none other than the house of God, and this is the gate of heaven."[39] The fragments are the raw material from which the omphalos feeling, familiar to archaic religion, springs.

Yet we glimpse already a centrifugal movement, which encompasses more in nature than specific place, and whose shape approximates a circle. Wordsworth's perspective opens, in the last-quoted lines, to a larger fellowship coterminous with the cycle of the seasons or of the day, and whose locus now centers in *two* things: the ruined cottage and himself. The "I" and the permanent (also least human) processes of nature are given equal weight; a solution which anticipates the later Wordsworth. There is an exclusion of intermediate (mythical, humanizing) links in favor of the equipoise and occasional strange blending of two immutables. One of these is traditionally the soul, the personal immortality of man revealed by the very corrosion (the ruined cottage) of the merely human; the other is an impersonal immortality felt in the larger presences or *pan* aspects of nature.

At the next stage, in the perfected MS of "The Ruined Cottage," the speck of glass and similar curiosities have disappeared. The omphalos feeling is now conveyed by casual descriptive details and a structural accumulation of event. Thus the cottage stands "beneath a shade / Of clustering elms that sprang from the same root" and is explicitly reduced to "four clay walls / That stared upon each other."[40] By the door the poet discovers the quiet form of the pedlar. The story of Margaret will be the circle replacing to a degree that of nature, yet seemingly anchored like it in that strangely central ruin. Margaret's imagination is as "bound" as the poet's, though to a spectral hope as well as to specific place. According to Wordsworth the lines describing that hope "fast rooted at her heart" were the first to be composed:

> On this old Bench
> For hours she sate, and evermore, her eye
> Was busy in the distance, shaping things
> Which made her heart beat quick. Seest thou that path?
> The greensward now has broken its grey line;
> There to and fro she paced through many a day
> Of the warm summer, from a belt of flax
> That girt her waist spinning the long-drawn thread
> With backward steps—yet ever as there passed
> A Man whose garments shewed the Soldier's red
> Or crippled Mendicant in Sailor's garb
> The little child who sate to turn the wheel
> Ceased from his toil, and she with faltering voice
> Expecting still to learn her husband's fate,
> Made many a fond enquiry.[41]

Thus Wordsworth's poem begins by hovering around the ruined walls of a cottage, a faint path nearby, and perhaps an overgrown well. These raise the story of Margaret or are linked to it in the same way as a heap of stones builds into the tale of Michael. At their center is something too central: fixed and scarcely human. The story then evolves as a humanizing glance. The tale of Margaret has the same locus (an adherence to specific place) as the poet's original experience, and her hope is as disproportionate to what it half creates as that original speck of glass to Wordsworth's "sickly heart." Yet Wordsworth never seizes the extreme pole of the idealist or apocalyptic position. For him this disproportion argues *two* vigors or centers of life: of the imagination, which is radically in excess of natural fact; and of nature, which has the power to deceive or attract imagination. This subtle knot, never resolved, makes Wordsworth the poet he is.

Margaret, who lets her child and garden die, has not survived her "betrayal." Older feelings keep her archaically tied to specific

place, and make her cottage the fatal center of a circle she cannot
expand. Her newer consciousness binds her with equal force to an
abstract hope. The two bonds are not opposite—this might gen-
erate conflict and life—but the same consciousness fruitlessly dou-
bled. Imagination cannot blend its power with nature's, because
the concept of Nature has not emerged from the fixation on specific
place, nor has that of the Imagination emerged from the blindness
of fixed hope.

Wordsworth, however, distances himself from Margaret in the
same way as the pedlar's tale achieves a distance, by inclusion, from
the spot syndrome. Instead of centering transparently on Mar-
garet, the tale reflects also the narrator, and tends to become a
story about the relation of teller to tale. This reflexive (and mod-
ern) emphasis[42] is achieved by the introduction of the poet as a
third person, which allows the accent to fall on the way the pedlar
confronts Margaret's passion. The poet-listener is affected by the
story's influence on the pedlar as much as by the incidents them-
selves:

> . . . when he ended there was in his face
> Such easy chearfulness, a look so mild
> That for a little time it stole away
> All recollection and that simple tale
> Passed from my mind like a forgotten sound.[43]

The story the pedlar tells is never a rape of truth, a ransacking
of the past, or a horror of revelation. It allows us to think about the
way in which passion—or vision—is to be faced. Instead of violating
nature (those silent overgrowings) it acts as a veil that uncovers a
veil. "Vision as thou art," Wordsworth will say of the Highland
Girl, "I bless thee with a human heart." Though the pedlar de-
scribes in Margaret a consciousness born of betrayal and careless of
nature, his own grows patiently around her sufferings.

If we review the poet's progress from *Descriptive Sketches* to
"The Ruined Cottage," a simple fact emerges. His starting point,
the germinal inspiration, is the same in 1795 (and later) as in 1791
(and earlier). It is always the omphalos feeling, a concern with
specific and fated place. However much his "consciousness about
consciousness" progresses, it begins at the same stage. Even *The*

*Prelude,* which raises him to a general conception of the growth of a poet's mind, will take its origin in the memory of peculiar and place-bound experience. It is as though the poet were subject to a dependency well-known from fairy tales in which a creature who has changed its shape has to return periodically to its original form. It seems to be Wordsworth's fate to return to spirit of place as if that alone were the well-spring of poetry.

Yet what a difference between those early fragments haunted by spirit of place and the pedlar discerning in nature the "secret spirit of humanity"![44] It cannot be said that "The Ruined Cottage," like "Salisbury Plain," utilizes a human machinery. The presence of man is more integral: the true subject of the poem is the perfected mind of man facing a still imperfect world. By the spiritual alchemy we have traced via the MS history of "The Ruined Cottage," Wordsworth separates his imagination from nature without abandoning nature, then remarries the two without abandoning imagination. Starting with the omphalos feeling, which shows both powers primitively linked, he first individualizes them. Instead of one dangerously static point two centers now appear: the "I" and the "alien" (place). This division is repeated as the "I" generates together with its persona (the Pedlar) the relation of a second person (Margaret) to a central place (the garden). But the "alien" also doubles: the pedlar tells his story at the site on which it occurred. He looks *through* the ruined cottage to the passion of Margaret just as when Margaret's garden was beginning to wilder. The result is a spectrum bounded at one side by the apocalyptic imagination and at the other by an alien nature. Their joint symbol is the naked, self-staring ruin. The middle ground of the spectrum, however, is occupied by the pedlar and his attitude toward nature, and there "All things shall speak of Man."[45] Human filters are made to intervene between the strange imagination and its strange object: poet→pedlar→(Margaret→ Cottage)→the ruin. The theme of the completed poem is the humanized imagination, and the manuscripts of the poem show how Wordsworth's imagination humanizes itself within an act of confrontation as pure as it can be. Ultimately poet and pedlar still stare at a ruin which stares at itself.

# 5.  *Lyrical Ballads*

Considering the *Lyrical Ballads* initially not in their own light but in that of Wordsworth's previous development, it is striking that many are built around a "spot," whether in nature or in the psyche. In a curse poem like "Goody Blake and Harry Gill" the spot is primarily a mental thing: something heard fixes itself through imagination on the physical organism. In "Michael" or "The Brothers" it is primarily a place, a straggling heap of stones or an unmarked grave, both slight yet drawing the mind by a premonitory fear or strong associations. In "The Thorn," Wordsworth's most experimental poem, the spot appears first as something in nature (stanzas 1–7) but then as something in the narrator: an *idea* that bodies forth its own dark symbols. We feel that even if the good Captain had not seen the curious-looking growth he would have invented it. What he describes responds to a need of his mind, nourished by superstitions and ballads. In many poems, finally, a person is seen returning to the place of his birth, or to one associated with a birth, and which is now actually or by implication a grave. The story of Michael, for instance, who goes to that unfinished sheepfold which is like a broken covenant to him, engenders in the poet further stories of a "return," one of which is later absorbed by *The Prelude* (1805, VIII.222–57). It tells of a shepherd lad who recovers a stray lamb by remembering that though storms drive it miles astray, "If he [the lamb] can crawl he will return again / To his own hills, the spots where, when a Lamb, / He learn'd to pasture at his Mother's side."

A similar return should be mentioned because of its direct link to Wordsworth's biography. In "Hart-Leap Well" a shepherd informs the poet of the local tradition concerning a deserted and desolate spot with three pillars. The pillars mark the dying leaps of a hart commemorated by its hunter who had a pleasure dome erected on that spot. In speculating on what gave the animal its dying strength, and why it chose to come to this place to die, the shepherd repeats an already familiar thought:

> For thirteen hours he ran a desperate race;
> And in my simple mind we cannot tell
> What cause the Hart might have to love this place,
> And come and make his death-bed near the well.
>
> Here on the grass perhaps asleep he sank,
> Lull'd by this fountain in the summer-tide;
> This water was perhaps the first he drank
> When he had wandered from his mother's side.
>
> In April here beneath the scented thorn
> He heard the birds their morning carols sing;
> And he, perhaps, for aught we know, was born
> Not half a furlong from that self-same spring.[1]

Now "Hart-Leap Well" was written at about the same time as "Michael" and "The Brothers," shortly after the poet had settled at Grasmere in the late winter of 1799–1800. These poems form a natural group allied by contiguity of theme and genesis. By coincidence Wordsworth became acquainted with the tradition of Hart-Leap Well on his journey from Sockburn to Grasmere, and we know that Grasmere meant for him not a new abode but a final homecoming, the end of a separation from his native region. The story of Hart-Leap Well, meeting him at the threshold of his return, affected him exactly like an omen, and in "Home at Grasmere" he describes the "awful trance" that overcame him at Hart-Leap Well.[2] He too is returning, like the hart, to his native place; and the visionary trance, as well as the hart's final, gigantic leaps, suggest the *preternatural* strength of his own homing instinct. It is an emblem of the vigor with which the separated imagination seeks its native country, which is not nature, but which might be nature.

It is not difficult, however, to reconcile our special perspective

with responses to *Lyrical Ballads* that are more traditional. The
realism of these poems has always been acknowledged to contain
an element of surrealism, though I have not used the term because
it now identifies a different type of literature. As Coleridge re-
marks: a Wordsworth ballad deals with nature yet excites feelings
analogous to the supernatural. I do not believe that any technical
explanation, as that Wordsworth draws "impressive effects out of
simple elements,"[3] will help to explain the uncanny atmosphere
of many of the lyrics. What we need is a thesis that relates the
realism of this poetry to its visionary effect or 'supernatural natu-
ralism.'

Too little has been said about the men and women in this poe-
try. They exhibit what Wordsworth calls in the 1802 Preface a
"power of real and substantial action and suffering." Yet their ac-
tion, or suffering, is of a peculiar kind. The poems that caused
Wordsworth's notoriety, and which are not, of course, restricted to
*Lyrical Ballads* (consider "Alice Fell," a lyrical ballad in spirit but
published in the *Poems* of 1807), are basically similar in showing
us people cleaving to one thing or idea with a tenaciousness both
pathetic and frightening. This physical or imaginative cleaving,
which is the central passion, results from a separation, if we use
the word in its strongest sense, as when the mystics speak of a sep-
aration from God. Blake said about Cowper and himself that their
madness was a "refuge from unbelief" but in Wordsworth's suffer-
ers it is more a "refuge from imagination." They cleave to one
thing or idea in order to be saved from a still deeper sense of sep-
aration. It does not matter whether a child is deprived of its tat-
tered cloak or a woman of child and lover—the wound that opens
is always the same, and even when the loss is ordinary, the passion
is extraordinary, and points to so deep and personal a sorrow that
we call it natural only to dignify human nature.

Something of that sorrow is shown in "The Last of the Flock,"
and of the cleaving, too deep to be conscious, in "We Are Seven."
The passion for property, in the former poem, is a spiritual pas-
sion, and may argue against Godwin that property is a need of the
soul.[4] No polemical context, however, can explain the intensity of
the shepherd's love for his flock, which mingles with that for his

children (stanza 8), or the iterated sacrifice of fifty sheep, one by
one. The relentless progress from fifty to nothing is like the back-
ward counting in some folk-songs: "there were ten little Indians . . .
and then there were none." Whether or not related to primitive
sacrificial rites, this stylized series (cf. the number emphasis in "We
Are Seven") does suggest an ominous game—there are also, after
all, the ten children of the shepherd. Lamb or child, there is no dif-
ference to his heart, because each loss is unique. Every new sacri-
fice is prophetic, and brings home the idea of separation, not only
perhaps from his children, but from all that stands between the
self and its nakedness. In this sense, certainly, property is a spiritual
need, and like all *realia* (nature) serves to keep imagination in
check. The dignity of the shepherd in his grief suggests, at the
same time, how infinitely capable of loss a man may be; so that
our final image is the perseverance of an individual.

"We Are Seven" conveys this perseverance by means of a dia-
logue between the rational questioner and the obtuse little girl.
Beerbohm's cartoon, "Mr. Wordsworth at cross-purposes in the
Lake District," catches the incongruity of the situation. The ques-
tioner, desiring to make conversation with a beautiful child ("her
eyes were fair, and very fair"), becomes rather involved. The per-
sistence shown by the girl is the counterpart of the perseverance of
the shepherd; they are of similar spiritual stock. But the thought
of separation is not even able to arise in the girl so that the num-
ber of siblings remains to her the same—an immortal, ever-
unbroken set. ("The set is broken," is Wordsworth's cry on hear-
ing of his brother's death.)[5] However much counting is done, it will
always be "seven in all."

What gives the child its strength to avoid the thought of separa-
tion is not explicit in the poem. The first stanza, contributed by
Coleridge, suggests that to know of death one must experience it
first in oneself. This may be true; yet to suppose that the child is
not able to realize the idea of death because it "feels its life in every
limb" seems naive. To suppose, on the other hand, that the little
girl (not so little, eight years old) still dwells in the realm of imag-
ination, and that the imagination does not know of death, is to
simplify Wordsworth's doctrine. The imagination does bring in-

timations of immortality, but through a divestment of the natural
world—"fallings from us, vanishings."[6] The indomitableness of the
spirit is revealed less in a marriage with than in a nihilation of
familiar nature. The woodland child, however, is not in this pre-
carious realm but under the spell of a nature that still weaves a
charm against her own, too powerful imagination.

This charm invests the world with the promise of wholly satis-
fying the mind, or, what is the same, bestows on nature an illusion
of deathlessness. (The girl is the same age Wordsworth was when
his mother died, and when Nature began to be all in all,[7] yet the
precise age probably matters less than the inherence of an illusion
which recurs in "A slumber did my spirit seal.") If the girl, in
dress and being a nature sprite, knows the fact of death yet will not
think of it as a separation, it is because she too is in the bosom of
nature, indeed, uncannily close to the dead:

> "Their graves are green, they may be seen,"
>     The little Maid replied,
> "Twelve steps or more from my mother's door,
>     And they are side by side.
>
> My stockings there I often knit,
>     My 'kerchief there I hem;
> And there upon the ground I sit—
>     I sit and sing to them.
>
> And often after sunset, Sir,
>     When it is light and fair,
> I take my little porringer,
>     And eat my supper there. . . ."

It seems to be Nature that prevents in the child the thought of
absolute separation.[8] Nature is taking the child to itself, as it will
Lucy. There is a beautiful ominousness in the proximity of birth
and death, of the wild woodland maid and the grave "Twelve steps
or more from my mother's door." The closeness of the cottage to
the churchyard, quite usual in a small English village, is still re-
markable because of the tendency here to center everything on the
grave. Such proximity to the grave, while intimating how lightly

the mystery of death rests on the child, also projects an archaic image of the living who stay as close as possible to the dead. We are furnished once more with a symbol of centroversion, or of the mind gravitating to a central spot. Birth and death seem to occupy what is virtually the same place, so that the danger of never reaching self-consciousness, or a significant separation of imagination from nature, is felt. Yet the memory of this instinctive resistance to the cognate thoughts of separation and selfhood is precisely what sustains the man who knows he has been strong *in* and *against* imagination: "How awful is the might of souls, / And what they do within themselves, while yet / The yoke of earth is new to them, the world / Nothing but a wild field where they were sown."[9] The child's unconscious faith should have admonished the questioner to look once more, and consciously, through death.

Tenacity, persistence, resolution—it is hard to find the just word—is also the key-note of one of the strangest poems in *Lyrical Ballads*. The first two stanzas of "The Thorn" depict a growth that has struggled to the height of a two-year-old child despite lichens and moss bent on dragging it down. The narrator leads us ritually, from this thorn, to a neighboring pond, and to a hill of moss also associated with an infant (it is said to be the size of an infant's grave); finally to a scarlet-cloaked woman who is supposed to sit there lamenting. All times of the day and night, we are told, in all weathers, she goes there and no one knows why. The narrator's absurd precision ("I've measured it [the pond] from side to side: / 'Tis three feet long, and two feet wide") intensifies the relentless narrowing of focus to a single, grave-shaped plot. In that plot the extremes of birth and death meet: the aged thorn, the "fresh" hill of moss, and the gradually emerging suspicion that the woman buried there her new-born child. All symbols, in fact, point to an exclusion of modes intermediate between birth and death, of human life as such:[10] a marriage promised which does not take place; a child still-born or buried as soon as born; the thorn looking as if it could never have been young and only the height of a two-year-old child; the story itself, in which nothing is concluded, contrasting the narrator who talks too much and the keening woman who says too little. As in the "Old Man Travelling," very different in technique and one of the perfect pieces of the collection, two kinds of death are juxtaposed: the being insensibly and slowly subdued to nature ("animal tranquillity and decay") and the premature cutting-off which entry into the human world proper seems to entail.

The poem, therefore, in an unexpected way, again defeats the idea of separation—it works against the image of man as a fully individuated being. While action, associated with the world of men, allows but a brief moment of self-consciousness (in the words of *The Borderers*, "Action is transitory—a step, a blow, / The motion of a muscle—this way or that— / 'Tis done, and in the after-vacancy / We wonder at ourselves like men betrayed"), passion, associated with nature, allows a different kind of consciousness, perhaps human but also a defeat of the human ("Suffering is permanent, obscure and dark, / And shares the nature of infinity").[11] In Wordsworth there is more revolt against "what man has made of man" than against what nature has made of him. The power of nature to retard, or to transmute from action to passion the brief moment of truly individual being, is what raises the largest emotions: pity, perplexity, wonder. Wordsworth depicts (it is his true realism) the powers man struggles with in his progress toward self-consciousness, and that powers of such scope are ranged against him indicates even in defeat his importance: "What am I that thou shouldst contend with me?"[12] Any survival, in these conditions, is miraculous: that wretched thorn is a symbol of the emergent self conserving its being despite everything (including its own strength, its mass of knotted joints) that conspires to bury it. So man must outlive his own imagination, then nature that beguiled it, then the world that betrays it and him forever.

The slow and teasing narrative Wordsworth gives his "loquacious narrator" exposes a mind shying from, yet drawn to, a compulsive center of interest. The narrator, later identified as a sea captain (another ancient mariner), helps the poet to achieve a certain distance from the darkness at the center but is still within its penumbra. His tale, like nature itself, wants to bury the whole matter;[13] there is a reluctance to come to the point. Yet his repetitiousness soon infers an intent of its own, and we suspect that his

mind cannot free itself of some *idée fixe*. As he warms up to his tale
he fluctuates more obviously between disclaiming firm knowledge
and thirsting for it; at one point (stanza 9) he even urges his
hearers to go to the spot for evidence. Just as the woman in his
story is drawn to thorn, pond, and mossy hill by a mysterious
interest, so his imagination is drawn to the image it perhaps cre-
ates: both to the inhuman crime he senses and to the more than
human, the mad persistence of the woman.

The persona enables, therefore, a double·plot on the level of
lyric; for the action narrated and that of the narrator's mind run
parallel. There is, as in "The Ruined Cottage," a humanizing dis-
placement from incident to character, from plot interest to psy-
chology. But in "The Ruined Cottage" this displacement occurs
before the final version of the poem, while here it is evolved be-
fore our very eyes. What "The Thorn" offers, courageously if not
wisely, is a caricature of Wordsworth's own imagination-in-process.
The captain is the ocular man in Wordsworth, searching for a
sacred or secret spot, spying on nature (his telescope is a big eye),
and only clingingly passing from nonhuman to human, from thorn
to woman. He exorcizes his quasi-apocalyptic obsession with clear
and centered evidence.

There are other pieces, however, in which Wordsworth has
trouble with the tone, yet cannot defend himself by pointing
to the chosen persona. He signals the fact that "The Thorn"
is not spoken in his own person,[14] but are the narrators of "Simon
Lee" or "The Idiot Boy" any less garrulous? There is no essential
difference of style, except for the moral at the end of "Simon Lee,"
which supplies a point to the rambling tale and evokes in the
reader a gratitude proportional to the old man's:

> I struck, and with a single blow
> The tangled root I sever'd,
> At which the poor old man so long
> And vainly had endeavour'd.
>
> The tears into his eyes were brought,
> And thanks and praises seemed to run
> So fast out of his heart, I thought

> They never would have done.
> —I've heard of hearts unkind, kind deeds
> With coldness still returning.
> Alas! the gratitude of men
> Has oftner left me mourning.

Both poems, of course, undermine the "moving accident."[15] The title, "Simon Lee, the Old Huntsman, *with* an incident in which he was concerned" (my italics), already shows this; while the only real happening during the idiot boy's adventure is "The cocks did crow to-whoo, to-whoo, / And the sun did shine so cold." Yet the reason Wordsworth wants to take our attention away from the incidents is to direct them to the feelings which, as he said, give importance to the action.[16] He must have meant the *represented* feelings, which include not only those of the subjects (Simon Lee and Betty Foy) but also of the poet-narrator, who allows himself an intrusive and emotional presence, comments on incidents, is variously affected by them.

To an extent this principle is very old, a recovery of Chaucer's freedom imported from narrative into lyric and applied to less colorful situations. In the eighteenth century, however, it was the novel that encouraged this kind of personal author. Interpolations like

> My gentle reader, I perceive
> How patiently you've waited,
> And I'm afraid that you expect
> Some tale will be related . . . ("Simon Lee")

are Sterne in spirit. The almost bouncy good humor, found especially in "The Idiot Boy," would also remind an eighteenth-century reader more of novel or satire. Thus Wordsworth was fated to displease both the gentle reader of his day and ours; the former because he committed a solecism (a breach of decorum or social contract) by elevating to poetic dignity words, matters, and attitudes permitted only on the pedestrian or comic level of prose; and the latter, because the tide (though turning) has run, in poetry and fiction, against the intrusive author. In comic poetry, as in prose, the commentary Wordsworth practices has always been allowed; but despite the mock-epic element in "The Idiot Boy" a basic seriousness is uneasily patent, and the swift changes from teasing narrative to genuine emotion, as at the end of "Simon Lee," must have been felt as a breach of style.

Though we can explain some of the difficulties in appreciating the more experimental of Wordsworth's ballads, this does not mean that the experiments are not failures. The reaction of Wordsworth's critics is essentially correct. His style in "Simon Lee" and "The Idiot Boy" is full of joyfully unrepressed "turns" or tautologies in evidence from the time of "The Vale of Esthwaite." In a note on "The Thorn" appended to the 1800 edition of *Lyrical Ballads,* Wordsworth justifies certain tautologies in principle.* His note bears out at least one point concerning his style that I have made before: its redundancies, sometimes beautifully appropriate, have a direct psychical function, being at once "symbols" of a passion, i.e. expressing the clinging or craving mind of the speaker, and "things," i.e. expressions that do release the mind and allow the passion to broaden into words, or the words, by psychical transference, to take on a life of their own.

If Wordsworth's repetitions were limited to these purposes, a case might be made for his defense, or would not have to be made. Yet in "Simon Lee" and "The Idiot Boy" the repetitions acquire another, and perhaps contrary function. They are not expressive, primarily, of passion, but of potential activity, of the poet's supremely nonchalant confidence that he can find "A tale in everything." A third, if minor complication, is that the tautologies, when referred back to the ballads, belong to a still different order of effects. They have, as in the refrain, a steadying, musical, "eternal" recurrence. This effect Wordsworth also seeks to exploit, as is shown by his remarks on the pleasure that meter affords in tempering passion.[17] It is the mixture of these different effects that often produces in us a perplexed response, if not a decided feeling

---

* "Repetition and apparent tautology are frequently beauties of the highest kind. Among the chief . . . reasons is the interest which the mind attaches to words, not only as symbols of the passion, but as *things,* active and efficient, which are of themselves part of the passion."

of incongruity. There is also something incongruous in the poet's obvious pleasure while narrating "The Idiot Boy." It may temper the painfulness of the subject or heighten the level of interest but it draws too much attention to Wordsworth's own "burring." The release he feels in telling the story is too wastefully apparent, and we suspect deeper causes for his delight than he is willing to acknowledge. In purely artistic terms, however, Wordsworth's fault in some of the ballads is that of overloading a rhetorical device: he has not found his best medium.

With most ballads there is no trouble. The Complaints, of which "The Last of the Flock" has been mentioned, and such plain-song lyrics as "It is the first mild day of March," strike a firm and personal note. Many have interesting connections with traditional genres. The "Lines written at a small distance from my House, and sent by my little Boy to the Person to whom they are addressed" derives from the Horatian epistolary poem, yet is a long-distance conversation (and invitation) rather than a letter, and stands midway between the verse-epistle and such conversational poems as Coleridge's "The Nightingale." The "Lines left upon a Seat in a Yew Tree . . ." has a direct link to the Inscription, a genre popularized by the Greek Anthology, and is a first cousin to the epitaph, having thus a local provenance as well.[18] The Yew Tree poem is, in fact, a recognizable epitaph with the formal address to the passing Traveler. About the ballad proper little can be said that is not already known: again the literary model had its local survival in the broadsides of Wordsworth's day. A ballad generally meant a poem based on a well-known tale (a "tradition") or on one that might become popular;[19] and Wordsworth's originality lies in drawing that tradition from his own casual experience as in "We Are Seven," a lyric marked by its subtle absorption of the ballad refrain into the story. Thus antiquity, contemporary usage, and personalization contribute to every poem. Other lyrics, for which it would be difficult to find relevant anticipations, for example the "Lines Written in Early Spring," revive spontaneously an ancient practice. They are poems of thanksgiving, marking or creating a *date*, excerpting from the flow of time a particular moment. They are part of the "living calendar" kept by Wordsworth and his sister from the time of Alfoxden, when the poet's A.D. truly began. It is also curiously moving that the "Lines Written in Early Spring" sustain until the last stanza an antiphonal structure as if they were a hymn or catechism:

> To her fair works did nature link
> The human soul that through me ran;
> And much it griev'd my heart to think
> What man has made of man.
>
> Through primrose-tufts, in that sweet bower,
> The periwinkle trail'd its wreathes;
> And 'tis my faith that every flower
> Enjoys the air it breathes.

Most of the plain-songs, as I have called them, do in fact express a creed. The *Lyrical Ballads* were the first fruits, with "The Ruined Cottage," of a conversion; and it is a gospel fervor that men like Hazlitt, Mill, Arnold, and William Hale White brought to them. The creed itself is fittingly simple: faith in the regeneration of man, during this life, and by the mildest means. Wordsworth's "conversion," the story of which is given in the following chapter, was linked to the discovery that "All shall survive." It laid the specter of epochal or absolute separation and made him reject all "hot" reformations. There are, if we trust nature, infinite chances for man's feelings to be renewed (a favorite Wordsworth metaphor is that of "revolving life," "the blessed power that rolls / About, below, above"); this renewal, moreover, as the "universal birth" and "stealing" influences of spring attest, is gentle to the point of not requiring the compulsion of externally framed laws or the gratification of reason:

> Love, now an universal birth,
> From heart to heart is stealing,
> From earth to man, from man to earth,
> —It is the hour of feeling.
>
> One moment now may give us more
> Than fifty years of reason;

> Our minds shall drink at every pore
> The spirit of the season.[20]

The juxtaposition of "one moment" and "fifty years" is justly exuberant, and has not been understood by either detractors or apologists. The true subject of the credal lyrics is rebirth—human renovation—and that depends on whether the heart can still give itself as in youth. Receiving is an active virtue to which vernal nature prompts, but the vigor of the heart's response to the present moment is unfathomable and can be gauged only by the future. This "silent" activity of the heart is mentioned in the stanza that follows:

> Some silent laws our hearts may make,
> Which they shall long obey;
> We for the year to come may take
> Our temper from to-day.

"In this moment there is life and food / For future years" ("Tintern Abbey"). The "one moment" is germinally a "spot of time" (*Prelude* XII.208).

Though we may recognize that Wordsworth's "one moment" is really "any moment," and interposes the generosities of nature between the precarious descent of grace and the now-or-never of political fervor, it is doubtful that many of the poet's contemporaries saw this. Wordsworth's implicit rejection of the "one blow" or revolutionary theory of human reformation is not remarked on.[21] But from the point of view of the history of Christianity *Lyrical Ballads* represents the furthest possible extension of the concept of the Light of Nature;[22] and this his readers did sense. "Come forth into the light of things," says the poet, "let Nature be your teacher." For those who followed Wordsworth this was religion in a new dress, the dress of feeling. Religion was once more opened to all, as in the primitive Christianity of St. Paul. Wordsworth extends Romans 1:19 to its limit and supports the simplest affirmation of the New Testament, that immortal life is in every man's reach. The new sensitivity to nature is indissociable from a new idea of Revelation or an old idea renewed. Wordsworth joins

Goethe and anticipates Carlyle in viewing nature as the "open se-
cret" or "commonplace mystery."[23] He does not deny the super-
natural but says nature is already so much. Why multiply entities,
or suppose special intervention, when nature is supernatural in
its powers to renovate man?

To call Wordsworth's creed quietistic is therefore to mistake it.
Though he reprehends self-assertions which divide us still further
from nature or ourselves, he does not say: "Regard the lilies of the
field: they do not toil neither do they spin." His counsel of wise
passiveness has a different foundation. Those lilies—or "apostolical
daisies" as *The Simpliciad* called them[24]—are almost hyperactive.
While they do not labor for the morrow they do take pleasure of
today and consciously or not communicate this:

> The budding twigs spread out their fan,
> To catch the breezy air;
> And I must think, do all I can,
> That there was pleasure there.[25]

The famous verses that prescribe a "wise passiveness" portray at
the same time a universe active beyond will or consciousness:

> The eye it cannot chuse but see,
> We cannot bid the ear be still;
> Our bodies feel, where'er they be,
> Against, or with our will.
>
> Nor less I deem that there are powers,
> Which of themselves our minds impress,
> That we can feed this mind of ours,
> In a wise passiveness.[26]

Such poetry does not depreciate but rather extends what Words-
worth calls elsewhere the "active principle."[27] He broadens the lo-
cus of individual, feeling life beyond man. There are energies in
man and around him that act in their own mode or naturally: they
cannot be subdued to the self. Man's body is not "his" alone. The
old grey stone, on which William sits in "Expostulation and Re-
ply," emblems this neutral countenance of earth, and stands against

the narrower spiritual locus of books. Activity, feeling, individuality, are not exclusively human. Nature has "passions" of her own.[28]

Here we touch a last point concerning the creed of *Lyrical Ballads*. The renovation of man is usually considered as the result of factors that are political, divine, or rational, or a combination of these. Wordsworth excludes the first (political) factor as insufficient, and doubts the directness of the second, but the third is explicitly attacked. The polemics enter only at this point. That man cannot be reasoned out of his old self or into unselfishness is just about the only restriction of redemptive possibilities he allows; and even this is not obtrusive in the 1798 edition. Yet reason, no doubt, is discredited; Wordsworth's nature has reasons the reason cannot know of. Human consciousness, deep as life itself, and to some degree against life, must be bound to nature and man by a stronger chain than ratiocination, one that has its beginning in the child's contacts with beauty "old as creation." The soul needs the "inscrutable workmanship" of its early association with nature in order to resist the crude interventions and immediate demands of reason—in this respect, as Hazlitt reported, Wordsworth is indeed a necessitarian.[29]

The "reply" in the poem quoted above is, in fact, to an "expostulation" traditionally ascribed to Hazlitt. Like most moral philosophers of the day, Hazlitt wished to transcend the skeptical eighteenth-century emphasis on self-interest, and to discover a more altruistic, yet still rational, theory of benevolence. He treated the matter in his first book, the *Essay on the Principles of Human Action* (published 1805),[30] and again in *Characteristics* (1823), a collection of aphorisms in the tradition of the French *moralistes*, who, with Hobbes, had sunk morality in self-interest. When Wordsworth attacks book-philosophy he is nearly always attacking "moral philosophy": those who emphasize the role of self-interest or seek to counter this emphasis by process of reasoning. Wordsworth's definition of the moralist as "A reasoning, self-sufficing thing, / An intellectual All-in-All,"[31] reflects the precise object of his contempt. Reason cannot renovate, and anyone who thinks it can, even though he use it to construct a theory of altruism, is still an egotist at heart. Half a century later Ruskin takes for his epi-

graph to the third volume of *Modern Painters* another Words-
worth hit at 'philosophers' who prize their soul "No more than as
a mirror that reflects / To proud Self-love her own intelligence."[32]

Wordsworth's position, then, is that only an elemental contact
with nature, still open to most at the beginning of the Industrial
Revolution, can restore the social (as opposed to selfish) principle
in man separated from it by sin, accident, or a necessity inherent
in maturation itself. Should this early relationship with nature be
present, something as light as one impulse can lead to restoration,
as Wordsworth learned at Alfoxden. The past may revive, and with
it the consciousness of what we were: natural beings in the strength
of nature. Presumably, the present moment may also have an un-
fathomable persistence. It need not die into the void of years. That
is the faith expressed in "Tintern Abbey," which leads Wordsworth
from present through past to even beyond his own death:

> Nor, perchance,
> If I should be, where I no more can hear
> Thy voice, nor catch from thy wild eyes these gleams
> Of past existence, wilt thou then forget
> That on the banks of this delightful stream
> We stood together.

Yet the voice we hear is full of haltings, of inner falls. It is the
voice of a man who has been separated from the hope he affirms and
who balances it in the moment against the possibility of further
separation. However consoling Wordsworth's creed may be, or
however far removed from it we may be, this voice of the *individ-
ual*, weighing the evidences of loss and gain, moves us today as it
did Mill and Arnold. They responded not to the naive but to the
alienated poet, to the nature-poet despite everything.[33] The specif-
ics of Wordsworth's creed are only as powerful as his attitude and
quality of consciousness. I have said that the feeling of certain four-
line stanzas is hymnic or antiphonal—

> To her fair works did nature link
> The human soul that through me ran;
> And much it griev'd my heart to think
> What man has made of man . . .

—but change the perspective slightly and what we hear is the rise-and-fall rhythm so characteristically Wordsworth's, with the shorter last line drawing the mood to a prematurely pointed close. Are there any verses more perilous in their balance than the following?

> A day it was when I could bear
> To think, and think, and think again;
> With so much happiness to spare,
> I could not feel a pain.[34]

The stutter of the indefinite article ("A day . . . a pain"), the feeling of hiatus set up by monosyllables in sequence, and that last verse, too short, defeating expectation, as the alexandrine in other poems (e.g. "The Female Vagrant") is too long: the poet's very articulation of happiness informs us of the heavy weight momentarily lifted from him.

I have grouped *Lyrical Ballads* according to various, interlocking designations. Theme has been important, and so has genre; there is also a distinctive series of polemical or credal lyrics. And having opened with the theme of separation I return to it once more. There is indeed one group of poems that treats directly of what Wordsworth calls "the mighty gulph of separation." I should like to call them lyrics of passage, because they are *rites de passage*.[35] They center in a death or a radical change of consciousness which is expressed in semi-mythical form; and they are, in fact, Wordsworth's nearest approach to a personal myth. I refer to the Lucy poems, which may be truer counterparts of Coleridge's "Mariner" (the greatest Passage poem of them all) than *Peter Bell*.

Unusually little is known about their genesis. They seem to have sprung up independently, during that German winter of 1799, the thought of England fastening on Wordsworth's heart. Coleridge's guess that "A slumber did my spirit seal" is an epitaph written after a premonition of Dorothy's death bespeaks their strangely elegiac mood. In genre the nearest important equivalents (near and yet so far) are Herrick's laments on the death of virgins.[36] The Lucy poems are more mysterious, however; their mode lying between ritual mourning and personal reminiscence. We wish to know about Lucy as a person, yet feel she represents more than a person. Who is Lucy, what is she?

Lucy is a boundary being,[37] nature sprite and human, yet not quite either. She reminds us of the traditional mythical person who lives, ontologically, an intermediate life, or mediates various realms of existence. Nymphs, both watery and human, are an example; heroes, insofar as both human and divine, another. Because of this ambivalence in mode of being, they seem to possess a supernatural element.

Wordsworth's Lucy, however, is an intermediate modality of consciousness rather than an intermediate being. She is seen entirely from within the poet, so that this modality may be the poet's own, and Lucy the "inner maiden." Except for this inwardness she belongs to the category of spirits who must still become human,[38] and the poet describes her as dying at a point at which she would have been humanized. This is especially clear in the third and fourth poems* of the group; and in the latter of these, "A slumber did my spirit seal," Wordsworth achieves the most haunting of his elisions of the human as a mode of being separate from nature. The first stanza describes him as without "human fears," probably because of a feeling of immortality associated with Lucy which also plays an important role in "Strange fits of passion"; in the second stanza she is dead, yet equally invulnerable because subsumed in a life beyond the touch of his thought.

Moreover, in the group as a whole, Lucy's fulfillment by nature and her passing into it (her death) coincide. She never is fully a person, or we never see her as one: even her growing-up, in the third poem, is narrated by Nature, not directly portrayed. She seems to jump over the crisis of self-consciousness and separation —but only, like the Boy of Winander, by dying into nature. Yet it

---

* I follow the later ordering: (1) "Strange fits of passion," (2) "She dwelt among th' untrodden ways," (3) "Three years she grew in sun and shower," (4) "A slumber did my spirit seal." In the 1800 *Lyrical Ballads,* which is the original ordering, the first, second, and fourth poems are printed together, and the third poem is the last, following at some distance.

must be remembered that we view her exclusively through the eyes of the speaker, so that the emphasis falls always on what she is to *him,* which strongly internalizes her meaning. The delusion that she is deathless is an unexplained magical ingredient of his thought.

This delusion he calls a "slumber" because it is not something entering his consciousness explicitly, but a dream or a supposition so deep (cf. "We Are Seven") that its existence is not revealed until the delusion is actually destroyed. This the first poem already makes clear. The lover in that poem (the persona of "the lover" will not drop away till the third and fourth poems of the group) identifies the moon and his love not by any conventional trick of thought but by so unconscious a "transference" that only when the moon drops is he startled into an idea which is the residue of that identification. It is like waking from a dream with a thought or terror whose antecedents remain unknown. In the fourth poem of the group, the beautifully inobvious use of the transferred epithet, "I had no human fears,"* shows that the illusion of Lucy's death-lessness is naturally within the poet, even if prompted by a real person; this is followed, moreover, by a second confirmatory trans-ference, when the slumber is depicted as having passed, as it were, from the poet to the object of his thoughts. Now Lucy *is* what she *seemed* to be.

Yet the poet expresses no shock at finding his illusion so rigor-ously betrayed by the fulfillment. Even the startled cry of the first poem is avoided. Lucy's death or the thought of her death (be-cause of the internal perspective we cannot distinguish) occurs in the blank between the stanzas. The poem may have its structural irony, but the poet's mood is meditative beyond irony. The first stanza describes the illusion and the second simply speaks its epitaph. A new "sealing" of the wounded consciousness has al-ready taken place.

The nearest Wordsworth comes to revolt is in a subdued parody of the divine fiat:

* "I had no such fears as would have come to me had I considered her as a human being."

> Thus Nature spake—The work was done—
> How soon my Lucy's race was run!

The soft delusion of immortality is related to nature, which weaves it to deceive imagination, though Wordsworth never lays the blame in any explicit way. The reason for his suspension of judgment will become clear. Blake, of course, would not have hesitated. His marginalia on this aspect of nature do not have to be imagined; they are to hand in his numerous visions of Beulah. For Wordsworth, however, nature's deception is a necessary lure "To make her Foster-child, her Inmate Man, / Forget the glories he hath known."[39] Not to forget them entirely, but to naturalize imagination, to prevent it from losing its anchor in this world. The immortality which apparels Lucy and makes her in the colloquial sense "divine," is actually nature's greatest success in blending with an imagination that can only be satisfied by the eternal and undecaying.

But if Lucy avoids the crisis of separation, the poet does not. She dies at the threshold of humanization, but he survives with "The memory of what has been, / And never more will be." The emphasis, I would repeat, is not on her death, but on the consciousness of the survivor. What he loses is more than a loved person. It is something *unique*, and the loss he feels includes the consciousness *that* it is unique. Two Matthew poems, written at almost the same time, suggest there are things the heart cannot replace. Substitution (in contemporary terms, sublimation) is questioned. Should another Lucy appear, "A blooming Girl, whose hair was wet / With points of morning dew,"[40] the poet, like Matthew, might look at her and look again, yet would not wish her his. The loss is primarily within himself, a fact of consciousness. After his brother's death, Wordsworth will say plainly: "A power is gone, which nothing can restore; / A deep distress hath humaniz'd my Soul."

Humanization, in the Lucy poems, or later in *The Prelude* and the Great Ode, is conceived as a precarious transition from imagination to the philosophic mind. This transition is also the subject of other Romantic ballads. The simplest of them is Goethe's "Erl-King," which describes a young and mysterious death, a child being lured from his father and the human world. The child's death expresses a prior allegiance that reasserts itself and prevails. The realm of nature spirits or imagination triumphs over the demythologized mind.

A more complex case is Keats' "La Belle Dame sans Merci." Keats' pale knight suffers a fate similar to that of the child, though the result is death-in-life rather than death: the solitude of self-consciousness, the awareness of irremediable loss. The mature man, in this ballad, is wakened once more to the nostalgia of the sensual, to something that indeed seems divine. For our sacrifice of the sensual, which is also a sacrifice of imaginative energy, is the Cerberus fee we pay for becoming human—only the gods escape it.

The last case I should like to mention is that of "The Ancient Mariner." In the Lucy cycle, death and the humanizing consciousness of death are almost simultaneous: Wordsworth does not dramatize the interval. It is precisely this interval which is dramatized by the Mariner's "passion," by everything that follows the precipitating crime. This crime, which signals the death of innocence and the beginning of an endlessly precarious process of humanization, leads back to the human through a new sense for the supernatural. Yet the Mariner's fall and redemption—his whole adventure—is inevitable: it does not represent a special case or special fate, but gives the generic pattern of how man is redeemed into humanity.

To return to the Lucy poems: Lucy's death is also more than loss, for it brings a new consciousness to birth. It is through Lucy's death that Wordsworth learns that nature does betray the heart which loves her. Yet the betrayal is not absolute; it has its point of comfort. It reveals not merely a delusion but also nature's strength in having fostered this according to a teleological principle. The imagination must be naturalized (nature must delude it) precisely because imagination is of more than natural origin. Thus if the poet has lost he has also gained. "She died and left to me / This heath, this calm, and quiet scene, / The memory . . ." The lines indicate a legacy: "left to me" has this connotation, if only in passing. The poet is calm because he has learned the dignity of his mind as well as the deep intent of nature.

Yet between the mode of the Lucy poems and that of the other ballads there is a very essential difference. Should "The Ancient Mariner" be an attempt at German sublimity, then the Lucy poems, conceived in Germany, are in a purely English mode. I do not mean they present an intentional answer to Coleridge or to Wordsworth's own, now firsthand, acquaintance with the German ballad revival. But they certainly cannot be called "sublime" since the strange and the familiar, the (German) sublime and the (English) pathos are mixed so evenly. And this is not irrelevant: it expresses in mood, or as a formalized mode, the precarious and blended quality of *human* consciousness, which is always in transition between natural and supernatural. Whereas the poems by Coleridge, Keats, and Goethe are clearly secondary ballads (in the sense that we talk of secondary or artificial epic), and try to recapture the force of a naive imagination and a native tradition, the awareness behind the Lucy poems is modern in every way. Their poet is not a bard or the anonymous ballad voice but a person still meditating and deepening the experience of which he talks. The reader's attention is not drawn toward magical incidents; these are only as important as the poet's expressed reaction to them. Instead of a transcendent 'poetic' rendering of experience, we are offered a recognizable if heightened 'normative' response. The voice we hear shares in the still sad music of humanity, and the mystery it depicts is the commonplace mystery of humanization.

# 6. Toward *The Prelude*

A series of fragments in blank verse from the Alfoxden period (July 1797 to July 1798) are probably our best link between "The Ruined Cottage," *Lyrical Ballads,* and *The Prelude.* They are roughly contemporaneous with the first-mentioned poem but relieved of the burden of sustained narrative. Published only in 1949, they have attracted relatively little notice because they appear to be overflows from "The Ruined Cottage" rather than a new departure.[1] It is remarkable, however, that Wordsworth is now recording various impressions in situ: the fragments indicate that a present sensation has become the matter of his song. It is perhaps the first time a poet has kept his eye so steadily on the object (which is also a subject, himself) and attempted a direct transcription of his personal response to nature. In "The Ruined Cottage," of course, the response of the pedlar is also in situ, which links many of the fragments to this poem. But instead of channeling the sensation that holds him into a conventional or public form, Wordsworth shapes the poetry it rouses as a consecration of native moment and place. Feelings that might serve other poets for simile or ornament are here explored to see whether they themselves cannot be the poem.

Though Wordsworth does not succeed in this, the discoveries rising from his attempt are important. He begins to see some of the "curious links" mediating between his present emotion and the past. Even while he tries to seize a present joy, an understanding grows in him of the role of the involuntary memory, and he is led to introspection. Yet because modern lyric poetry is essentially occasional, and takes for granted the celebration of ordinary things and private moods, one can easily overlook the significance of

Wordsworth's interest in the moods of his mind. What gave him the initial confidence that the "shadowy exultations"[2] he felt at Alfoxden were important? The fragments record only insubstantial experiences, momentary spells or sensory fixations, and Emerson can remark of a far more interesting event: "How much self-reliance it implies to write a true description of anything, for example, Wordsworth's picture of skating; that leaning back on your heels and stopping in mid-career. So simple a fact no common man would have trusted himself to detach as a thought."[3]

To make feelings that are more fugitive or episodic than this the substance of poetry required surely an extraordinary egoism—egoism in the sense of assured self-consciousness. This is accompanied, however, by a supporting yet opposite mood, a thankfulness that makes Wordsworth look out as well as in, and enables genuine nature poetry. The fragments are thanksgivings: a giving back to nature what the poet feels he has received. His renewed life is linked to nature's own life, till confidence in nature and in self appear interwoven rather than contraries. In many a walk, writes Wordsworth:

> At evening or by moonlight, or reclined
> At midday upon beds of forest moss,
> Have we to Nature and her impulses
> Of our whole being made free gift, and when
> Our trance had left us, oft have we, by aid
> Of the impressions which it left behind,
> Looked inward on ourselves, and learned, perhaps,
> Something of what we are.[4]

The fragment's continuation suggests a further reason for trusting such privileged moments. They lead to firmer self-consciousness, but also to "all shades of consciousness." Just as the poet's mind is not 'by pleasure less,' so in its fullness it does not make nature less. The assurance given to Wordsworth—which helps to restore his confidence in his mission of poet—is that the mind need not violate nature. Thought did not necessarily destroy the original impression of delight; on the contrary,

> by such retrospect it was recalled
> To yet a second and a second life,
> While in this excitation of the mind
> A vivid pulse of sentiment and thought
> Beat palpably within us, and all shades
> Of consciousness were ours.[5]

These verses provide an immediate context for his statement, a year or two later, that poetry "takes its origin from emotion recollected in tranquillity,"[6] and qualify what has been previously said of Wordsworth making a present joy the matter of his song. There is, clearly, an interval between "trance" and "retrospect" though we cannot tell how large it is. The fragments do not allow a precise judgment on when the recollectings in tranquillity occurred, whether shortly after the original emotion or at an unpredictable distance. It is even difficult to tell when the original experience took place. Sometimes, obviously, in the present:

> these populous slopes
> With all their groves and with their murmurous woods,
> Giving a curious feeling to the mind
> Of peopled solitude.[7]

Many instances are less clear. Whether the following passage portrays an experience originating in one of the many moonlight walks Dorothy and her brother took at Alfoxden, or whether it is an old memory surging up from childhood, or whether—the most likely interpretation—that memory is activated by a present scene, cannot be absolutely determined:

> there would he stand
> In the still covert of some [? lonesome] rock,
> Or gaze upon the moon until its light
> Fell like a strain of music on his soul
> And seem'd to sink into his very heart.[8]

The difficulty in determining whether Wordsworth is describing a past or a present experience points to something rather significant. We have complementary evidence from the fragments that the poet is on the brink of a discovery which made *The Prelude* possible. At Alfoxden, which seemed to have revived dead or alienated memories, he learns that the present depends deeply on the past. There is the story of the Athenian afraid to leave Athens because where else would he find sun and moon? Wordsworth had been forced to leave his native regions in a spiritual as well as physical sense; he had thought himself alienated from his past, both because of personal misfortune and, ontologically, as a man. Now Alfoxden—but Alfoxden is more than a place, it includes the steady company of Dorothy and Coleridge—restores once and for all his faith in continuity. Knowing that "All shall survive"[9] he leaves Alfoxden easily, and goes to Germany, and thence to Sockburn and Grasmere.

Wordsworth called Alfoxden the turning point in his career as a poet. What occurred must have been like a conversion, though it was in the making since 1793 and heralded by the intense poetic activity at Racedown in the spring of 1797. It is a self-discovery— a conversion to himself—and leads beyond "The Ruined Cottage" to a poem on Wordsworth's own mind. Not that things will suddenly cease to be problematic; on the contrary, Wordsworth is not completely happy with his best subject, himself. He keeps running after the false fire of an epic theme. Yet the promise of Alfoxden is never extinguished, and it takes him far beyond the simple conviction that the past is redeemable. His gliding, for example, from present to past (that fusion or indeterminacy of times) is accompanied by a deeper understanding of the function of place. "For I would stand . . ." says the poet, and "stand" gains a new emphasis here as in other fragments. The obsession with specific place lifts from him or blends into a more generous conception of nature: he feels he can stand, cast roots, in many places. What happens here and now has happened before, and is elsewhere, everywhere, "on earth, / Or in the heavens, or in the heavens and earth."[10] This multiplying locus assumes a tremendous sweep and molds for itself a subtler form as the blank verse of the fragments becomes an exercise in fluidity. The strongest contrasts become blendings; new corridors are opened and hidden subsistencies revealed. Past and present, time and place are involved but not these alone: even the senses are felt to converse or to exchange functions. In what follows I shall try to indicate the range of Wordsworth's vision, which never leaves "the very world, which is the world / Of all of us,"[11] yet reaches from the minute articulations of syntax and rhythm to the visionariness of Snowdon.

### Perception and Recollection

The gradual movement into the past or the mind which many fragments exhibit is by no means a simple retreat from the present. It is the living discovery that "Each most obvious and particular thought . . . Hath no beginning."[12] Mythically extended, as in the Great Ode, Wordsworth's discovery harmonizes with Plato's theory of recollection. But in one of the earliest fragments it appears as a gliding, at all levels, from immediacy to mediacy:

> Yet once again do I behold the forms
> Of these huge mountains, and yet once again,
> Standing beneath these elms, I hear thy voice,
> Beloved Derwent, that peculiar voice
> Heard in the stillness of the evening air,
> Half-heard and half-created.[13]

In this fragment, which shows the poet in the renewed presence of the river of his childhood,* the heavy present "do I behold," joined to the precisely visual but distancing notation of "the *forms* / Of these huge mountains" (my italics), betrays an analytical pressure similar to that which extends "Five years have passed" into "five summers, with the length / Of five long winters" ("Tintern Abbey"). The second subject predicate "I hear thy voice" initiates a further verbal lengthening that reveals the factors mediating to the ear. Wordsworth's 'analysis' slows perception to a more natural pace. He seems to speak a perfect mind-time, one that allows immediate feeling to expand both inwardly and outwardly.[14]

This general expansion is related to a shift from sight, which is

---

* The fragment may commemorate a visit to Derwentwater in 1794. But it could also describe the unexpected awakening of the memory of Derwent in the presence of an Alfoxden (or other) scene.

direct, to the ear, which catches life at a distance. But the ear is still too direct or local. A modulation of the verb changes the "I hear" and its direct object "thy voice" to a construction ("that peculiar voice / Heard in the stillness of the evening air") which slightly de-emphasizes the central "I" while bringing forward the roles of moment and place. The vanishing point of all this "mediatizing" is, of course, the past. Wordsworth becomes aware of every current feeding immediate consciousness, including sensations that he feared were lost. The purely spatial distance between Wordsworth and the Derwent is temporalized by the evening darkness, and we realize that time, like space, is an actively mediating power. The past is not *temps perdu.*

The phrase "Half-heard and half-created" suggests, finally, an effluence from the sense of hearing itself, either as it affects the things perceived with "an absolute / Essential energy"[15] of its own, i.e. with an energy not reducible to the conscious self, the ear having an activity the mind does not know of, or because the poet's memories of Derwent waken half-consciously into the new perception. Nothing is denied its own mediatory role, yet nothing acts independently of anything else. Cognition is recognition as generation should be regeneration: the whole man participates.

### The Continuities of the Self

As the foregoing suggests, Wordsworth does not believe in single, independent things, yet the "I" he uses freely, and without which *The Prelude* could not have been written, expresses a consciousness of self clearly distinguished from consciousness of nature. It is not, however, a persona-consciousness, for a persona dramatizes an attitude or a public presence while Wordsworth's "I" represents itself only. There are glimpses, of course, of a more public and prophetic voice, yet in these fragments the first person is usually an immediate construct answering immediate feelings, as if mood and person were born simultaneously and sustained each other's life. An inner confidence allows him to meet nature, or his own emotions, without a persona, and the energy of this blank verse (an idling energy of extraordinary power) also reflects this confi-

dence. Because Alfoxden has removed the terror of discontinuity,
the poet threads past, present, and future:

> Along the mazes of this song I go
> As inward motions of the wandering thought
> Lead me, or outward circumstance impels.
> Thus do I urge a never-ending way
> Year after year, with many a sleep between,
> Through joy and sorrow; if my lot be joy
> More joyful if it be with sorrow sooth'd.[16]

After Alfoxden the starting point of Wordsworth's poetry is
this dynamic and excursive consciousness of self. It is a heart
"Joyous, nor scared at its own liberty"[17] that opens *The Prelude*.
The initiative has passed from nature to the poet, but only because
anything in nature can quicken him. Sure of the renovating im-
pulse of nature, he is sure of himself, and for the first time he looks
at nature steadily. It is a power analogous to the mind and which
the mind cannot subdue to itself. Nature is an other; to the natural
man *the* other; its divinity is precisely to escape a purely human,
selfish use. But how is nature's otherness to be thought of? Here
Wordsworth's sanity shines through. He values local superstitions
and accepts all kinds of "animating thought."[18] There is no harm in
generously adding to nature; the danger is in subtracting from it
by fixed abstractions; anything which enlarges nature yet does not
diminish soul is legitimate. Though Blake would deny the pos-
sibility of such coexistence, because for him Nature's life is Imag-
ination's death (and vice versa), Thoreau, without knowing *The
Prelude,* almost caught the Wordsworthian relation of poet and
nature:

> He [the poet] must be something more than natural—even
> supernatural. Nature will not speak through but along with
> him. His voice will not proceed from her midst, but, breathing
> on her, will make her the expression of his thought. He then
> poetizes when he takes a fact out of nature into spirit. He
> speaks without reference to time or place. His thought is one

world, hers another. He is another Nature,—Nature's brother.
Kindly offices do they perform for one another. Each publishes
the other's truth.[19]

The only really satisfactory formulation, however, comes in an
unpublished passage summarizing Wordsworth's whole develop-
ment, and from which I excerpt the portion that most succinctly
refers to the biographical period here under discussion:

> And now
> The first and earliest motions of his life,
> I mean of his rememberable time,
> Redound upon him with a stronger flood;
> In speculation he is like a Child,
> With this advantage, that he now can rest
> Upon himself; authority is none
> To cheat him of his boldness, or hoodwink
> His intuitions, or to lay asleep
> The unquiet stir of his perplexities;
> And in this season of his second birth,
> He feels that, be his mind however great
> In aspiration, the universe in which
> He lives is equal to his mind, that each
> Is worthy of the other; if the one
> Be insatiate, the other is inexhaustible.[20]

### The I and the Other

The otherness of nature is not that of a mysterious solid, "a solid
without fluctuation."[21] Indeed, Wordsworth cannot be said to dis-
cover nature as such but rather the reality of the *relation* between
nature and mind. He is now made certain of two things: that there
is an indissoluble relation between them, and that this relation is
regenerative. In this season of "second birth" everything turns on
the possibility of rebirth, and the view that nature is cosubstantial
with mind contributed vitally to his own restoration.

The apogee of Wordsworth's trust in the reciprocity and even
"blending" of consciousness of self and consciousness of nature ex-
tended from Alfoxden to the first years of his residence at Grasmere
(1800–02). It was at Alfoxden that he composed his manifesto on

that wedding of mind and nature for which his proposed epic "The Recluse" was to be the spousal verse:

> I, long before the blessed hour arrives,
> Would sing in solitude the spousal verse
> Of this great consummation, would proclaim
> Speaking of nothing more than what we are
> How exquisitely the individual Mind,
> And the progressive powers perhaps no less
> Of the whole species to the external world
> Is fitted, and how exquisitely too,
> Theme this but little heard of among men,
> The external world is fitted to the mind
> And the creation, (by no lower name
> Can it be call'd), which they with blended might
> Accomplish: this is my great argument.[22]

It is significant that the manifesto does not announce a poetry dealing with the past. Wordsworth's eye is on present and future; he takes it for granted that the past is recoverable. The past, of course, is not only a body of experience to which that name is collectively given, but also the spirit which informed it. Wordsworth speaks exactly when he says that what redounded on him were "the first and earliest *motions* of his life."

Settling at Grasmere in the winter of 1799–1800, Wordsworth begins to implement his manifesto. Here Book I of the "Recluse," entitled "Home at Grasmere," is written, as a kind of prologue to the manifesto, and a new launching. By that time, of course, there have already been stirrings of another poem, rough drafts of what is to be *The Prelude*, whose hesitant and reverted eye would displace the forward singing "Recluse." "Home at Grasmere" remains the sole sustained example of Wordsworth making "A present joy the matter of a song";[23] only in this poem, swelling to over 700 lines, are the relations between self and nature relatively unproblematic. Let us look a moment at this "brief epic" of mutuality.

### Home at Grasmere

In "Home at Grasmere"[24] Wordsworth approaches a personal myth-making. It is his freest poem; the only poem in which his zest equals in a naturalistic context the inventiveness of a Blake or a Shelley. His muse riots; his creative energies almost evoke the terrestrial paradise. The speaking, vocative ("Thou") relationship he establishes with the valley, and the occasional viewing of spiritual feelings as phenomena, anticipate Shelley; while his picture of the whirling swans can transpose into pastoral the harmony of the spheres. Our being's heart and home, in this exuberant poem, is with nature, and infinity is with nature. Yet the valley is still Grasmere and the poet is too conscious of all his "little realties of life."

The result is often embarrassing as well as exuberant. The fault Coleridge has noted, that Wordsworth's conceptions are sometimes too large for their subject, is seen both here and in a later, related fragment, "The Tuft of Primroses."[25] Nature cannot really bear this unusual wantonness of spirit. Instead of remaking nature in the fire of imagination, instead of using the corporeal world as only one analogue among many, the other analogues being mythical, Wordsworth refuses to depart from common-sense perception or the corporeal understanding. That refusal involves him in a violation of the lesson nature itself had seemed to teach as far back as *Descriptive Sketches:* that the world cannot become a place of repose for imagination. Yet the mixed sweetness and energy of "Home at Grasmere" make it in Wordsworth's canon what *Alastor or the Spirit of Solitude* is in Shelley's and *Endymion* in that of Keats, though composed when Wordsworth was thirty and a mature poet. It is as if Wordsworth had reached too slowly a point Keats and Shelley reached too quickly. After the poem's failure, or its breaking off, he has only two paths open to him: a greater reliance on the autonomous imagination (traditionally expressing itself in myth and such genres as the quest-romance) or an inquiry into the problematic character of his imagination, that "redundant energy, / Vexing its own creation."[26]

A typical difficulty in the poem is the personification. Wordsworth seems to return to the time when everything appeared instinct with life, even the loose stones on the highway: "I saw them feel, / Or linked them to some feeling."[27] He is not, it is true, as gross as in *Descriptive Sketches,* where everything may become a

separate and animated entity; for each personification is soundly
justified. The principal person, for example, is Grasmere, and his
addresses to the valley result from a spreading joy (spreading from
nature to man) which the valley itself encourages: "Thou art
pleased, / Pleased with thy crags, and woody steeps, thy Lake, / Its
one green Island and its winding shores; / The multitude of little
rocky hills."[28] Yet there remains a mild grotesqueness, not miti-
gated by Miltonic or divine precedent,[29] in this self-regarding,
complacent nature: it is too much like Wordsworth counting his
possessions. And this surely is happening. The poet, afraid of the
solitude he freely denies to exist, afraid of his mind which needs
more than this nest of nature, this one valley, lingers embarrass-
ingly over all its peculiar beauties, and ends by displaying that
obsession with specific place which shows consciousness of self
buried in nature:

> No where (or is it fancy?) can be found
> The one sensation that is here; 'tis here,
> Here as it found its way into my heart
> In childhood, here as it abides by day,
> By night, here only . . .
> Something that makes this individual Spot,
> This small Abiding-place of many Men,
> A termination, and a last retreat,
> A Centre, come from whereso'er you will,
> A Whole.[30]

It is the spot syndrome all over again; and Grasmere becomes a
crude omphalos.

Yet when Wordsworth calls his valley "a haunt of pure affec-
tions," fusing place and spirit of place, or when he describes his
wintry initiation, "Stern was the face of Nature; we rejoiced / In
that stern countenance, for our Souls thence drew / A feeling of
their strength," or when he makes it difficult for us to distin-
guish between emanations of nature and of the heart—

> Joy spreads, and sorrow spreads; and this whole Vale,
> Home of untutored Shepherds as it is,

Swarms with sensations, as with gleams of sunshine,
Shadows or breezes, scents or sounds . . .[31]

—we recognize that interfusion of human and natural which is
among his greatest effects. In such a world the self can be itself and
never lonely. The separated consciousness is, by such continuities,
"the human Soul of universal earth."[32]

### The Survival of Apocalyptic Thoughts

The truly personal poetry first written at Alfoxden nourishes the
sense of self and of nature simultaneously. It does not matter
whether the inspiring impulse is from within or without: from
now on Wordsworth considers them interchangeable and uses
whether/or formulations.* The "I" must never seize the initiative
too strongly, and must be willing to be born in the moment and
precariously from moment to moment. No strong mythic or social
persona is needed when consciousness is a "con-naissance"[33] of self
and nature. Wordsworth's trust in nature is absolute not in the
sense that he waits on nature, but because his trust in himself vis-
à-vis externals is absolute. His wise passiveness disdains that "vi-
olence from within" which Wallace Stevens (like Blake) opposed
to the violence intrinsic to externals, to every fact as fact.[34]

Some doubts remain, however, and swell into moments of dark-
ness. Though Wordsworth defines the poet as a man speaking to
men, similar in kind, more sensitive in degree, he knows that to
Chaucer, Spenser, and Milton, "poet" meant more than that. To
Milton especially. For every Chaucer there is a Milton; and while
the one laughs in the hawthorn shade, the other, surpliced and
ceremonious, sings of a beauty that has terror in it.[35] Wordsworth
cannot long refuse the persona of poet. He dreams of epic whereas
his present trust limits him to lyric—"sweet passions traversing my
soul / Like Music,"[36] as the Alfoxden manifesto puts it. Then also,
even as he writes, his spirit rises up to show itself more independent
of nature than he knows. What makes these moments difficult to
recognize as belonging to the autonomous imagination is that they

---

* Cf. above, p. 169: "As inward motions of the wandering thought / Lead
me, or outward circumstance impels."

tend to take the form of nature rising up against him. There are spirits, he says in the earliest MS of *The Prelude* (1798–99, and so contiguous with Alfoxden), who form a favored being with gentle visitations; but there are also those that use severer means, interventions of a grosser kind, and, he concludes, "of their school was I."[37] *The Prelude* softens this admission somewhat by allowing equal power to gentle and severe. Yet even when Wordsworth, in "Home at Grasmere," believes he has found a nature adequate to his idea, the apocalyptic tendency survives in the returning obsession with specific place and such strangely excessive deepenings of the landscape as when Grasmere valley is described as the counterpart of the vault of heaven, "By which, and under which, we are enclosed / To breathe in peace."[38] Whether the image of a womb or a grave predominates here is hard to say. A similar deepening occurs more gradually at the beginning of "Tintern Abbey" where the poet's eye is drawn to a solitary hermit imagined at the heart of the landscape.

### Contrasts and Blendings

Is there an essential difference, then, between Wordsworth's evocations of "secret Power" in *Descriptive Sketches* and these survivals? I have argued that by 1798 the poet had come to firm self-consciousness and separated his imagination from nature. Yet the autonomy implied by this separation is only accepted when it appears not to be *contra naturam*. Such symbols of secret power or deepest solitude, therefore, as the hermit in "Tintern Abbey," may reflect the buried (naturalized) self held precariously within the confines of a nature it denies.[39]

But now Wordsworth is more conscious than in *Descriptive Sketches* of what happens to him in the moment, and this consciousness flows differently into perception. The Wordsworthian 'descent' does not begin with images or forcible personifications immediately transcended for others (the poet's mind being thrown restlessly from point to point), for the hermit comes into view *after* a slowly expanding movement of the mind over the landscape and into itself, and is presented as a fiction or intimation rather than as a direct percept. Though we are led, as in *Descriptive*

*Sketches,* to transcend the immediately visible, what lies beyond sight is not too great for it. It is the last term of a continuum, a blending of natural and human at the deepest stratum of what has gone before. Wordsworth's natural seeing resolves gradually every line where being ends, converting fixities into incremental contrasts or blendings, till sight transcends paradigmatically even itself, and becomes hearing: an eye "made quiet by the power of harmony."

### Eye and Object

The opening of "Tintern Abbey,"

> Five years have passed; five summers, with the length
> Of five long winters . . .

is representative of this incremental pattern on the level of verse. For the continuous purging of fixities is verbal as well as visual, and related to the sustaining swell of Wordsworth's new medium. We can now attempt a closer analysis of that medium.

One of the données or spontaneous forms in ordinary perception is the object. Another is the objectified sense of self (the "I") which is to consciousness what the object is to perception. Both forms, if too readily accepted, limit imagination. They impede "The one Life within us and abroad"[40] even while making consciousness of that life possible. The imaginative life of the poet— and this is clearest with the rise of non-objective art—is less dependent than that of other men on the form of the object. In visionary poetry like Blake's this relative independence is supported by an attack on the "daughters of memory" and a strong condemnation of naturalistic art. Blake insists on outline, but outline is spiritual form, not natural form. In nonvisionary poetry, however, the mind must begin with the given (object or objectified sense of self), and struggle with it organically or dialectically. Some modern art, of course, is so extreme that it leaves the reader to bring the object to it. The artist, knowing that the mind cannot function without recognizable objects (representations), that the object will creep back anyway, either conceives his work in opposition to the very idea of an object, obliging us to pass through a purgative series of hypotheses, or, as in a new kind of allegorical riddle, has an object in mind which we must divine in order to admire its transformation. The painter who cubes a grasshopper into pure shape and color, or the striking periphrases of Valéry and Hart Crane have this purpose.[41]

Since object-consciousness and self-consciousness are related, it is quite possible to determine Wordsworth's position in this "history" of nonobjective art. Here, for example, in one of the completer Alfoxden fragments, is a movement from image to imagelessness (from object-consciousness to a further, nonobjective stage) and then to a fluctuation between them:

> To gaze
> On that green hill and on those scattered trees
> And feel a pleasant consciousness of life
> In the impression of that loveliness
> Until the sweet sensation called the mind
> Into itself, by image from without
> Unvisited, and all her reflex powers
> Wrapped in a still dream [of] forgetfulness.
>
> I lived without the knowledge that I lived
> Then by those beauteous forms brought back again
> To lose myself again as if my life
> Did ebb and flow with a strange mystery.[42]

The poet passes beyond specific place (object) or an emotion that has fixed him to it. The word "gaze" and the demonstratives of the second line[43] suggest his visual and trance-like adhesion, but "gaze" becomes "feel" and the particulars ("green hill . . . scattered trees") merge as "the impression of that loveliness." The syntax then relaxes, suggests a turning inward, and the poet remarks explicitly that the object-cause, the "image from without," is no longer felt. A moment of intense unself-consciousness ensues: "I lived without the knowledge that I lived."*

---

* The "I" is strangely doubled, suggesting perhaps that the "I" that sets the boundaries, as between self and non-self, has been elided, but not the I AM of the primary imagination.

The next and last stage is not, as it may seem, a mere return to duality. If the données of ordinary perception are reconstituted, it is with the difference that "the one Life, within us and abroad" is now directly sensed and even activated by changing polar distinctions. Outer and inner, active and passive, subject and object are felt as a fluctuation expressed by the doublets of Wordsworth's style: I lived I lived, again again, myself my life, ebb and flow.

### Centroversion

The movement beyond specific place is often accompanied by renewed localizations. There is in fact a continual fleeing and seeking motion centering on the "one":

> solemn dreams,
> Dreams beautiful as the fair hues that lie
> About the moon in clouds of various depth,
> In many clouds about the full-orb'd moon.[44]

The Wordsworthian turn[45] is in particular evidence here as the poet gravitates toward central stasis yet gently converts this impulse into a "circle." Though he begins with the definite subject of dreams, the simile which is to describe it draws away from the subject toward an emergent symbol. This symbol, the moon, harmonizes the idea of center-point and circle. A similar centrifugal-and-centripetal pattern is discerned in the deployment of phrases. Much of the fragment can be plotted as a series of rhythmic phrases whose ABBA (chiastic) form draws motion out of convergence. Solemn (A) dreams (B), dreams (B) beautiful (A) is such a pattern expanding from three syllables to four; while the next two lines are a fine self-rounding instance with the repeated nouns made fuller; moon, full orb'd moon; in clouds, in many clouds. Almost any passage of "Tintern Abbey" will show this style perfected. There is a drawing out of words into doublets, gradual expansions that blend thought with thought, link feeling to feeling, yet the whole, though constantly expanding, falls inward like circles emphasizing their concentricity:

> that blessed mood,
> In which the burthen of the mystery,

> In which the heavy and the weary weight
> Of all this unintelligible world
> Is lighten'd:—that serene and blessed mood.

### Eye and Ego

Most of the fragments are descriptive of night or of stillness. Wordsworth becomes conscious of what happens when his eye is subdued. Or rather, it is the directness of the eye which is subdued, its desire for a "moon," for a subsuming object or sight-symbol:

> The moon is in the East, I see her not;
> But to the summit of the arch of heaven
> She whitens o'er the azure of the sky
> With thin and milky gleams of visible light.

The poet glimpes a principle of compensation; sees more not seeing the moon. But when the eye has even less, it begins to be precariously visionary, prospecting a secret power:

> The leaves stir not,
> They all are steady as the cloudless sky;
> How deep the Quiet: all is motionless,
> As if the life of the vast world was hushed
> Into a breathless dream.[46]

Silence or darkness also yields another reaction. It allows an intrinsic energy of the senses to come forth. In the relative absence of external stimuli their *"own* divine vitality"[47] appears. Wordsworth knows what kind of vitality this is; yet his descriptions indicate one thing, and his major theoretical fragment, probably under the influence of Coleridge, something different.

Coleridge urged on Wordsworth a long philosophical poem which would have demonstrated that "the senses were living growths and developments of the mind and spirit, in a juster as well as higher sense, than the mind can be said to be formed by the senses."[48] The way Coleridge formulates the problem is determined by the polemic against Locke, and is therefore both clear and crude. Wordsworth's major theoretical fragment may be harmonized with Coleridge's position:

> There is creation in the eye,
> Nor less in all the other senses; powers
> They are that colour, model, and combine
> The things perceived with such an absolute
> Essential energy that we may say
> That those most godlike faculties of ours
> At one and the same moment are the mind
> And the mind's minister.[49]

This seems to be pure Coleridge, for the idealist viewpoint is used to exalt rather than depreciate sense experience. Insofar as the senses are organs ("living growths") of the mind, they are exactly what Wordsworth says: at once the mind and the mind's minister. Coleridge furthered the organicist point of view,[50] and tended to distinguish, like Wordsworth and even Blake, between the senses and sensation, and to put the blame on the latter to save the former. "If the doors of perception were cleansed, everything would appear to man as it is, infinite." Sensation is, at its best, "vision nascent, not the cause of intelligence, but intelligence itself revealed as an earlier power in the process of self-construction."[51]

Yet Coleridge, as the last quotation shows, combined his organicism with a hierarchical and progressivist principle imported from German philosophy and reinforced by seventeenth-century and Neoplatonic likings.[52] The passage on the Scale of Nature (*Paradise Lost*, V.469 ff.) which Coleridge quotes at the beginning of chapter 13 of *Biographia Literaria* is the most impressive English statement of that principle. Wordsworth, on the other hand, tenaciously respectful of individual stages, refuses to go beyond sensation as vision nascent. He will not, or cannot, make it vision consummate via transcendental schemes or giant personifications. Though the professions of faith in which *The Prelude* abounds are sometimes very close to Coleridge and Blake, they remain effusions that convince by the passion of statement and not by a realized imagery.

When Wordsworth, then, attributes to the senses an "absolute essential energy" he may mean something different from (though not opposed to) Coleridge, something more simple and rooted in

immediate experience. The remark, linked to his growing con-
sciousness of individuation as a universal principle, means (1)
that like the personal "I" the senses are individuated, yet thereby
also independent of the personal "I"; and (2) that by virtue of
their intrinsic life they continue to function when conscious
thought or nature itself seems to sleep. This is the most pointed
idea of the fragments, and it contextualizes such halcyon mo-
ments as

> The clouds are standing still in the mid heavens;
> A perfect quietness is in the air;
> The ear hears not; and yet, I know not how,
> More than the other senses does it hold
> A manifest communion with the heart.[53]

It also reveals that the doctrine of "The eye it cannot chuse but see,
/ We cannot bid the ear be still . . ." refers primarily to this in-
trinsic and impersonal energy of the senses rather than to a general
necessitarianism.[54] Wordsworth is reaching beyond the selfish eye
to its radical and purer energy; he is once more learning to see the
human from the point of view of Being:

> I felt the sentiment of Being spread
> O'er all that moves and all that seemeth still;
> O'er all that, lost beyond the reach of thought
> And human knowledge, to the human eye
> Invisible, yet liveth to the heart. (*Prelude* II.401–05)

*The Night Watch*

One fragment brings an especially mysterious working out of
Wordsworth's theme. Night falls, and the poet continues his
watch:

> I stood
> Within the area of the frozen vale,
> Mine eye subdued and quiet as the ear
> Of one that listens, for even yet the scene,
> Its fluctuating hues and surfaces,
> And the decaying vestiges of forms,

Did to the dispossessing power of night
Impart a feeble visionary sense
Of movement and creation doubly felt.[55]

According to the fragment a fading scene gives to the night causing
it to fade a visionary sense which is "doubly felt." Felt by the
night? And why "doubly"? The answer is that the poet, recover-
ing at Alfoxden his earlier power to attribute life to all things,
feels nature feel. This results in a radical kind of personification.
Intuiting the "passions" of nature Wordsworth removes himself
as the exclusive center of an activity which seems to take place pri-
marily between nature and nature, between the hues and surfaces
of the landscape and the power of night. Strange elision of the hu-
man intermediary![56]

The fragment illumines, therefore, the passage from *The Prel-
ude* quoted earlier, which begins, "I felt the sentiment of Being
spread . . ." The "I" of the poet widens to become aware of the "i"
of other beings: even of the "i" of the eye. Yet to multiply stand-
ard personification might increase our sense for the life of nature
at the risk of diminishing the "sentiment of Being," since our con-
ception of personal existence is anthropomorphic. Wordsworth,
however, desires to link the "Life within us and abroad" to some-
thing larger than ego- or object-consciousness; excessive "anthro-
pomorphitism" is, in fact, the principal cause of his dislike of what
the eighteenth century praised as "forcible" personification, and
this dislike coincides with his protest against pagan religion which
is said to subject the mind to the bondage of definite form.[57] (The
fragment, incidentally, helps to confirm our previous determina-
tion of the theme of "The Vale of Esthwaite" and of *An Evening
Walk*. Wordsworth faces the coming of night, and only an emer-
gent "sentiment of Being" is strong enough to retard and per-
haps vanquish his deepening night thought, his fear of apocalypse.)

### Eye and Ear

In the night watch fragment, Wordsworth represents the eye as
potentially *listening*. It is possible to overlook this, for the poet

does not reduce his intuitions to one emphasis. But apposing another fragment in which the silent light of a night-scape becomes a speaking light, inward and musical, this fact is clarified:

> there would he stand
> In the still covert of some [? lonesome] rock,
> Or gaze upon the moon until its light
> Fell like a strain of music on his soul
> And seem'd to sink into his very heart.[58]

It is as if the eye were transcending itself to recover the sound-value of things, "By form or image unprofaned." Again, as we have noted, Alfoxden seems to retrieve an earlier power or experience:

> I would walk alone,
> Under the quiet stars, and at that time
> Have felt whate'er there is of power in sound
> To breathe an elevated mood, by form
> Or image unprofaned; and I would stand,
> If the night blackened with a coming storm,
> Beneath some rock, listening to notes that are
> The ghostly language of the ancient earth,
> Or make their dim abode in distant winds.
> Thence did I drink the visionary power.[59]

"Visionary power," he will also say, sharpening the paradox, "Attends the motions of the viewless winds."[60]

If Wordsworth insists on a quieting of the eye, and on the part nature itself played in this, either *a contrario* as at the time of *Descriptive Sketches,* or by disclosing new antennae, as at Alfoxden, it is because sight (object-consciousness) overbears the other senses. He does not want to blind a faculty but to cleanse a gate of perception; and Alfoxden makes him aware that eye and ear are as deeply in touch as past and present. Yet Alfoxden was not the first place of discovery although it did bring on its fullest realization. The "fellowship of silent light / With speaking darkness"[61] Wordsworth discovers first during his ascent of Snowdon.

*Eye and Ear on Snowdon*

The Snowdon vision, according to the poet's own declaration, is one of several events vital in the growth of his mind and the recovery of his (poetic) spirits. Its import, daring if taken literally, is that there exists an imagination in nature analogous to that in man. Nature exhibits "the express / Resemblance of that glorious faculty / That higher minds bear with them as their own."[62] Wordsworth did take the experience literally, and instead of offering at the end of his poem an eighteenth-century Allegory of Imagination, he presents us with a concrete Act of Imagination. He does not consider what he sees as a projection of his mind on nature. The episode returns him to the faith that "the forms / Of Nature have a passion in themselves."[63] Nature is not a universe of death that lives only from or within our life. It has a greatness commensurate to that in man: this greatness, this imagination, is revealed on Snowdon.

It is important to dwell on Wordsworth's belief that Snowdon was Nature's "naked work / Self-wrought, unaided by the human mind."[64] His literal animism even makes him say that the vision was given "to spirits of the night / And three chance human wanderers"—it was, that is to say, no private revelation but one for any man and even for others than man. At a later date nature's unusual *activity*[65] might have disturbed the principle of reciprocity, but at this time in Wordsworth's development (circa 1791–93) it redressed the balance between nature and the self by opposing "Nature's Self" to "Reason's naked self."[66] In his crisis years, as *Prelude* X through XIII recount, Wordsworth had been tempted to divorce head from heart, himself from nature; they are the years in which his belief in an autonomous intellect threatened to cut him off from former sources of strength. Only experiences which could not be laid to the fantasy of an excited mind, but which would indubitably be nature's "naked work / Self-wrought," were therefore of power to restore him.

Yet Wordsworth is of the mind's party without knowing it, and Snowdon remains one of the most complexly deceptive episodes in literature. When the poet emerges from the mountain mist (*Prel-*

*ude* XIV.35) two things force themselves one after the other on his senses. The first is the moon single in the firmament: it seems insulated from the lower sphere on which it gazes sovereignly. The second is the roar of waters rising from that sphere: an event as striking as the moonscape's previous silence. The meditation following the vision (*Prelude* XIV.63 ff.) calls this strange reversal a "mutual domination," an "interchangeable supremacy." Nature, Wordsworth suggests, forced a shift in his attention from one apparently supreme agent to another, from moon to abyss; a shift which makes him aware of an antiphony between them. The active principle cannot be localized.

One aspect, however, not clarified by the meditation, and which may be the most important, is that the ascent of the voice of the waters does not indicate a true mutation in nature, a genuine Second Act. For the voices, if we examine the vision closely, cannot be sudden except psychologically: i.e. in their breakthrough to the poet's mind. If he does not hear the stream of sound, which must have been there all along, it is because his senses were fixed by an obsessively visual image. So strong is the usurpation of sight that it masks the continuous sound, and the re-entry of the latter into consciousness appears like a breakthrough. Though the vision, therefore, is about nature, it is also about the poet's perception of nature, since not heaven and earth but only the poet's mind is turned.[67] The domination of which Wordsworth speaks is exerted first on eye then on ear, with neither given ultimacy but with sight more dangerous because more easily fixating the *flow* of attention.[68]

Thus Wordsworth's greatest visionary sight is based on the simplest kind of psychical error. To us this makes it more solid: such accidental epiphanies, almost a modern staple, and popularized by the contemporary novel, sharpen our sense of self-determination, but also our sense of fatality, since blindness to oneself at this level infers greater—immeasurable—blindnesses further on. Many poems in the *Lyrical Ballads* similarly "build up greatest things / From least suggestions." Yet the Snowdon episode is not written with the slightly bemused, almost deprecating tone of a Wordsworth ballad. It approaches a Miltonic sublimity. Wordsworth would have found it difficult, perhaps wrong, to stress at this point the simplicity of his error. And to return the emphasis from the objects to the energy of perception in any explicit way might tempt us to locate the whole drama solely in the human mind, and this would defeat his refusal to over-objectify the locus of perception, as well as his awareness that the *correspondence between eye and ear* is but one crucial revelation given by the experience.

"A Voice to Light gave Being" Wordsworth writes much later in "On the Power of Sound" (1828). His reference to the Logos is secondary; it re-enforces a personal knowledge. The Alfoxden fragments and the vision on Snowdon intimate that the individuated energies of eye and ear might prove the source of a larger, reciprocal vigor. Snowdon in particular shows an interchange rather than reunification of these senses. The sea lends, as it were, its voices to the moon, and that broods (like the Spirit of God in Genesis or *Paradise Lost*) on a lower sphere from which it had seemed utterly distinct. This potentiality of interchange points to the ethics of metaphor and perhaps of poetry as a whole. In MS W, which is of special importance because it gives the Snowdon episode as originally written for the five-book *Prelude,* Wordsworth comments that higher minds

> from their native selves can deal about
> Like transformation, to one life impart
> The functions of another, shift, create,
> Trafficking with immeasurable thoughts.[69]

### Between Worlds

Snowdon remains an exceptional episode, not in what it discloses but in the form in which the disclosure reaches Wordsworth. He is careful to point out that the "circumstance most awful and sublime" (1805 *Prelude* XIII.76) is not necessary: the imaginative mind may also be roused by least suggestions. It could even be argued that the form of the Snowdon vision and its content are at odds, for nature both thrusts itself on the senses and seeks to liberate imagination from sensory thrall.

Yet Wordsworth has previously made it clear that nature may

have to pit the senses against each other to undo their individual
tyrannies and achieve "the great ends of Liberty and Power"
(XII.139). His mind, to be genuinely imaginative and free, must
transcend the impressive *object* (moon and abyss) as the focal
point of its inspiration. The twofold fixation, therefore, on the vis-
ual moon, then on the sounding abyss, does not issue here in a
double fixation but in the awareness of continuity and interchange.
Snowdon thus foreshadows a modern poetry that relies on a delib-
erate and liberative synaesthesia, or on nonobjective (syntactical)
forms. And yet, adhering to common sense and common terms,
Wordsworth refuses to start at a point beyond object-consciousness.
He dooms himself to stay within the limits of the corporeal un-
derstanding and of immediate experience.

This is not a lesser but a greater task than that of modern poetry,
for starting at a more primitive point in perception Wordsworth
raises himself to the same transcendence of object-consciousness.
His respect for the natural contours of an experience and the out-
lines of objects is never artificially suspended, yet by means of a
principle of contrast or reversal that seems to inhere in experience
itself, all fixities are resolved. Through contrast everything is made
distinct yet nothing is defined into absolute independent single-
ness.[70] No sphere or event, in the Snowdon vision, has exclusive
properties. The moon's light flashing through the mist is paral-
leled by the voices roaring up; these voices are "one" (*Prelude*
XIV.60) like the moon itself or the radiant silence they pierce;
the moon, moreover, in its fixity and solitude, stands symmetrical
to the "fixed, abysmal, gloomy, breathing-place" in the vapor;
while the vapor itself is a consummate mimic of properties. Even
the senses exchange energies and perhaps functions. Discontinuity
yields to communion, and if moon and chasm are apocalyptic
spots, dangerously fixed points, the second is more vital and be-
comes almost immediately a strait between two worlds, a "breath-
ing-place" and "thoroughfare."

We see by this that Snowdon is an omphalos vision and that
Wordsworth again turns from apocalypse. He achieves a view of
the border between realms of being. The oscillating up-down
pattern of attention (counterpointed by the strongly horizontal

stretching of the mist "far as the sight could reach") recalls the original of all such visions for minds nourished by the Bible: "And he [Jacob] dreamed, and behold a ladder set upon the earth, and the top of it reached to heaven: and behold the angels of God ascending and descending on it."[71] On Snowdon the ladder descends, as it were, into a nether sphere: the Deep or *Tehom*, which the Bible mentions hesitantly at the beginning of Genesis, reopens as strongly as in the Psalms; and the notion of a "breathing-place," seen suddenly as in a dream near where the poet stands, helps to enforce the impression that he has passed into himself, and sees his body's life from the inside, or from the pulse-point of the macrocosm. He stands, in any case, where the sustaining (ascending and descending) circulation between worlds is visible.

This circulation, in the lineaments of a style Alfoxden bore, some of the preceding paragraphs have traced. The only difference between the sublime shadowings on Snowdon and the "subtle intercourse"[72] Wordsworth describes at Alfoxden is that in the former even the least sensitive man cannot choose but feel, while in the latter nature acts imperceptibly. Which mode seemed the greater miracle to Wordsworth? The "wondrous influence of power gently used." It was his rediscovery of the subtle links that join past and present, or restore the alienated heart, which prompted the great thaw of Alfoxden and led into *The Prelude*. That poem begins with a "gentle breeze" which reappears at the second beginning of *The Prelude*, the story of the poet's restoration:

> Ye gentle breezes lead me forth again
> Soft airs and gladdening sunbeams lead me on
> To the green haunts of chearfulness and peace
> And health and liberty, to pathways roads
> And fields with rural works to open earth
> And the calm bliss of an unbounded sky
> The woods the villages the pleasant farms
> Smoke rising up from tufted trees and brooks
> Muttering among the stones[73]

In this almost unpunctuated variant there is no stop to the breeze of a rhythm running over so many things, joining by simple enumeration and the least effort of grammar one thing and the next. Is this not Sabrina of *Comus* dancing over "The Cowslip's velvet head / That bends not as I tread"? Snowdon, however, is more naked in its display of powers, more abrupt in its passings from mist to light, moon to abyss. The spirit of that place has a resemblance to Wordsworth's moments of terrible beauty and skirts the Miltonic Sublime. Yet there remains a significant distance between Wordsworth at his most Miltonic and Milton. This distance is worth defining; it touches on Wordsworth's general problem in writing an epic poem, i.e. a long poem on the greatest possible subject with a style appropriate to its subject.

### The Sublime Scale   1: Milton

Raphael treats Adam to pre- and postprandial discourses. The former of these politely justifies his sitting down to eat with Adam, the latter learnedly explains angelic digestion. Both are parts of a comprehensive argument teaching the concept of an orderly ascending Scale of Nature. Raphael's moral parallels to a nicety Wordsworth's notion of fruitful reciprocity:

> For know, whatever was created, needs
> To be sustain'd and fed; of Elements
> The grosser feeds the purer, Earth the sea,
> Earth and the Sea feed Air, the Air those Fires
> Ethereal, and as lowest first the Moon;
> Whence in her visage round those spots, unpurg'd
> Vapours not yet into her substance turn'd.
> Nor doth the Moon no nourishment exhale
> From her moist Continent to higher Orbs.
> The Sun that light imparts to all, receives
> From all his alimental recompense
> In humid exhalations, and at Even
> Sups with the Ocean. (*Paradise Lost* V.414–26)

Here too we glimpse "the emblem of a mind / That feeds upon infinity" (*Prelude* XIV.70 f.). Wordsworth's metaphor is as serious as Milton's larger machinery bearing on the theme of angelic diet. To ascend to God via the food for thought provided by created

things ("Light after Light well used") is the hope held out to
Adam. The ascent, moreover, does not violate creation like Satan's
bound that overleaps all bound. It is a gradual movement up. "By
steps we may ascend to God" (*Paradise Lost* V.512).

Yet Wordsworth does not proceed in a hieratically straight line
from grosser to purer; nor does he extend cosmologically what
he sees. The analogical and myth-making imagination, by which
Milton travels beyond the confines of ordinary experience, is only
superficially present in him. When he writes of "affections by com-
munion raised / From earth to heaven, from human to divine"
(*Prelude* XIV.117 f.) he talks the cant of his time or shows his
nostalgia for the Miltonic; it has little bearing on his poetic pow-
ers. On Snowdon the descendental movement is as important as
the ascendental; the episode at once posits and destroys such
dichotomies. High and low, mist and light, light and sound, sound
and silence are patently present without interrupting a unifying
flow of power. The same holds true of Wordsworth's largest
dichotomy: Nature and Mind. We look at something he calls Na-
ture, yet we feel we have entered the Body of the Mind. Though
Milton's world has its great and alternating extremes, there is never
this kind of fluctuation or reversibility; and in Wordsworth it
can occur without extinguishing the light of sense. His Sublime is
the subtle magnified.

Yet without a mythical or cosmological scheme positing a con-
tinuity between human and divine, it is difficult to see how epic
can be written. Epic is total in its aim, a vision of "First and last
and midst and without end." For Wordsworth, however, conti-
nuity is too crucial to be posited a priori. It is recovered, or re-
vealed from moment to moment; and only by an act of faith or
sentiment, and never of imagination, fixed as certain and ordained.
The terror of discontinuity or separation enters, in fact, as soon
as the imagination truly enters. In its restraint of vision, as well as
its peculiar nakedness before the moment, this resembles an ex-
treme Protestantism, and Wordsworth seems to quest for "evi-
dences" in the form of intimations of continuity. But it is likely
that this radical Protestantism, and Wordsworth's sensibility, have

a modern and corrosive self-consciousness as common ancestor, rather than being in a relation of cause and effect to each other.

*The Sublime Scale*   2:  *The Heterodox Imagination*

At the end of his life Yeats returned "To where all ladders start, / In the foul rag-and-bone shop of the heart."[74] Yeats had previously tried many ladders, sublime scales to vision. They can all be classified as products of romance, or heterodox mystical, traditions. A mysticism that made use of any myth, Christian or not, and which had been absorbed to a surprising extent by Catholic thought and even practice, sprung up into a new and independent existence when Protestantism removed Catholic dogmas from the imaginative life, yet only to purge that life more strongly. Between Spenser and Dr. Johnson all forms of "sacred" imagination grew suspect. Both in England and France, though for complexly differing reasons, a great divide came to separate devotional and secular art, one which nourished, if it did not actually produce, Neoclassicism. In England, with which we are now concerned, Spenser managed a hidden and Milton a superbly patent (though not unproblematic) harmonizing of Poetry and Divinity—the passage previously quoted from *Paradise Lost,* simple as it appears to be, reflects a large store of appropriated pagan speculation.[75] Even Marvell, a more generous Protestant than many, and not unaware of esoteric currents of thought, was made uneasy by Milton's mixture of profane and sacred; and although he claims it as an astounding, also qualifies it as an "inimitable," feat.[76]

English Romanticism is, from a certain point of view, a renascence of the Renaissance: a return to the spirit of Spenser and Milton, to their redemption of imaginative thought wherever it is found.[77] The imagination, like the Spirit of God, can seize on heathen as well as Christian, and only the enlightenment spirit of "insolent light" (as Novalis called it) is profane.[78] Yet a return to the temper of the great myth-making poets does not mean necessarily a return to their materials. We should imitate, says Edward Young, Homer the man, rather than his work; Milton, after all, gave us a Milton, and not simply an English *Aeneid.*[79] So the Romantics, starting with Collins, looked for the flame and not the matter it consumed.

Blake held that all religions are a derivation from the Poetic Genius. The poet's task is no longer, as in the Renaissance, to integrate Classical and Christian, but to winnow from both the sacred flame of original imagination. Though Blake maintains the inferiority of pagan modes of thought, and claims to prefer Christian sources, he refuses to distinguish between sacred and secular prophecy. All imaginative men are his guides: Milton with Ezra and Isaiah, and Shakespeare, and Paracelsus.[80] What matters is the spirit of these men rather than the specific, perhaps devotional, materials they organize—a spirit that prefers, before all temples and codes, the imaginative heart. The greatness of *Paradise Lost* is to recover the Bible as a work of the Poetic Genius: it is a meeting of imagination with imagination.

On this basis Blake managed a last flourishing of the Sublime. He felt free to add to the reopened canon his own "Bible of Hell." Instead of totally refusing, like Wordsworth, esoteric and cosmological imaginings, he appropriated them with greater freedom than Milton. Blake's system is strongly antinomian with respect to received materials, and with respect to itself repudiates the absoluteness of traditional eschatology. Despite the "ladder-vision" inherent in most previous cosmogonies, Blake remains as radically Protestant as Wordsworth in his rejection of any continuity between human and divine assured by intermediaries or intermediate forms. He too casts out "heaven" and "futurity."

Yet his rejection of links between human and divine is in the name of a continuity between human and human: no ladder is ultimately necessary because nothing stands between man and his redemption except man himself. It is we who have falsely separated divine from human, and created systems or snares to ladder it back. The concepts of Nature and the Divine are a perversion of the joining concept of the Human. The labor of redemption, therefore, is to rehumanize both by perpetual mental fight. It is to reappropriate them to Original Man that the apocalyptic hammers, furnaces, and winepresses work in Blake's poetry. To overvalue his source materials or to take too literal a view of his system is therefore to "dishumanize" once more the imagination of man.

Wordsworth did not have a principle of conversion to purge existing myths from ancient error and to lead that error back to the mind of man which first engendered myth. According to Blake all myths are creation myths and tell of man's self-alienation. They are the records of our fear of ourselves, of our recoil before our own imaginations, but therefore contain the traces of the energy we have disowned. His own system is a myth to redeem all myths, and to reintegrate, like Isis, the body of Osiris, the "human body divine." Yet for Wordsworth myths are externals rather than fallen Eternals, and lacking Blake's basic principle, as well as his massive irony, he allows but a single cosmic extension of sight: a mild *anima mundi* mysticism probably fostered by Coleridge in those long communion walks between the summers of 1797 and 1798 at Alfoxden. It underlies his profession concerning the "active principle" which opens the last book of *The Excursion* but was first written at Alfoxden:

> There is an active principle alive
> In all things, in all natures, in the flowers
> And in the trees, in every pebbly stone
> That paves the brooks, the stationary rocks,
> The moving waters, and the invisible air.[81]

This is his sole compromise with the heterodox imagination.

Even so it is less a ladder vision (a progressive Chain of Being) than a sense of circulation whose roots can be traced in his own development, through tapping archaic emblems of world harmony.[82] In *The Prelude* the *anima mundi* theory blends with what seems to be a secondhand Spinozism (also, surely, from the enthusiastic Coleridge) to provide a quasi-philosophical dignity for his view of nature. What Yeats claimed to return to, Wordsworth never abandoned in his greatest decade: the heart, where all visions begin, and where they remain rooted. He rises "as if on wings" but only to look back on himself: "the world which I had been / And was" (*Prelude* XIV.381 ff.). From Blake's point of view, doubtless, Wordsworth's refusal of imaginative system is related to a fear of imagination, not by any means a disesteem of imagination, the Enlightenment concern that it may lead to intellectual error, but too great a fear of the very "fear and awe" Wordsworth rapturously acknowledges on looking into the mind of man. This fear, according to Blake, engendered the withdrawal of Urizen and our fall from eternity into the body of this death.[83]

### The Sublime Scale    3: Science

A visionary extension of sight was also offered by eighteenth-century science. As early as his revision of *An Evening Walk* (probably 1794, and certainly before any meeting with Coleridge) Wordsworth had linked two kinds of "favoured souls," those who look imaginatively on common nature, and those

> to whom the harmonious doors
> Of Science have unbarred celestial stores,
> To whom a burning energy has given
> That other eye which darts thro' earth and heaven.[84]

The continuation, too long to quote, makes it reasonably clear that Wordsworth conceives the man of science on the Thomsonian model as one who adds philosophy to science just as he has added science to fancy, so that the "illimitable tracts of mind" also become his habitat.

At Alfoxden, similarly, we find Coleridge planning one of his many phantom projects, a long poem called "The Brook" which would have traced a river from source to delta with suitably impassioned reflections on man, nature, and society.[85] Coleridge does his research from nature and walks almost daily to the top of Quantock to study the course of his stream. A year before he had already contemplated Hymns to the Sun, the Moon, and the Elements, including, of course, a Hymn to Water; and J. L. Lowes has amply shown the heterogeneous *materia* accumulated by him for that purpose.[86] That the sublimer subject of the hymns and the humbler one of "The Brook" should flow side by side is no more surprising than that Wordsworth should associate local and celestial in his picture of the compleat Poet-Scientist-Philosopher: "Home their gay garden and the world their field."[87]

The quick shift between humble subjects and sublime was encouraged by Didactic Poetry, a mode hard to distinguish from Descriptive Poetry, and modeled on Virgil's *Georgics*. It was Virgil who explicitly justified the "sublime enumeration of all the charms or Tremendities of Nature"[88] in a famous passage translated by Thomson,[89] who had himself attained a certain sublimity by mingling cosmos and cottage, as well as description and didacticism. To this mixture Coleridge's early *The Destiny of Nations*, nakedly Thomsonian in style, added a joining metaphysic which he may have tried to settle on Wordsworth at Alfoxden:

> Infinite myriads of self-conscious minds
> Are one all-conscious Spirit, which informs
> With absolute ubiquity of thought
> (His one eternal self-affirming act!)
> All his involvéd Monads, that yet seem
> With various province and apt agency
> Each to pursue its own self-centering end.[90]

Yet despite the richness of Coleridge's mind, the force of literary tradition, and ancient example, all such scientific speculation and research flowered only as a single brief and great poem—the briefest and most imaginative of epyllia—"The Ancient Mariner."

Did this turn of events reflect Wordsworth's influence? It is certainly true that while Wordsworth eloquently asserted the compatibility of poet and scientist in the 1802 Preface to *Lyrical Ballads*, he did not himself explore the cosmic dimension opened by science. Though willing to follow, as that Preface suggests, wherever there might be an "atmosphere of sensation," science's human significance was still too remote or uncertain for him. His emphasis on the poet "following" the man of science suggests a rather passive role; but it is honest, and he will never flounder in either the "Empyreal Air" or the "intense inane." He remains an Antaeus bound to his native element; and only today, as the extension of sight offered by science and the human capacity for it separate, is Wordsworth's attitude justified. The scientific spirit which promised eighteenth-century thinkers a greater imaginative as well as material appropriation of the earth, overbears the contemporary imagination which sinks under present discoveries as once under apocalyptic thought.

The science which Thomson and Coleridge cultivated was, in any case, not fully distinguishable from myth and the subterranean influence of heterodox traditions. It was visionary thought masking as natural philosophy; Lowes has shown this too well for anyone to have to demonstrate it again. That so myth-motivated a drive for knowledge should produce "The Ancient Mariner" is therefore quite appropriate, and Wordsworth's attitude also falls into place. It is not science he distrusts but its admixture of myth or apocalyptic thought. Speculative natural philosophy could not displace those direct relations with nature which were to be his mainstay of vision and renovation.

### Myth without Myth 1: The Mountains of the Moon

Yet the myths feeding into such moments as Snowdon are incalculable. Though the vision appears to be generated by the elements themselves—being a gift of nature, or, more miraculously still, of the autonomous imagination blending with nature—the Abyssal Vision has a history going from well-known biblical sources (Genesis and Psalms) through Virgil, Boehme, Thomas Burnet and other metaphysician-travelers of the profound.[91] It culminates, prior to Wordsworth, in one of the really exciting though still self-flagellating bursts of sublimity in Thomson's *Seasons,* as the poet addresses the Genius of Science and is rewarded by a short if powerful response:

> Hung o'er the deep,
> That ever works beneath his sounding base,
> Bid Atlas, propping heaven, as poet's feign,
> His subterranean wonders spread! Unveil
> The miny caverns, blazing on the day,
> Of Abyssinia's cloud-compelling cliffs,
> And of the bending Mountains of the Moon!
> O'ertopping all these giant-sons of earth,
> Let the dire Andes, from the radiant Line
> Stretched to the stormy seas that thunder round

> The Southern Pole, their hideous deeps unfold!
> Amazing scene! Behold! the glooms disclose!
> I see the rivers in their infant beds!
> Deep, deep I hear them labouring to get free!

Only after myth—which is the "deep" working beneath Thomson's Science—has had its say, does the more learned vision unfold:

> I see the leaning strata, artful ranged;
> The gaping fissures, to receive the rains,
> The melting snows, and ever-dripping fogs.
> Strowed bibulous above I see the sands.[92]

Still nearer home, the crucial stanzas in "The Ancient Mariner" on the rotting Deep can also be resolved into a number of traditions where science sports with myth. There were theories about the watery abyss hidden in the earth and from which the Flood originally came, theories about a central fire, about the center itself (the regenerative omphalos); and the central Deep has its connection with the great river-serpent or Tiamat of the Babylonians, to which Coleridge's water snakes are distantly (perhaps bookishly) related. This could lead us, in turn, to the old serpent of the Nile, the watery Mountains of the Moon, and the whole area of Nile mysticism[93]—from which Wordsworth preserve us.

Yet from what precisely does Wordsworth preserve us? That his mountain vision is not presented as myth does not exclude the existence of a mythic, archetypal, or "topocosmic" dimension.[94] It must be acknowledged at the same time that the man writing *Prelude* XIV is very different from Milton, Thomson, or Coleridge. He does not 'pass into' vision by specific rituals such as sleep or calling the muses or adopting a special persona. He maintains an unusual continuity between perception and vision. This continuity extends to all levels, so that, while we hardly feel the presence of an observer, and are almost deceived into thinking Snowdon a symbolic landscape, it undeceives us on close inspection, and remains tied to eyes and ears, to a personal, distinct act of the mind. Again, though we must talk of high and low, and of a tripartite, separated realm of moon, mist, and deep, this does not affect their intercourse. It even seems, ultimately, as if the poet were within his own mind as well as in nature. "What is Above is Within, for everything in Eternity is translucent," says Blake, "The Circumference is within."[95]

Man on Snowdon is not, however, a microcosm redeeming his alienated (macrocosmic) part. He is a mesocosm: at the boundary of all realms, and himself their boundary. Wordsworth preserves the self from all (including mythic) encroachments because the self is not this or that but *between*. He guarantees man his own realm without separating him fatally from nature or supernature. Man himself is an omphalos, the mediterranean being. If such myths as of the Mountains of the Moon hover suggestively over the scene it is because as one reputed source of the Nile they were also just that: a boundary image, the symbol of a border between natural and supernatural.[96]

### Myth without Myth  2:  The Man in the Mountain

With rare exceptions Wordsworth's poetry stops short of the supernatural and draws its energy from boundary images. Perhaps the symbols affecting us most have this janus-faced quality; one side toward nature, one away from it. Perhaps a symbol is essentially of this structure. Or imagination, brought beyond its proper bound, yet confined by nature, ends in a "Purgatory blind."[97] It is easy to fall at this point into mystery or pure speculation: a comparison may save us from both.

One of Virgil's famous personifications is of Mount Atlas in the fourth book of the *Aeneid*. Virgil depicts the mountain as also a man, as the Titan Atlas doomed to support the skies, head in clouds, beaten by wind and rain, his beard ("barba horrida") crusted with ice, and rivers pouring from the forehead. The powerful image was not understood in the eighteenth century. Joseph Warton, though a precursor of Romantic sensibility, calls it "very sublime and picturesque," as if it were ornamental in function, while Spence in his *Polymetis* thinks the description an excellent model for a fountain-statue—to which Warton adds that it might indeed have been copied from such a statue by Virgil.[98] Both of these learned men cannot give serious imaginative consideration to Virgil's use of myth: they are infected, like Wordsworth himself at the beginning of his career,[99] by the picturesque and its external view of nature and of art.

Yet Virgil's Atlas, at once man and mountain, and standing at the boundary of heaven and earth,[100] is imaginatively and cosmically the very type of a boundary image. From a formalistic point of view Virgil introduced Atlas to make Hermes' descent more vivid, as the latter speeds to Aeneas with Jupiter's message. But the formal reason is almost an excuse, though not for a "picture" in Warton's sense. We recall that the epic is approaching its first major crisis or turning point, and that Aeneas must decide to sacrifice Dido to a higher imperative. Virgil, writing about the emergence of a new order and the necessary sacrifice of the old to the new, and dealing epically with both gods and men, with all natures, here widens the field of vision by instinctive analogy. For Atlas is a vanquished Titan: an instance of the older cosmic order becoming the involuntary servant and basal energy of the new. Hermes rests on Atlas but a moment, and compared to him is a liberated figure skimming through air and over sea.[101]

Atlas retains nevertheless a dangerous and solid immortality. Though frozen by age, or bound like Saturn, he stands like an eternal shadow at the gate of the two realms. Virgil's art enhances that ambiguity. His description of Atlas is subordinated enough to be passed over as a picture or conceit. We still sense, however, the Titan's giant agony, and his remnant of mediating power, as he stretches through all the spheres, from ocean to heaven, containing a being at once human, divine and natural. He is, in fact, a direct ancestor of Hermes, as Virgil lightly mentions, and the god's touch-down, equally light, at least affirms the nexus.

There is no hint in Virgil of the legend Ovid tells concerning Atlas' transformation. Perseus, another divine messenger, is said by Ovid to have changed Atlas by means of the Gorgon's head (*Metamorphoses*, Book IV). Virgil's Titan is not a man first then a mountain. He is both at once, and it is the blended image, the stonified (to use a Blakean term) humanity that affects us. Virgil's personification is grounded in a venerable myth and raises an archaic image; and a true reading cannot undo the triple effect and prefer, like Warton, the poet's craft rather than the myth, or, like Ovid, a personalized myth rather than the archaic image.

The Romantics, in England as in Germany, see Nature as circumscribing imagination or as the product of a self-blinded imagination. Whether that imagination is inside or outside of man (the latter concept makes nature a fallen god or emanation) is less important than their refusal to accept the Newtonian (deistic) object-nature deprived of all individual relation to the mind. Blake, whose Albion is an Atlas-figure, felt that if the "stony" in man could be purged—the Newtonian world-picture entirely expunged —then Albion would regenerate and the mountain bring forth its man. Other Romantics who stir the slumberous mass of the Greek divinitic᾽ may also do it less for the sake of nature than for the sake of imagination, which had never existed without a middle ground of some kind and now realizes the danger of being polarized into starry intellect and earthquake passion. The mixed imaginative essence of the ancient gods—the fact that human and nonhuman coexisted in them—and the beautiful thought that some of them fell into nature and might revive from that base, helped to restore faith in the revival of what Wordsworth calls Nature, and Keats, with conscious paradox, "the unimaginable *lodge* / For solitary thinkings."[102]

The conception of this lodge or middle ground differs from poet to poet. Blake accepts "Beulah" only as a place of repose for the mental warrior, afraid that the latter might lay down his weapons before the imagination is rehumanized. Shelley and Keats create it (each in his own way) by a mythopoeic mixing or weaving of natures, but their minds never enter this act totally enough to be deceived, or lightly enough not to be disillusioned. Wordsworth alone refuses to create imaginary beings of a mixed nature, yet it is he who comes closest to the blended or boundary image of Virgil.

The strongest parallels to Virgil's image are Wordsworth's pictures not of mountains but of old men. I will cite only one of the best-known. The Leech-gatherer of "Resolution and Independence" is described as follows at his first appearance:

> As a huge stone is sometimes seen to lie
> Couched on the bald top of an eminence;
> Wonder to all who do the same espy,

By what means it could thither come, and whence;
So that it seems a thing endued with sense:
Like a sea-beast crawled forth, that on a shelf
Of rock or sand reposeth, there to sun itself;

Such seemed this Man, not all alive nor dead,
Nor all asleep—in his extreme old age:
His body was bent double, feet and head
Coming together in life's pilgrimage;
As if some dire constraint of pain, or rage
Of sickness felt by him in times long past,
A more than human weight upon his frame had cast.

Himself he propped, limbs, body, and pale face,
Upon a long grey staff of shaven wood.

Here the blended image is not created by personification grounded
in myth. Instead, by simile, the man is brought nearer the stone,
which is itself brought closer to the man by a comparison within
the comparison. The effect is more gentle and graded than in Vir-
gil; and even as the man and a massive nature slowly coalesce, our
sense for "margins" or intermediate horizons is increased. It is as
if these approximations could extend infinitely, man and nature
drawing imperceptibly, gently, closer. Wordsworth's own comment
on the stanzas is worth quoting:

> In these images, the conferring, the abstracting, and the modi-
> fying powers of the Imagination, immediately and mediately
> acting, are all brought into conjunction. The stone is en-
> dowed with something of the power of life to approximate it
> to the sea-beast; and the sea-beast stripped of some of its
> vital qualities to assimilate it to the stone; which intermediate
> image is thus treated for the purpose of bringing the original
> image, that of the stone, to a nearer resemblance to the figure
> and condition of the aged Man; who is divested of so much of
> the indications of life and motion as to bring him to the point
> where the two objects unite and coalesce in just comparison.[103]

Thus, though the landscape reveals a human form (the Hermit
of "Tintern Abbey," this oldest man of "Resolution and Inde-

pendence"), there is no wish in Wordsworth, as there is in Blake, to see nature purely under the aspect of the human. The ultimate figure remains a borderer,[104] at once natural and human. The Leech-gatherer is also amphibious in other respects: he commutes in the poet's imagination between natural and supernatural. He is so intimately connected with nature and the very landscape of the poem that his voice is like that of a stream and blends with the sound of waters in the air; yet this same image of the voice which is as the sound of waters refers us to the apocalyptic figure of the Ancient of Days and intimates a destruction of nature.[105] It is strange that even the poem's setting is a border region. Though not explicitly identified, the lonely moor of this encounter is a kind of no-man's land near the Scottish Border and has previously entered Wordsworth's poetry.[106]

### A Poem of the Thirty-Second Year

Though a storm in nature sets the scene, and is followed by a mental storm as Wordsworth thinks of "mighty Poets in their misery dead," the Leech-gatherer comes to save Wordsworth from dejection as gently and surely as that opening storm passes into a beautiful dawn. In each case restoration is the opposite of cataclysmic. Those sudden thoughts of the poet as Ephemerid, dead among his dead dreams, are purged by the appearance and imaginative elongation of a man who seems to have been made too slowly ever to decay. Despite age, poverty, and loneliness, he is still so much one being or a "Being made / Of many Beings,"[107] that he seems neither all living nor all dead. If he is dying, it is into the life of nature, and if he seems so alive, it is because he gives the impression of having already died, in the sense that his great dignity and steadfastness appear no longer as purely mortal qualities but as indestructibles nourished by an ancient communal faith as well as by an individual's hope. Let all the pools dry up—he would still poke about that moor in the faith of Matthew 6:25 ff.

That the words of Matthew are in the poet's mind is clear from a previous stanza ("My whole life I have lived in pleasant thought"): the Leech-gatherer, moreover, whom Wordsworth feels to have been sent to admonish him, is of the purest Protestant stock, a grave and hardy Scotsman who lives by those lines of Scripture, taking what God's mercy provides, and not fearing for the morrow. But Wordsworth, approaching the christological age, approaching also his marriage, is deeply unsure of the future. His questionings, more explicit in the Intimations Ode and *The Prelude*, are as to whether the "marvellous Boy" in him can survive being changed into the "philosophic mind," whether poetry must die with maturation. It is not only that his imaginative powers might be suppressed by the concerns of daily life; that is a danger, but a lesser danger; the real concern is that they might be displaced from life and become apocalyptic. He is at a turning point in life; he needs guidance; and a "divine" messenger comes to him. The Leech-gatherer actually puts him into the temptation he fears: he could take this experience as being discontinuous with ordinary experience.

But though the Leech-gatherer comes suddenly, solitary to solitary, in a moment which is precariously visionary, he also comes gently, as an argument for continuity. His example persuades the poet that faith in nature can survive maturation and even decrepitude. Change is not destruction, transition is not violence, and the passage from one mode of being to another should resemble the storm at the beginning of "Resolution and Independence" which passes into the calm, sunny energies of a new day.

### The Subtle Scale

At the outset of *Prelude* VI Wordsworth has occasion to describe in a few lines the changing of late summer into autumn. This produces, between 1804 and 1850, interesting variants. It is their aim to render the advent of a new season without defining it into absolute, independent singleness. The passage from one season to another as from one state of being to another is thought of as a gentle transfer of energies. Thomsonian personification, which portrays the seasons as separate entities and too distinctive powers, is rejected.

In this, Wordsworth may simply be relying on his senses. He is true to a nature which gives a certain impression of simultaneity, of what Hölderlin calls "Allgegenwärtigkeit" and Dr. Johnson "appearances subsisting all at once."[108] Yet it is hard to tell whether truth of description is the consequence or the cause of Wordsworth's argument, which stresses as always that transformations can occur without injury. True power propagates itself imperceptibly, not by supernatural or secret agency, but by a "universal birth." The variants return us to our starting point, to the confirmation Wordsworth received at Alfoxden that renewal is neither violent nor apocalyptic but a daily fact and a "natural" possibility.

There are six significant variants (I include the 1805 and the 1850 versions as variants). They are quoted here in probable chronological order, but without the inference that every case will show a correlation between that order and refinement of thought. The poet is preparing to return to Cambridge after the long vacation of 1789:

1.          I turn'd my face
   Without repining from the mountain pomp
   Of Autumn, and its beauty enter'd in
   With calmer Lakes, and louder Streams (MS A, 1805)

2.          I turn'd my face
   Without repining from the beauty and pomp
   Of Autumn, entering under azure skies
   To mountains clothe(d) in golden robe of fire,
   To calmer lakes and louder streams (MS B)

3.          I turn'd my face
   Without repining from the beauty and pomp
   Of Autumn azure skies and mountains clothed
   In [crested ?] fire with mild magnificence
   Of calmer lakes and louder streams (MS B)

4.          I turn'd my face
   Without repining from the mountain pomp
   Of Autumn, undisturbed by ruffling winds
   And entering with the mild magnificence
   Of calmer Lakes and louder Streams (MS A² and C)

5.          I turn'd my face
   Without repining from the coves and heights
   In the soft sunshine of their golden fern
   Attired; from Autumn's mild magnificence
   Her calmer Lakes and louder Streams (MS D)

6.                    I turned my face
     Without repining from the coves and heights
     Clothed in the sunshine of the withering fern;
     Quitted, not loth, the mild magnificence
     Of calmer lakes and louder streams. (1850)[109]

The most significant change is the disappearance of overt per-
sonification. The 1805 text has only a mild picture of autumn as a
person, and may have been chosen for that reason over variants 2
and 3, which are alternatives added in MS B (contemporaneous
with A) and could represent choices excluded from A rather than
revisions. Variant 2 has the strongest personification, extending to
both autumn and the mountains; variant 3 removes it, making au-
tumn an adjective and increasing the impression of simultaneity
by the simplest kind of connective (paratactical) syntax. But the
resulting sentence is heavy and dangling. The fourth variant equi-
librates the sentence once more by restoring the break after au-
tumn; yet, wishing to carry over the idea of "pomp" from previous
versions, reintroduces personification through the metaphor in
"undisturbed by ruffling winds." The fifth variant strengthens per-
sonification though lessening the idea of pomp; and only in the fi-
nal text of 1850 is there no trace of personification of either au-
tumn or mountains except for the vestigial "clothed."
     Absence of personification certainly helps to make the last ver-
sion the best (if we overlook the stilted "Quitted, not loth . . ."").
Yet it is difficult to consider personification reprehensible in itself;
and on studying the texts we see that its removal is really the emer-
gence of something else which accounts more positively for the
felt improvement. There is a more general conceptual shift from
advent to presence, from picture-simultaneity to parousia, from
hierarchy to reciprocity. Why this shift should please us is a diffi-
cult question. Does it please necessarily? What if a bad poet should
hold the pleasing notion and a good poet the less pleasing? All I
can say is that Wordsworth's shift is more than "conceptual" in
the sense that a whole series of relations, rather than one concept,
is involved.
     The pleasure, when it comes, is from sensing that the poet has
refined the idea of power. Through his changes the peculiarly an-

thropomorphic notion that power is localized in *one* place or person, and transmitted consciously or visibly, is broken down. "Power" seems to become "life" through the intermediary of nature as it is pictured here. That "Autumn," moreover, is now the implicate of described relations rather than a hypostatized entity, suggests that the increased value of the last version is linked to an increased economy of statement or thought related perhaps to Occam's razor. A gross idea of *power* but also a gross *idea* is purged, and the aesthetic pleasure we receive in addition to or mingled with the pleasure of truth comes when the mind is released from an oppressive and somehow superfluous notion.

The variants allow us to trace rather precisely the stages of refinement. The first three versions contain two doublets: beauty and pomp, calmer lakes and louder streams. At first (1805) the pomp is associated with the mountains and beauty implicitly with the lakes. This distinction reflects faintly a sense of hierarchy dividing the scene into higher and lower, or stern and mild, or sublime and picturesque. Yet running "beauty and pomp" into one phrase already diminishes that sense of hierarchy which is further muted by the second doublet. It depicts a contrast natural and dynamic (rather than static and mind-imposed) in character.

The last three versions also have two doublets.* The second of these, "calmer lakes and louder streams," remains the same, while "coves and heights" substitutes for "beauty and pomp" in two of the three versions. This substitution replaces not only abstract with concrete but again an artificially discriminated with a more natural pair. Yet the sense of contrast and the distinction between pomp and beauty are reserved. The fourth variant, which does not yet have "coves and heights," maintains them by distinguishing between two types of the same quality: there is a sterner and a milder magnificence. "Mild magnificence," moreover, is itself a contrastive phrase and a subtle paradox. Though referring originally to the lakes (version 4) it begins to subsume the whole scene and achieves its perfect emblem in a striking image of the 1850 text which actually refers to the mountains: "Clothed in the sunshine of the withering fern." In this image we have the culminat-

* Variant 4 has only one doublet but retains two contrasts.

ing tendency of all the revisions, which is (1) the purging of ar-
tificial in favor of natural contrasts, and (2) the depiction, related
to this, of a perfectly easy, organic transition mixing death and
birth, and so diminishing the idea of change as discontinuity.

The genesis of that final image is intriguing and may help to
gather the threads of our discussion. The image originates in the
poet's description of the mountains as "clothed in golden robe of
fire" (variant 2). But this is too pompous both in concept and
style and therefore mellows to "In the soft sunshine of their golden
fern / Attired" (variant 5). Fern, the specific and natural, replaces
robe of fire, the abstract and artificial; while the slight contrast of
"golden . . . fire" which anticipates the crescendoing "calmer . . .
louder" is replaced by a beautiful redundance, a kind of hendiadys
putting almost equal weight on its two parts: "soft sunshine,"
"golden fern." It is also interesting that this is a new doublet, two
things being drawn out of one in the usual Wordsworthian man-
ner. And though "sunshine" is a metaphor intimating the color
and radiance of the fern, we now feel the presence of two loci (sun
and fern) that produce in blending a deeper and milder thing
than each in isolation. A quality is diffused but not lessened by the
diffusion; the original fire is no longer drawn from only one source
and no longer the attribute of only one thing.

But to achieve the final image a further abstract or artificial
element must be removed, and two adjectives, soft-golden, com-
bined as "withering." Now the redundance and the doublet are
gone, but in their stead a more natural contrast reveals (like
"calmer lakes and louder streams") a compensatory or dynamic
interchange. Wordsworth's "sunshine of the withering fern" min-
gles the notes of life and death and of cause and effect. The fern
gives off the sunshine, but the sunshine is related to its withering.
Life and death, darkness and light are now, as in the greater epi-
sode also described in Book VI, "features / Of the same face, blos-
soms upon one tree." The Sublime is the subtle magnified. In this
smallest instance, taken from the beginning of *Prelude* VI, Words-
worth incorporates his knowledge that nature renews itself un-
violently in man and beyond him. *Natura tota est nusquam magis
quam in minimis.*[110]

# 7.  The Prelude

## The One Great Theme

A mighty maze is *The Prelude*, but not without a plan, if we believe its author. Doubting yet not lost, he treads the complexities of his theme.[1] He sometimes falters, however, and at two points honestly confesses he has lost his way.[2] Can we follow after him though there is no common myth to guide us, no clear enunciation of The Argument? A poem without proper name, of obscure origin, mazy as a river, stretches its casual magnificence to epic length. It has never been subdued to one great theme.

Wordsworth begins by taking stock of himself as a man destined to be a poet.[3] If Milton spent the greater part of his life actively preparing for his epic, one can hardly grudge Wordsworth his hesitations or license to inform us of them; yet do we need a diffidence dressed out in thirteen books? No true comparison is possible between the well-placed reflections that open Book IX of *Paradise Lost*, or Spenser's "mee, all too meane" stanzas prefatory to *The Faerie Queene*, and this enormous testimonial Wordsworth gives himself in a mixture of self-reproach and self-affirmation.

But at the end of Book I the uncertainties that launched him seem to fall away or become less important. He disingenuously admits that the poem is reviving the poet. He is satisfied to tell the story of his life. "The road lies plain before me;—'tis a theme / Single and of determined bounds" (I.640–41). He chooses it in preference to "ampler or more varied argument." What that theme is we are still not explicitly told, and already halfway through Book II the road no longer appears quite so straight: "Yet is a path / More difficult before me; and I fear / That in its broken windings

we shall need / The chamois' sinews, and the eagle's wings"
(II.272–75).

A revived sense of the majesty and difficulty of his subject brings
back the old epic metaphor of high flying—naturalized, of course.
But still the theme eludes us, and we know only that here is a man
whose mind moves as he writes, who thinks aloud in verse (as
Matthew Arnold remarked disparagingly), or who thinks into the
human heart (as Keats said approvingly), a poet, therefore, who
confronts heuristically maze within maze. The road he thought
more certain than the trackless realms of visionary epic proves
just as difficult and shadowy.

It has become clear, however, that Wordsworth had no intention,
originally, to write so largely of himself.[4] Though he believes that
the past flows into the present—that a man is never alienated from
his former sources of strength—this did not require a confessional
poem about his own life. That his visionary powers had survived
could be proved in the traditional way, by engaging on a heroic
or high-philosophical poem. "I have come through" is not heroic
argument unless associated with the generic triumph of great
men or of a definite idea of man. Enchantments faced and over-
come by a strong mind; zeal unquenchable; the vanquished war-
rior founding a new race; the survival of the spirit of liberty de-
spite the holocausts of history; the individual, whether de Courges,
Gustavus, or Wallace, acting on his own initiative to perpetuate
justice and freedom: these are the subjects that could have roused
Wordsworth (I.166 ff.). Poet, hero, and visionary are obviously of
the same company, three manifestations of heroic temper. Yet the
historical-legendary themes he mentions, or others self-invented,
or the "awful burthen" of the philosophic song toward which
Coleridge was urging him,[5] in making his imagination shrink
rather than expand, compel him to set forth why he thinks him-
self a poet.

His reasons are relatively easy to follow. Nature from the first
intended him to be a poet. The Derwent flowed through infant
dreams and began to attach him to things of this world. The
forms of nature in all their variety then elicited the strength of his
soul. His childhood and youth were visionary in the sense that na-

ture drew him out, released the life in him, and gradually made it conscious. In a dramatic paragraph of Book III he cries that only this outgoing is true "heroic argument." Nature, he suggests, was the occasion rather than cause of his love, and his soul went out to her unself-consciously, by creative acts of purest generosity. "Of genius, power, / Creation and Divinity itself / I have been speaking . . ." (III.173 ff.). But at the very point of finding his theme, he apparently bids it farewell, for he knows that the generous and heroic age is past, and that he must tell of what happened afterward—in Cambridge, in France, and amid "the many shapes / Of joyless daylight."

It is only, however, when separated from his early unself-conscious relations to nature that Wordsworth begins to understand her role. In this "second act," while Imagination sleeps (III.259 ff.), nature begins to shine surprisingly through time and alienation. Various experiences, including "spots of time"—strong memories dating from the first act of his life, surviving in him as fresh as when they happened, and often unconsciously restorative—guide him like stars. The past of "genius, power," etc. is still with him. In the depth of his estrangement, such memories of nature, and of his own strength vis-à-vis nature, preserve him for another day when imagination might meet the world once more as at least its equal.

Now this may appear to be "a theme / Single and of determined bounds." Wordsworth's great claim is that the imagination can be naturalized, and that the "heroic age" of its naturalization saves it from being lost to human life. Without this intermediate stage, when the child faces nature by himself, and feels her mystery as his own,

> How awful is the might of souls,
> And what they do within themselves while yet
> The yoke of earth is new to them, the world
> Nothing but a wild field where they were sown . . . (III.180–83)

the imagination would have to go underground, buried by the necessities of custom and social life, or become apocalyptic. If imagination, however, blends in childhood with the forms of nature, not only does its influence survive via strong reminiscences, but a hope is set up that it might be humanized, even as it had been naturalized.

The only trouble is that Wordsworth's own imagination refuses to accept this argument. It rejects the history imposed on it. Imagination can never be fully attached but remains a force that isolates man, and from which he draws the consciousness of individual being:

> Points have we all of us within our souls
> Where all stand single; this I feel, and make
> Breathings for incommunicable powers. (III.188–90)

Nature, time, memory, and poetry itself, can only fitfully bind an imagination which is radically in excess of nature as of every socializing principle.

If the word "imagination," because associated with "image," seems inappropriate to describe the special consciousness that brings a man home to himself, another term should be coined. Yet in one sense the term is quite appropriate, for what is popularly understood by imagination is the first, strong, "imaginal" reaction to this pointed and mortalizing state of mind. The images we associate with imagination are an antidote to self-consciousness drawn in part from consciousness itself. It is certainly true that wherever you find self-consciousness raised to a certain pitch there you will find imagination: cause and effect are so close, that they are, by metonymy, interchangeable.

### The Early Manuscripts and the "Spots of Time"

The textual growth of *The Prelude* is similar to that of "The Ruined Cottage," which it follows closely in time. The development of the poem from first to final state presents a real analogue to organic process: it is a development by accretion, extension, and interpretative division of one type of experience which is the nuclear cell of the whole. This experience is again related to an obsession with specific place. Wordsworth recalls various places that affected him in time past and still strongly modify his consciousness—so strongly, in fact, that they are places in his mind as well as in nature. They have "such self-presence in my mind, / That, musing on them, often do I seem / Two consciousnesses, conscious of myself / And of some other Being" (II.30–33). Named "spots of time," and distributed over several books of the completed *Prelude,* they are found massed together and linked desultorily in the earlier manuscripts.[6]

It is hard to decide whether the first or second member of the partitive construction "spots of time" should be emphasized. If we derive the origin of the notion from Wordsworth's attraction to specific place (the omphalos or spot syndrome), and notice that "spot" is subtly used in two senses—as denoting particular *places* in nature, and fixed *points* in time ("islands in the unnavigable depth / Of our departed time")—the emphasis would fall on the initial word. But the natural pull of the phrase, and the fact that these spots are not only *in* time, like islands, but also creative *of* time or of a vivifying temporal consciousness, throws the emphasis to the second noun and evokes a beaconing "time-spot." The concept is, in any case, very rich, fusing not only time and place but also stasis and continuity. The fixity or fixation that points to an apocalyptic consciousness of self is temporalized, reintegrated in the stream of life.

How did Wordsworth raise himself from his obsession with specific place to the key notion of spots of time? I suspect the intermediate concept to have been that of *genius loci,* or "spirit of place." The renovating energy flowing from the spots of time is really spirit of place reaching through time with a guardian's care. The *genius loci* was a guardian as well as indwelling spirit of his abode. To link that kind of genius to the genius of the poet—the spirit, namely, that inspires or guards his "genial" powers—is an easy matter, and the early MSS of *The Prelude* show several at least implicit instances of it.[7] There are apostrophes not only to powers of the earth, beings of the hills, and spirits of the springs, but also to "genii" who form the poet by means of gentle or severer visitations.[8] The "powers" and "presences" retained in the final versions of *The Prelude* reflect the same belief purged of some of its anthropomorphism. There is also one direct and beautiful association of poetic genius and guardian genius. MS 18a (Goslar, 1798–99)

has an abortive beginning to what is now Book II, an address to
Coleridge that reads: "Friend of my heart and genius . . ."⁹
Wordsworth uses the notion of spirit of place as liberally as any
writer of the Renaissance. It is only necessary to remember that
"Nutting"* stems from the same time, that it contributes an over-
flow passage to MS JJ and another to the "second beginning" of
*The Prelude,* in which a gentle breeze heralds the poet's turn from
crisis to peace and restoration; that in MS 18a (which contains,
except for JJ, the earliest sketches for *The Prelude*) a version of
"Nutting" is found in which the "dearest Maiden" there addressed
is named Lucy;¹⁰ and that the Lucy of the Lucy poems, likewise
from that rich winter harvest in Germany, is perhaps an embodi-
ment of *English* spirit of place:

> and she shall lean her ear
> In many a secret place
> Where rivulets dance their wayward round,
> And beauty born of murmuring sound
> Shall pass into her face.¹¹

One may also recall that the crime of the Mariner is basically one
against spirit of place, and that it was Wordsworth who suggested
it to Coleridge.¹²

This "efficacious spirit,"¹³ one that lurks in the spots of time, re-
news the poet vis-à-vis nature. He again meets the world with a
sensitive, creative soul, as in his youth. Yet it renews the poet in
two different ways, perhaps insufficiently distinguished by Words-
worth. One of the "tutelary" functions of the *genius loci* was to
prevent or revenge desecration of its abode. Now Wordsworth, by
his own confession, was guilty of a peculiar sin against Nature dur-
ing the years of crisis. His description of this sin leads, in fact, to
the passage on the spots of time in the final (1805 and 1850) texts
of *The Prelude:*

> Oh! Soul of Nature! that dost overflow
> With passion and with life, what feeble men
> Walk on this earth! how feeble have I been

* "With gentle hand / Touch—for there is a Spirit in the woods."

When thou wert in thy strength! Nor this through stroke
Of human suffering, such as justifies
Remissness and inaptitude of mind,
But through presumption, even in pleasure pleas'd
Unworthily, disliking here, and there,
Liking, by rules of mimic art transferr'd
To things above all art. (1805, XI.146–55)

His violation of nature was too abstract an idea of nature, one in-
herited from his age, and tending to foster a "picturesque" and
dissective attitude.

Wordsworth's sensitivity to spirit of place eventually countered
this abstract view and restored him as nature's inmate. A comple-
mentary influence of the *genius loci* is, however, more interesting,
though harder to understand. Related to revenge as well as to
preservation, it is mediated by the sterner aspects of nature. In the
early manuscripts, the episode of the drowned man fished up with
ghastly face introduces two other memories, which are the ones
specifically named "spots of time." The first tells how Words-
worth, then less than six years old, riding with a servant through
a desolate region near the Scottish border, is accidentally parted
from him, and experiences a dread-inspiring impression of place.
The second is from later childhood, from just before his father's
death, and again recalls an ordinary scene invested with visionary
dreariness.[14] To these, which in *The Prelude* proper are trans-
ferred to the later book telling of Wordsworth's restoration, we
can add other incidents retained as part of Books I and II: the
robbing of birds' nests, the boat-stealing, and similar wanton or
willful acts.

The common factor in all these is a violation of nature (a secret
or patent violence directed against nature) linked to the develop-
ing self-consciousness of the child. In episodes where the violation
is patent we can say that the spirit of place rises up in revenge
against the violator. But where it is secret, as in the two spots of
time (for no clear desecration has occurred), we must assume that
the boy's very *awareness* of his individuality—a prophetic or an-

ticipatory awareness nourished by self-isolating circumstances*—
reacts on him as already a violation. A sudden self-consciousness,
transferred to outward things, is raised against him under the mask
of nature. Only this could explain Wordsworth's statement that
the spots of time give "Profoundest knowledge to what point, and
how, / The mind is lord and master—outward sense / The obedient
servant of her will" (XII.221–23). Wordsworth must think that
both experiences, despite the important role of sensation, really
manifest the child's imagination as a power unself-consciously ac-
tive. I knew, he says, prefacing these events, "Too forcibly, too
early in my life, / Visitings of imaginative power" (XII.202–03).

This leads into a last and crucial point about the spots of time.
It is quite clear the child does not know that what he sees and
feels is an effect of the power of his imagination. The impact of
the scenes on him is inseparable from overwhelming sense-impres-
sions. For the retrospective poet, however, the power that belonged
to the external world is now seen to have belonged to the mind.
The boy's imagination accepted nature's images so forcefully that
he is deceived, not able to dissociate nature's strength from his
own, and even blind to all but the latter. The question therefore
arises why this should be so, why, from a providential perspec-
tive, the child is granted but a masked suspicion of the mind's
power.

The reason is that such ignorance shields the child from paralyz-
ing recognitions that might prevent growth of mind. Though the
imagination is often said to be a life-giving or animating power, it
is not, in Wordsworth, life-giving initially. The poet's later strength
has its origin in experiences that intimate (negatively) a death of
nature and (positively) a faculty whose power is independent of
nature. This faculty of imagination is profoundly conservative. It
strives to retain, as the Intimations Ode says, giving the experience
a mythical turn, recollections of a previous, immortal existence.
Nature, on its side, does the best it can to act as Heaven's substi-

* The death of his father, in the second spot of time, seems to have con-
firmed the boy's solitude, which is not happily accepted, but felt as a chastise-
ment.

tute, and the imagination, deprived of directly numinous data, seizes on nature's imagery to fill the vacuum. But imagination remains too strong for the milder, perishable beauties of nature. The shadow of its power often erases the reality of the familiar world or is affixed to parts of it with overwhelming psychic effect. Were it not, at the same time, in the gift of Nature to provide the mind with a substitute Heaven, the child might not forget its former "home," and so never be an "inmate of this active universe" (II.254).

The spots of time, then, bring the child closer to confronting the power or mystery of its own imagination. They have significant points of resemblance to Wordsworth's adventure in the Alps followed by the retrospective appearance of "Imagination . . . That awful Power." In the first spot of time, for example, he is separated from his guide; a perplexed up-and-down movement ensues; he sees "characters" that subsist against a background of decay; pool, beacon, and woman are, in fact, perceived singly and with the sharpness of individually engraved signs; even the rhythm of the travelers in Book VI, now hurried, now halting, finds its counterpart. The three things (pool, beacon, girl) suggest, moreover, a *stasis* (the transfixed, halted consciousness) verging on powerful motion. "A naked pool that lay beneath the hills"—"lay" divines the weight, the ominous quiescence. "The beacon on the summit"—fixed solitude, but also a steadfast monitory light, potentially guiding. "A girl, who bore a pitcher on her head . . ."—another solitary, rigid figure, but moving against an invisible force.

The halted Alpine traveler was transfixed by a consciousness that erased the idea of this world as the end of his journey. He recognizes that his home is with infinity. The recognition, however, frees him for the world it denies because he is now absolutely sure of imagination's autonomy. It has shown itself distinct from nature, as an unmediated, apocalyptic force. The visionary dreariness of the spots of time also foretells the insufficiency or even the destruction of nature. A terrible beauty is born; familiar features become stark hieroglyphs.

The great difference between the episodes is that the young boy does not yet recognize his own imagination. Nor, as he flees "Faltering and faint, and ignorant of the road," does nature appear as his guide: on the contrary, it repeats in larger letters the writing on the turf. Nature's only guidance is to intimate an imperishable *consciousness* which outlives even nature.[15] The boy senses this; both his future loss and the grandeur it implies; but he does not come face to face with his imagination. The experience, however, remains etched in his mind, as freshly visible among the moldering effects of time as the name under the gallows.

Yet without this transference to nature—the fixity of the memorial writing being repeated in the fixtures of nature (pool, beacon, girl) and so engraved on the mind—the event could not have reached through time. That the imagination appears here *sub specie naturae* is already a freeing from deadly stasis, and to talk of "projection" catches the point but misses its import. The transference to nature reveals that imagination may receive a new content without ceasing to be "the dread watch-tower of man's absolute self."[16] Naked pool, Beacon, and Woman are monitory enough. The reaching through time, or temporalizing of this "spot," is therefore a second kind of liberation analogous to the first (the transference to nature). Because the fixating strength of imagination is transferred to the images as images, the boy seeks nature as well as imagination, and is driven toward *this* world. His emotions become more transitive, his sympathies expand, and when Wordsworth, thirteen years later, roams the same region, it is still alive to him though in a different way (XII.261–71).[17]

There is a last and curious turn to the whole sequence. Even as the poet praises nature, and time's mercy, a confession usurps him. It resembles, in its ecstatic and vacillating manner, the sudden apostrophe to Imagination in Book VI, leaping from past to present:

> Oh! mystery of man, from what a depth
> Proceed thy honours. I am lost, but see
> In simple childhood something of the base
> On which thy greatness stands; but this I feel,
> That from thyself it comes, that thou must give,
> Else never canst receive. (XII.272–77)

It is impossible, initially, to say whether the "but see" and "but this I feel" are contrary or complementary. One feels only the "turns and counterturns, the strife / And various trials of our complex being" (XII.148–49). The eddying of the style shows Wordsworth almost face to face with Imagination, as in Book VI. For the ground of his argument, which is also the ground of Nature, its ability to sustain the Imagination, is being taken from him. There is the same apostrophe, the same quick change of persons, even the same cry "I was lost" (VI.596), "I am lost" (XII.273). That cry of confusion evokes the traveler, lonely and halted, who has momentarily lost the guidance of Nature.

Yet Wordsworth recovers almost at once, and clutches a certainty revealed from the depths. His cry is followed by two strong adversatives, like a regaining of balance. The first "but" (line 273) affirms: *I am not lost,* my soul can still see the basis in nature on which its vigor rests. The counterturn replies: but (line 275) whatever strength nature had in childhood was really given to it by imagination. Hence *you are not lost,* because this power is within you, and only lent to nature through an amply rewarded generosity. But then *nature also is not lost,* for should you keep your instinctive childhood trust, and continue to go out to her, will she not repay that generosity again, sustain imagination as before?

Though this is followed by a further vacillation, it is clear that the intent of *The Prelude,* to review the sources of the poet's faith in himself, is often diverted. The poem reviews instead the sources of the poet's faith in nature, even though the latter is at most "something of the base" of his strength as poet. The confusion cannot be helped. For Wordsworth's childhood experiences work in two conflicting ways, they (1) prophesy the independence from nature of his imaginative powers, *and* (2) impress nature ineradicably on them. His genius as a poet arises primarily from the first of these actions; through the second, he becomes an inmate of the world, a man speaking to men. The first reminds him his home is with infinity and only there; the other binds him to this world.

*The Prelude* leaves many things obscure. Yet its theme is ultimately clear, and its argument no argument but a vacillation between doubt and faith. The soul has dwelt with nature in the past, and nature gave the soul what it required; then if it dwell with nature again, can nature give it once again what it requires? "I would enshrine the spirit of the past," writes Wordsworth, "for future restoration" (1805, XI.342 ff.).

## Books I–IV: The Binding of Imagination

The reciprocal generosity of nature and imagination is referred to in a famous passage of "The Recluse," published as a kind of manifesto-preface to the 1814 *Excursion*. It is a passage to which Blake took violent exception. Wordsworth there proclaims as his "high argument" (1) that the mind is exquisitely fitted to the external world, (2) that the external world is also fitted to the mind, and (3) that the blended might of mind and nature accomplish something deserving of the name of creation. Blake will not believe such "fitting and fitted." He rejects Nature categorically as a source of Inspiration.[18]

Yet for Wordsworth, as *The Prelude* makes clear, the interaction of nature and mind remains a mystery, "The incumbent mystery of sense and soul." There is no mechanical "epistemological" fitting of the one to the other.[19] Wordsworth supposes, in fact, that the soul is born into this world an alien. To be of the world and not only in it, the individual is forced to create his own bonds, to forget himself to nature. Here the principle of generosity begins to operate in memorable time: a soul that does somehow *go out* to nature receives an eternal recompense. Its might is fertilized by that of the external world. In its celestial soil (to use a Wordsworthian metaphor) nature sows and plants images "for immortality."[20]

This seems to me a mythical or transcendental and not a strictly associationist point of view. The necessitarian terminology, moreover, often found in *The Prelude,* emphasizes rather than lightens the mystery in this progress of the soul. It suggests that the external world is only associated to the soul, that it bears no intrinsic relationship, but that if the association has been established in childhood by an act of the soul's generosity responding to or uncovering nature's, it becomes indefeasible, and impels the child along a beneficent course. "There is a dark / Inscrutable workman-ship," according to Wordsworth, "that reconciles / Discordant ele-ments, makes them cling together / In *one society*" (my italics, I.341–44). *The Prelude* seeks to reveal as much of this soul-making as is possible.[21]

The generosity and beneficence of the socializing process is al-ready apparent in that the child has so many varied chances to people his mind with live images. They are seeded in him, as the first book says, through beauty or fear, vulgar joy soon forgotten or repeated happiness, quaint accidents or mysterious calms. The external world is secretly fastened to the boy's affections by in-numerable means, when he does not even know that something so beautiful and majestic needs to be fastened. He enjoys river, wood, and field as objects of danger or desire, unthinkingly, without con-scious love. Yet there are hints of a calmer, more reflective at-titude.

Book II (47–197) describes the coming of the time when nature will be sought for its own sake. It used to enter the sphere of child-hood passions almost incidentally, as a kind of backdrop, but now the young sports find they cannot do without it. At first it was nothing but a wild field where they were sown; now they take a conscious pleasure in it. Though still wantoning through rough and smooth, and feeling their animal energies rather than nature, they occasionally become aware of the charm of a particular place or of the whole fabric's glory.

It may seem strange that Wordsworth begins the story of his de-velopment with nature rather than human nature. The reason emerges from the fact that he adheres closely to rememberable time. No incidents antedate the age of five, and most are from ten and later. It is not surprising, therefore, that we hear next to nothing about the influence of father and mother (the latter dies when Wordsworth is eight, the former when he is thirteen). The poet's memories coincide with the onset of the "latency period" which is marked by a strong oblivion of early and too human con-tacts. And by the time the poet emerges from it he is already with-out father and mother. Only once, in Book II.232 ff., does he go behind memorable time, to suggest, by way of speculation, that it is

the mother's love which first links the newcomer to the objects of
his world:

> No outcast he, bewildered and depressed:
> Along his infant veins are interfused
> The gravitation and the filial bond
> Of nature that connect him with the world. (II.241–44)

The mother is nature concentrated in "one dear Presence." Yet
when his mother dies, or the unconscious bond with nature is
loosened, the world begins to attract him in its own right:

> For now a trouble came into my mind
> From unknown causes. I was left alone
> Seeking the visible world, nor knowing why.
> The props of my affections were removed,
> And yet the building stood, as if sustained
> By its own spirit! (II.276–81)

This is, of course, as it should be: the invisible sowing of links
has taken hold. That these links are hidden from the inquisitive
eye simply goads that organ on, and helps to expand the poet's
curiosity about nature. By his seventeenth year his sympathy and
sense of mystery have broadened so much that all seems in kinship
with his soul: "in all things / I saw one life, and felt that it was joy"
(1805, II.429–30). The naturalization of the soul is complete. But
why, then, that occasional tone of doubt, that mention of "broken
windings," or such gestures as "If this be error, and another faith
/ Find easier access to the pious mind" (II.419–20)?

Part of it is due to religious scruple, for he is according nature a
large role in man's maturing and salvation. But part of it stems
from a correlative scruple, his knowledge that to be truly a poet,
he must come to know his soul also as separate from nature. More-
over, that the imagination is naturalized does not mean it is hu-
manized. Nature must lead him to love man, and to the recogni-
tion of his transcendent soul, at the danger of being surpassed.

The *narrative* weight of *The Prelude*, therefore, is not on child-
hood, but on this difficult process whereby the soul, having over-
come itself through nature, must now overcome nature through
nature. Thus Wordsworth is careful to bring to our attention, at

the very point that he describes the farthest expansion of the
bodily senses, other times in which they were forgotten or led to
moments of pure consciousness, "by thought or image unprofaned."
The problem of how the senses lead beyond themselves, or bear
witness to the unsubdued imagination, is an extremely complex
one; contradictions hedge it about. To thread the "broken wind-
ings" of Wordsworth's argument requires indeed the chamois'
sinews and the eagle's wing.

Only representative aspects can be mentioned here. The poem
is certainly structured with this central problem in mind. Book II,
which takes the poet to his seventeenth year, marks the approxi-
mate end of the soul's broadest identification with the life of the
world. The remaining books depict Wordsworth becoming con-
scious of his own powers without "divorcing" nature (Bks. III–
IX); growing self-consciousness, divorce from nature, and the crisis
coincident on that (IX–XII); and the factors that restored his faith
in the importance of nature to imagination (XII–XIV). These
divisions are no more than serviceable; there is much overlapping,
and one does well to heed the poet's own caution that "Each most
obvious and particular thought . . . Hath no beginning."

The first two hundred lines of Book III, for example, soon over-
lap and revert to the theme of the opening books; not until
Wordsworth employs once more the traveler metaphor is the break
fully accomplished (III.170 ff. and 197 ff.). At Cambridge there is
a falling-off from his intensely sympathetic relationship to nature.
But this is surprisingly interpreted as a falling-off from a height of
communion between the poet and himself. For only now, through
the contrast of college life and its dazzling yet transitory charm,
does Wordsworth realize what nature meant to him. It wooed
imagination so successfully because it allowed the latter a kind of
self-communion with permanent and immortal presences:

When the first glitter of the show was pass'd,
And the first dazzle of the taper light,
As if with a rebound my mind return'd
Into its former self . . .
                              now I felt

The strength and consolation which were mine.
As if awaken'd, summon'd, rous'd, constrain'd,
I look'd for universal things; perused
The common countenance of earth and heaven;
And, turning the mind in upon itself,
Pored, watch'd, expected, listen'd; spread my thoughts
And spread them with a wider creeping. (1805 *Prelude* III.94–114)

On returning, in the first long vacation, to Esthwaite, another "re-bound" occurs. It again makes him conscious of his debt to nature, but specifically of her renovating power. His soul, in nature's presence, puts off its veil gently, rather than, as so often in childhood, starkly (IV.131 ff.). The experience anticipates the episode that climaxes this part of *The Prelude*. After a night of dancing and revelry Wordsworth is surprised by a dawn whose simple magnificence strikes him more deeply than if he had not lapsed. Though he does not realize the full meaning or inner force of the experience ("bond unknown to me / Was given") it makes him a dedicated poet. Since Wordsworth does not indicate explicitly what moved him, we must rely on what in his description of the scene moves us:

> Magnificent
> The morning rose, in memorable pomp,
> Glorious as e'er I had beheld—in front,
> The sea lay laughing at a distance; near,
> The solid mountains shone, bright as the clouds,
> Grain-tinctured, drenched in empyrean light;
> And in the meadows and the lower grounds
> Was all the sweetness of a common dawn—
> Dews, vapours, and the melody of birds,
> And labourers going forth to till the fields. (IV.323–32)

The prospect may intimate (if anything conceptual) a marriage of heaven and earth. Yet its charm, its moving quality, is not entirely encompassed by that notion. What affects us more directly is the effortlessness of this rebirth, the joy and lightness on the face of creation. Think of Spenser, whose long-rising dawns can make us feel the reality and resistance of night:

Early, before the worlds light giving lampe
His golden beame upon the hils doth spred,
Having disperst the nights unchearfull dampe,
Doe ye awake. (*Epithalamion*, 19–22)

In Wordsworth's picture the sea laughs, and the solid mountains
are no heavier than light. Dews, vapors, the melodies of birds, the
going out to labor, are put together as if of the same weight, which
is no weight, but spontaneous, volatile motion. It is a *contrast* that
moves us: of great power exercised gently, of transcendent power
exercised daily. There is no reason, however, why contrast should
move qua contrast. If there is shock or delight it comes from an ex-
cess of energy suddenly in the mind; from a freeing, an expansion
of the mind that had fixed part of its strength unnecessarily. Why
does the image before us do this? Perhaps we are accustomed to
think of power—of naked, transcendent Power—as catastrophic and
deadly. Yet here it kindles the natural world without any destruc-
tion. All things are renewed in their accustomed place, and go
about their task as if immortal.

If the poet's conception of power derived mainly from "*that*
beauty, which . . . Hath terror in it" (XIV.245 ff.), then this virtue
in nature to move him so easily after his alienation, to return him
by unviolent means to his former self, bore the strength of a revela-
tion. A "morning-knowledge" comes to him which suggests that
the power of his soul is like the power which revives nature, and
him through nature, unapocalyptically.

It should be added that this is not the ultimate analogy Words-
worth finds between the soul of man and of nature. There are
visionary moments in which the two powers seem actually to inter-
change or blend their functions. The tranquillity which means de-
cay in the natural world but fixed faith in the spiritual, is, in such
moments, one and the same. Immobility, or fixity without life,
and immutability, or fixity beyond life, blend into a single image
marked by a "ghastly mildness." Wordsworth's meeting with the
discharged soldier (IV.385 ff.) is of this kind and closely resembles
his encounters with the blind London beggar, the Leech-gatherer,
and other old men. Each of them is "A Borderer dwelling between

life and death," so ghastly is their calm, and so vitally steadfast
their mind. "A milestone propp'd him," says Wordsworth of the
Soldier, "and his figure seem'd / Half-sitting, and half-standing."
We cannot tell where his life is, or that of the blind, steadfast beg-
gar "propp'd against a wall" (VII.619–49). What sustains them?
Their acceptance of the injuries of time evokes the idea of a soul
that is invulnerable, because it dwells in Abraham's bosom or na-
ture's. One of these is life, the other death, but in such border
figures life and death, like natural and supernatural faith, are no
longer separable.

### Book V: Akedah and Apocalypse

The episodes that conclude Book IV show the farthest point
reached by the poet in becoming aware of his own powers (of
imagination) without disowning nature. I shall call them and
similar episodes *akedot* (singular, *akedah*), from the Hebrew
word meaning a bond or tying.* Some such term is needed to dis-
criminate conveniently between two types of experience, one of
which separates from, and one of which joins to nature. For the
former the term "apocalypse" is often used. Wordsworth's own
phrase, "spots of time," combines (for his own good reason) the
idea of both akedah and apocalypse, and so does not help at this
point: one should respect, besides, his particular use of the term,
and not generalize it avidly. It is of interest, however, that the epi-
sodes designated by it, though among the most apocalyptic ex-
perienced by Wordsworth, are his strongest supports for the
idea of akedah, or of the marriage of imagination with nature. A
true though rather simple view of the structure of *The Prelude*
would be gained by showing how the poet continually displaces
or interprets apocalypse as akedah.

* In Jewish religious thinking *akedah* always refers primarily to the sacrifice
(viz. binding) of Isaac, which adds another "knot" to the covenant between
God and man, the first coming after the flood, and this one intending especially
the Hebrews. In Christian thought Isaac becomes a figure for Christ whose
completed sacrifice adds the strongest knot yet to this covenant. I have chosen
the term quite conscious of the fact that a Blakean can have his fun by com-
paring this binding to the binding down of man by Nature, which "The Men-
tal Traveller" describes vividly.

*Prelude V* was originally to conclude the poem, and did not deal
with "Books." It told instead of another, perhaps the most striking
moment of akedah experienced by the poet, and later placed at the
end of the lengthened poem. This experience, the ascent of Snow-
don, has been considered. In it the poet comes face to face with his
Imagination yet calls it Nature. It is the *Prelude's* supreme instance
of the avoidance of apocalypse.

Of the books that take the poet from the long vacation of 1789
to his settling in revolutionary France at the end of 1791, two are
progressive and two recapitulative. The theme common to all is an
initiation—in Wordsworth's terms, love of nature leading to love of
man. The recapitulative books (V and VIII) stress the nonviolent
character of that initiation, not only by the experiences described
in them, but also by their leisurely and reflective pace. Book V, for
instance, goes in apparently desultory manner from the announced
subject of books to a praise of nature accompanied by an attack on
book-learning. No wonder R. D. Havens complains that Prelude V
"is not unified or homogeneous."[22] He is, nevertheless, mistaken,
for there are two kinds of books mentioned, one praised and one
depreciated. The books *praised* by Wordsworth have an effect on
the child deeply analogous to nature: they provide a nature for
imagination, to which the child can go out, to which it can forget
itself (V.345–47; 523 ff.). This second nature, "the great Nature
that exists in works / Of mighty Poets" (V.594–95), keeps up the
generous relations of mind and external world in a dubious hour:

> That twilight when we first begin to see
> This dawning earth, to recognise, expect,
> And in the long probation that ensues,
> The time of trial, ere we learn to live
> In reconcilement with our stinted powers. (V.513–17)

The books of adventure, poetry, and imagination to which Words-
worth refers gradualize our break with nature; they delay the
overquick maturation of the child. But the books *attacked* (V.347
ff.) are those that interfere with this slower, natural maturing, be-
ing part of an adult conspiracy to control the child and plunge it
as quickly as possible into manhood.

The child's second birth—into mankind—is no less precarious than its first into nature. Wordsworth, repeating the traveler metaphor, describes this birth as a pass-over, an "isthmus, which our spirits cross / In progress from their native continent / To earth and human life" (V.536–38). Like all mythical crossings, it is fraught with dangers. The poet needs a guide, and this paradoxically is Nature herself, who grounds the child in human life without grounding his imaginative powers. Such, at least, is the tenor of Wordsworth's argument in Books V–IX, and again in XII–XIV; but it is counterpointed by the fact that (1) at certain moments in his life, and (2) in certain greater moments of his poetry, nature is engulfed. Akedah reverts to apocalypse; the poet confronts a power in him that denies the reality principle he is establishing, or nature as sufficient for imagination.

The three main episodes of Book V are the poet's dream (50–140), the story of the Boy of Winander (364–406), and that of the drowned man (426–59). They are marked to an extraordinary degree by motifs of confrontation and engulfment. This is true even though they overtly celebrate nature or the "nature" in books. That they share a motif opposed to the overt line of argument is partially due to a pressure of insight mounting in the poet during composition itself; perhaps the same pressure which, in the next book, produces the *Prelude's* most dramatic instance of confrontation and engulfment (VI.592 ff.).[23]

The dream of Book V is, in fact, the closest Wordsworth comes, before this climax, to understanding directly the autonomy of imagination, though his insight is still restricted by the existential and narrative mode of a dream-vision. The dangers of confrontation and engulfment occur only in the 'sacred' space of the dream: the poet himself stands firmly in nature and narrative.[24] The special character of any dream not an hallucination is that it is separated from life by a *cordon sanitaire* of the dreamer's consciousness. This cordon, while it prevents total usurpation, also prevents total integration, so that a dream might be called a *spot* of eternity. A more total revelation can only occur by a sudden, dangerous violation of consciousness; or it is possible that the imagination is colored so deceptively by nature that the poet lives a waking dream. It is these two kinds of climax toward which *The Prelude* moves: intentionally toward the ascent of Snowdon, where imagination takes the colors of nature; and unforeseeably toward VI.592 ff., the purest instance of apocalypse and usurpation. The dream is a third kind of experience, sharing existentially the hypnotic and fixating character of apocalyptic moments, but thematically the freer traveler-notion of an experience apparently in time and space.

Wordsworth's dream transcends the subject it is supposed to illustrate. The perishability of books contrasted with the imperishable character of nature (the book of God) is at most its occasional cause. Read in the context of *The Prelude* as a whole, rather than in the frame of its own preface and epilogue, it shows its kinship with experiences by which imagination reveals its distinctness from nature. There is a moment of loss linked to loss of the way, an ominous guide, and a curiously apocalyptic landscape.

For the purpose of analysis the dream may be divided into three parts. (1) At its outset the poet discovers himself in a "boundless plain / Of sandy wilderness, all black and void." (2) A guide appears holding symbols of what binds element to element, man to man. The stone-symbol denoting (in the language of the dream) geometry, infers dispassionate eternal relations; the shell-symbol or poetry, passionate human relations. These the Guide wishes to save from a destruction prophesied by one of the things he would save, for the shell emits

> A loud prophetic blast of harmony;
> An Ode, in passion uttered, which foretold
> Destruction to the children of the earth
> By deluge, now at hand. (V.95–98)

(3) Though the Dreamer wants to associate himself with the Guide the latter hurries on heedless of him, yet looks back fearfully. The Dreamer, then, also looking back, sees "a bed of glittering light," is told that this is the Deluge, and unable to catch up with the Guide wakes in terror.

The darkening of nature (1) at the dream's outset is a moment of "visionary dreariness" comparable to I.393–400 or XII.254 ff. The Guide (2), who has a stronger presence here than in any other episode, is the initiation-master, who guides the poet, but only to a more radical loss of Way. His symbols, the emblems of the human spirit, of revelations achieved by man himself, suggest two *akedot* or fundamental ways in which man binds the world to himself. They exalt not only the human mind but also nature,[25] and are therefore both nature-things (stone, shell) and mind-things (books). Poetry paradoxically foresees a destruction of these bonds. The chase (3) in which the Dreamer is both pursuer and pursued, mingles emotions of fear and of desire. Just as a desire to cleave to the Guide is engendered from the poet's fear (1805, V.115), so, on following the Guide, a visionary fear arises. One question that must be answered before the dream can be understood is exactly what the dreamer desires or fears, the two being linked as in "blast of harmony" (V.95). A clue furnished as to the character of that link by other episodes is that they also center on the "anxiety of hope" (XII.313): hope is heightened to the point where its imaginative and even apocalyptic character appears.

I shall propose that the dream is sent by Imagination to lead the poet to recognize its power, and that what the dreamer desires and fears is a direct encounter with Imagination. In other episodes it is nature, or imagination *sub specie naturae,* which compels him toward this end. But in VI.592 Imagination comes athwart directly, and here in the classical guise of a dream-vision. The moment of "darkness . . . solitude . . . blank desertion" (1) ensues when the mind is proleptically bereft of nature and the imagination stands revealed as a free power. The poet is perhaps less afraid of the deadness of nature than of the consequence: that he must now come face to face with the "desert-shape" of imagination. The guide (2) is an unstable dream-atom personating the hope, which survives or rises by reaction, that the human mind can separate its nature-involved powers (poetry and science being depicted as such in the dream) from nature's imminent death. Yet to accept this hope is still to recognize the mind as a power separate from nature, and opens the way to a new fear of nature's death—generated this time from within a mind that fears its power to do without nature. It is this fear which grows on the Dreamer as he cleaves to his Guide (3). He pursues the hope that man's mind may be saved though radically involved in nature: yet the flood growing in pursuit denies that chance of salvation for a more terrible one. The flood is Wordsworth's recognition of a power in him (imagination) which implies and even prophesies nature's death.

A striking feature of the dream is the doubling of (apocalyptic) terror as first a wilderness and then a flood. The wilderness "all black and void" suggests a *dry* chaos, i.e. one deprived of the potentiality of life, "Old Ocean, in his bed left singed and bare" (V.33, cf. II Peter 3:10). Unlike this desert the deluge suggests a *wet* chaos, i.e. the trauma of birth or rebirth. The flood, in any case, cannot denote merely a regeneration of nature (Old Ocean coming back), unless nature's life implies the spirit's death. This is far too Blakean an insight, although I would put nothing past a dream. All one can say with certainty is that the deluge bodes more than nature's death, and that this "more" is either the life of (resurgent) nature and death of the spirit, or the life of imagination and death of that part of the spirit involved in nature.

These alternatives are a Scylla and Charybdis. Both link life of one sort with death of another. What inclines me to identify the flood as imagination is a consideration of method as well as the tendency of the whole dream. The flood is not a static symbol to be discriminated from other static symbols (Arab, desert), but part of an action that coordinates all symbols. It is quite possible that the ambivalence of the flood is due to our concentrating on symbol instead of action, though the dreamer's mind may also have "fixed" at that point.[26] The dream, in any case, establishes a relation between desert and deluge based not only on the connotations of either symbol but also on the vacillating axis of the poet-dreamer's glance. The poet sits with "eyes toward the wide sea"; the sea is replaced by a wilderness stretched "before me"; the flight is characterized by the Arab's backward glances that compel the dreamer also to look back; the Arab flees unheedful of the poet, "before me, full in view"; and the poet wakes up with the sea once again "before me." The symbols of desert and deluge are thus developed as functions of the dreamer's ambivalent desire for *confrontation*.

The additional evidence for this can be summarized as follows.

The desert is the ocean already singed and bare: by dream-prolepsis we evade the drying-up or actual moment of apocalypse. Ensconced in the desert, however, the dreamer's fear of confrontation revives, and the image of the Arab-Guide materializes to still it (the latter appears, significantly, "at my side, / Close at my side"). When the Arab hurries ahead the poet's fear grows once more, and he is forced to turn with the Arab's glance, to *face* the pursuing flood. But then he wakes, and the flood seems to have passed over, for he discovers the sea before him. The moment of confrontation is again avoided; yet the flood which rises behind the dreamer is probably engendered by his fear-and-desire: the result (an image of engulfment) replacing the cause (the idea of confrontation).[27]

Lastly, everything in the dream has its double, and I suspect that this reflects a vacillation similar to that of the poet's glance and also relates to the quest of confrontation forced on the dreamer. Besides the doubling of the apocalyptic landscape as desert and deluge, we find the dyadic forms of Poet and Arab (linked by their simultaneous backward glance, V.127), Arab / Quixote, shell / poetry, stone / geometry, shell and stone / books. If we were to pair the characteristics of this dream with those of Wordsworth's waking epiphanies, this vacillation ("Of these was neither, and was both at once") or at times fission of the major symbols could correspond to that quick *grammatical* change of persons found, for example, in VI.592–99 and XII.267–77. The latter is, of course, a common rhetorical feature of impassioned speech, yet its very commonness in moments of passion marks it as a more than arbitrary feature. Could it be explained, like the doublings in the dream, as the expression of a mind attempting to escape from fixed locus? Is the mind, usurped by a fixating access of consciousness (imagination), dividing defensively into at least two parts to escape complete engulfment? This might produce a kind of poetic schizophrenia. The structure of the major symbols in this dream is linked, in any case, to recognized oneiric modes of evasion or displacement.

The second reminiscence of Book V, that of the Boy of Winander, emphasizes in its original version the akedah aspect of nature, the many expedients by which she holds a child's affections. The reminiscence is a masked passage of autobiography and belongs

really in Book II. The present book directs the episode polemically
against those "mighty workmen" (the metaphor of workmanship
of I.342 being ironically continued) who substitute books or single
expedients for nature's many. The theme of confrontation, how-
ever, is clearly emphasized by the curious "half-hour" look; that of
engulfment also appears, but not till the third episode, which
casts an interesting backward light.

The drowned man rising from the Lake of Esthwaite embodies
the horror of all ghost stories. The narrative mood, however, is
preserved, and no actual shock of confrontation occurs as in VI.592
which has a comparable "rising up." The incident is one of the
original spots of time; and Wordsworth struggles valiantly to shift
its emphasis from apocalypse to akedah. It is certainly curious that
Hawkshead should have revealed this skeleton in nature's cupboard
"the very week / When I was first intrusted to the care / Of that
sweet Valley." The other spots of time, placed in Book XII, are
said to contribute to akedah ("love of nature's works") by blend-
ing in with future states of consciousness despite their strongly
accidental character and independent life. The present episode,
lifted from its original context, is reasoned differently. The land-
scape of fairy story and romance, says Wordsworth, had antici-
pated such terrors; that ghastly face was, therefore, a poetic rather
than soul-debasing spectacle. This interpretation of the episode
harmonizes with the argument that imaginative literature con-
tinues the child's 'natural' maturation by keeping it from being
plunged too quickly into the adult world.

Yet, held together by the fact of sequence, rather than by the
loosely sustained theme of Book V, the stories of the Boy of
Winander and of the drowned man reflect on each other. In one
a buried child appears, in the other a man engulfed. A similar
thing is "faced" in both episodes as the poet looks at stillness, as
his glance becomes an auscultation, an uncertain sounding of the
deep. Strange currents of symbols, half-formulated symmetries,
heighten our disquiet: the green peninsulas shaped like *ears,* a fish
leaping to snap the *stillness,* the *sounding* of the lake. This quiet-
ness of nature (which also shrouds the appearance of the old sol-

dier) is both beautiful and ominous. We come to expect a prophetic "rising up."

Blake would argue that fear of one's imagination is derived from the religion of nature. While Wordsworth's nature is more than the deistic Abstract Void, it is still a void of a kind, a breeding place for terrible conceptions because nature can never wholly satisfy imagination. Wordsworth might reply that the terror he knows does not come from nature but from a power blind to nature, which breaks, as in childhood, nature's gentler bonds. But Blake would snap (in this Spirit Dialogue) that Wordsworth is of his party without knowing it. The calm that leads to fear is the void-in-nature, or at best gentle Beulah, the lower Paradise, a land of revery and sexual repose. True imagination, however, needs a more active body. The man bound by nature is an Orc, and the energy which breaks that bond is also Orc's, not apocalyptic but revolutionary, so that Wordsworth's man, characterized by natural rather than spiritual energy, will never escape the cycle of generation which he mistakes for regeneration. At this, if madness is a category known among spirits, Wordsworth would stalk off, an affrighted shade; or else, conciliating wrath, answer: nature, for both of us, is not an absolute, but a merciful middle ground, a limitation of the bottomless pit.

### Books VI–X: From Love of Nature to Love of Man

While the first two books deal almost exclusively with the naturalizing of imagination, the third introduces the interworld of college life, and with it the theme of initiation to human nature. Book IV shows Wordsworth's consciousness growing in two directions: toward himself as a man, and toward himself as a poet. In Book V these themes mingle, and the drift of *The Prelude* becomes harder to follow. For though the making of a man and the making of a poet are not the same thing, they are somewhat desperately conjoined by Wordsworth. Up to Book V, for example, he praises nature for its role in domesticating, without dulling, the child's imagination. Now, by a subtle shift, nature is mainly praised for preventing too quick an initiation into human nature, or what the

German tradition calls "Menschwerdung." But it is clear that
these functions of nature are not necessarily coincident. Even
should the child of nature have its soul shaped to majesty and calm,
so that it gains a distance from its kind, does it follow that this
negative self-confidence will encourage the positive quality of "love
of man"? The result may simply be an embalming of childhood;
while the imagination, even if it survives, may do so in a mode that
could never actively turn toward humanity.

Yet Wordsworth believes that nature can lead one's imaginative
hopes toward man. Books VI through IX interpret the fact that
the imagination, though naturalized, exceeds nature, as a providen-
tial widening of imaginative interests that are to wean the poet
from nature and turn him toward social life. Only at the depth of
his crisis does Wordsworth adequately recognize the imagination
as a power satisfied by neither nature nor man. He learns, in other
words,

> That 'tis a thing impossible to frame
> Conceptions equal to the soul's desires.[28]

While he ends, therefore, by distrusting imagination in its supernal
nakedness, he paradoxically trusts it in a previous mode, when it
had still gone out to nature. The only human balance is for imag-
ination to be generously chastened by nature, and Wordsworth
falls back on memories of how the soul and nature did fertilize
each other in childhood, and on the faith drawn from this, that
they will "marry" again through the influence of his song.

Wordsworth is preserved for a long time from too pointed a
sense of his mortality. He remains, vis-à-vis man, in a state of in-
nocence, feeling so much and no more. "I looked upon these
things," he says of the stirring events of 1790 (he is twenty years
old), "As from a distance; heard, and saw, and felt, / Was touched,
but with no intimate concern . . ." (VI.767 ff.). The strange im-
munity remains with him in the "underworld" of London de-
scribed in Book VII, for he moves among that chaos and confusion
like Aeneas in his cloud.[29]

By coincidence, *The Prelude* and *Paradise Lost* are symmetrical
here. In Book VII of *Paradise Lost,* Raphael changes his story
from things heavenly to things earthly, and Milton notes the fact

by an invocation. In Book VII, likewise, Wordsworth changes
from the more heavenly pitch of Nature to the more earthly of
London, though this is, in truth, his second descent (see III.196).
A preamble parallels Milton's invocation, but it is a sad and wintry
poetry, especially in comparison to the joyous burst of verses that
opens *The Prelude,* and it refers less to a change of subject than to
a change in the subject (the poet): "too slowly moves the promised
work." The comparison with Milton reveals also a curiously
"retrograde" movement in Wordsworth's narrative, for while Mil-
ton goes neatly from a point far from the human (Hell and
Heaven) to a point chiefly human (the Fall and after), and while
the anticipations of *Paradise Lost* are all forward, toward creation
and mankind, Wordsworth moves back and forth in time, never
accepting epochal structure, but counterbalancing change by a
mention of the survivals of the past, so that the child never quite
assumes the fatality of manhood. It is not until his brother's death,
when *The Prelude* is practically finished, that Wordsworth will
associate irremediable loss and humanization.

Books VII–IX, in particular, mark a period in Wordsworth's life
that parallels the time between Fall and final loss of Paradise. The
poet walks among dangers as if innocent, fallen in a sense, yet
saved from too steep a decline. The immunity already mentioned
comes from his previous relationship with nature, so that even the
great city is "thronged with impregnations like the Wilds / In
which my early feelings had been nursed" (VIII.633 ff.). Ref-
erences to Milton multiply, and an explicit passage at the end of
the eighth book confirms the parallel:

> every thing that was indeed divine
> Retained its purity inviolate,
> Nay brighter shone, by this portentous gloom
> Set off; such opposition as aroused
> The mind of Adam, yet in Paradise
> Though fallen from bliss, when in the East he saw
> Darkness ere day's mid course. (VIII.655–61)

The finest passage of Book VII (except for Wordsworth's de-
scription of the blind beggar, who is an embodiment of immuta-
bility rather than immunity) is also related to this sense of inno-

cence preserved. Having recorded that he saw among the many amusements of London a play based on the pathetic story of the Maid of Buttermere, he prepares to continue his pedestrian narrative,

> when, with sundry forms
> Commingled—shapes which met me in the way
> That we must tread—thy image rose again,
> Maiden of Buttermere! She lives in peace
> Upon the spot where she was born and reared;
> Without contamination doth she live
> In quietness, without anxiety;
> Beside the mountain chapel, sleeps in earth
> Her new-born infant, fearless as a lamb. (VII.317–25)

Here again, as in VI.592, something that happens in the moment of composition enters the narrative as a special event. The poet is waylaid (the metaphor is practically his) by an image which demands more than a "memorial tribute." Wordsworth then describes a "real" scene of analogous significance, perhaps one of the shapes (VII.318) mentioned. It is of a boy about two years old, sitting admired and unself-conscious among gamesters and their women. He seemed, says the poet, in a phrase that condenses the Great Ode, "A sort of Alien scatter'd from the clouds" (1805, VII.377). Wordsworth continues with a superb though frightening sequence of thoughts on this child, who reappears to his mind's eye as eternally nature's, arrested in his development:

> I behold
> The lovely Boy as I beheld him then,
> Among the wretched and the falsely gay,
> Like one of those who walk'd with hair unsinged
> Amid the fiery furnace. He hath since
> Appear'd to me oft-times as if embalm'd
> By Nature; through some special privilege,
> Stopp'd at the growth he had; destined to live,
> To be, to have been, come and go, a Child
> And nothing more. . . .

> But he perhaps
> Mary!* may now have liv'd till he could look
> With envy on thy nameless Babe that sleeps
> Beside the mountain Chapel, undisturb'd! (1805, VII.394–411)

The last lines recall Wordsworth looking at the Boy of Winan-
der's grave, and perhaps the entire motif of the child reared and
absorbed by nature. Lucy is another such; and the thought of death
which associates itself with her is not free of ambivalence. It is an
easy thought in the sense that if she were not to die life would be-
tray her, as it probably did the "lovely boy." Yet if death prevents
one kind of betrayal, it confirms another, for nature placed *on*
Lucy and *in* the poet an illusion of immortality.

Despite London, and a shock suffered before that (VII.382 ff.),
the poet retains his distance from human kind well into his second
visit to France (November 1791). He tells us he was tranquil
amidst the turmoil of revolution and city life,

> careless as a flower
> Glassed in a green-house, or a parlour shrub
> That spreads its leaves in unmolested peace,
> While every bush and tree, the country through,
> Is shaking to the roots: indifference this
> Which may seem strange. (IX.87–92)

From VIII.348, moreover, we know that man remained subordi-
nate to nature until not less than twenty-two summers had
passed, i.e. the change began, or began to be noticed, during 1791–
92. Of the two major events of this time only one, his meeting of
Beaupuy, is mentioned; his love for Annette Vallon is not. An-
nette is either censored or not deemed critical; as for Beaupuy,
Wordsworth sees in him an *alter ego,* transferring to his person
the immunity characteristic of himself:

> He through the events
> Of that great change wandered in perfect faith,
> As through a book, an old romance, or tale

---

* Mary of Buttermere.

Of Fairy, or some dream of actions wrought
Behind the summer clouds. (IX.298–302)[30]

I conclude by noting how many contrasts are offered in Book IX
between a world maturing or decaying slowly, "by reverential
touch of Time / Dismantled" (IX.468 f.), and a world of revolu-
tion, of "violence abrupt." The contrast anticipates the sudden
change described later, which broke the gradualism of nature. But
before tracing the story of that crisis, I must change from the theme
of initiation to that of imagination. The progress of the poet's
imagination toward self-consciousness covers a dual period of time,
going from 1790 (the Alpine journey) to the end of his visit to
France (December 1792), but also from those days to the actual
moments of composition in 1804. As the poet continues with the
story of his life, which is chiefly the story of his imagination, he
also proceeds toward imagination, which, as if contradicting his
words, frees itself of the nature that is supposed to have bound and
mellowed it.

### Books VI ff.: Imagination Unbound

I will mention in passing the attraction of geometry and abstract
thought, noted already in Book V.65 ff., and connected by Words-
worth himself to the desire for "an independent world, / Created
out of pure intelligence" (VI.166–67). About the same time the
curious power of Fancy wakes in him (VIII.365 ff.), characterized
by a similar independence of space and time, but showing it
through willful distortions, or through exaggerated humanizations
of nature. A further sign of the imagination threatening its ties is
revery, that abstracted, dream-like void which enables Words-
worth to pass unscathed through London. The poet thinks it a gift
of nature, yet it removes him as much from nature as from man.
"Of that external scene which round me lay, / Little, in this ab-
straction, did I see," he remarks of a previous strong moment of
revery (IV.160 ff.). This vacancy of the poet's has a character all
its own, and I do not want to simplify it. But a fading of the im-
mediate external scene is always present. When Wordsworth meets
the Blind Beggar (VII.619 ff.), such revery is, in addition, cli-
maxed by the abrupt entry-into-consciousness of an external figure

marked by its naked or solitary aspect. The solitary figure (even a single tree, VI.76) is a common part of the Wordsworthian landscape; yet if it forces the eye, and so returns him to the realm of externals, it also embodies the idea of something absolute—independent of nature even when within nature. It is a border image, or omphalos.

In some ways Wordsworth's London sojourn has the effect of intensifying by repetition his Cambridge experience. He is made aware that imagination is dulled rather than delighted by "the increasing accumulation of men in cities, where the uniformity of their occupations produces a craving for extraordinary incident which the rapid communication of intelligence hourly gratifies."[31] That is why so much space is given in Book VII to fairs and festivals, to primitive and sophisticated amusement, in a word, to distractions. Their existence shows the imaginative impulse asserting itself blindly, yet being reduced to superstition and torpor by too quick or crude a satisfaction. The imagination, in Wordsworth's view, is marked by activity not only in the presence but also in the absence of immediate external stimuli, and even creates that absence when necessary. Struggling to remember what exactly among this mass of city events stirred his mind, Wordsworth finds that the casual incident (e.g. his encountering the blind beggar) had more effect than the "moving accident" (the stage spectacle), and this reminds him of the freedom his imagination demands. Twice in this book he uses the metaphor of imagination sleeping; once to defend his apparent trivialities,

> More lofty themes,
> Such as at least do wear a prouder face,
> Solicit our regard; but when I think
> Of these, I feel the imaginative power
> Languish within me; even then it slept,
> When, pressed by tragic sufferings, the heart
> Was more than full; amid my sobs and tears
> It slept, even in the pregnant season of youth . . . (VII.465–72)

and once to emphasize that his mind wearies at the given, the complete spectacle:

From these sights
Take one,—that ancient festival, the Fair,
Holden where martyrs suffered in past time,
And named of St. Bartholomew; there, see
A work completed to our hands, that lays,
If any spectacle on earth can do,
The whole creative powers of man asleep!—
For once, the Muse's help will we implore. (VII. 675–82)

By appealing "for once" to the conventional Muse, Wordsworth gives his judgment on all purely descriptive poetry, which makes of her, as Blake would say, the daughter of Memory.

The ultimate insight as to the independence of imagination from nature comes during the poet's reflections on Crossing the Alps. His memories are disrupted by a rising-up of imagination that deflects emphasis from the gloomy though sublime spectacle of the Ravine of Gondo, and bestows it on a less obvious, indeed trivial, event—a feeling of melancholy. The moving accident is once more replaced by the casual incident, but also a *scene* by a *sequence*. The poet's mind, held captive by its anticipation of nature's finale (VI.624 ff., the "Characters of the great Apocalypse") frees itself suddenly from that remembered glory as from too immediate a stimulus, or more precisely it frees itself both from a particular moment and a particular kind of sense stimulus. The gloomy strait spoke directly to eye and ear, but the poet's hopes pointing to the clouds (VI.587) and his ensuing sadness (VI.617), which in 1804 seem more significant than the vision previously attained, spring from so internal a source that they appear constitutive rather than caused. The revelation of 1804 is the last event in a series that brings the mind anagogically to an understanding of its independence from nature.

Wordsworth permits us to trace at least three stages in this liberative series. Each can be given an approximate biographical span, though all mingle in some respect. The first stage may be identified with the period of *Descriptive Sketches*. At that time Wordsworth gains a first knowledge of how the mind is released from a not unnecessary tyranny of the senses, and especially of the eye. He records a defeat of the eye which leads him from visible to less visible, from place to unbounded. The eye is frustrated by the endless visual contrasts it discovers. The second stage may be identified with the period in which VI.621–40 is composed (1799). It presents a new interpretation of the relation between mind and eye. The dynamics of contrast receives here its supreme symbol, yet the very strength of natural oppositions, winds against winds, the commingling of darkness and light, tumult and peace, rising and sinking perspectives, stuns the senses and swells into the knowledge of something unbounded: eternity, apocalypse. The passage is a most unusual example of how the dynamics of contrast and of blending cooperate, since insight still proceeds from sight, from the blended might of all the oppositions. In the last stage, however, the poet's mind is roused not by sight or by the idea of sight, but by the idea of a blindness (to nature) so powerful that even a supremely visual moment like VI.621 ff. serves only, in the final account, to call it forth.

This contrast, of sight revealing a power in the mind independent of sight, finds its next and strangest instance in Wordsworth's meeting with the blind beggar. Book VII had begun with an array of images suggesting increase of light through darkness: the glowworm, the hermit's taper, a tree's dark boughs tossing "As if to make the strong wind visible." In the 1850 *Prelude* an image of the same kind is used to explain the effect of the beggar on the poet:

> As the black storm upon the mountain top
> Sets off the sunbeam in the valley, so
> That huge fermenting mass of human-kind
> Serves as a solemn back-ground, or relief,
> To single forms and objects. (VII.619–23)

Such a comment merely strengthens the mystery of the "power of contrast" (VII.481), and it does not explain why the poet is caught by precisely *this* single form. For the real and hidden contrast, too deep for Wordsworth's consciousness, or else displaced, is between the blind man's face and his label ("upon his chest / Wearing a written paper, to explain / His story"). These natural foci of any observer are shocking because here they are *not* in contrast. Face and label are equally fixed or affixed: we expect the beggar's face and eyes ("his steadfast face and sightless eyes") to be centers of life whereas they are as much a surface as the paper he wears. As in the central episode of the sixth book, it is both a mental anticipation and the expectation of a strongly visual significance which is defeated,[32] and this again causes a quasi-apocalyptic feeling of reversal turning the mind around or into itself. "Caught by the spectacle my mind turned round / As with the might of waters" (VII.643 ff.).[33] Wordsworth, once more a halted traveler, divines the power behind the beggar's fixity of stance, and the image of great waters hints at the engulfing solipsism of Imagination.

### Books IX–XII: The French Revolution

Two things make it difficult to follow Wordsworth's involvement in the French Revolution. One is the rhythm of his mind, which avoids the epochal, though often tempted by it. Another is his truth in recording events not objectively but phenomenologically, as "storm / Or sunshine" to his individual mind (X.121). Both tendencies are related to his fear of the Absolute.

It is for a good reason that the poet hesitates to consider his crisis as an epoch or a cut in time that separates before and after. He may be "engulphed" (IX.4) once again even as he writes; the very act of confrontation, moreover, if too direct and hasty, would already be against Nature and show the soul's impatience—a divine impatience. Hence Wordsworth engages in a host of dilatory tactics and relaxes his style overmuch. Too causal, too pedantic, too matter-of-fact; always looking back once more before proceeding; and welcoming too suspiciously those "shapeless" anticipatory motions of the soul which are its poetry, he creates a highly undramatic narrative and associates its mazy rhythm with Nature's own:

> Even as a river,—partly (it might seem)
> Yielding to old remembrances, and swayed
> In part by fear to shape a way direct,
> That would engulph him soon in the ravenous sea—
> Turns, and will measure back his course, far back,
> Seeking the very regions which he crossed
> In his first outset; so have we, my Friend!
> Turned and returned with intricate delay. (IX.1–8)

A second "traveler" simile follows, delaying while talking about delay. This double simile prefaces in true epic fashion the book in which our poet's notes must change to tragic. By genial coincidence, it is now the ninth book, as if *The Prelude* again were synchronized with *Paradise Lost*. Wordsworth cannot avoid any longer the story of his great change, and echoes in "Oh, how much unlike the past!" (IX.22) the classical tragic formula: *quantus mutatus ab illo*. His gradualism does not cease, and his argument does not alter; but he is forced to recognize, despite turns and windings, forward and backward glances, the apocalyptic implication of his break with nature.

Wordsworth at first considered the French Revolution as a fulfillment rather than abrogation of natural law. It was a gift of nature's "come rather late than soon" (IX.248). The influence of Beaupuy is significant here. Though respectful of custom, he persuades Wordsworth that man may take destiny into his hands and speed natural process (IX.396–552).[34] Wordsworth begins to think of man as one who adds to or helps nature, but the truly revolutionary implications of this thought are still masked by the background to the conversations of the two men, who walk the green sides of the Loire, or in forests of continuous shade, whose dialogue is softened by reminders of the permanent and ancient. Book IX ends with examples of how in France state law had usurped natural law: the story of Vaudracour and Julia, whatever its biographical obliquities, has the clear narrative purpose of showing that human life and progress had been *unnaturally* repressed. Vaudracour's inertia, described in IX.574 ff., is of the same kind as that of the hunger-bitten girl pictured so eloquently in IX.509 ff.: both sufferers have been violently separated from hope, and so accept their fate with terrible quietness. It is nature that is dynamic, open; and man who by "monstrous laws" has repressed man.

The fine, lingering beginning of Book X,

> It was a beautiful and silent day
> That overspread the countenance of earth,
> Then fading with unusual quietness ... (X.1–3)

counterpoints the story of Vaudracour,

> hidden in those gloomy shades,
> His days he wasted,—an imbecile mind. (IX.584–85)

By now it is October 1792, a month after the massacres, and Robespierre is in power. But Beaupuy's example and philosophy still sustain Wordsworth, and various concepts of natural law, commonplaces of English political thought, support his feeling that tyranny cannot last (X.191 ff.).[35] He realizes, at the same time, that man's destiny often hangs on single persons (X.154–56); and at this critical point, more conscious than ever of his power as an individual, and in this consciousness ready to give himself to the Revolution, Wordsworth is obliged to return to England.

Up to this time his view of the Revolution has been modified but not changed in any radical way. He still considers it a work of nature, though he has a sharper awareness of the individual's role as *agent provocateur*. There are, however, premonitions that different forces may be at work. In his lonely Paris room the memory of the massacres oppresses him:

> Until I seemed to hear a voice that cried
> To the whole city, "Sleep no more." (X.86–87)

This is the voice Macbeth hears, having violated the order of nature triply, by killing his king, his guest, and a sleeping man. Wordsworth is near to understanding the more-than-natural character of the Revolution; but the change does not come till after his return to England.

In February 1793, or shortly after this, he at last suffers the shock for which he reserves the name "revolution": Britain, birthplace of the idea of liberty, of just revolutions, goes to war against France:

>               No shock
> Given to my moral nature had I known
> Down to that very moment; neither lapse
> Nor turn of sentiment that might be named
> A revolution, save at this one time;
> All else was progress on the self-same path
> On which, with a diversity of pace,

> I had been travelling: this a stride at once
> Into another region. As a light
> And pliant harebell, swinging in the breeze
> Of some grey rock—its birth-place—so had I
> Wantoned, fast rooted on the ancient tower
> Of my beloved country, wishing not
> A happier fortune than to wither there:
> Now was I from that pleasant station torn
> And tossed about in whirlwind. (X.268–83)

At one blow, Wordsworth is cut off from hope in *natural* process. The power of the shock he felt is conveyed by images of uprooting and up-routing. The imagery is similar, therefore, to what issues from his direct encounter with "Imagination." It is only now, by means of this inner shock, that he begins to glimpse the fact that the French Revolution may be a work of the apocalyptic imagination. Britain's betrayal achieves this paradoxical result in two ways: it opens his eyes to other betrayals of "nature," and it leaves him with a hope deprived of the possibility of earthly realization. What Britain betrays is, of course, not only her ideological offspring in France but the pride and patriotic love of her own sons. Her unnatural action "turned an angry beak against the down / Of her own breast."[36] The hope inspired by the Revolution is not destroyed in Wordsworth, but it is radically displaced. It has, in fact, no home or sphere of action left for it, and was bound to become apocalyptic, or skirt that temptation:

> A woful time for them whose hopes survived
> The shock; most woful for those few who still
> Were flattered, and had trust in human kind:
> They had the deepest feeling of the grief. (X.386–89)

But this is to anticipate matters. At first the betrayal intensified Wordsworth's developing ideas on man's role in history. He now pursues a certain ideal of Man rather than man as he is, conditioned by environment and institutions. England has put the moral force of the past and of institutions in doubt, and Wordsworth withdraws his trust from both. Already taught by Beaupuy to re-

spect the individual's role in the shaping of destiny, he vests his
hope exclusively in abstract individual man. The full turn-about
of his mind can be judged by comparing such lines as

> Oft, as my thoughts were turned to human kind,
> I scorned indifference; but, inflamed with thirst
> Of a secure intelligence, and sick
> Of other longing, I pursued what seemed
> A more exalted nature; wished that Man
> Should start out of his earthly, worm-like state,
> And spread abroad the wings of Liberty . . . (XI.247–53)*

with what he had said about his interest in man just prior to meet-
ing Beaupuy:

> Tranquil almost, and careless as a flower. . . . (IX.87 ff.)

The believer in nature as the source of liberty, whether moral or
political, has become an apocalyptic revolutionary.

He is helped to this change by wild theories, "speculative
schemes" (XI.224). They have been identified with Godwinism,
yet Wordsworth's phrasing indicates something widerspread, in
the air ("afloat"), which Godwin shared or systematized. Their
common factor is religious fervor expressing itself in several dog-
mas. One of these holds that the reformation of the individual
must precede that of society, social being built on personal liberty
(XI.240). But this, which might actually limit political activity, is
joined to a principle of moral action subordinating natural law,
positive law, or custom, to "Reason's naked self." All that is
needed to come to a decision is "the light of circumstances, flashed
/ Upon an independent intellect" (XI.243 ff.). By this means, says
Wordsworth, using a significant metaphor, his hope found a new
*ground,* and was able to grow once more.

We do not know exactly when this new ground—abstract individ-
ual man—proved to be a groundless myth. But we do know that a
new crisis supervened when Wordsworth called on his reason to
pass the judgments he thought it capable of. Everything is dragged

* The 1805 text says that Wordsworth "sought / To accomplish the transi-
tion by such means / As did not lie in nature . . ." (X.842–44).

by him to the bar of the mind, even finally the mind itself which
cannot discover the formal or absolutely clear proof it needs. Will
and choice are atrophied by an excess of cases and an absence of
case rules.

In Book XI Wordsworth treats the crisis purely from its moral
side, but in XII.102–46 he links it also to an epistemological diffi-
culty. Common to both is the need for judgments of an immediate
and absolute nature, for Othello's *ocular proof*. The difficulty of
such proof is exposed in *The Borderers* (1796–97), which has its
Iago in Oswald, and whose locale, the border region, represents the
absence of the "blind restraints of general laws" (XI.241). In this
need for eye judgments (curiously emphasized in *The Borderers*
by the figure of the blind victim) one can see the survival of the
apocalyptic urge, though my interpretation at this point may be
clearer than Wordsworth's, who multiplies explanations and ad-
mits (XI.282 ff.) the need for an additional poem "flinging out
less guarded words."

If Wordsworth is guarded in the history of his crisis, he is noth-
ing less than obscure concerning its resolution. Or rather, while
the resolution itself is clear, its *history* is telescoped. The poet, at
the end of Book XI, drops all pretense of historical method, and
he does this either to avoid epochal structure once more, or be-
cause his restoration is indeed a mingling of past, present, and fu-
ture, of fact and faith. He often speaks from an eschatological
viewpoint, and so prophesies rather than speaks:

> I, long before the blissful hour arrives,
> Would chant, in lonely peace, the spousal verse
> Of this great consummation.

*The Prelude* is a similar prelude: a history with a hope, it looks
forward to the time when this hope will be realized, and the mind
of man wedded to the goodly universe.

### Books X–XI: Restoration (1)

There is no evidence, from Wordsworth's poetry, that the period
of dejection was unbroken, and the recovery sudden. The poet's
retrospective mingling of crisis and cure may have its basis in fact.

Even without data already brought from other poems closer to the period of crisis, *The Prelude* can show how resilient the idea of nature was. Wordsworth's recovery, as *The Prelude* presents it, begins with Book X rather than XII. Books X and XI were, of course, a single narrative in the 1805 version, with the poet approaching crisis, looking after its depiction both forward and backward, describing the great betrayal a second time, then passing immediately to a résumé of the main forces leading to his recovery. But in Book XII (1805, XI) he returns, as if compulsively, to a third mention of the crisis, now followed by his deepest retrograde movement in time, one that resurrects events from the age of five and thirteen. We are given, then, three separate accounts of Wordsworth's crisis, each followed by a movement showing the persistence or actual revival of his dealings with Nature.

After the first account of his crisis, the poet moves forward in time, and the Revolution begins to appear as something clearly against nature. His imagery is sarcastic and strong in this knowledge:

> In France, the men, who, for their desperate ends,
> Had plucked up mercy by the roots, were glad
> Of this new enemy. (X.331–33)
>
> Domestic carnage now filled the whole year
> With feast-days. (X.356–57)

Sleep, he admits, rarely came "charged with natural gifts." His dreams turned against him; and he has thoughts comparable to those of the Hebrew prophets, who viewed history as a divine turning of nature against man in the form of a new flood of sin (X.437 ff.). He had previously used an allusion to Macbeth, and now another image of the monstrous reversal of the order of nature comes to him, and he compares the town of Arras persecuted by her son Robespierre to Lear reproaching the winds. When he learns of the death of Robespierre (the incident concludes Book X in the 1850 *Prelude*) it is in a place of some of his happiest moments, where nature first began to be sought for her own sake; while the calm day on which he hears the news augurs a restoration of nature's normal course. The last line of Book X, recalling how the young and spirited horsemen

> beat with thundering hoofs the level sand . . .

repeats verbatim the last line of an episode in Book II, so that the continuity with childhood seems already established.

The second description of Britain's treachery is prefaced by Wordsworth's most famous lines on the Revolution. Clearly, ardently humanistic, they show that he believed his desires in accord with nature, that what he foresaw was the millennium. France, it seemed to him, was an exemplary occasion to find a best realization for the skill and powers of man. Not France alone, but the whole earth wore the beauty of promise. Theory was Romance, and the mistakes, even massacres, affected him only as if *natural* by-products:

> Not caring if the wind did now and then
> Blow keen upon an eminence that gave
> Prospect so large into futurity;
> In brief, a child of Nature, as at first. (XI.165–68)

For Wordsworth, who associated England's history, even her landscape, with the idea of liberty, there could have been no greater bosom-betrayal than her attack on France. The betrayal struck, as his images show, not at hope, which is immortal, and finds its channels, however perverse, but at the marriage of hope and *this* world, of imagination and nature:

> This threw me first out of the pale of love;
> Soured and corrupted, upwards to the source,
> My sentiments; was not, as hitherto,
> A swallowing up of lesser things in great,
> But change of them into their contraries . . .
>                     What had been a pride,
> Was now a shame; my likings and my loves
> Ran in new channels, leaving old ones dry. (XI.176–85)

By 1795 Wordsworth is writing fragments that lead to *The Borderers* and "The Ruined Cottage," and which describe what happens when the rebellious heart, being denied the common food of hope, "to its own will / Fashions the laws of nature."[37] His own worship, under the influence of Godwin, of the naked individual reason, is part of a tremendous hunger for a new subjective absolute. When that fails he turns to science, feeling it to be a realm where reason can work without disturbance from material accidents or spiritual wilfulness. He is now as far from Nature as can be, having first broken with natural process, and now with nature itself in all her homely and personal aspects. His thirst for "an unimpregnable intelligence" has carried him beyond the human.

It is then that Dorothy's influence is interposed, together with nature's own. Wordsworth was reunited with his sister in February 1794, and that Spring they spent several weeks in the Lake Country, entering Grasmere together for the first (but not the last) time:

> Then it was . . .
> That the beloved Sister in whose sight
> Those days were passed, now speaking in a voice
> Of sudden admonition—like a brook
> That did but *cross* a lonely road, and now
> Is seen, heard, felt, and caught at every turn,
> Companion never lost through many a league—
> Maintained for me a saving intercourse
> With my true self; for, though bedimmed and changed
> Much, as it seemed, I was no further changed
> Than as a clouded and a waning moon:
> She whispered still that brightness would return,
> She, in the midst of all, preserved me still
> A Poet, made me seek beneath that name,
> And that alone, my office upon earth;
> And, lastly, as hereafter will be shown,
> If willing audience fail not, Nature's self,
> By all varieties of human love
> Assisted, led me back through opening day
> To those sweet counsels between head and heart. (XI.333–53)

With Book XI we reach the end of the forward movement in time: Books XIII and XIV will add two more incidents from the period of dejection and recovery, but neither takes us beyond August 1794, the news of Robespierre's death. It is clear that the poet feels the "leading back" more important. His recovery is a rediscovery of self: he finds that he is not radically altered, nor alienated from his former being, "I was no further changed / Than as a clouded and a waning moon." At the beginning of XIII he says explicitly that even when the "spirit of evil" reached its height, he kept to nature, which maintained his "secret" happiness (XII.43).

Yet in what follows, which gives a final description of his crisis, Wordsworth admits that a natural graciousness of his mind had been shaken. Just as the hope in reason had disqualified every other standard including finally reason itself, so it had doubted poetry. Now this, mentioned last, was not an incidental result of his perplexity. For the burden of Books XII–XIV is less the restoration of his faith in nature than of faith in himself as a poet. His crisis had divorced him from a destiny which he now rediscovers—helped by nature, by Dorothy (who is a nature spirit), and Coleridge.

That some uncertainty of self and vocation remained is clear from Wordsworth's opening to *The Prelude*, and from what the poem itself teaches him: that his imagination is not only not naturalized but perhaps utterly transcendent. Yet he bends back the energy and freedom of his mind to nature. He does not trust, despite Milton, the Miltonic sublime; or else is not sure any longer that his readers will bring to poetry that instinctive humanizing which Renaissance practice required. His distrust, then, may be directed less against poetry (as Charles Williams thought)[38] than against the apocalyptic impulse. Spenser and Milton still expected their ideal reader to blend the humanizing power of his mind with their own transcendental imaginings; but Wordsworth's poetry is too nervous ever to relinquish contact with the earth.

### Books XII–XIV: Restoration (2)

In the dedication scene of Book IV (see above, pp. 223 f.) Wordsworth's surprise and gratitude come from the fact that he recovers a sense of native powers as unviolently as day follows night. This gentleness of restoration[39] is the very theme of his invocation to nature at the beginning of Book XII, "Imagination and Taste, How Impaired and Restored." He celebrates "the wondrous influence of power gently used" manifest everywhere in rural nature, and his very voice is struck with a kind of nature-envy:

> And you, ye groves, whose ministry it is
> To interpose the covert of your shades,
> Even as a sleep, between the heart of man
> And outward troubles, between man himself,
> Not seldom, and his own uneasy heart:
> Oh! that I had a music and a voice
> Harmonious as your own, that I might tell
> What ye have done for me. (XII.24–31)

He wants his poetry to be like nature in function and effect. It should purge our imaginative belief in the necessity of apocalypse or violent renovation, and purge it gently. His own voice is to be wind-like and almost inscrutable, yet having the strength to shift, at a touch, "stupendous clouds."

Wordsworth was so anxious to stress the gradually restorative action of nature that the original five-book *Prelude* would have ended with the dedication scene (which bound him *unknowingly* to poetry), and the vision from Snowdon.[40] These incidents, together with his childhood experiences, were enough to maintain and then to restore the continuity between his past and present self. They were operative even in his apocalyptic stage when he hoped that the future would be divided "as by a gulph" (XII.59) from the past. And the expanded *Prelude* adds only one further incident (the "spots of time" would have been part of Books I and II): the adventure on Salisbury Plain which took place in the summer of 1793 and is incorporated into Book XIII.

Yet this adventure, like the "spots of time," has its apocalyptic side, and raises the question of the role of terrible beauty. Can we understand Salisbury Plain in relation to Wordsworth's recovery of his sense of mission? I suspect that the experience was needed to assure him that nature could engage—as she had done in his youth—the darker as well as milder emotions. In order to be sure of nature, sure of her ability to satisfy imagination, he has to see once more her terrible countenance.

On Sarum's Plain Wordsworth met his own past and recognized its survival. The experience, as told in Book XIII, shows the two-fold structure of his earliest relation to nature in its mingling of fearful (318–35) and mild (336–49). Moreover, the verses composed in memory of Salisbury Plain, and not published till 1842 as *Guilt and Sorrow*, bring additional evidence that Wordsworth had to recognize and face the apocalyptic character of his imagination, before he could understand the basically non-apocalyptic role of nature and so begin to celebrate the marriage or "ennobling interchange" (XIII.375) of both.

"Salisbury Plain" is dominated by the idea of confrontation, even in its plot structure. Wordsworth links two separate stories, that of the Female Vagrant and that of the Sailor, both of which depict human beings deprived of home (including hope in this world) by war, greed, cruelty, and fatal imaginings. The scene enabling the linkage is Salisbury Plain, which becomes a kind of Egdon Heath. The sailor is first confronted by a clanging gibbet (reminding him of his possible fate), then by the dreadful fantasy of druidic sacrifice at Stonehenge, by the Female Vagrant in the "Dead House," and by his own crime recalled on seeing the wound an angry father gives his child;

> and, as the boy turned round
> His battered head, a groan the Sailor fetched
> As if he saw—there and upon that ground—
> Strange repetition of the deadly wound
> He had himself inflicted.[41]

After this he meets, by coincidence, his dying wife. Though nature plays no direct part in the story, she does attain to a kind of instrumentality as the dark background to these confrontations leading the wanderer back into his past.

It is probable, therefore, that Wordsworth on the plain passed once more ("strange repetition!") through a previous experience or recognized the survival of his childhood strength of imagination; and that though still in crisis, shunning man, and desolate of heart with respect to nature, he begins to hope that his imagination will find in nature and "natural tales" its proper object. For though "Salisbury Plain" has its gothic and ghostly moments, it is also a tale of natural guilt and sorrow. Wordsworth is already recovering faith in himself as a poet with a special mission, with "a power like one of Nature's" (XIII.312).

The last episode of *The Prelude* is introduced abruptly at the beginning of Book XIV. It may have taken place in the same summer as the walk across Salisbury Plain, or two years earlier. The date, for once, hardly matters. Snowdon, its ascent, the vision, the meditation, points to the utmost Wordsworth can achieve as poet. The episode does not confirm that he is a poet (like the dedication scene of Book IV) or that nature may, as in childhood, evoke and receive the strongest imaginings (the spots of time, Salisbury Plain) —these things have already been settled, or do not need reconfirmation. The episode embodies instead what Blake would have called the Spiritual Form of the poet. Wordsworth sees Imagination by its own light and calls that light Nature's, and this deception or transference, a greatest avoidance of apocalypse, is still the best possible ending for *The Prelude*. If it does not reveal, as Wordsworth thought, the nature of all Imagination, it does manifest his own. His special poetic mission is made absolutely clear by the power and character of the episode.

What Wordsworth sees is a Pisgah-sight, though from within as well as above the earth. Even without the after-thought (XIV.63 ff.) we feel it to be a vision of Creation or of the *continuous* act of Creation. It is hard to determine why this impression rises so surely: perhaps because the human observer pales deceptively into the margin, suspended as he is between the powers of sea, mist, and sky? Or is it because the lines of the sight are so unusually sharp for Wordsworth, so hieratically vertical as well as horizontal? There is, moreover, in the double suddeness of light and sound, and the circumstance of mist, an effect like the tearing of a veil by which the poet stumbles on a naked vision. This, combined with reminiscences from the Psalms,* raises us to a direct Adamite view of power, of the action that generates and *is* power.

---

* E.g. "Deep calleth unto deep at the noise of thy waterspouts." Psalm 42:7.

Yet, as often in *The Prelude,* a slight mismatching of argument and illustration is felt. Wordsworth has been talking in the previous book about the new world that seemed to have opened to him, and which produced a poetry of heightened "everyday appearance" praised by Coleridge as an index of great original powers:

> [You said] my mind had exercised
> Upon the vulgar forms of present things,
> The actual world of our familiar days,
> Yet higher power; had caught from them a tone,
> An image, and a character, by books
> Not hitherto reflected. (XIII.355–60)

Coleridge is thinking of verses like "The Female Vagrant," begun probably in 1791, worked into "Salisbury Plain," and published in the *Lyrical Ballads* of 1798. Yet though the ascent of Snowdon is as ordinary as, perhaps, the materials of the vision, Wordsworth mentions the presence of circumstances "awful and sublime." Snowdon occasions a unique rather than characteristic Wordsworthian moment, and seems to naturalize the supernaturalistic imagination of a Milton. It remains an unparalleled success in Wordsworth's canon, and discloses a poetry greater than his staple.

Of the vision itself one could truly say that it opens the earth. It justifies Wordsworth's "The earth is all before me," which advertised, at the beginning of *The Prelude,* that he wished to begin where Milton left off. After so much poetry which is *about* experience, Snowdon comes not as prelude or spousal verse but as a poetic consummation. Out of such passages the Bible of Experience is made; they have a life of their own and support weights of interpretation. We enter them far more deeply than anything of Milton's, who is still the greater poet. For where Milton cannot work with nature he works against it, or finds a second nature; and if he loses the earth, at least preserves strength of imagination. But in Wordsworth the very force of the naturalized vision, whether in childhood or as in this "mounting of the mind," cannot be forgotten, and it produces ultimately a retrospective faith rather than a forward poetry.

There are interesting Miltonic echoes here,[42] but it is a question of the apocalyptic imagination in general rather than of Milton's in particular. Yet Milton was important to Wordsworth because the Idea of Creation remains central to *Paradise Lost*. There is the sevenfold gorgeousness of Milton's seventh book; there are also many subtler returnings to man in the midst of unearthly imaginings. Milton's moral is human; and Wordsworth and Dorothy, engaged to Grasmere as to a terrestrial paradise, wept over the Flood and its teaching

> that God attributes to place
> No sanctity, if none be thither brought
> By Men who there frequent, or therein dwell.[43]

It is not an accident that *The Prelude* ends with a vision in the Mount, one that centers with Miltonic intensity on the nexus between "upper" and "lower" involved in the very idea of creation.

At first the upper sphere dominates, with the moon in single glory, the hills like worshippers, the real ocean usurped on, and the second ocean of mist meek and silent. Then, in a reversal, the lower sphere recovers its realness and breaks so strongly upward that its voice seems to be felt by the starry heavens. The meaning of this reversal, which included a shift from visual to aural, has been considered. The moon, if we keep Miltonic hierarchy in mind, seems to emblem a *creative return* of the "sovereign" mind —of the self-sustained imagination, single in glory and separated from a nether sphere. A similar movement is also shown by the waters, which 'return' upward. In 1805 Wordsworth had been tempted to identify "The Soul, the Imagination of the whole" (XIII.65) with the rising voice of waters (or the breach) rather than with the moon; yet it should not be identified fully with either, because the vision yields the image of an action inclusive of both symbols or moments.

The "homeless voice of waters" (1805, XIII.63) and its dark thoroughfare are reminiscent of the threat of engulfment which elsewhere shows the poet recognizing the transcendent character of imagination. Yet in this case the moon with its fixity, singleness, and impassibility, is initially a more obvious sense symbol for

the apocalyptic mind; and in passages which Wordsworth thought
to include as further illustration of his "argument," the same
curiously single and impassible figure is seen, the "large unmuti-
lated rainbow [that] stood / Immoveable in heav'n" during a storm,
or the explorer sitting calmly on the open deck of his bark until
"engulph'd and seen no more."[44] If the moon in its fullness is
evocative of a fixed, unchangeable world above this one, then the
unfolding vision, by shifting to the "fixed, abysmal, gloomy breath-
ing-place," seems to correct a displacement and bring the poet
closer to what is the real source of revelation, as deep as that was
high, and also "fixed." But when the poet says that *Nature* had
lodged the *Imagination* of the whole in that gulf, a new displace-
ment occurs, this time not organic but interpretative. The entire
vision, moreover, as distinct from its two moments, justifies these
dynamic shifts that displace first the locus and then the meaning of
the poet's apocalyptic feelings. In a vision of life, or of creative
power mingling with life, it must be so; and Wordsworth's attribu-
tion to Nature of something which is more properly Imagination's
is a similar displacement, a true and vital generosity analogous
to religious faith.

   *The Prelude* ends with tributes to Dorothy, Coleridge, and Cal-
vert.[45] These three were foremost in enabling the poet to "maintain
a saving intercourse / With his true self." Calvert's gift was not
directly spiritual (he left Wordsworth a legacy sufficient to let him
live without a profession), but his sister, and also the "Friend" to
whom *The Prelude* is addressed, played crucial roles in restoring
his sense of mission. Wordsworth was united with Dorothy early in
1794, and he met Coleridge probably in the latter part of 1795. I
have neglected both Coleridge and Dorothy[46] because *The Prelude*
places its greatest emphasis on the way Nature (i.e. time prior to
the time of crisis) kept its secret hold on the poet; and even Words-
worth's beautiful tribute to Dorothy in Book XII sees her mainly
as a Spirit of Nature. But *The Prelude* is, of course, a verse-epistle
to Coleridge, who, during a critical portion of its writing, had gone
to Malta. "Far art Thou wander'd now in search of health / And
milder breezes," is Wordsworth's farewell to him in the sixth book
of this "Poem . . . Addressed to S. T. Coleridge." "Oh! wrap him in

your Shades, ye Giant Woods / On Etna's side" is the hope ex-
pressed in the tenth book. For it is Coleridge who presently needs
the "restorative delight" of Nature and the faithful trust of his
friends. *The Prelude*, whose subject is the possibility of man's re-
newal through Nature, addresses itself ardently to the person now
most in need of that renewal.

To discriminate finely between Dorothy and Coleridge in the
matter of Wordsworth's recovery is less important than to de-
termine the direction of both their efforts; and Wordsworth him-
self stresses the common factor. It was Dorothy who softened the
"Miltonic" element, his love for what Anna Seward would have
called the "terrific graces":

> but for thee, dear Friend!
> My soul, too reckless of mild grace, had stood
> In her original self too confident,
> Retained too long a countenance severe;
> A rock with torrents roaring, with the clouds
> Familiar, and a favourite of the stars:
> But thou didst plant its crevices with flowers. (XIV.247–53)

Coleridge's "kindred influence" also domesticated this apocalyp-
tical penchant:

> Thus fear relaxed
> Her overweening grasp; thus thoughts and things
> In the self-haunting spirit learned to take
> More rational proportions; mystery,
> The incumbent mystery of sense and soul,
> Of life and death, time and eternity,
> Admitted more habitually a mild
> Interposition—a serene delight
> In closelier gathering cares. (XIV.282–90)

Wordsworth hints at yet another reason why Coleridge was so im-
portant. It was he who introduced Wordsworth to the *moral* impli-
cations of associationism. Or was it simply that one poet should find
another of his kind, and not be alone any more with his genius?
Coleridge, in any case, removed a burden of solitude, and taught

Wordsworth to associate less fearfully with "the life / Of all things and the mighty unity / In all which we behold, and feel, and are" (1805, XIII.253 ff.).

The Prelude tells us what lies behind fiction: the hope that the hopes of man can be wedded to this earth. Croce somewhere disdains this belief in what he terms "the marriage of mind and mud." Wordsworth's position is indeed so simple that it is tempting to make it more complex by stressing epistemological subtleties of object and subject. But his trust in Nature remains a trust in the human mind, which finds inexhaustible rewards in the world, and is renewed by natural rather than supernatural means. His poetry substitutes, therefore, the "produce of the common day" for sensationalism and supernaturalism, and his abiding bitterness at England's betrayal is due to the fact that it deprived many of his generation of this ordinary food of hope, that it forced them toward violent schemes and vain imaginings.

# 8.   1801-1807: The Major Lyrics

The years that followed the second edition of *Lyrical Ballads* were not immediately taken up by Wordsworth's 'poem on his own life,' but saw the appearance of many short and middle-sized lyrics. Coleridge, in fact, lamented that his friend should squander himself on occasional poetry: "Of nothing but 'The Recluse' can I hear patiently."[1] It was not till the beginning of 1804 that Wordsworth resumed his long poem with enough zest and vigor to complete it by June of the following year.

The lyrics composed between 1801 and 1807 were gathered in a collection called *Poems in Two Volumes* (1807). Here some of Wordsworth's most familiar pieces are found: poems on the Solitary Reaper, the Cuckoo, the Daisy, the Daffodils; 'ballads' on Alice Fell and the Sailor's Mother; the better-known sonnets, and such larger-scaled lyrics as "Resolution and Independence" and the Intimations Ode. It would be wrong to treat this collection as a natural unity. It is, as the title indicates, a composite volume written over a number of years and with no single aim. In this it differs from the *Lyrical Ballads*, many of which, composed in one fervid year, are consciously innovative. Yet the *Poems* of 1807 do have some distinguishing characteristics, and many of them were actually composed in a short period of time, the spring of 1802. I propose to consider individually, yet in the approximate order of their composition, several of the poems spanning the period between the 1800 *Lyrical Ballads* and the *Poems* of 1807, hoping to salvage some gradations that would be lost if the two collections were compared only generally.

## "Michael"

"Michael," the last poem to enter *Lyrical Ballads,* was finished in December 1800, and is one of Wordsworth's great poems of fortitude. It can set the tone for the group of lyrics on which our consideration will center: "Resolution and Independence" (1802), the Intimations Ode (1802–04), the "Ode to Duty" (1804) and the "Elegiac Stanzas . . . on Peele Castle" (1805 or 1806). "Michael" is somewhat of an anomaly, for it might have been as appropriate for *The Prelude* as for *Lyrical Ballads.* It is a 'ballad' in that it begins with a heap of stones with which no one but Wordsworth could have shaped a story, is unenriched by strange events, and intends to delight only a few "natural hearts." Forty lines of prologue apologize mildly for its "homely" and "rude" character. Yet the prologue also resembles those frames of authorial comment in *The Prelude* which allow episodes to point their own meaning yet link them thematically to the growth of a poet's mind. "Michael" may have been conceived as Wordsworth was thinking back to his youth and composing drafts for the poem on his own life. It supplements Book V of *The Prelude* and covers the time when children, though still careless of books, begin to develop their sympathetic imaginations by listening to tales like "Michael."

As in "The Thorn," Wordsworth opens in the person of a guide who leads us to a strangely inhuman place (a heap of stones) which his story humanizes. "The Thorn," of course, maintains a tension between inhuman and human significancies. Here the resolution is clearer. The stones are shown to have been the site of a covenant, the birthplace and grave of a human hope. When we have finished the story, they are no longer an accidental or indifferent part of nature, a "spot . . . shut out from man," but in a landscape where, had we but eyes to see, "All things . . . speak of Man."[2] That Wordsworth begins in the person of a guide is apt, for just as nature (or this tale) had originally guided and expanded his imagination, so he intends to lead *our* imaginations to an equal humanity of vision.

Though the story, once we come to it, is cleanly told, with the least intervention of the author, the poet begins by insisting that it is not an object made for its own sake. The story had a function in his life; it is this function he means to explain and perpetuate. He establishes, in fact, a strange identity between himself and his main character. Both Michael and Wordsworth wish to save the land, the one for Luke, the other for the imagination. Michael desires Luke to inherit a land "free as the wind / That passes over it"; and Wordsworth tells Michael's story for the sake of "youthful Poets, who *among these hills* / Will be my second self when I am gone." The underlying concern, conscious in Wordsworth as shepherd-poet, is for the human imagination, which cannot be renewed unless it has a nature to blend with, not any nature, but *land* as free and old as the hills:

> Those fields, those hills—what could they less? had laid
> Strong hold on his affections, were to him
> A pleasurable feeling of blind love,
> The pleasure which there is in life itself.[3]

Thus "Michael" is a Pastoral in the most genuine sense: its care of nature is also a care of the human (as distinguished from supernaturalistic) imagination. The urgency of its task is heightened by the spirit of the time. Industrialization is causing great changes, changes affecting also the minds of men; and Wordsworth, writing toward the beginning of this epoch, is not less than prophetic. The Industrial Revolution, in his eyes, is divorcing man from the earth as effectively as a debased supernaturalism. He sees that what is happening is indeed a revolution, cutting men off from their past, and their imagination from its normal food. The popularity of gothic novel and German ballad are only two examples of the "craving for extraordinary incident" and the frantic thirst for novelty which he decries in the 1800 Preface to *Lyrical Ballads*. He therefore begins his story with the simplest object imaginable, the most recalcitrant to a novelty-seeking mind. A truly great, unblunted imagination, Henry James said, is better served by the minimum of valid suggestion than by the maximum.

The care of nature is everywhere in "Michael," at the level of
property and the level of words:

> And when by Heaven's good grace the Boy grew up
> A healthy Lad, and carried in his cheek
> Two steady roses that were five years old;
> Then Michael from a winter coppice cut
> With his own hand a sapling, which he hooped
> With iron, making it throughout in all
> Due requisites a perfect Shepherd's Staff,
> And gave it to the Boy; wherewith equipt
> He as a Watchman oftentimes was plac'd
> At gate or gap, to stem or turn the flock;
> And, to his office prematurely called,
> There stood the Urchin, as you will divine,
> Something between a hindrance and a help;
> And for this cause not always, I believe,
> Receiving from his Father hire of praise.

The description of how Michael makes the boy a staff is Homeric
in its respect for weapon or implement; while the staff itself, given
at a certain age, is a mark of new or coming dignity, as well as a
necessary tool. That Michael cuts it with his own hand bespeaks
his direct relation to the lad, and is as significant as when he later
asks Luke to lay one stone of the sheepfold "with thine own hands."
Labor, or the products of labor, are not yet alienated from man as
they will be through the Industrial Revolution. The fold, again, is
no impersonal object but associates son and flock in the same way
as parental affection and love for the land are fused in Michael's
heart.[4] The "patrimonial fields" are made dearer by Luke's pres-
ence.

The chaste and natural diction of the narrative is standard; there
are greater passages in "Michael" but none falls below this in its
pastoral care for words. We find, of course, slight heightenings; a
kind of alliteration and doubling as in "gate or gap," "hindrance
and a help," "turn or stem"; but these are colloquial not latinate
in origin, and probably echo the old northern tradition of allit-

erative verse. In respecting them, Wordsworth continues a living idiom in touch with the past. He also diverges slightly from natural word order, just enough to give sinew to the line, and to postpone by the interposition of an adverbial phrase the object (sometimes the subject) of the verb. This serves to throw the emphasis steadily forward in a kind of self-qualifying conversational movement:

> And when by Heaven's grace the Boy grew up
> A healthy Lad,

and so we feel the mind still thinking, still alive, while it narrates. The interpositions, at the same time, by diminishing the transitive effect of the verbs (there is a considerable proportion of intransitive verbs and copulas in any Wordsworth passage), equalize the energy of the various parts of verse-line and sentence. Verbs are naturally strong, emphasizing action or event; but the poet works against this to build up the dignity of every phrase in a manner almost formulaic:

> He / as a Watchman / oftentimes / was plac'd
> At gate or gap, / to stem or turn / the flock.

But when we add to this muting of the 'verb active' that the plot of "Michael" is very slight—the focus is totally on the way Michael's feelings for his son are blended with his feelings for nature, and when Luke is sent to the city it is to keep the land free, and Luke's fall is treated as quietly as the Boy of Winander's death—a certain doubt may mingle with our admiration for the story. Does not Wordsworth give us a picture of suffering rather than of significant action, and does this not falsify his purpose of expanding the human imagination? The food of hope, as he himself remarks in a poem close to this time, is "meditated action,"[5] yet here there is an absence of action.

It is clear, however, that the story touches on a kind of loss and suffering which occurs in some form to everyone. The changes wrought by the Industrial Revolution are only the occasional cause for the disaster. The *universal* aspect of the loss suffered by Michael is of a hope which has attached itself to a person and seems to die with that person. Through Luke the old man's heart was born again; after Luke's defection, one wonders whether Michael can continue to live. It is then that Wordsworth shows in what way nature is essential to human actions and meditations. His picture of the old man is not simply of suffering or muted despair, but of natural resilience and the habit of fortitude. The inalienable sources of vigor in a man who has lived "in the strength of nature" are brought out: there is not a hint of the need for or even possibility of a specifically religious consolation. We feel, of course, how close to heartbreak the old man comes; we feel it in the absolute tact with which the poet begins to describe him after the disaster, when Wordsworth is like one who may not come near the quick of the grief, and approaches his subject by generalization and indirection:

> There is a comfort in the strength of love;
> 'Twill make a thing endurable, which else
> Would overset the brain, or break the heart:*
> I have conversed with more than one who well
> Remember the Old Man, and what he was
> Years after he had heard this heavy news.

Yet Michael does not break; he continues his habitual labors, still looks up to sun and cloud, listens to the wind, and will live "the length of full seven years."

Though we are told about the seven years in connection with Michael's unfinished labors at the sheepfold, there remains his persistence which suggests an immemorial covenant between man and the land. Michael does not hasten the end, and abides his time without abandoning the land even in imagination. Like the Old Cumberland Beggar he dies as he has lived: "in the eye of Nature." His patriarchal strength, his strange and lonely fidelity, make him the poem's center. Yet Michael is not an obsolete possibility of the human spirit: the covenant that holds the mind of man to the earth springs only from such as he. Abraham was not unlike Michael. He needed Isaac, his only child, the child of his old age, to perpetuate a similar fidelity. But the land cannot retain its hold on Luke's imagination. Can it, then, retain its hold through Wordsworth, who is restoring the covenant once more by wedding the mind of

---

* This line is quoted as it stands in 1820 and after.

man and this goodly earth? The poet is Michael's true heir. "I
look into past times," says Wordsworth in a related fragment, "as
prophets look into futurity."[6]

## "Resolution and Independence"

In February 1801, having sent Charles Lamb the new second
volume of *Lyrical Ballads*, and received Lamb's criticisms, Words-
worth dispatches a strong reply to his correspondent. It must have
been a pompous, not to say condescending letter, such as he could
write only too well. We know of it through Lamb's good-natured
report:

> I lately received from Wordsworth a copy of the second vol-
> ume . . . with excuses for not having made any acknowledg-
> ment (of my play) sooner, it being owing to an 'almost insur-
> mountable aversion to letter-writing.' This letter I answered
> in due form and time . . . adding unfortunately that no single
> piece had moved me so forcibly as the *Ancient Mariner, The
> Mad Mother*, or the *Lines at Tintern Abbey*. The Post did not
> sleep a moment. I received almost instantaneously a long let-
> ter of four sweating pages from my Reluctant Letter-Writer,
> the purport of which was, that he was sorry the 2nd vol. had
> not given me more pleasure (Devil a hint did I give that it
> had *not pleased me*), and 'was compelled to wish that my
> range of sensibility was more extended, being obliged to be-
> lieve that I should receive large influxes of happiness and
> happy Thoughts' (I suppose from the L. B.)—With a deal of
> stuff about a certain Union of Tenderness and Imagination,
> which in the sense he used Imagination was not the charac-
> teristic of Shakspeare, but which Milton possessed in a de-
> gree far exceeding other Poets: which Union, as the highest
> species of poetry, and chiefly deserving that name, 'He was
> most proud to aspire to.'[7]

What concerns us is mainly that "deal of stuff about a certain
Union of Tenderness and Imagination." Wordsworth uses some
such formula repeatedly after this time, often varying the specific
terms but always reflecting a distinction similar to that of "sublime"
and "pathetic." The formula can guide us in an approach to "Res-

olution and Independence," which was composed in May 1802, in the midst of a new surge of poetic activity equaled only by that of 1797–98. It is not difficult to translate Wordsworth's terms into those generally used in this book: the desired union is that of the supernatural and the naturalized (or sympathetic) imaginations. The covenant of mind and nature, the marriage of heaven and earth, center on the possibility of converting, yet not subduing, the one imagination to the other. The reason why Wordsworth ascribes that union to Milton rather than to Shakespeare is that he saw in Milton his own greatest predecessor, a religious poet who had succeeded in weaning his imagination from sublime and terrible without abandoning them. Shakespeare, however, was a "human and dramatic" rather than meditative and religious poet. The distinction is openly made in the preface to the *Poems* of 1815. "The grand store-houses," says Wordsworth, "of enthusiastic and meditative Imagination, of poetical, as contra-distinguished from human and dramatic Imagination, are the prophetic and lyrical parts of the Holy Scriptures, and the works of Milton; to which I cannot forebear to add those of Spenser."[8]

Now it is actually Spenser who is more helpful than Milton in clarifying the mode of "Resolution and Independence." Its basic situation is Spenser modified. The poet walks out into the country on a beautiful day; he is depressed (in Wordsworth's case depression has given way to joy only to turn back into depression) and comes upon a mysterious sight which restores him. This is the very scheme of Spenser's *Prothalamion;* though what is important here is not the *Prothalamion* but what Spenser has done with the type it represents.[9] Behind Spenser's mode there lies the dream-vision converted so calmly yet daringly into a waking vision that dream blends with reality and an autonomous product is created which we rather helplessly define as "allegory." Spenser walking along the Thames near London's bricky towers is no dreamer, unless we adduce Goethe's definition of the poet as one who dreams with open eyes. For without any "methought I saw" he views in open sight a marriage procession in which the bridesmaids are water-nymphs:

> All lovely daughters of the flood thereby
> With goodly greenish locks all loose untyde,

and the brides-to-be are swans floating down the Thames as fair and white as Leda. This is a direct exercise of the mythopoeic imagination in the context of a realistic scene, and no facile retranslation of the swans into the barges that carried the Lady Elizabeth and the Lady Katherine Somerset can undo the metamorphosis. It is Spenser's courage we admire, his passing from personal cares at court to a magnificence which redeems the courtly life, but which stands or falls with his unashamed direct exercise of the poetical faculty. Behind this faculty, however, here so personally exerted, is the "prothalamic" imagination in general, which brings together not only man and woman, but also myth and reality, human and divine, nature and human nature.

This 'union' is also achieved by "Resolution and Independence" in very different circumstances. On the deserted moor, a man appears to Wordsworth "unawares," and the sight is ghostly enough to make him suspect a divine apparition. Yet though he tends toward apocalyptic thoughts (see above, pp. 202–03), a precarious intermingling of vision and matter-of-fact is all the while maintained. Wordsworth's mode differs, of course, from that established by Spenser's fiat. It is not even a mode, strictly speaking, but an uncertain consolidation of thoughts. Spenser's refrain, for example, "Sweet Themmes, runne softly, till I end my song," is the very emblem of literary and natural continuity, and indicates by its steady return how much time is at man's disposal, how everything will flow along in order and degree, and how the world is too well established on the flood for any "end" to be feared. But Wordsworth's greatest lyrics are acts of a living mind open to the terror of discontinuity. His encounter with the Leech-gatherer is unrelieved by myth or allegory or any steadying indulgence. The waters do not flow easily; the strange repetitions (sts. xvii ff.) have no aim that is not mental and precarious; and the continuity, even on the level of rhythm (that last, draggle-tailed alexandrine), is uncertain. We feel the poet's distraught perplexity, as if this could not be, or could not last.

How open Wordsworth's mind is in "Resolution and Independence," how receptive to new thought even during composition, can be shown more specifically. Though he begins with an emotion recollected in tranquillity, the tranquillity soon disappears and his mind not only recalls the past but also responds once more to what it has recalled. The past event is not so totally in the past, not so determinate, that it cannot confront the poet in a new way. This new and further confrontation must then be honored in addition to the old. There is the question of the poet's original recognition, and then of his insight as he tells, so to say, his story back to himself. The two do not coincide in all respects.

Wordsworth's earlier and formal recognition is found in the concluding stanzas of the poem and is expressed in part as an absorbing mental echo (st. xvi) and image (st. xix). I quote the latter:

> While he was talking thus, the lonely place,
> The old Man's shape, and speech, all troubled me:
> In my mind's eye I seem'd to see him pace
> About the weary moors continually,
> Wandering about alone and silently.
> While I these thoughts within myself pursued,
> He, having made a pause, the same discourse renewed.

An *after-image* of this kind plays an important role in many of Wordsworth's poems. It expresses the possibility of the renewal (or at least recurrence) of a certain experience by including that possibility in the very structure of the experience. As a mental reflex, the after-image elongates the encounter, and as an image *of* something, it may also suggest an indefinitely extended action. Not any action, of course: it is the image, itself repeated, of a repeated and persistent action which moves the Leech-gatherer closer to the figure of the Wandering Jew and brings about Wordsworth's recognition of his firmness.

The after-image or echo may occur at a distance from the original experience, and still be part of it. If in "The Solitary Reaper" the inward echo follows immediately on the actual hearing of the girl's song, in "I wandered lonely as a cloud" the daffodils flash in the mind some time after the poet has seen them. The lapse of time seems to be a relatively unimportant factor, since Wordsworth's point is that the renewal of the image—or of the inner person through the image—occurs despite time. The overcoming of time can be shown by either a delayed or an immediate response. When Wordsworth says of the cuckoo, hailing its return, "I have heard, / I hear thee and rejoice," the doubling (reflecting) is immediate. Yet since in listening to its call the poet *begets again* the golden time of his youth (st. VII), the simple repetition of "hear" together with the tense change from past to present, indicates in one formula his inward response, and the renewal of the past in the present—in short, the gentle and immediately renovating influence of nature.

The after-image could be defined as a re-cognition that leads to recognition. It is found as early as "The Ruined Cottage," in which the poet describes the echoes left in him by the pedlar's story.[10] The *Lyrical Ballads* also show the poet or his personae responding to the very incidents they describe, yet no such *formalized* structure of recognition appears. Only one lyric before 1802 depicts the after-image as a formal part of the structure of experience,* yet does this so well that chronology seems unimportant. "The Two April Mornings," in which again an old and a young man meet, is totally conceived in terms of a contrast between recurrence in nature and recurrent powers of feeling. An April dawn brings back the memory of another April dawn thirty years ago, when Matthew met a girl resembling his dead daughter yet "did not wish her mine." The poem, like "Tintern Abbey," is realistic (compared to the lighter lyrics) in its acknowledgment of time, for it seems to indicate a limit to nature's renovating influence. But it ends with a beautiful reflective doubling similar to that which concludes Wordsworth's meeting with the Leech-gatherer:

> Matthew is in his grave, yet now,
> Methinks I see him stand,
> As at that moment, with his bough
> Of wilding in his hand.

* "Tintern Abbey," however, assumes that nature persists in the mind through after-images or deeply blended feelings. It is just possible, moreover, that the second stanza of "A slumber did my spirit seal" is an after-image. As in the optical phenomenon, to which I owe the term, the image is not merely a repetition but also a complement, and both these characteristics are present in the transformed yet symmetrical quality of the second stanza image.

I come, then, to the second kind of insight, in which the mind
moves under the renewed (recollected) rather than original im-
pact of an experience.[11] Though the after-image is often delayed,
and so approaches the second kind of recognition, some distinc-
tions can be made. The second kind of recognition is based on an
experience to which the mind has already formally reacted. More-
over, while this initial reaction (an after-image) helps to dissolve
the finiteness of the experience, the renewed recognition is more
complex, and suggests both its continuity with the after-image
(thus increasing the sense of infinite repercussion) and a possible
discontinuity. The second type of recognition is, in fact, an un-
predictably organic movement of the poet's mind in the very mo-
ment of recollection, yet Wordsworth allows it to enter into the
experience he is remembering. Before an event which includes his
first insight has been fully described, a second insight forestalls
and even transcends it. The most dramatic instance of such dis-
placement is *Prelude* VI.592 ff., and in "Resolution and Independ-
ence" we find a similar, though less dramatic re-vision:

> There was a roaring in the wind all night;
> The rain came heavily and fell in floods;
> But now the sun is rising calm and bright;
> The birds are singing in the distant woods;
> Over his own sweet voice the Stock-dove broods;
> The Jay makes answer as the Magpie chatters;
> And all the air is fill'd with pleasant noise of waters.
>
> All things that love the sun are out of doors;
> The sky rejoices in the morning's birth;
> The grass is bright with rain-drops; on the moors
> The hare is running races in her mirth;
> And with her feet she from the plashy earth
> Raises a mist; that, glittering in the sun,
> Runs with her all the way, wherever she doth run.
>
> I was a Traveller then upon the moor;
> I saw the hare that rac'd about with joy;
> I heard the woods, and distant waters, roar;
> Or heard them not, as happy as a Boy:

The pleasant season did my heart employ:
My old remembrances went from me wholly;
And all the ways of men, so vain and melancholy.

In line 3 the poet crosses spontaneously from the past tense to the present and does not return to the past till stanza III, "I was a Traveller then upon the moor." His mind, rejoicing in the beautiful dawn like birds, sky and hare, seems to have imperceptibly entered its own conception.[12] This crossing over, from past to present, happens during composition, and shows that time itself can still dissolve at the touch and even the mere memory of nature.

Yet in the original incident the poet's extreme joy was followed by a reversal: "As high as we have mounted in delight / In our dejection do we sink as low" (st. IV). Knowing this, Wordsworth cannot entirely liberate himself from the fear of a reversal even in the moment of recollection. If he passes with line 3 beyond mutability, for his mind can still dissolve time, or the barriers between past and present, his verses continue to reflect a slight hemming which is expressed by the repeatedly end-stopped (semicolon) lines. In stanza II, with the picture of the hare, the mood overflows and is close to breaking down the end-stopped line; but it is still restrained by residual stops and a certain syntactical heaviness. In stanza III, then, the semicolons return (they lessen in frequency but continue to dominate the rhythm till stanza VIII); the past tense is reinstated; and we sense—fully now—the burdened mind, as it revolves heavy thoughts and anticipates the reversal of which it eventually speaks. When the present tense returns momentarily in stanza V ("Even such a happy Child of earth am I . . .") it does not betoken a spontaneous transcendence of time but reports the speech of a man vainly reasoning with himself.

"Resolution and Independence" is the most characteristic of Wordsworth's greater lyrics because of this openness of mind which makes it in mode what it is in subject: a self-confrontation. Though it is proper to refer to the *Prothalamion* as the nearest literary model, Wordsworth restores the archaic situation from which both his and Spenser's poem derive. Behind the dream-sight is the prophetic situation, the "chance" omen sent against a man whether or not he can interpret it. The uncertainties of interpretation in Wordsworth's case are remarkable; I can only repeat that though a steadying recognition is gained from his meeting with the Leech-gatherer—an open meeting indeed, beside a pool "bare to the eye of heaven," and radically Protestant in its sense that nothing stands between man and man except God—the possibility of reversal, of recognition turning into peripety, is never absent. It can be urged that the poem's high point comes not at the end but at the beginning, when the heart *is* renewed toward nature and enters the recollected image.

### The Intimations Ode

Once more, to the poet of the Intimations Ode, a thought of grief comes on a fine spring morning. And, again as in "Resolution and Independence," instead of saying immediately it was this or that which grieved him, Wordsworth goes on to think aloud, as if thinking and grief had now an intimate link, and the one would always issue, at some point, in the other. This time, however, the recognition that restores him is elusive. There is no Leech-gatherer: it is all a dialogue of the soul with itself in the presence of nature. The joy must spring from deep within thought; the consolation perhaps from the very grief he feels. We sense the constant possibility of reversal even more than in "Resolution and Independence."

The irregular rhythms, a privilege of the ode form, work independently of specific stanza or stage of argument to express the flux and reflux of a mind for which reversal is no longer simply the structure of experience but its own structure, its very *style* of thought. Wordsworth does mention in the third stanza a "timely utterance" which gave him relief, but what happened is kept vague, and the event, in any case, could not have been determining, since the grief returns in the next stanza. There is, finally, again encouraged by the ode (the sublimest of the lyric genres), a larger pattern of flux and reflux: even though each stanza tends to mingle rising and falling rhythms, stanzas III and IV are, as it were, a "Counter-turn" to stanzas I and II, while stanza V is a kind of epode or "stand" in which the passion seems to level out into a new generalization or withdrawal from personal immediacy.[13] Related to this larger pattern is the Ode's admixture of reflection, question, invocation, petition, and praise, which approaches the Psalms in sublimity, and also recalls the confessional style of St. Augustine.

The subject of the Ode, Lionel Trilling has said, is growing up. Yet though it is true that the subject is conceived, except for the organizing myth, in naturalistic terms, Wordsworth's high style and the religious intensity of his emotions must be considered. There is a Hebrew prayer which praises God's mercy in restoring the soul every morning to its body, even as He restores it to the dead. Some of the terror of discontinuity behind the gratitude of this prayer is also in Wordsworth's Ode. The poet fears a decay of his "genial" responses to nature, and he fears that this decay has affected his powers of renovation. Growing up is not enough; the development of abstract sympathies is not enough; these must be linked, else they cannot be actualized, to the renewal of earlier feelings, to *joy* in nature.[14] It is easy to gain the world and to lose one's soul.

This deeper concern with renewal explains why Wordsworth is so affected by what appears to be a very little thing: a wrong echo. On this May morning, his heart responds with a thought of grief instead of equal gaiety. All other creatures have the proper harmonic echo, the immediate internal response to nature's influence. The young lambs bound "As to the tabor's sound"—there is no tabor, but Wordsworth sees their joy as a responsive joy. He calls them and the other participants in nature's jubilee "blessed Creatures": "And God created . . . every living creature that moveth . . . and God saw that it was good. And God blessed them, saying, Be fruitful and multiply." God responded to them, God *recognized* them, but the poet's heart is dull. We remember the opening of "Resolution and Independence," where everything echoes and responds: the Jay to the Magpie, the Stockdove to its own call, and even the glittering mist to the hare wherever the latter runs.

That Wordsworth should take a momentary grief as an omen

questioning his power to be renewed, to be 'naturally' renewed, is typical of his spiritual state at this time. *The Prelude* also begins with a failed response (overcome more lightly), and the fear that his "genial spirits" might be decaying was already quietly expressed in the meditations of "Tintern Abbey." We have to do with a recurrent, not an unusual, fear. The Ode, in fact, begins with a general statement, and only then proceeds to mention the particular moment which perhaps was the occasion of that generality.[15] Each failure of joy, each feeling of indifference or alienation, newly accuses the poet. Much later in his life, when he seems to be more resigned to what he here still resists, and an "Evening of Extraordinary Splendour" surprises him, he will querulously demand: "This glimpse of glory, why renewed?"[16] But in the Ode he rises to an answering vigor of imagination.

There is first the "timely utterance" which frees him for other utterances:

> The Cataracts blow their trumpets from the steep,
> No more shall grief of mine the season wrong.

The second verse is surely the inner call by which, in this restored continuum of inner and outer events, he replies to the cataracts. It is followed by a movement like the Psalmist's "Awake the dawn," when he accepts the fact that the initiative is with him, and indicates his readiness to join "in thought" what others may still feel at heart. "Thou Child of Joy / Shout round me, let me hear thy shouts . . ." "Then, sing ye Birds, sing, sing a joyous song." There are, finally, those "intimations of immortality" which remind him of actual continuities and permanent points of relation with the Nature he has known.

These affirmative movements are interrupted, of course, by renewed questionings and qualifications (extending even into imagery and rhythm), so that the continuity of the Ode is as precarious as the "natural piety" which is its subject. But though this precariousness is just—the Ode is prayer as well as celebration—one contradiction seems not to have been expressed clearly enough by Wordsworth, which may perhaps explain why so many have felt the Ode to be confused, or not completely unified. There are, if we look closely, two quite different "intimations of immortality." Whereas one implies the mortality of nature:

> questionings
> Of sense and outward things,
> Fallings from us, vanishings;
> Blank misgivings of a Creature
> Moving about in worlds not realiz'd . . .

the other implies its immortality:

> the primal sympathy
> Which having been must ever be.

In stanza ix especially, when Wordsworth says that his thanksgivings are less for the visionary gleam than for the visionary dreariness, and goes on to describe the latter as:

> those first affections,
> Those shadowy recollections,
> Which, be they what they may,
> Are yet the fountain light of all our day,
> Are yet a master light of all our seeing;

it is hard to follow him. He seems to be willfully confusing moments of darkness and fear in which nature seemed alien to the child with moments of splendor and beauty which first developed the child's affections and drew them to nature in a more intimate way.

The confusion is willful, I think, and may be resolved; but not by the Ode alone. It needs an understanding of Wordsworth's conception of the progress of the soul. Wordsworth shares with St. Augustine the knowledge of a personal mercy which is part of a mercy to mankind. Both have been rescued 'unto life'; but life for Wordsworth is the freeing of his soul from solipsism. Before the child is naturalized, and sporadically at later times, its soul moves in another world than "nature," or if in nature, then one that is colored by a sublime and terrible imagination. The soul's eventual turning to nature is therefore a real conversion, and proof of self-transcending powers. Man's growth into humanity is founded on this conversion. A child is an "Alien scatter'd from the Clouds," but the strength which its imagination exhibits in going out of itself and blending with a lesser nature is the source of all further strength: it is for Wordsworth *the* act of re-generation.* Every step in growing up is but an extension of this constitutive sympathy. The mature man, therefore, bases his faith in self-transcendence on the ease or unconsciousness with which the apocalyptic imagination turned in childhood toward life. Then the crisis was to go from self-love (unconscious) to love of nature, and now it is to go from self-love (conscious) to love of man. Each transition is precarious; but the second cannot occur without the first, and the first is the sign that the second is possible. "The Child is the father of the Man."

By the time the poet understands nature's role, only intimations of his unself-conscious powers of relationship remain. The nature to which he appeals in his great envoi:

> And oh ye Fountains, Meadows, Hills, and Groves,
> Think not of any severing of our loves!

is dying to him; and the perilous progress of the Ode comes from Wordsworth's resistance to this appearance of death. I say "appearance," because, were nature really lost to him, the excursive or self-renewing vigor of his soul might be impugned. Wordsworth cannot give up nature without giving up his faith in renovation. The whole issue turns on faith and hope.

## "Ode to Duty"

The "Ode to Duty" is more in need of interpretation than the other poems so far considered. This is not only because it has failed to attract devoted attention, but also for an intrinsic reason. Wordsworth is speaking in the Ode in his "character of philosophical

---

* The ancient Natura, as in the fertile Chaos of Spenser's Garden of Adonis (*Faerie Queene*, Bk. III, canto VI), clothes the soul with a "first being" sufficient to let it enter the changeable world. But Wordsworth's Nature gives the soul its "second being," which is more essential insofar as it lays the ground for all further second being or rebirth.

poet";[17] and our immediate difficulty with it stems from a diction of generality, not to say vagueness, which its "philosophical" character seems to have imposed. What identity, first of all, do we give the Duty to which Wordsworth desires to submit? It cannot be only conscience, since he says approvingly that it is in the quietness of thought he supplicates, undisturbed in soul or by compunction. Nor can it be only obedience to the dictate of positive or divine law, even though the Miltonic personification which opens the Ode, and the description of Duty as lawgiver in the first and seventh stanzas, must be considered. But this (the sterner demand) is at once qualified:

> Stern Daughter of the Voice of God!
> O Duty! if that name thou love . . .

> Stern Lawgiver! yet thou dost wear
> The Godhead's most benignant grace . . .

Wordsworth, no doubt, is asking for a guide stricter than conscience or consciousness; even the regular form of the Ode, Horatian rather than pseudo-Pindaric, indicates his wish to escape the eternal flux of the inner life. Yet the chief emotion expressed by him, and expressed movingly, is for a *self-devoted* dedication,[18] and this eliminates the possibility that Duty's compulsion could stem from authority or the dictate of external law. Duty is "stern" only in the sense that she is, or could be, a "great Task-master"* for Wordsworth.

This leaves us with the rather simple idea that Duty is conscientiousness: due attention to the world and its cares. As Wordsworth will say many years later: "The education of man, and above all of a Christian, is the education of *duty*, which is most forcibly taught by the business and concerns of life."[19] This meaning of Duty at first escapes us because the poet's style of address is so high. Yet his elevated style has surely the same intent as certain stanzas to the daisy, also in the 1807 volume, although these are more playful.[20] Just as he exalts the humble daisy, he here dignifies the

---

* See Milton's sonnet "How soon hath Time," and cf. "Ode to Duty," st. IV: "I shov'd unwelcome tasks away."

simple duties imposed by life, or those "lowliest duties" which his heart, like Milton's, accepts to lay upon itself.[21] It is, most probably, the image of Milton in Wordsworth's mind, rather than an abstract ethics, which determined his conception of Duty. The Milton referred to is the poet of the great political and personal sonnets as well as the visionary of *Paradise Lost*. Between 1802 and 1804 Wordsworth wrote a volley of sonnets, many of them "Dedicated to Liberty" and mingling the personal and the prophetic strains. We know that the first impulse to these was given by a rereading of Milton in May 1802: previously Wordsworth had eschewed the sonnet form. We remember also what the poet had written to Lamb in 1801, about Milton and the "Union of Tenderness and Imagination." Milton's sonnets were confirmatory evidence of a great spirit, of a visionary spirit, submitting his imagination to daily and historical event. Here was a man whose soul dwelt apart like a star, yet with an ideal of service that informed both poetry and life. This ideal was maintained despite blindness and despite adversity. The presence of Milton in the "Ode to Duty" is confirmed by its allusions to his writings. There is the opening line, there is a direct quotation from a prose tract in the sixth stanza, and in the last a patent echo of Raphael's warning that Adam should keep his imagination on earth and cultivate his garden: "Be lowly wise; / Think only what concerns thee and thy being."

In "Resolution and Independence," whose title, in relation to the Ode, speaks for itself, Wordsworth had already broached the subject of Duty in this sense of planning, sowing, building, loving. They are, strangely enough, selfish cares, which arise when our unconscious faith in nature diminishes, and we realize to what extent our futures and those of the "kind" depend on the individual person. To this point Wordsworth had come in 1802, with or without Milton; and in the Ode of 1804 the same problem is once more resumed. Stanzas II and III acknowledge that there are those who continue to rely on the "genial sense of youth" (they are still deified by their own spirits), but that Wordsworth himself, and perhaps everyone at some time, needs the additional security of a self-determined rather than instinctive involvement in the things of this world. The Ode's true subject is, once again, the humanization of the spirit.

Like Collins in "To Manners" or Gray in "To Adversity" (Wordsworth acknowledges the latter as his pattern) the poet goes out to meet the inevitable, accepts the necessity for transcending a previous mode of being, and calls up his calling. There is strength in this attitude, but also the pathos that a man should come to need a bond stronger than nature to keep his spirit with nature. The "empty terrors" and "vain temptations" which the first stanza mentions abstractly are those of the autonomous imagination: they are apocalyptic fears and gratuitous desires. The poet's later confession, "Me this uncharter'd freedom tires; / I feel the weight of chance desires;" reveals more cogently the personal circumstance, but is no clearer. Wordsworth expects the reader to infer the particular experience from the generalizing (or biblical) expressions, which is good Neoclassical procedure: in this Wordsworth *has* changed. He no longer conveys the impression of speaking "from the depth of untaught things" but deals out what everyone should know, perhaps too well.

The bond stronger than nature Wordsworth calls duty and also reason. It is by no means opposed to nature but supports nature's earlier agency. Explicitly discussing in his *Answer to Mathetes* (1809) the stage of life in which youth passes into manhood, he admits that the "sacred light of childhood" cannot be more than a remembrance to the maturing man. He then continues in a passage of unusual clarity: "He [the youth] may, notwithstanding, be remanded to nature, and with trustworthy hopes, founded less upon his sentient than upon his intellectual being; to nature, as leading back insensibly to the society of reason, but to reason and will, as leading back to the wisdom of nature. A re-union, in this order accomplished, will bring reformation and timely support; and the two powers of reason and nature, thus reciprocally teacher and taught, may advance together in a track to which there is no limit."[22] Reason, here, is not a radically new source of strength—not discontinuous with the older faith in nature—but it does involve a methodic or ceremonial *prise de conscience;* and it is this which the "Ode to Duty" exhibits. The Ode moves us, if at all, by its dignified self-consciousness, by the invented ceremonial of the self giving the self away, and to a power it has called for that purpose: "I call thee: I myself commend . . . thy Bondman let me live!" Byron's Manfred will not better this tone, although he resists all the powers he summons.

Thus Wordsworth's "awful Power" of Duty is simply the inner strength of voluntarily dedicating oneself to the household bonds of life. Take away the idea of voluntary obedience, substitute for it a decision to rely on external authority, and you make nonsense of Wordsworth as you do of Milton. In Psalm 19, which moves structurally from the glory of nature to the light of "the law," both testimonies are praised because they renew the heart: "The law of the Lord is perfect, converting the soul: the testimony of the Lord is sure, making wise the simple." The emphasis remains on the inner man. Wordsworth remembered another verse of Psalm 19 in his beautiful lines on Duty in the seventh stanza:

Thou dost preserve the Stars from wrong;
And the most ancient Heavens through Thee are fresh and strong.

Compare the Psalmist's description of the sun as a "bridegroom coming out of his chamber, and [who] rejoiceth as a strong man to run his race." The stars too are preserved and the heavens renewed by the virtue of voluntary obedience. Even if such lines, as Wordsworth admitted, transfer "in the transport of imagination, the law of moral to physical natures,"[23] this does not dispute the truth they suggest but indicates the changed mode of its venue, which is no longer as if directly from nature but from nature via the resolved or meditative soul. Yet the weakness of the Ode remains: the style in which it talks about Duty makes us suspect a virtue that does not arise from human nature, or which transcends it.

I should not be understood to say that there is no change in Wordsworth between 1798 and 1804, between:

Some silent laws our hearts may make,
Which they shall long obey;[24]

and his address to the "Stern Lawgiver." The only question is what kind of change there is. In 1804, obviously, it is not the heart alone which makes these laws, and they are by no means silently made.

But the views held respectively in 1798 and 1804 are still reconcilable, for laws are made in both cases (resolutions might be a preciser word) and they are made freely by the person unto himself. That they are "silent" in one case and rather vocal in the other ("Stern Daughter of the Voice of God . . .") is to be explained by the greater need in 1804 of a formal act of will, since nature, though disclosing to man his powers for relationship, binds only to herself, whereas Wordsworth is now concerned with a formal self-surrender "to labours by which his livelihood is to be earned or his social duties performed." Still, in both cases, the "act of obedience [is] to a moral law established by himself."[25]

Where then is the change? Primarily in the style, where it appears to be. Let us characterize that style more closely on the basis of the two Odes. It has already been said that there is a certain vague or perhaps "philosophical" generality in some of Wordsworth's expressions, and which might be attributed to his subject or to the genre of the Sublime Ode.[26] The heightening, actually, is due to the genre which is consciously chosen to revalue the subject: childhood and practical duties are not traditional themes for elevated treatment. Unfortunately, when Wordsworth calls Duty a "Stern Lawgiver," the serious parody can be overlooked: only a close and puzzled reading shows that he means his determination to take common household duties as seriously as if they were indeed divine law. The ordinary reader of 1807 (and of today) would surely think that the Duty referred to is a 'sublime' personification of the moral law as it expresses itself in outward code or inward conscience. And it is quite possible that in his desire for a greater affiliation with the poets of the past or with the present public formed by them, Wordsworth slipped into a conflation of an original thought and the traditional perspective from which he wanted only the style.

Symptoms of a generalizing diction already appear in the Intimations Ode. The phrase "timely utterance" has confuted a generation of interpreters. Why did the poet not specify of what nature, other than timely, the utterance was? He is keeping the experience at a certain level of generality. He does not specify, for the same reason, the content of the "thought of grief." Though he begins his Ode with a specific sentiment, it is still expressed in very general terms, and we learn nothing about the conditions in which it arose except that the season was spring. It happens that "timely utterance" is a well-chosen phrase, for it emphasizes the restoration of a natural cycle, and the whole vital necessity of being drawn out of oneself. Yet like many other expressions it skirts vagueness. "Fields of sleep" is another difficulty in the same stanza: what does it stand for? The West? The west wind that awakens nature yet recalls the region nearest the setting sun? A mingling of the themes of birth and death would not be inappropriate, but again one is uncertain as to whether the phrase has real mystery or is a periphrasis avoiding a more specific term.

The change of style, then, is due to a poet consciously fashioning his own diction of generality. If it is asked why Wordsworth modifies his style in this way, and runs the risk of falling back into Poetic Diction, the answer is that he thinks of himself as entering a new stage of life, in which his mission is to propagate his knowledge, and draw closer to his kind. There is no change of heart, but there is a self-conscious attempt to assume that *his* truths are also *general* truths, or will be accepted as such in time, so that certain intimate features of his experience should not obtrude. His mission is to reveal the multifariousness and curious depth of that which binds man to man and man to nature, and not that which separates them. "In spite of difference of soil and climate, of language and manners, of laws and customs; in spite of things silently gone out of mind; and things violently destroyed; the poet binds together by passion and knowledge the vast empire of human society, as it is spread over the earth, and over all time."[27] Wordsworth, in beginning to look on his thoughts as representative, tends to confuse, as Coleridge remarked, self-established convictions with generally accepted truths.[28] This, ironically enough, would be an evasion of self-consciousness in the very poem that ceremonially affirms the self in order to limit it.

### *"Peele Castle"*

When we read in Wordsworth's poem on his brother's death, "A deep distress hath humaniz'd my Soul," and remember what he had said in a less personal but hardly less tragic context, "By our own spirits are we deified," the question arises again what his attitude is toward this relentless humanizing of imagination. And although the man who speaks to us is standing on lowly ground, conscious of his solitary and individual state, we are reminded of a vaster and truly epic theme, which his destiny as a whole presents. For here is Adam given his sights of death, or Gilgamesh confronted with his mortality. It is the same perplexed or rebellious or finally consenting response.

"Peele Castle" not only urges the poet's consent to mortality but seems already to confirm it. Wordsworth admits, speaking now in his own person, radical loss and absolute change: "A power is gone, which nothing can restore." For the first time also he does not talk of recompense until the last line, which in its brevity and isolation is like the inscription on a tomb. If in the "Ode to Duty" he still deifies his own spirit in the very act of voluntary submission, here the blow has fallen and has made what he thought a sacrifice an irreversible doom.

Yet the energy with which Wordsworth accepts loss, his direct unequivocal affirmation of it—there are no mixed rhythms, no qualifications as in the Intimations Ode—and his conscious sympathy with the pictured storm, amount to almost an *amor fati* and reveal how much of power is left. We are obliged to ask what has been lost (he says "*a* power") and what it is that remains so clear and unimpregnable in him. I think the answer to the first part of that question is definitely not his faith in nature. It is quite true that nature led him on, to a conception that proved false; but it is clearly his own soul which betrayed him through the "fond delusion" that nature is more than it can be. A distinction between the roles played respectively by nature and the soul in this betrayal may seem niggling, but the contrast is, after all, between a past and a present *conception* (picture). While the first few stanzas describe nature directly, the next five mention the picturing response of a mind that would have added *its* light ("the light that never was")[29] to nature and so perpetuated an experience in trust and hope. Although the heart goes *with* nature in this perpetuation (it extends the image from day to eternity instead of from day to day) it also goes *beyond* nature in its desire for steadfastness. By changing to the conditional mood when the mental representation is described ("Ah! THEN, if mine had been the Painter's hand . . ."), Wordsworth tells us quite precisely what is lost: this kind of potentiality, this capacity for generous error and noble illusion, which made life correspond to the heart's desire. The sea from now on could smile and smile and still be thought a villain. True steadfastness is only in "fortitude, and patient chear."

"Peele Castle," therefore, repeats in an open and personal way the thought of radical loss haunting the Lucy and Matthew Poems. It is not epochal in Wordsworth's growth except in the manner of a grammatical period: the delusion, like a sentence, has run its course, and must be formally concluded. The last part of the poem, beginning with the address to Beaumont and ending with the "Farewell" and "Welcome" (faint echoes of Collins), ritually signals the poet's entry into a new mode of life. But if the implication of these imperatives is different from those addressed to Dorothy at the end of "Tintern Abbey" ("Therefore let the moon / Shine on thee in thy solitary walk; / And let the misty mountain winds be free / To blow against thee") their mood is comparable. Both evoke the 'meeting soul' which goes out to whatever demand realizes it.

This also partially answers the question what in Wordsworth resists and is clarified by loss. In terms of the two contrasting states of mind and the image dominating each, the answer is simple: the rugged castle resists, the "dread watch-tower of man's absolute self," in Coleridge's memorable phrase.[30] That a more lucid self-consciousness has been attained is suggested by the unusual progression, in the poem, from milder to sterner nature, as well as by the very structure of the poem. The structure of "Peele Castle," with one significant difference presently to be mentioned, is that of 'X' revisited: the poet confronts a previous stage of life and comes to a new consciousness of human destiny.

The character of this consciousness is brought out on comparing "Peele Castle" and "Tintern Abbey." Both look back (revisit) approximately the same stage of life but from a vantage point differing by seven years. Since the experience reviewed is almost identical, we can measure the difference in the poet who reviews it. The summer of 1793 (revisited in "Tintern Abbey") and that of 1794 ("Peele Castle") were equally important for the recovery of Wordsworth's faith in nature or natural process. His description of Peele Castle stresses the continuity of day with day and of each thing with its neighbor:

> So pure the sky, so quiet was the air!
> So like, so very like, was day to day!
> Whene'er I look'd, thy Image still was there;
> It trembled, but it never pass'd away.

It is all a balm shed on the wounds of time. And, by "Tintern Abbey," Wordsworth's faith in natural continuity has become so strong that he can already associate loss with humanization (he hears "The still, sad music of humanity"). His sensibility is being transformed, not radically weakened. He believes, moreover, that his former self may be revived or continued by his sister. The long coda in which he expresses this belief owes something to Coleridge's habit of accepting separation from joy as long as he can think of participating in the joy of other persons.[31]

But with John's death in 1805 that imaginative kind of hope becomes too painful. The poet in fact concenters himself against the temptation of hope. He does not even return, in "Peele Castle," to the original site: he accepts his loss and is not tempted to try his soul. "Not for a moment could I now behold / A smiling sea and be what I have been." This modification in the structure of the poem of revisit indicates that an irreversible stage has been attained. There is no nostalgia for a previous mode of being except in the last, lingering "Farewell," and in the elegiac return of certain sounds and words. Wordsworth's new strength is in not dallying with the hope that his soul may revive once more toward the past. He faces only to future in the assured consciousness that, if he cannot bear the divine glimpses which the past offers, he can sustain the human sorrows to come.[32]

"Peele Castle" itself shows no diminution of imaginative vigor. Like Milton's Nativity Ode, it is an envoi which displays what may be forfeit and takes from it a dying splendor. An eloquent modulation of tenses moves us through the past and a response to nature then possible, to the present which kills this possibility, and finally to Beaumont's picture which allows a new, though intellectually prompted, empathy. There is, in other words, not only a generous constatation of what was and could have been, but also a demonstration of the resolute mind in the act of embracing what is and will be. Nothing is denied by the poet: a lost magnanimity is fully acknowledged, and a present imagination given a new image to enjoy.

Yet Wordsworth's implied program is perilously close to renouncing everything that could engage the imagination. First, the challenge of past modes of being. Next, the possibility of surmise itself, especially concerning a sympathetic nature, one that participates in the growth and destiny of the human soul. Wordsworth does not deny the notion, here or elsewhere; but he is even more cautious about it than Milton, who used it in "Lycidas" to provide a frail if imaginative moment of comfort. Perhaps he is afraid of returning to the "spot" in his mind that still wounds him, the drowning of his brother, its irreversibility, and the feeble wishfulness of every notion of supernatural-natural sympathy. This should not have affected all imaginings, but it does. Every self-transcending hope or fancy turns back into a pang of loss. "O do not Thou too fondly brood," he writes in further elegiac verses on his brother, "On any earthly hope, however pure!"[33] This lesson he will urge in *The Excursion*, where excessive hope is revealed as a form of violence against nature, a form of the apocalyptic imagination.

There is a final restraint to be mentioned. Whereas Milton, after enjoying the surmise of nature's sympathy, spurns it for a transcendent consolation, which is Lycidas' redemption, Wordsworth will not engage imaginatively even in that. A poetry of statement —"Not without hope we suffer and we mourn"—is the most he will allow. His letters after John's death do show him turning toward the idea of another world,[34] but in "Peele Castle" the consolation is purely human. If he has religious thoughts (I have just quoted the only verse which tends that way) he does not tap them; he is yet strong enough in himself. There may come a time for them, but it has not come. Nor will Wordsworth allow his imagination to dwell seriously on post-existence even after he has found the doctrine necessary, except in "Laodamia" where the Classical background liberates him.

## Toward The Excursion

The *Lyrical Ballads* of 1800 and the *Poems* of 1807 can be taken as the terminal points of two periods of development. Comparing, broadly, Wordsworth's progress between 1793–1800 to that between 1800–1807, it can be said that though the poet seems to approach a new crisis in the later period, no crisis actually ensues. The changes that occur or threaten to occur are interpreted as logical steps in the humanizing of imagination, and Wordsworth accepts them, often with grief, as in the course of nature. Even the growing dimness affecting his senses, and the need to evoke a previous strength of relationship by reason or recollection, are linked to a scheme of progress in which nature plays the founding role. If nature is not enough to bind the soul, then reason and duty must be added, and if these are not enough, then the restraining bonds of religion are appealed to. At times Wordsworth goes further and suspects that his weakness is bound up with a weakness overtaking mankind, and auguring a dangerous epoch, perhaps the Apocalypse itself. But his usual attitude is that the loosening of certain natural or unconscious or organic bonds merely shows forth the transcendent vigor of the individual soul, which nature almost satisfied, but which must be progressively bound to earth by the addition of more conscious ties.

The question that remains is whether the humanized imagination is really still imagination. How can there be a genuine rebirth (Wordsworth's "renovation") without a threat against the steadfastness of one's being? How can there be an imaginative life without the dangers of love or hope or of a sympathy so extreme that it annihilates the self and substitutes another? Is not humanization, as Wordsworth conceives it, at the level of self-certainty rather than of self-transcending rebirth?

It is rather clear that Wordsworth's master tendency is to bypass the *Person* or *Imago* in desire. If he must be 'born again' it is not through a person but through nature—through a Lake-Country blend of water and the spirit. In his educational theory Wordsworth attacks the necessity of preceptors, in theology he neglects the personal intermediary, and his dislike of mythology is based in part on its multiplication of persons. He desires to liberate nature from human shape, and says of a brook that might have been depicted as a Naiad:

> It seems the Eternal soul is clothed in thee
> With purer robes than those of flesh and blood.[35]

He is equally doubtful of the "personal forms" found in Christian mythology:

> Jehovah—with his thunder, and the choir
> Of shouting Angels, and the empyreal Thrones.[36]

He is the first major poet who considers that a sense for the otherness of nature (the "non-human mystery" as Lawrence will call it) is a spiritual fact linked vitally to the growth of the mind.[37]

But it also leads him to problematic figures like Michael and Matthew. They are men *in* whom a person (Luke or Lucy) has died, yet who survive because of desires unconsciously fertilized by the broader, impersonal field of nature. One cannot say that Matthew's heart fails him at the sight of the "blooming Girl" or the poet's offer to be his son, but neither does it rise to the occasion. Matthew has overcome, with the help of nature, the grievous feeling that something unique is lost, is irreplaceable; he lives so much in the realm of natural recurrence that his sense for the unique is elided.[38] And yet—Matthew, like Michael, is still vulnerable. It is a thirty-year-old memory which halts him that fine April morning; and when Wordsworth tells us about Michael at the sheepfold:

> 'tis believed by all
> That many and many a day he thither went,
> And never lifted up a single stone

we feel, not the weight of the stones, but that which presses on Michael to give them this weight. The typical act does not seem to lessen pain but evokes an undying consciousness.

It can be charged, likewise, that Wordsworth did not distinguish sufficiently between resilience and renovation (his contemporaries thought that he neglected to portray the operative grace of believing in a personal Redeemer), but I think this is a matter still to be clarified. It centers on the question of the Personality of the Spirit. How is man renewed? How does the summons or the renovation —*gird up now thy loins like a man; for I will demand of thee, and answer thou me*—come to the poet and go from him to other hearts? Wordsworth's answer, involving a concept of nature, modifies the personalistic and apocalyptic views of divine agency, but without approving the deistic God ("impotent, lost in his own immensity") who drove Nerval into alienation, and against whom Blake prophesies. Blake, of course, remains an uncompromising personalist, who would have denied that Wordsworth was capable of sowing regeneration, since the more than human is the more-human, and a nature which is not humanized, not "men seen from afar," is but the "deistic abstract void." Wordsworth's view is closer to Goethe's. Man can never know, says Goethe, how anthropomorphic he is; and anthropomorphism is a prison-house. Influenced by Spinoza, Goethe wished to reconcile a divinely impersonal Nature with a personal Mediation. "For a very long time, indeed," writes Coleridge similarly, "I could not reconcile personality with infinity; and my head was with Spinoza, though my whole heart remained with Paul and John."[39]

To be more exact is not within my power. It seems to me correct to say that Wordsworth thinks of nature as chastening imagination, as purging it of a too personal "master folded in his fire."[40] His attitude may be quite unknowingly a renascence of negative theology. To see only the human in nature (or, for that matter, in man) is like seeing only the personal in God: it must produce an apocalyptic self-consciousness, a too-human or super-human image, and so fix the person to one self-image. *The Excursion,* now on the horizon, is a large-scale argument for the importance of nature in breaking that image. Nature, ideally, does not obliterate self-consciousness, but enables such various and mild renewals that happiness is less a separate quality of consciousness than an integral quality of being.

*The Excursion,* however, is not successful even on its own

terms. It ends with the main disputant still unregenerate, and with the issue of renovation unresolved after nine books. Yet it evokes, like all of Wordsworth's poetry, a sense of the *rock* on which humanity is founded. That rock is Matthew or Michael, Leech-gatherer or Wanderer, pastoral people, in contact with earth and whose eye is on the earth. They are not heroic; they perform no miracles; their mind is never free of nature. Yet since we can measure the strength of a thing by what might repress it, they bear witness to the vigor of imagination by showing that nature *almost* holds it in check.

# 9. *The Excursion*

## *The One Great Defect*

Concerning *The Excursion,* the worst has already been said by Jeffrey, Hazlitt, and others.[1] One must admit that to read carefully its nine books is a massively depressing experience, and it is hard to think of a corrective for *that* despondency. Though a radical slenderizing would save *The Excursion* from dying (like a dinosaur) of its own weight, nothing can remove the haunting suspicion that it is a second-rate work which might have continued *Paradise Regained* to become the greatest humanistic poem in the language. The betrayal of possible sublimity is impossible to forgive; for even if we exclude Book I and passages originating in Wordsworth's prime, there are still in the remainder of the poem tokens of a habitual poetic greatness that preserve it from settling to the splendor of a period piece. Yet, however condescending and ungrateful it is to diagnose failure, an understanding of where Wordsworth fails (rather than, immediately, why) may disencumber his poem of that mass of conjecture which failure as well as success brings on.

*The Excursion* offers us not a vision, but a voice. Its failure, and to some extent its distinction, reside in that. In Milton also, as Macaulay noted, the imaginative impact is mediated by aural rather than by visual suggestions.[2] From Milton we receive, to put it plainly, the vision of a voice—its power, the power of the Word reverberating for good or bad. But Milton still orients us graphically by using a very simple kind of myth and cosmos. It is simple, at least, when compared to Dante's. There are subtlety and precision in Milton, but on a massive scale; and the reader need only accept a few imaginative axes. Hell, for instance, is not the opposite of heaven but its parody; so that Satan's pain is the remembrance of light forever lost, and the mocking presence of "No light, but rather darkness visible." It follows easily enough that the hope buoying Satan is a false hope, and, like the light, a real Tantalus punishment. In this way Milton elaborates his imaginary world by means of a few graphic axioms.

Now *The Excursion*, however low we rank it, has an aim not unlike these greater poems; yet its visionary element is almost denuded of visual supports. After the first book (this reservation will come often) the visual and visionary divide, the first being curiously neglected, and the second being rendered by an oblique and self-conscious voice. The Wanderer only occasionally makes us feel the earth he stands on or the heaven he stands under, and for whose sake he sermonizes:

> —Voiceless the stream descends into the gulf
> With timid lapse;—and lo! while in this strait
> I stand—the chasm of sky above my head
> Is heaven's profoundest azure; no domain
> For fickle, short-lived clouds to occupy,
> Or to pass through; but rather an abyss
> In which the everlasting stars abide. (III.92–98)[3]

Such moments are a welcome relief to the effusions of this strange old man, who instead of letting silence speak, as it does powerfully through Leech-gatherer or Cumberland Beggar, betrays it. The visionary element of the poem should fuse with "the speaking face of Nature," yet after Book I it is increasingly an abstract voice that carries the burden of vision, and, as it were, stoops to the visual or to nature. Sometimes, in fact, Nature ironically punctuates the Wanderer's speech with its truly visionary sounds:

> List!—I heard,
> From yon huge breast of rock, a voice sent forth
> As if the visible mountain made the cry.
> Again! (IV.402–05)

Wordsworth's separation of visionary and visual results usually in the atrophy of both. It is a further step in his flight from the autonomous imagination. His flight could also, of course, have led *into* the visual. Those who "peep and botanize" on their mother's grave, or whose dull eye hangs on its object in brute slavery (IV.1254), are refugees from their own mind. But Wordsworth, unlike these, never denies the power of imagination. On the contrary, imagination has something sacred about it, which is why he hesitates to come near. Though *The Excursion* is predicated on the possibility of natural visionary experience ("his spirit shaped / Her prospects, nor did he believe,—he *saw*"[4]), and though such experience is given as proof of the argument that man's imagination can bind itself fruitfully to the world, Wordsworth shies from entering the area of his greatness. By removing himself as much as possible from the immediacy of his senses, and especially of the eye, he omits the sphere where imagination may seize on the seen and make it a haunting image, a "questionable shape." He reverts to lecturing on a venerable discipline, that of the Platonic-Christian journey from visible to invisible, from the *res factae* (Romans 1:19–20) to the intuition of an active principle "howe'er removed / From sense and observation . . ." (IX.3–4).

Yet poetry is distinguished from even the most poetical philosophy by the fact that it exists only where a poet is led beyond his thoughts. He *enters* his poem, like Dante or Milton. Dante is "guided," and Milton "flies" on wings for which he asks support in the words of the Prophet: "Instruct me, for Thou know'st." If Wordsworth flies, it is *from* open vision, like Jonah or his own Solitary. What he and his sufferers see we never entirely learn; their vision is subsumed, veiled like a holy thing which might break out. The power of vision, and its fearful or pacifying effects on the human person, are rendered by him; but rarely the substance. Vision, in this poem, is always a suffering, whether conceived in joy or in pain: for the soul is raised by it to a height it cannot keep, and the human energies striving to regain that height fall into despondency and thence into an "appetite of death."[5] (It is sometimes asked what Lear dies of, whether from thinking his daughter is alive, or from the realization that she is dead. But surely he dies, like Gloucester, of imagination. Lear, imagining

Cordelia is alive, cannot bear to fall from that height. So it is with Wordsworth's sufferers.)

The poet's flight from vision causes a warp of obliquity felt throughout *The Excursion.* It lends him strength for the story of Margaret, which he unfolds with preternatural slowness, yet wearies us elsewhere, because we are always brought close to some substantial drama, yet never allowed to see it. Milton again proceeds very differently. While saying "Dream not of other Worlds" (*Paradise Lost,* VIII.175), he nevertheless dreams of them, purging our unearthliness by indulging it, or substituting a clearer vision for a murky. Wordsworth, however, fails to respect his earlier conviction that

> Dumb yearnings, hidden appetites, are ours,
> And they *must* have their food. (*Prelude* V.506–07)

Though we infer the existence of such yearnings from the tragic stories included in *The Excursion,* inference by itself is no satisfaction for the soul, which needs at least an admixture of direct vision, that "taste of eternity"[6] hope adds to faith. The defect of *The Excursion* (after the first book especially) is to *show* us death and to *word* hope. Only the story of Margaret, the purest example of Wordsworth's art, uses inference successfully; it reveals the indomitableness of a woman's hope by showing the death of whatever she abandons in that hope.

Wordsworth's flight from vision may be a simple orthodox trembling or the result of a terror like that of the Prophets. *The Excursion* is less free of religious scruple than *The Prelude,* and often comes close to supporting Dr. Johnson's caveat about religious poetry.[7] Yet understanding Wordsworth's fear, we can lay the ghost of the charge that he averts his face from "half of human ken." It is not from man that Wordsworth turns but from the apocalyptic response to his mortality. Margaret and the Wanderer share a too vivid sense of mortal being. The Wanderer, nevertheless, keeps his imagination actively linked to the earth, but Margaret falls prey to *secret love,* to a near-apocalyptic displacement of hope. The verse prospectus to *The Excursion,* therefore, though an epic flyting, is no bravado. The poet passes unalarmed the myths of traditional apocalyptic poetry because the mind in its daily working creates things more awful than these. Previous imaginings of terror or beauty merely adumbrated what the mind achieves naturally when wedded in love to this world, or what it imagines and suffers when divorced from it. The story of Margaret certainly breeds such fear and awe "As fall upon us often when we look / Into our Minds, into the Mind of Man."[8] The poem declines, however, into a massive communion with the dead, noble raptures spoken above their graves. It is the living mind and the live moment we need communion with, not the storied dust of the dead.

While the figure of the Solitary still redeems Books II and III, the next book initiates a funeral sermon on human aspirations, and VI and VII ("The Churchyard among the Mountains") add an involuntary parody of the epic *nekya* or descent to the dead. I doubt that there exists another poem of such length in which death and tragic mutation become so literally the ground of the whole. The intended locus, of course, is the mind of man; which contemplates and is not cast down, which recognizes in suffering the disabled passion of hope. Death cannot be winged, however, and it is a realized impotence—"I blessed her in the impotence of grief" (I.924)—that is truer here to strength of heart than the joint fluencies of Pastor and Wanderer.

### Genre, Subject, and Argument

*The Excursion* is a strongly consistent poem in terms of genre, subject, and argument. All three are deeply meditated, and the genre in particular is a difficult blending of new and old that needs clarification.[9] It certainly has roots in the topographical and contemplative poetry of the eighteenth century. Thomson, Akenside, Cowper, and Dyer are ancestors of note. Their poetry, in turn, is best seen as a development of the *Georgics*, a poem containing the same attention to country lore, a similarly loose yet didactic structure, and a respect for the mind that remains close to "the great and permanent objects that act upon it."[10] But the ambulatory scheme, as well as the compression of time (though into five days rather than a single day) owe something to Milton's *Il*

*Penseroso* and *L'Allegro,* which influenced Wordsworth as early
as "The Vale of Esthwaite." Wordsworth seems to return to a first
line of development starting with his earliest long-poem venture,
affecting *Descriptive Sketches* and *An Evening Walk,* and inter-
rupted, as it were, by his experiment in autobiography.[11]

Why did the *Georgics* and associated poems appeal to Words-
worth? That they dealt with man's relation to nature is less impor-
tant than that Virgilian nature is a *divinity* which has to be wooed
and wounded, conquered and worshiped, at the same time. The
sense of Nature as a living and unpredictable presence, now gra-
cious now fearful, emerges already from Thomson's *Seasons,* which
are strongly imitative of Virgil. Yet Thomson, like Dryden in his
translation of the *Georgics,* too often substitutes poetic machinery
for divine. Though he is especially good in the ominous parts, we
admire him more for the energy or luster of his language than for
the actual subject. The style of a didactic poem, said Joseph War-
ton, "ought certainly to abound in the most bold and forcible
metaphors, the most glowing and picturesque epithets, it ought to
be elevated and enlivened . . . by every figure that can lift a lan-
guage above the vulgar and current expressions."[12]

Virgil's brilliance, needless to say, is also not subdued to his sub-
ject, but he has an inestimable advantage over his seventeenth-
and eighteenth-century imitators. The body of knowledge he deals
with has not yet "selved" from myth; cult and cultivation are
still close to each other. For Dryden and Thomson, however, agri-
culture as such is a recalcitrant theme and practically divorced from
folklore or myth: it is a subject that can only reveal the energy of
the contemplating mind. Thomson, in fact, in a poem much freer
of its original than a translation could ever be, clearly shifts the
ground of interest from cultivation to culture of mind. The cult
of nature is pursued only insofar as it raises the mind above nature.

Wordsworth's "labor" is also primarily an attention to nature
that yields imaginative fruits. The *agricola* now is the poet himself,
who observes how nature has fructified imagination. And, like
the true farmer, he observes or analyzes not for the sake of analysis
but in order to take advantage of the earth. His past life, which he
so carefully husbands in *The Prelude,* is analogous to the body of

myth or knowledge garnered by Virgil, and presented by him as a token of hope. Despite the divinity of nature, its unpredictable and even "monstrous" behavior, labor is repaid, the earth is grateful. If the future is like the past, adds Wordsworth, nature will fructify imagination now as then. Thomson does not reach this simple and highest theme. He labors nature to extract from it natural religion, and though Wordsworth is by no means free of the habit, it remains subordinate. Whether or not nature leads the mind to God, it suffices imagination. This seems to him the greater miracle.

The conception developed from the *Georgics,* that nature is the proper ground of man's imagination as well as of his labor, was only as influential as the form of the poem. Virgil's manual is devoid of action in the ordinary sense. So is *The Excursion.* Virgil can build his poem on the four branches of husbandry, and within each book follows the seasons or weaves together admonition and myth. Wordsworth, of course, structures his narrative less didactically and adopts once again the frame of a country walk. This frame, however, allows him to link story to story in the Virgilian manner, i.e. like a poet who is still essentially a combiner of legends. Wordsworth, like Burns, attaches his imagination to folklore, and in this he continues the tradition of Chaucer, Spenser, and Shakespeare more securely than the purely myth-making poet.

Yet he succeeds only partially, after *Lyrical Ballads,* in staying in touch with folklore and "local superstition." He is perhaps too interested in the workings of the naive mind and not enough in the person whose mind it is. Wordsworth's natural metaphors are important enough to found a whole theory of imagination, yet too thin to satisfy imagination itself. The Idiot Boy's "and the sun did shine so cold" or the poor woman's "that waggon does not care for us"[13] are telling cries, with something of the economy and density of the repressed imagination, yet the pressure of Shakespeare's mind engenders them continually. Chaucer and Shakespeare are often greater poets of natural life than Wordsworth; they know nature is a constipated or frozen form of imagination and refuse to worship its randomness. The poet, said Shakespeare, is "of imagination all compact"; but lack of compactness so distinguished

Wordsworth from other great poets that John Stuart Mill called
him the poet of unpoetical natures.

It is nevertheless true that the stories, reflections, and conversa-
tions of *The Excursion* are strongly linked to *place,* and are in
that sense natural. Wordsworth raises them from an inert land-
scape as a magician does rabbits. The living memory sees some-
thing merged with nature, a disused well, a discarded book, a
grave. In this unapparent or quiet vestige, Wanderer and Pastor
recognize a story that is all too human.[14] Nature is potentially
humanized; there is nothing which does not declare *man* to the
excursive and meditative mind. "All things shall speak of Man,"
says Wordsworth in an early passage, revised for *The Excursion*.[15]
And going back still further, to the lispings of "The Vale of
Esthwaite," we find the alienated poet ("doubting what to call his
own") wandering in fancy around the vale of his lost childhood,
seeking to read nature, and to draw a tale from every rock.[16] In
*The Excursion* also, it is not an ideal but a storied landscape he
discovers.

Yet, as the poem proceeds, and more ghosts are raised, nature
takes on the aspect of a large graveyard. Only the creative memory,
or the excursive mind, can see it as anything else. The emphasis is
shifted, by the momentum of the poem, from the individual fates
that are charactered, to the more comprehensive question of how
a man can face death or mutability and remain uninjured. Wan-
derer and Pastor appear then as examples of the uninjured mind
(IX.784). Their strength lies not in the ejaculative piety the age
demands but in the way they confront and subsume death. It is
their mind, or rather the quality of their imagination, that matters,
and the stories they revive are never told for their own sakes. There
is no riot in them, no "vain dalliance with the misery / Even of the
dead" (I.628); nothing is told merely to pleasure the time. The
stories of Wanderer and Pastor are drawn from nature (specific
place) and return to it; they are products of imagination blended
with spirit of place, and endow nature paradigmatically with some
of the richness of interest necessary to keep imagination well-
grounded.

Wordsworth's subject, then, is the mind of man—the uninjured mind. At the dramatic center of the poem stands the Solitary: can his mind be restored to health? Wordsworth is honest enough not to resolve the question. We do not know, by the end of the poem, what breach has been made in the Solitary's despair. The Solitary almost steals the show, opposing his own *mens immota*, his sense of injured merit, to the contrary firmness of Wanderer and Pastor. His instinctive movements toward retreat (V.73, VIII.30) are, after all, not so different from the Wanderer's tendency toward repose. When the latter talks of "the sublime attractions of the grave" it is hard to tell the unction of the phrase from its imaginative daring. Each of these friendly opponents has a fixed faith which is not always distinguishable from the fixity of death.

In pitting Solitary against Wanderer, Pastor, and Poet, somewhat like Job against his three friends, Wordsworth came very close to creating a poem of true spiritual debate. That he did not succeed better is due to a variety of causes; but the lineaments of the conception are there, and often mock the finished product. The Solitary is to be delivered from Despair, and *The Excursion* is therefore linked thematically with Book I, canto ix, of the *Faerie Queene,* Book X of *Paradise Lost,* and Wordsworth's own crisis described in *Prelude* X. ff. As in Spenser, Despair causes a wish to escape the human condition. Self-annihilation seems preferable to self-confrontation, and it could be achieved by a return to mere nature ("sleep / Doth, in my estimate of good, appear / A better state than waking; death than sleep: / Feelingly sweet is stillness after storm"[17]) or by the abandonment of reality for pure vision. The Red Cross Knight, taken up the holy mountain and shown the New Jerusalem, does not want to descend, and has to be reminded of his mission and georgic origin. The Solitary has a similar mountain experience.[18]

But, unlike Spenser or Milton, Wordsworth wishes to combat despair by purely human arguments. It is almost as if he meant to humanize his predecessors. The Wanderer, clearly, is a champion of natural wisdom; and though his arguments are supplemented by the Pastor's, and these are doctrinally phrased, both afford the Solitary the same kind of comfort. Starting at opposite points, from experience and from revelation, Wanderer and Pastor arrive at one conclusion, and blend their voices in thanksgiving. It is unfortunate, however, that the poet, to realize this plan, must give the Wanderer (who supposedly takes his wisdom from "mute insensate things,") the eloquence of a preacher. Equally unfortunate is the fact that religion and eloquence are still close enough so that as the Wanderer waxes in eloquence he also grows in religion. The poem, instead of keeping to the dilemma of the Solitary, becomes on occasion a defense of the Established Church.

Despite this betrayal of subject, *The Excursion* continues *Paradise Regained* in the same way as the *Prelude* dovetails *Paradise Lost*. It is "Recover'd Paradise" that Wordsworth, anticipating the blissful hour, means to sing. He ranges through the "highth or depth of nature's bounds." The deeds he sings of can be qualified as "Above Heroic, though in secret done."[19] The increasing Miltonisms, moreover, seem to me to derive more from Milton's later style, which attempts no more than a "middle flight."[20] But more important, perhaps, than the connection with *Paradise Regained* is the deeply fortuitous link with Dante's *Purgatorio*. It is not my purpose to salvage Wordsworth's poem by giving it a sublime context. Yet having considered its genre and subject, we come, finally to the "argument," and this does run parallel to Dante's. Not only is Earthly Paradise the crown of this part of Dante's journey as of Wordsworth's, but the sins purged are essentially those of *disordered love*. "Set love in order, thou that lovest me," is the verse of Francis of Assisi on which, according to E. G. Gardner, Purgatorio rests.[21] In Wordsworth it would be more exact to talk of disordered hope or imagination; it is the unredeemed strength of hope and the ravage of too intense imagination for which Margaret, the Solitary, and the Solitary's wife suffer:

> the innocent Sufferer often sees
> Too clearly; feels too vividly; and longs
> To realize the vision, with intense
> And over-constant yearning;—there—there lies
> The excess, by which the balance is destroyed. (IV.174–78)

Imagination itself is the illness. It is also, of course, the strength of man. Margaret's hope in her husband's return is so fierce that it withdraws her from all life. Like an unweaned child she is "unwilling to be fed" by aught else. If the poet, at the end of the Wanderer's tale, is so moved that he cannot thank the old man, but turns aside and blesses Margaret with "a brother's love," it is less because the touch of suffering makes him kin than because he has recognized, through her, the visionary power of hope: a power in which he shares for good or evil.

Despair being related to the vigor of imagination, Wordsworth can give no facile antidotes. He begins, in fact, with the example of a despondency that was not able to be "corrected." Margaret dies desolate. The Solitary remains, at the end of the poem, a moot case. The Pastor's examples of the calming or strengthening influences of nature are also not without their complexities. Wordsworth knows he is dealing with a "sickness unto death" coterminous with the best and strongest part of man. "Oh, Sir! the good die first, / And they whose hearts are dry as summer dust / Burn to the socket" (I.500–02). No wonder Shelley remembered these lines and made them part of the preface to *Alastor*. The poet's reaction to the Wanderer's story shows that the consolation must come from the same source as the grief, from a recognition of the supernatural vigor of desire, hope, imagination.

What, then, except blind faith leads Wordsworth to think the imagination can ever be naturalized? If hope, says the poet in his verse preface, truly blends with the world, despondency or visionary despair will cease, the earth will satisfy imagination wholly, and be as Paradise Regained. Yet Margaret shows rather the inhuman or too human strength of hope. Here we touch on something in the poem that has not been fully understood. It is not Margaret or the other sufferers who prove that Wordsworth's faith is not misplaced. It is the Wanderer: the quality of his mind, the way he faces human suffering, and the genealogy of his strength. Wordsworth's anticipatory poem, his "spousal verse," rests on this simple man, bred simply, a pedlar by profession, and not exceptional in any point of provenance or fate.

### Book I: The Wanderer

The Wanderer's attention is exquisitely directed toward nature. He has the same eye for detail as the Sea Captain of "The Thorn," and perhaps the same imagination of disaster, but his pacing of the tale is perfect, and shows a restraint which speaks the habitual

quality of a mind familiar with evidences of death and neither
shunning nor anticipating them. His "realism" thus assumes an
energy and morality of its own. He looks at nature as a seer, and
what he sees is linked startlingly with death—"I see around me
here / Things which you cannot see: we die, my Friend, / Nor we
alone . . ." (I.469–71). This leap of the imagination is among the
finest things in the book, not only because (as in Shakespeare) it
betrays the prophetic soul, but because the Wanderer rarely allows
himself such inner haste. Though the passion of Margaret is deeply
moving, we are equally affected by the Old Man's ability to keep
his eye on death, and to describe, with an intensity of sight so
purged that nothing morbid or sentimental remains, the gradual
extinction of a human soul. His is the strength lacking in Marga-
ret's husband, who cannot bear to look on the misery of his loved
ones.

The poet shares in this "harvest of a quiet eye."[22] The subdued
visual intensity of the whole first book shows that Wordsworth is
refusing to stand in the service of "*that* beauty, which, as Milton
sings, / Hath terror in it" (*Prelude* XIV.245–46). The poem's
opening landscape exemplifies his restraint:

> 'Twas summer, and the sun had mounted high:
> Southward the landscape indistinctly glared
> Through a pale steam; but all the northern downs,
> In clearest air ascending, showed far off
> A surface dappled o'er with shadows flung
> From brooding clouds; shadows that lay in spots
> Determined and unmoved, with steady beams
> Of bright and pleasant sunshine interposed;
> To him most pleasant who on soft cool moss
> Extends his careless limbs along the front
> Of some huge cave, whose rocky ceiling casts
> A twilight of its own, an ample shade,
> Where the wren warbles, while the dreaming man,
> Half conscious of the soothing melody,
> With side-long eye looks out upon the scene,
> By power of that impending covert thrown
> To finer distance. (I.1–17)

We move noticeably from high noon to the depth of a cavern, from which the eye *returns* to the scene, but soothed now by shade and melody and "finer distance." The texture of the passage is subtle, modulating starker intimations ("glared," "brooding," the half-felt personifications) or static properties (the shadows "determined and unmoved," the past tense and general dance of *d's*) into a more purely picturesque, softened and reciprocally blended prospect. In the first version of this landscape from *An Evening Walk*,

> When, in the south, the wan noon, brooding still,
> Breath'd a pale steam around the glaring hill . . .

not only is the personification more inclusive, but the rhyme, the fine jingle of "brooding" and "glaring," and the ritardando of "wan noon brooding" tense the very rhythm of the lines between stark-still and forward motion.

The visual theme is quickly attached to the person of the Wanderer. When we first see him his face is toward the setting sun, and the second time he lies supine, shaded from the noonday sun, his eyes half-shut. But there are also contrary indications, showing the unsubdued nature of his eye. "Time had compressed the freshness of his cheek / Into a narrower circle of deep red, / But had not tamed his eye" (I.426–28); "He had rehearsed / Her homely tale with such familiar power, / With such an active countenance, an eye / So busy . . ." (I.614–17). His picture of Margaret speaks for itself:

> evermore
> Her eyelids drooped, her eyes downward were cast;
> And, when she at her table gave me food,
> She did not look at me. Her voice was low,
> Her body was subdued. (I.791–95)

The Wanderer's spirit *clings* to Margaret, "so familiarly / Do I perceive her manner, and her look, / And presence" (I.780–82). But the essential difference between him and Margaret is that he has retained his excursive power; he is not bound up in vision but still pastures wide, letting nature wean his eyes. Nothing is more beau-

tifully rendered than his broadening glance (I.710 ff.) that mounts
gradually into recognition:

> From the bench I rose;
> But neither could divert nor soothe my thoughts.
> The spot, though fair, was very desolate—
> The longer I remained, more desolate:
> And, looking round me, now I first observed
> The corner stones, on either side the porch,
> With dull red stains discoloured, and stuck o'er
> With tufts and hairs of wool, as if the sheep,
> That fed upon the Common, thither came
> Familiarly, and found a couching-place
> Even at her threshold. Deeper shadows fell
> From these tall elms; the cottage-clock struck eight;—
> I turned, and saw her distant a few steps. (I.738–50)

The Wanderer, clearly, possesses that chastity of recognition
which Henry James' characters are in search of. To know, or even
to desire to know, is connected with guilt. The visual theme passes
here into a higher mode still based on the old cry for ocular proof.
But the Wanderer restores to knowledge some of its innocence, its
mixture of good, for even if knowledge is always of death, or of
good *and* evil, his mind remains inviolate, and does not lust for
what it knows it will find.

Wordsworth's lengthy account of the Wanderer's childhood
(I.108 ff.) traces the genealogy of an inherently moral imagination.
Brought up in nature, by nature, the Wanderer stands before us
as the embodiment of natural wisdom. Although God-fearing par-
ents and the Scottish Church tended him closely, his religion some-
times seemed, the poet says, "Self-taught, as of a dreamer in the
woods." He would be a mute inglorious poet had Wordsworth not
come to make him speak too much. His mind is satisfied by nature,
not now, in the moment, which may be evil or lacking, but because
nature, instead of being an object or something alien "out there,"
is indistinguishable from his yet living past.

The Wanderer has known communions with nature too strong
to be forgotten, moments of terror too stark to be entirely remem-

bered, and silences too deep to be profaned. By weaning his senses and, in particular, his eyes, nature teaches him that he must separate from many things, yet offers him the compensation of an active spirit. As he grows, and is unsatisfied with dimmer perceptions than those that used to lie on his mind and perplex his bodily sense, he develops an ability to fasten images on his brain, and to raise, by meditation, their affective power. At the same time he turns eyes and ears outward, searching the external world, whose variety both rewards and draws him. Taking away one kind of food, and offering him another, nature gradually binds him to her in faith. He trusts her generosity and his power (through her) of renovation. He becomes what Wordsworth so aptly calls him, "A Being made / Of many Beings" (I.430–31).

The slow maturation of nature does not save the Wanderer from solitude or evil, but enables him to face these without exhaustion. "Disesteem of life" cannot reach him. Nature has made him so active toward her that he is endlessly renovated through an outward going. Like the Red Cross Knight after his trials and his passage through Caelia's House, the Wanderer is able to get up after each fall, to rebound. His ultimate reward is to look *through* death. "If the doors of perception were cleansed," says Blake, "everything would appear to man as it is; infinite." The Wanderer's home is with nature only insofar as it breathes "immortality, revolving life, / And greatness still revolving; infinite" (I.228–29). He is the proper antagonist for the Solitary, who lives sullen in the bosom of nature, and who makes his entry in Book II.

### Books II–III: The Solitary

The Solitary has lost his "excursive power,"[23] and with it his chances to be renewed. After the death of his two children and his wife, the failure of his faith in political action, and the decay of earlier vitalities of feeling (all have correlatives in Wordsworth's life), he becomes a recluse, avoiding contact with other men and literally burying himself before his time. His place of abode is like an urn:

> We scaled, without a track to ease our steps,
> A steep ascent; and reached a dreary plain,

With a tumultuous waste of huge hill tops
Before us; savage region! which I paced
Dispirited: when, all at once, behold!
Beneath our feet, a little lowly vale,
A lowly vale, and yet uplifted high
Among the mountains; even as if the spot
Had been from eldest time by wish of theirs
So placed, to be shut out from all the world!
Urn-like it was in shape, deep as an urn;
With rocks encompassed, save that to the south
Was one small opening, where a heath-clad ridge
Supplied a boundary less abrupt and close;
A quiet treeless nook, with two green fields,
A liquid pool that glittered in the sun,
And one bare dwelling; one abode, no more! (II.323–39)

This funereal place, almost naked of charms, attracts the poet strangely. The "dreary plain," a Miltonic phrase descriptive of Hell, now reveals "a sweet Recess" (II.349), which is what Adam calls Paradise on learning that he must leave it.[24] As if to objectify some (not unattractive) thought of death, Poet and Wanderer hear voices rising in a dirge from that urn-shaped valley. By a significant prolepsis, voice precedes sight, and by a second prolepsis, the Wanderer, even before seeing the cortege, concludes that it is the Solitary who has died.

When, therefore, in the only dramatic surprise of the poem, the Solitary appears before them, it is a dead man they see. Practically his first words indicate the death-wish in him. "The hand of Death . . . has been here; but could not well / Have fallen more lightly, if it had not fallen / Upon myself" (II.542–45). His confession in Book III then links the "appetite of death" with the desire for repose. The Solitary's remaining hope is that the current of his life will soon reach "The unfathomable gulf, where all is still!" (III. 991)

Who is the Solitary, if not the Hamletian man in black, and a dangerous part of the poet's mind? In one of his earliest poems, "Lines left upon a Seat in a Yew-Tree," Wordsworth had sketched a similar recluse. "The man whose eye / Is ever on himself," he cautions us, "doth look on one / The least of Nature's works. . . ." Though the "beautiful abyss" in which the Solitary dwells is a kind of Grasmere, "Not melancholy—no, for it is green, / And bright, and fertile, furnished in itself / With the few needful things that life requires" (II.355–57), we also recognize in it features of the spot-syndrome which elicit or express the apocalyptic imagination and explain the poet's fascination with it. Sterner and milder beauties in alternation suggest a biblical or Miltonic reversal:

> Beneath our feet, a little lowly vale,
> A lowly vale, and yet uplifted high
> Among the mountains. . . .

This high and low, the verbal lingerings, something rising from the abyss, the reversal of an expected or natural order (sound preceding sight), and the further prolepsis of thinking the Solitary dead, indicate in a deeply ordinary way the stirrings in Wordsworth of "Imagination . . . That awful Power" even perhaps as he is composing. I need hardly add how many images of engulfment haunt the narrative at this point: we go from the abyss of II.373 to the unfathomable gulf of III.991.

Wordsworth's attitude toward the Solitary and his abode is full of ambivalence. For the Solitary, like himself, is a new Jonah, who escapes into the deeps of nature. What would he escape from? Imagination. It is not possible to think of him as shunning only the face of man. What he really shuns is the face of God, that is to say, his past strength, his dreams, his young intuitions. But solitude, instead of delivering from these as from the world, declares their greatness. He is forced to suffer a vision of glory (II.834 ff.) and remember his own. Describing a terrible moment in his sea-journey to America (it parallels an episode in "The Female Vagrant" and is linked to Wordsworth's experience on Salisbury Plain), the Solitary tells what may happen when a man is left to himself on the desert of the sea:

> O, never let the Wretched, if a choice
> Be left him, trust the freight of his distress

> To a long voyage on the silent deep!
> For, like a plague, will memory break out;
> And, in the blank and solitude of things,
> Upon his spirit, with a fever's strength,
> Will conscience prey.—Feebly must they have felt
> Who, in old time, attired with snakes and whips
> The vengeful Furies. *Beautiful* regards
> Were turned on me. . . . (III.844–53)

Two stories are linked to the meeting with the Solitary. The first concerns the man whose funeral the visitors unexpectedly see. A type of Cumberland Beggar, he has been adopted by a housewife of those parts, who gives him, in return for small services, food and shelter, "a blind dull nook . . . the *kennel* of his rest." One day, while in the mountains, he is surprised by a storm, and when finally discovered by a search party,

> We spake—he made reply, but would not stir
> At our entreaty; less from want of power
> Than apprehension and bewildering thoughts. (II.824–26)

And, although he seemed to have received no harm, "a silent change / Soon showed itself: he lingered three short weeks; / And from the cottage hath been borne to-day."

Everything suggests that the Old Man died of other than physical causes. He is found within the ruins of a small chapel on the central heights, almost buried in tufts of heath, and snug as a child. Protection from the storm, yes; but the place, the circumstances, his paralysis, and the manner of his passing away, hint at death by vision as well as by water. Perhaps the vision was merely the terror of the elements from which he hid. The result is still that silent or lingering death characteristic of those who are vision-struck, and no longer able to tolerate, after what they have been, their former selves.

If this is so, the fates of the Old Man and of the Solitary are mirror-images. And it becomes something of a probability when we notice a displacement common enough in literature. The vision which the Old Man may have had is experienced by the Solitary as he returns from the search for him. A step suddenly frees the Solitary from the "blind vapour" (the transferred epithet used pregnantly here) and reveals a scene analogous to that given from Snowdon. "By earthly nature had the effect been wrought / Upon the dark materials of the storm." He seems to see the glory-seat of God. Its footstool is the little valley in which he dwells. More important than the substance of the vision is its effect on the Solitary:

> my heart
> Swelled in my breast.—"I have been dead," I cried,
> "And now I live! Oh! wherefore *do* I live?"
> And with that pang I prayed to be no more! (II.874–77)

It does not matter whether the Old Man had the identical experience. The episode establishes without doubt in what way vision, or Imagination, is death-dealing. From that height the Solitary must descend. Thenceforth his life is death-in-life. He has not escaped the face of God.

The second story, covering the latter half of Book III, is of the Solitary's past. Much of it reflects Wordsworth's own experience, already broached in the eleventh book of *The Prelude,* but remaining unpublished. The part that is new incorporates the poet's loss of his two children in 1812, and was added to *The Excursion* shortly after that.

The Solitary, according to his story, is happily married for seven years, and his thoughts and wishes are finally "bounded" to this world, when his children die, and his wife, like Margaret, sinks into a curious inertia:

> Calm as a frozen lake when ruthless winds
> Blow fiercely, agitating earth and sky. (III.650–51)

She, as it were, unbinds herself from the earth, and becomes so aloof even from her husband that he confesses:

> The eminence whereon her spirit stood,
> Mine was unable to attain. (III.659–60).

In a variant, the Solitary calls her "an untranslated spirit." Yet she soon loses that exaltation and wastes away silently:

> Dimness o'er this clear luminary crept
> Insensibly;—the immortal and divine
> Yielded to mortal reflux; her pure glory,
> As from the pinnacle of worldly state
> Wretched ambition drops astounded, fell
> Into a gulf obscure of silent grief,
> And keen heart-anguish—of itself ashamed,
> Yet obstinately cherishing itself. (III.670–77)

Her manner of dying, then, is similar to that of the Old Beggar, and its cause is probably related. The woman, after losing her second child, is not sealed up in apathy or stoic response, but in *vision*. She enters a waking slumber impenetrable to human fears. Her love for the two children cannot be sublimated. It is so intense that only an intensified vision of their continued life has the power to replace them. Her mind is unable to accept the thought of death unless assured of a life superior to what is dead, and hope raises her mind to that imagining. But—

> 'tis a thing impossible to frame
> Conceptions equal to the soul's desires;
> And the most difficult of tasks to *keep*
> Heights which the soul is competent to gain. (IV.136–39)

The sorrow which ensues to consume her is not so much anguish at her children's death as a consequence of that—the drying up of her soul in the effort of continued ecstasy. Perhaps the idea of personal immortality has been so strongly abetted by scriptural consolation that she cannot pass from the belief in supernatural existence to a faith in other than personal subsistence. The "more than human" is identified by her with the "more human," the Person *eminenter:*

> Too, too contracted are these walls of flesh,
> This vital warmth too cold, these visual orbs,
> Though inconceivably endowed, too dim
> For any passion of the soul that leads
> To ecstasy; and, all the crooked paths

Of time and change disdaining, takes its course
Along the line of limitless desires. (IV.179–85)

### Book IV: Despondency Corrected

The tragedies of Margaret, the Solitary, and the Solitary's wife,
though the first is triggered by the cruelty of governments, the sec-
ond affected by both political and personal causes, and the last
purely domestic, share similarities that far outweigh their differ-
ences. They are tragedies, first of all, of common life, to which the
Pastor can add numerous examples in Books V ff. We do not hear
"Of carnal, bloody, and unnatural acts." Nor are the persons that
are overthrown distinguished in any way, or noble. They are com-
mon clay; and Wordsworth continues the aim of *Lyrical Ballads*,
which was to choose incidents and situations from ordinary life,
describe them as far as possible in language really used by men,
and trace through them the primary laws of our nature. Though
he does not really succeed in the matter of language, the first book
shows he might have achieved "words / Which speak of nothing
more than what we are."[25] And though, after Book I, the tenor of
*The Excursion* is diverted by various scruples, which include,
principally, a fear of the power of vision that is his very subject,
Wordsworth still succeeds in providing the first strong account of
imagination as the exalted and tragic part of *every* mind. The ap-
petite for vision, related to the appetite for death, needs a "cure of
the ground";[26] and the onus of arguing that cure, without dis-
paraging the nobility of the disease, falls on the Wanderer.

The despondency the Wanderer seeks to correct is less the op-
posite of hope than its strongest derivative. As a theological vir-
tue, hope was distinguished from faith and love; but the distinction
was always somewhat scholastic, and is not operative in Words-
worth. When the Wanderer says that we live by admiration, hope,
and love, he is not significantly substituting one virtue for an-
other,[27] but hinting at a psychological scale that proceeds from feel-
ings of awe to gentler sympathies. Wordsworth's experiences are
divided into two main kinds, which he often qualifies as sterner
and milder, separating man from or binding him to this world.
Now hope, in Wordsworth's poetry, as in traditional theology, is the

middle virtue, which looks beyond this world, yet still seeks its attachments and enjoyments in the here and now. It is represented by Spenser (and the emblem books) as looking heavenward while leaning on anchor or spade. *Agricolas spes alit,* says the motto,[28] which links the Christian thought to a Virgilian theme, and forms a homely proverb not alien to later Romantic laborers in the vineyards of vision. What Wordsworth calls Imagination is, in this perspective, hope recognizing itself as originally or ultimately independent of this world.

Such a recognition, however, is still dependent on a natural process of birth, or coming-to-mind, which brings back the world and makes hope reflexive. Hope, in fact, is never experienced in a purely unmediated way: the very term imagination is significant in pointing out that hoping is not without images. But no image can ultimately satisfy, and this produces a continual tension. For where nature is too strongly present, hope is not, as St. Paul indicates in a famous definition (Hebrews 11:1). Though Margaret's hope is still attached to this world, that it should be attached at only *one* point is dangerous: it lives at the expense of everything else. None of Wordsworth's visionaries escapes this monism; their imagination clings to the world by a single (usually human) bond, and seems to prefer death to diminution.

The Wanderer's most powerful argument against visionary despair is also the most Romantic, and is directed less against despair than toward the expansion of hope. The desires should be multiplied. The faculties in man should be multiplied. He who feels contempt for any living thing, Wordsworth says in one of his first poems, has faculties which he has never used; thought with him is in its infancy.[29] (Traherne, in his *Centuries of Meditations,* urges similarly a "sowing of needs.") The eye should not dominate the faculties and man should not be the sole center of our affections. All nature waits to rouse the sleeping energies of the spirit. Let us rise, says the Wanderer, pleading for a reappropriation of this world tantamount to resurrection,

> From this oblivious sleep, these fretful dreams
> Of feverish nothingness. Thus disciplined
> All things shall live in us and we shall live

> In all things that surround us. This I deem
> Our tendency, and thus shall every day
> Enlarge our sphere of pleasure and of pain.[30]

Though repetitious and verbose, the Wanderer's harangue is also affecting because of that. Its rhythm is that of the divided mind which seeks unity of being yet draws its energies from self-division. We feel its turns and counterturns generating a prophetic passion. Blake, also insisting on the liberation of the senses for the sake of expanded perception, would never have used dichotomies this way, at least not common dichotomies. He attempts to stand beyond "fitting and fitted." But if Wordsworth distinguished, as between imagination and nature, senses and intellect, it is not

> That we should pore, and dwindle as we pore,
> For ever dimly pore on things minute,
> On solitary objects, still beheld
> In disconnection dead and spiritless,
> And still dividing and dividing still,
> Break down all grandeur . . .[31]

but rather that we should learn, through the very momentum of such speech, the temper of a mind that could dedicate itself either to "one" thing in disconnection, or allow its divided powers to generate, by meditation, new broadsides of the spirit.

But the ultimate argument against visionary despair is the example the Wanderer sets. His attention to the *turnings* of thought and his respect for *vital accidents*, are Wordsworth's own and save this poetry from abstraction. The courage to go out, to take consolation from nature, or to multiply, by an attention to nature, the "spiritual presences of absent things," is not only an argument but has behind it the "strange discipline" of a lifetime. It shows the habit of perfection. The poet's greatness is revealed when his wisdom teeters on the axis of a moment, on a sudden turn of thought, as in the apostrophe to Imagination in the sixth book of *The Prelude,* or here, after he has heard the tale of Margaret:

> my heart
> Went back into the tale which he had told,
> And when at last returning from my mind

> I looked around, the cottage and the elms,
> The road, the pathway, and the garden wall
> Which old and loose and mossy o'er the road
> Hung bellying, all appeared, I know not how
> But to some eye within me all appeared
> Colours and forms of a strange discipline.
> The trouble which they sent into my thought
> Was sweet, I looked and looked again . . .[32]

The inward-turning mind could lose itself; it tends toward a vision-
ary image, and we feel strongly the "fixative" urge. But subtly, and
as if by a sleight of thought, the normality of the scene prevails, the
mind allows nature's calm to blend with its trouble, and lightens
into an image of paradise:

> The very sunshine spread upon the dust
> Is beautiful.[33]

Perhaps repose is too quickly achieved, but the preceding fluctua-
tion has shown how precious our mental balance is, and how pre-
carious.

It is all the more puzzling, therefore, to find the Wanderer in
Book IV arguing ex cathedra, and mixing the most original with
the most commonplace thoughts. When he says, for example,

> Happy is he who lives to understand,
> Not human nature only, but explores
> All natures,—to the end that he may find
> The law that governs each; and where begins
> The union, the partition where, that makes
> Kind and degree, among all visible Beings;
> The constitutions, powers, and faculties,
> Which they inherit,—cannot step beyond,—
> And cannot fall beneath; that do assign
> To every class its station and its office,
> Through all the mighty commonwealth of things;
> Up from the creeping plant to sovereign Man . . . (IV.332–43)

an idea expressed also in other poems is blended here not only
with a Virgilian topos (apt enough) but also with the concept of

the Chain of Being, which is superfluous. Yet I cannot believe that it is a mere indigestion of ideas that prompts Wordsworth to this. Perhaps he meant to appropriate to his purpose certain great commonplaces, because they also nourished Milton, his nearest example of the philosophic poet, and Spenser, and Shakespeare. Wordsworth is a poet even to his faults, though Coleridge's urgings that he should compose the "first and truly philosophical poem" are doubtless responsible for some of the weightiness in Book IV and after.

A few of the more important examples of this admixture of original thought with poetically consecrated notions should be given, both to redeem somewhat the latter stretches of *The Excursion,* and to localize their weakness.

> One adequate support
> For the calamities of mortal life
> Exists—one only . . . (IV.10–12)

begins the Wanderer's correction of despondency, yet his *one* is really *many*. Wordsworth stresses the One, which is absolute trust in a providence that converts all accidents to good, because, as in Spenser, the enemy to Hope is Mutability (cf. *Excursion* III.124 ff., 458). At the same time, and almost without transition, other traditional supports against despair are invoked. We meet the argument from design:

> How beautiful this dome of sky;
> And the vast hills, in fluctuation fixed
> At thy command, how awful! Shall the Soul,
> Human and rational, report of thee
> Even less than these! (IV.34–38)

This goes back to Romans 1:19 and Psalm 19. "In fluctuation fixed" is a rather beautiful argument in a minor mode against the power of mutability. There follows a reference to Duty, conceived in stoic terms as a moral vigor not subject to the storms of circumstance (69–73); also a eulogy of ideal or geometric forms, "Whose kingdom is, where time and space are not" (76); and this flows into an address to the deity as the self-sustaining support of all the Chain of Being (79–99). But everything then issues in the apparently contrary affirmation that the world shall pass away, with a further dark foreseeing that the poet's own sight will fail, though this is delicately redressed by a Miltonic note of fortitude:[34]

> Ah! if the time must come, in which my feet
> No more shall stray where meditation leads,
> By flowing stream, through wood, or craggy wild,
> Loved haunts like these; the unimprisoned Mind
> May yet have scope to range among her own,
> Her thoughts, her images, her high desires. (IV.103–08)

Such a personal and moody digest of ideas should deny to Wordsworth the Coleridgean title of *spectator ab extra*. Nor is there, except for the secret championship of the many against the one, real philosophical distinction in the ideas offered us. *The Excursion* becomes increasingly a Romantic commonplace book; and used as such may afford some enjoyment. Wordsworth himself seems to admit the desultory yet comprehensive character of his long poem. At one point he thinks of subtitling his work "views of Nature, Man, and Society." Some passages, in fact, like his defense of myth and superstition, which begins

> Yet rather would I instantly decline
> To the traditionary sympathies
> Of a most rustic ignorance and take
> A fearful apprehension from the owl
> Or death-watch: and as readily rejoice,
> If two auspicious magpies crossed my way;—
> To this would rather bend than see and hear
> The repetitions wearisome of sense,
> Where soul is dead, and feeling hath no place (IV.613–21)

became quickly the source of a Romantic *topos*, leading perhaps to Carlyle's words on mythology in "On Heroes and Hero-Worship" and certainly influencing Keats and Shelley. Ruskin also felt their power.[35]

It must be said, however, that the structure of Book IV is quite firm, and in one sense important. Wordsworth divides despondency into two kinds. The first kind is something universal and philosophical, and everyone knows it who has been haunted by the phantom of mutability. But the greater part of the book addresses itself to a more particular despair arising from "loss of confidence in social man" (IV.261). This was felt by Wordsworth and Coleridge to be the characteristic melancholy of their time, political in nature, and following on Britain's betrayal of the French Revolution as well as on the latter's self-betrayal.[36] The solitary had, in fact, recovered from his grave personal disasters, risen once more on the wave of hope, and again bound himself to the world during the period of enthusiasm for the Revolution. "Thus was I reconverted to the world; / Society became my glittering bride, / And airy hopes my children" (III.734–36). The metaphor recalls that marriage of mind and nature, of imagination and this world, which Wordsworth urges throughout, but here the Solitary uses it bitterly, knowing the failure of this second marriage.

The Wanderer's concern is primarily with men alienated from politics (in the largest sense of the word) by the events of his time. The Wanderer knows their dejection because he has shared it. He is the Wordsworth who has come through. The "gentle shocks" of nature, according to him, weaned his pride in revolutionary activities and returned him to gradualism. His counsel to the Solitary, therefore, is not simply, leave your solitude and return to the bosom of mankind, but, "A piteous lot it were to flee from Man— / Yet not rejoice in Nature" (IV.575–76).

There is no need to dwell on the particular persuasions used by Wordsworth's spokesman to restore the Solitary's faith in nature, i.e. in nature's power to regenerate the soul. Many are traditional, deriving from the debate between the active and the contemplative life. They place the emphasis less on the one than on the manifold. Take away this or that strength, remove this or that gift, the bounty in nature and the answering vigor of the soul are still infinite. The main line of argument adds little new to the drift of *The Prelude*. He who has dwelt with nature in the past may dwell with her again, and recover his feelings if he trusts himself abroad. Impulses cannot but come to him from the external world; it is up to the individual to have the imaginative power to value them, rather than letting reason, opinion, or a routine self-centeredness limit his "imaginative Will" (IV.1128). Most of these thoughts, which stress the great and fruitful principle of reciprocity, were actually conceived at Racedown and Alfoxden, in the seminal period of 1795–98.

### Books V–IX: Elegies in a Country Churchyard

The question as to whether solitude and nature are regenerative leads into the second part of *The Excursion*. The Solitary's skepticism is undaunted. Neither nature nor the rites of the church can really alter, according to him, a man's destiny or purify his heart. The Wanderer brings him to a place where nature and religion seem to join their forces, to the Churchyard among the Mountains. To no avail: in one of his most passionate statements, the Solitary conjures up a Homeric opening of Hades that would destroy all this cant about green graves and rustic virtues:

> If this mute earth
> Of what it holds could speak, and every grave
> Were as a volume, shut, yet capable
> Of yielding its contents to eye and ear,
> We should recoil, stricken with sorrow and shame,
> To see disclosed, by such dread proof, how ill
> That which is done accords with what is known
> To reason, and by conscience is enjoined. (V.250–57)

He insists that rustic loneliness breeds, except in a few rare natures, "selfishness, and cruelty, and vice; / Or, if it breed not, hath not power to cure" (V.889–90).

This gives the challenge direct to the Wanderer, who falls back on the revered support of the Pastor of this mountain village; and the greater portion of what remains of *The Excursion* consists in the Pastor's attempt at rebuttal. Standing in the churchyard, he resurrects in a series of "living epitaphs" the memory of the sufferings and triumphs of his dead parishioners.[37] It is heaping up of exempla in the medieval manner.

Yet many portraits from among this gallery of the dead are deeply moving. Anguish and pain are by no means slighted: this is clearly the poet of *Lyrical Ballads* changing into a pseudo-narrative mode. It is easy, of course, to prefer the company of living rogues to that of dead sufferers. Yet what Blake said of Chaucer's pilgrims, that they are "the Characters which compose all Ages and Nations" and that though some of the names or titles are altered by time, "the Characters themselves for ever remain unaltered, and consequently they are the Physiognomies or Lineaments of Universal Human Life, beyond which Nature never steps,"[38] is also applicable to Wordsworth's solitaries. The avaricious matron (VI.675–770), the deaf man, a unique portrait in literature (VII.395–481), the patient woman (VI.906–1052), and the prospector kept alive by "The darksome centre of a constant hope" (VI.212–54), remind us that if suffering is infinite, its types are recurrent.

Those famous misreaders of Wordsworth who say he advocates rural nature as a panacea should be condemned to read *The Excursion* once a day. It might not raise their estimate of the poem, but it would certainly be fit punishment. Nowhere does Wordsworth acknowledge more explicitly the difficulty in reforming human nature. The Pastor cannot even answer the Solitary in a very direct way. Instead of stating roundly that country life restores the soul to health, he argues negatively that it at least is not deleterious to greatness. Native grandeur of soul is present in lowliest as well as highest, and even the "perverseness of a selfish course" can exemplify it. Perverseness is perseverance of a kind, the product of a too rigid hope. But this almost irrelevant and commonplace point hides a deeper intention. The Pastor's first speech had already cautioned against a speculative or proudly objective standpoint vis-à-vis man. Angels, he says, taking up an old theme, see the object as it is, but we are what we see, and try vainly to distance ourselves from ourselves. It is impossible to judge men by the separated reason alone.[39] Love, admiration, fear, desire and hate, these are our organs; without them we are blind. Why should we read the forms of things with an unworthy eye? the Wanderer had asked in Book I. By showing that behind the most selfish course there is a perverted hope or a darkened imagination, the Pastor rebukes the *eye* of the Solitary. He confirms by the authority of his office, and by invoking scripture, the very vision of things radiating naturally from the Wanderer during his story of Margaret. Again the emphasis of *The Excursion* is put strongly not on argument but on how to acquire "The inward principle that gives effect / To outward argument" (V.572–73).

It may still be doubted whether the latter part of *The Excursion* adds anything essential to what the first books so sufficiently convey. The poet himself acknowledges that the Wanderer had already declared "by what exercise / From visible nature, or the inner self / Power may be trained, and renovation brought" (V.583–85). It is as difficult to defend Books V–IX as to justify their length. They seem to serve Wordsworth as a frame for pictures of humble men and a humble life, and as a repository for homeless passages from the fertile period of 1797–1800.

Only one intention of the poet's casts a glimmer of favor on these books. Though mazy and polemically inefficient, they do answer the Solitary in a curious way. For *The Excursion,* viewed as a whole, or progressively, shows that man stands in communion not only with the living but also with the dead. Behind its conventional religiosity is this more archaic feature.[40] From the beginning, the Wanderer's glance uncovers the truth of the dead and the evidence of the invisible, and the Pastor perfects this spiritual *katabasis* or resurrection by story of the dead. Both open the grave to intensify our vision of the coils of mortality. We are taught to look uninjured on death, vice, and selfishness, which are shown to be the estranged products of a love "all hoping and expecting all" (VII. 848, I Corinthians 13:7); a love asking of imagination more than earth can give.

> The riddle Nature could not prove
> Was nothing else but secret love,

writes Clare in his madness;[41] and against this heroism of the soul, which becomes an avarice of the past or of the impossible, the poet sets the expanded eyes of Pastor and Wanderer.

But the realm of the dead is greater than that of the human dead, extending to everything apparently inanimate. The "universe of death," as Wordsworth calls it, borrowing a Miltonic phrase for Hell, includes whatever is barren to mind. "Where man is not, nature is barren,"[42] says Blake; and Wordsworth, at about the same time, declares: "All things shall speak of Man." By this he does not mean an extension of the anthropomorphic viewpoint, or even, as in Blake, an infinite expansion of the concept of Man. It might have been better to say, "All things shall speak to Man." Only by such converse can the naked spirit be clothed, the burden of existence become fruitful, and the rape of vision cease. Wordsworth does not insist on Blake's *All* ("More, More, is the cry of the deluded spirit. Nothing but All can satisfy Man") but rather on the *Any*. The Wanderer's final oration evokes a world from which solitude, though not individuality, has been removed, because each thing has the capacity to communicate its being, to "go out":

> All beings have their properties which spread
> Beyond themselves, a power by which they make
> Some other being conscious of their life,
> Spirit that knows no insulated spot,
> No chasm, no solitude; from link to link
> It circulates, the Soul of all the worlds.[43]

This is not only a noble description of the Chain of Being envisioned at its fullest and most dynamic, but also a final cast at the Solitary. The solitary: is he not happier than he knows, less solitary than he knows? He is still a link in the chain that binds living and dead as one company. Who is to say what is living, what is dead, what is nature, what is imagination? Each link may be a life or the source of renovation. Yet the Wanderer never blurs all things as one. By genial enumeration—

> There is an active principle alive
> In all things, in all natures, in the flowers
> And in the trees, in every pebbly stone
> That paves the brooks, the stationary rocks,
> The moving waters, and the invisible air . . .[44]

—he multiplies the locus as well as the sentiment of life. The individual being is respected. Though Wordsworth appeals to the ancient idea of the *anima mundi,* he avoids all other hypostases, and the movement of his verse carries us away from demonic fixities and sublimely vague personifications. Rooted in so generous, so interactive a world, can hope decay? Only, says the Wanderer, if it divorces itself from that world:

> The food of hope
> Is meditated action; robbed of this
> Her sole support, she languishes and dies.
> We perish also; for we live by hope
> And by desire; we see by the glad light
> And breathe the sweet air of futurity;
> And so we live, or else we have no life. (IX.20–26)

This is the real Chain of Being: take the world from hope, and hope dies; take hope from us, and we die. There is no fallacy, for Wordsworth, in calling the light glad, for, even if it is we who are glad, the power to spread beyond ourselves and to make some other being conscious of life, is what distinguishes life from death and from apocalypse. The specter of selfhood-solitude is purged, and imagination circulates rejoicing through infinite arteries of links.

In 1807, at the end of his great decade, Wordsworth wrote *The White Doe of Rylstone*. As "Nutting" is a fit emblem to stand at the threshold of the fruitful years, so this romance can introduce the leaner years. Not published till 1815, it marks an epoch in Wordsworth's career, though less by the date of composition or publication than by its special character as a poem.

*The White Doe* is still a lyrical ballad. Its interest does not derive, even in part, from the report of heroic event or "moving accident," and this despite the fact that it tells of a Catholic insurrection in the time of Elizabeth and that it describes the strange apparition of the doe. Wordsworth, in later distinguishing his poem from the balladry of Sir Walter Scott, was careful to point out that its action culminates not in a catastrophe of the material sort but rather in the spiritual state of the heroine, who triumphs with the help of the doe over despair and solipsism.[1] Emily (the heroine) is set apart from the rest of her family (the Nortons) in that her acts are not "outward things / Done visibly for other minds, words, signs, / Symbols or actions."[2] As a Protestant heroine she has no sacramental banner to rally her: passive resistance, patience, and the creature-comfort of the doe are her only aids.[3] Her triumph of privacy is similar to that of Christ's at the end of *Paradise Regained*.

The ballad also perfects other haunting concerns of Wordsworth's earlier poetry. Its central relationship, that of Emily and the doe, reposes again on an elision of intermediaries. Emily faces alone, and eventually draws comfort from, a natural mystery. The action of the poem isolates her from family, from society, and almost from the human condition. Her womanhood, then her Protestantism, then the fate of the Nortons and the death of her

brother Francis (the only other Protestant in the family), bring
her spirit to a singular nakedness. She approaches 'the very heart
of loss.' Yet though Emily, in her privation, is admirable:

> held above
> The infirmities of mortal love;
> Undaunted, lofty, calm, and stable,
> And awfully impenetrable, (1625–28)[4]

she is also in danger of losing her contact with things earthly. The
white doe, appearing at this point, obliges the unwilling heart to
resume some connection of feeling with the world. Slowly, re-
luctantly, Emily is brought back; through the sympathy of the
doe her own sympathetic imagination revives. A "holy, / Though
stern and rigorous, melancholy" (1596 f.) becomes a "holy, / Mild,
and grateful, melancholy" (1757 f.). She is renaturalized, or at least
"faintly, faintly tied / To earth."

The simplicity of Wordsworth's invention and the greatness of
his conception survive the more adventitious and polemical fea-
tures of the ballad. Coleridge saw at once that there were really
two stories: the ballad of Emily (almost totally Wordsworth's own)
and the ballad of the revolt (based on historical tradition). He
finds portions of the latter *"comparatively* very heavy" and com-
plains of too great a disjunction between the stories.[5] The poem
as finally printed may incorporate Coleridge's suggestions for uni-
fying the stories, since Emily and the doe are clearly the center of
the whole, and rather skillfully linked, in theme and plot, to the
story of the revolt, which remains somewhat heavy. Both parts of
the ballad contain a basic symbol: what the doe is to Emily, the
banner Emily was forced to embroider is to the fighting Nortons.
Both banner and doe take at least a portion of their influence from
the human mind that communicates to them its own creative en-
ergies.[6] When, however, Wordsworth begins to differentiate these
symbols, a polemically motivated speciousness enters. He associates
the reliance on the banner (the "tilting Furniture" of *Paradise
Lost* IX.34) with the pagan or superstitious element in Catholicism,
and so insists on seeing the "Protestant" relationship between Em-
ily and the doe as intrinsically purer than the "Catholic" one be-

tween the Nortons and the banner. Though there is a difference
between these relations, to identify it with that between the two
rival faiths is hardly tenable. Might not a Catholic Emily have
looked in a similar way on the doe?

Wordsworth is distracted by his conception (basically Miltonic)
of the difference between the Protestant and the Catholic imagina-
tions. He might otherwise have treated the entire action in the man-
ner of "The Thorn" and guided us step by step toward a central
mystery, as the older ballads do.* We can imagine an alternate
structure to the poem: the narrator's mind clinging to Norton
tower, prospecting a "rock-encircled Pound" nearby (where the
doe first appeared), then ranging, like Emily herself, through Bol-
ton Priory, and finally converging on two graves, the one Emily
used to haunt, that of her brother Francis, and her own, "one se-
questered hillock green," which the doe now frequents as assidu-
ously as Martha Ray her stunted thorn. In the first canto Words-
worth uses a modified form of this approach in describing the
"superstitious fancies" of those who see the faithful doe. She is the
elusive object of strange surmises. His poem is still about the imag-
ination's proper relation to the creature or to itself.

But Wordsworth's more objective narrative procedure, which
gives so much space to the Catholic revolt, allows him to depict, as
in "Hart-Leap Well," at least two kinds of imagination, certainly
related, yet distinguished in terms of their origin and vital psy-
chological consequences. The two kinds[7] are no longer identified
as martial and mild (the hunter's and the poet's in "Hart-Leap
Well") but as Catholic and Protestant. The imagination of the
two Norton factions is shown to be connected to, if not actually
derived from, particular creeds. Though I am inclined to discount
the poet's religious bias, his distinction remains typologically valid,
and is concerned with how nature participates in the growth of
the mind.

Without a basic sympathy that allows the mind to associate
with 'the creature,' there would be no world for that mind,
nothing it could recognize as vital to itself. In that sense we are

* See, e.g., "Lully, lulley, the faucon hath stolen my make away!"

truly givers of the given. When Wordsworth, referring to banner
and doe, says that they derive their influence not from properties
inherent in them, but from the soul of man which communicates
to them its creative energies, he is not abandoning the principle of
reciprocity, the dialectic of love between man and nature, but em-
phasizing rather awkwardly the constitutive ("excursive") act of
the mind which underlies all subsequent parleyings. Precisely be-
cause the mind must always *still* be humanized—because its attitude
toward this world remains problematic—the great virtue of nature
(as of the doe) is to lead from self to other, or to remind the self
of its power for relationship. This leaves the question as to what
attitude our mind should take toward its own power. Conscious
that the influence of banner or doe is, essentially, of its own choice,
it could seek to withdraw all value from them and stand in awe
only of itself. Or, like child and primitive, it might forget itself to
them, and achieve an entire transcendence of self-consciousness.
Wordsworth, in *The White Doe,* attempts to distinguish between
a basically superstitious and a more humane attitude toward the
symbols or second natures which we 'participate.'[8]

Thus, while the Catholic Nortons are a corporate entity cen-
tering on their father ("The Norton"), and the spirit of their
spirit depends on that relation which culminates totemically in
the banner (which bears, again as a composite charge, the five
wounds of Christ), Francis and Emily have a more individual re-
lation to their conscience. The Norton's Nine-in-One must
similarly be distinguished from the One-and-One of Emily and
Doe: to see in the companionship of woman and animal a spiritual
totem, or prophecy of the corporate consciousness of nature and
man, is to fall into the very superstition that created the banner.
Wordsworth evokes the idea of a mystic participation, but only to
resist it. His progression from Nortons and Banner to Emily and
Doe leads to a third relationship: that of *our* imagination, *our* re-
sponse (which he controls somewhat palpably) to this "animal
form divine." He brings us from what he believes to be a Romance
and Catholic perspective to one that is more natural. His poem,
beginning with "superstitious fancies strong, / Which do the
gentle creature wrong" (215–16), ends with a view that involves

a kind of Protestant "Assumption" yet respects the creatureliness
of the doe.

Wordsworth may even have glimpsed the possibility of breaking
through to a new mode, of changing the 'Catholic' romances to a
'Protestant' form—more Protestant than Spenser's. He enters the
realm of Romance to harrow its Christian mysteries and to natu-
ralize them. The white doe is a romance apparition carried over
into his "mortal song" with daring literalness. The Pagan animal
guide, or the suffering Nature of the romances, is transformed by
him into the Protestant Comforter. Wordsworth's doe (like the
fawn in Marvell's "The Nymph complaining for the death of her
faun") helps the betrayed soul to renew its kinship with nature.
The doe's strange humanity, however, retains a natural basis:
having been raised by Emily and her brother, the doe is to that
extent humanized and already merged with Emily's life. It is al-
ways our own human sympathy which nature reflects by drawing
out our love toward itself.

Wordsworth's attempt to revive the Romance mode for a con-
sciously Protestant imagination had no issue in his own poetry,
or even in English poetry as a whole, which will follow the freer
romances of Keats, Shelley, and Scott. But in America, where Puri-
tanism still questioned the sacred and also secular rights of imag-
ination, a similar development is found. The possibility of a
consciously Protestant romance is what inspires or self-justifies
Hawthorne, Melville, and Henry James. If the Christian poets of
the Renaissance wondered how they could use Pagan forms and
themes, the neo-Puritan writers wonder how they can use the Chris-
tian superstitions. Not only do we find the often directly presented
schism between an old-world (Norton) and a new-world (Emily)
imagination, in which the old world is, sometimes nobly, under the
spell of "superstitious fancies strong," but the action centers on the
manner in which a strange central apparition, a romance phe-
nomenon, is imaginatively valued. In the European society in
which she moves, James' Daisy Miller is a white doe, and there
are those who do the gentle creature wrong, who kill her, in fact,
by knowing her wrongly. I have chosen, of course, a very simple
case; but there is no need to ascend the scale of Jamesian or Mel-

villean fiction to the final white mystery. Wordsworth's scruples concerning the imagination are Puritan scruples even though they are gradually associated with Anglican thought.

That Wordsworth was seeking to develop a new kind of romance, one that would chasten our imaginations, is already suggested by the stanzas dedicating *The White Doe* to his wife. A moving personal document, they trace the history of his relation to romantic fiction. He describes his and Mary's love of Spenser, their innocent enjoyment of "each specious miracle." But then a "lamentable change"—the death of Wordsworth's brother—pierces their hearts:

> For us the stream of fiction ceased to flow,
> For us the voice of melody was mute.

Romance and realism are suddenly opposed. The truth is too harsh, and fiction is even blamed for deceiving the mind, for veiling reality with "the light that never was."[9] Spenser, however, is so soothing, that he beguiles them once more, and the story of the Nortons, with its own "mild Una in her sober cheer," is composed.

But the death of Wordsworth's brother leaves its mark. Though Wordsworth returns to Spenser, the stream of fiction is troubled, it will never again flow lightly "in the bent of Nature." The poet seems to have interpreted his brother's death, like his father's, as a "chastisement" following an over-extension of imaginative hopes (cf. *Prelude* XII.309–16). The dream of happiness built on John's return was something *hyper moron*, secretly apocalyptic, or beyond the measure nature could fulfill. This is not to say that John's loss was the decisive cause for Wordsworth's decline as a poet—I have abjured speculation on this matter. Some speculations, however, are simply a way of describing the later poetry, and it is quite true that whether or not the decisive shock came in 1805, Wordsworth's mind is now much less inclined to "wanton" in "the exercise of its own powers . . . loving its own creation."[10] If we compare his dedicatory stanzas to Mary with those Shelley wrote to *his* Mary and which preface "The Witch of Atlas," the distance between one poet's light-hearted espousal of "visionary rhyme" and the other's weight of scruples becomes fully apparent. It is as if Shelley and Wordsworth had polarized Spenserian romance, the former taking its *dulce,* the latter its *utile.*[11]

It might not seem possible that the later poetry could be beset by even more scruples, but this is what happens. Wordsworth's attitude toward his mind's "exercise of its powers" suffers a further restraint. He begins to watch on *two* fronts: to be deluded that "the mighty Deep / Was even the gentlest of all gentle Things"[12] is as dangerous as to gaze into the bottomless abyss. He is now as careful about an idealizing impulse as about the apocalyptic intimation. The presence of a Sympathetic Nature, which is the one superstition for which he had kept his respect, for it is vital not only to poetry but also to human development, being a necessary illusion in the growth of the mind, this too is falling away. Yet the story of the white doe is his attempt to save the notion once more in some purer form. He knows that to give it up entirely is to return to a holy, but stern and melancholy, imagination.

Under the pressure of these many restraints, Wordsworth's mind has little chance to fall in love with or explore its own impressions. Self-discovery, which informs the meditative lyrics (the act of recall there is never a passive thing but verges on new and often disturbing intuitions) almost disappears. And, by a curious irony, the unpublished *Prelude,* which is his greatest testimony to the living mind, now discourages further self-exploration. Such later sentiments as:

> Earth prompts—Heaven urges; let us seek the light,
> Studious of that pure intercourse begun
> When first our infant brows their lustre won,[13]

do not rely, in their weakness, on the external authority of the church,[14] but on the internal authority of his own greatest poem, which is kept private, and as scripture to himself abets the flat reiteration of his ideas in a slew of minor poems. J. M. Murry is right in feeling that the later Wordsworth represents the process of self-discovery as much more orthodox from the beginning than it was; and Coleridge, severely disappointed by *The Excursion,* offers a similar diagnosis: Wordsworth's opinions, he said, were based on "self-established convictions" and did not have for readers in general the special force they had for the poet.[15]

There are, nevertheless, strange happenings in the later poetry, which has a precarious quality of its own. Though Wordsworth no longer dallies with surmise, he cannot entirely forego apocalyptic fancies, or the opposite (if more generous) error which attributes to nature a vital and continuous role in the maturing of the mind. The old imaginative freedoms continue to rise up, like Proteus or Triton, against the narrow-minded materialism of his time—a living Pagan is better than a dead Christian spirit. He is not beyond being surprised by his imagination. It continues to defy his censorship, even if he queries every fancy, every moment of "quickened subjectivity." I shall conclude by considering certain incidents from the later poetry that show in what relation to his own mind Wordsworth stands.

1.

In 1820, thirty years after his journey through the Alps, he takes Mary and Dorothy to the Continent. Dorothy keeps her usual journal, to which he probably turned in composing the "memorials" of that tour.* While in the valley of Chamonix (a place sacred to the poet) the travelers hear voices rising from the mountain's base and glimpse below them a procession making its way to the church. Dorothy describes the scene for us:

> [we saw] a lengthening Procession—the Priest in his robes—the host, and banners uplifted; and men following two and two; —and, last of all, a great number of females, in like order; the head and body of each covered with a white garment. The stream continued to flow on for a long time, till all had paced slowly round the church. . . . The procession was grave and simple, agreeing with the simple decorations of a village church; the banners made no glittering shew; the Females composed a moving girdle round the Church; their figures, from head to foot, covered with one piece of white cloth, resembled the small pyramids of the Glacier, which were before our eyes; and it was impossible to look at one and the other without fancifully connecting them together. Imagine the

* _Memorials of a Tour on the Continent. 1820._

*moving* Figures, like a stream of pyramids,—the white Church, the half-concealed Village, and the Glacier close behind, among pine-trees,—a pure sun shining over all! and remember that these objects were seen at the base of those enormous mountains, and you may have some faint notion of the effect produced upon us by that beautiful spectacle.[16]

Wordsworth is inspired by this to a 'progress poem' entitled "Processions. Suggested on a Sabbath Morning in the Vale of Chamouny" which traces the spirit of religious ceremonies from ancient times to the present. The Alps, archaic strongholds, allow him to recognize in Pagan ritual the impure basis of Christian pageantry. Shrill canticles have yielded to sober litanies; silver bells and pompous decorations to "hooded vestments fair"; and noisy feasts to an assembly breathing "a Spirit more subdued and soft." Moreover, as he looks on, another archaic vestige suggests itself, which is hinted at in Dorothy's account: that the procession is born of the mountain, like the white pillars above it. Indeed, the glacier columns, juxtaposed with the moving column of white figures, bring to mind the theory of Creation by Metamorphosis. The mountain, in this Blakean insight, is "men seen afar."

Wordsworth is strangely frightened at this—not at the mere thought of metamorphosis but at a reflexive knowledge connected with it. He realizes he has viewed more than a transformed archaic ritual, or ancient truth: he has seen the *source* of that truth in his mind's excited and spontaneous joining of the living stream of people to the frozen of nature. As in his greatest poetry, the mind is moved by itself after being moved by something external. He writes a stanza similar in tenor and directness to the apostrophe to Imagination in the sixth book of *The Prelude,* similar at least in its magnificent opening:

> Trembling, I look upon the secret springs
> Of that licentious craving in the mind
> To act the God among external things,
> To bind, on apt suggestion, or unbind;
> And marvel not that antique Faith inclined
> To crowd the world with metamorphosis,

> Vouchsafed in pity or in wrath assigned;
> Such insolent temptations wouldst thou miss,
> Avoid these sights; nor brood o'er Fable's dark abyss!

Wordsworth's reaction, visceral first, pontific later, differs from the usual religious decision to relinquish a profane subject or style. He does not say, in Herbert's sweet manner, farewell dark fables, or censor their use in Christian poetry. But he turns in the moment, and explicitly, from a power of his own mind without which poetry is not conceivable. It is not fabling merely, but "Fable's dark abyss"—the mind of man itself—he now fears to look on. He is afraid of fables because of their reaction on a mind that might brood too pregnantly on what they reveal of its power. Yet at the time of *The White Doe* he had still tried to 'convert' a fable by purifying its superstition and cleansing its mystery: the doe is not a metamorphosed spirit and her powers of sympathy are due to natural not supernatural causes. What a difference, also, between this sacred tremor and his earlier, almost cavalier attitude toward all mythologies! In 1798, and again in 1814, he professes to be unalarmed at their conceptions because of the greater "fear and awe" that fall on him when he regards "the Mind of Man— / My haunt, and the main region of my song." He did not fear his fear then as he does now, trembling before his own creative will.

### 2.

Wordsworth's diffidence is no sudden thing; we found it at the beginning of his career, and related it to an extraordinary, apocalyptic consciousness of self. At that time religion seemed to him too much a product of that same apocalyptic consciousness. Nature had to be defended against a supernatural religion as well as against the barren eye of Science. Was it ever meant, he asks,

> That this majestic imagery, the clouds
> The ocean and the firmament of heaven
> Should lie a barren picture on the mind?[17]

In the later poetry, however, religion has changed its role. It now protects rather than threatens nature. He begins to identify with

the Anglo-Catholic concept of the *via media* his ideal of Nature, of
England, even of Poetry. The poet, he had said in 1802, is "the rock
of defence for human nature; an upholder and preserver, carrying
everywhere with him relationship and love." He now sees the
church as part of that rock: an *ecclesia* mediating by a divine prin-
ciple of mercy the sterner demands of God, State, and Imagination,
demands which have often threatened human nature, and led to
individual or collective fanaticisms. Religion and imagination are
intervolved (Wordsworth and Blake are in perfect accord on *this*),
and whereas Catholicism incites an apocalyptic response:

> Mine ear has rung, my spirit sunk subdued,
> Sharing the strong emotion of the crowd,
> When each pale brow to dread hosannas bowed
> While clouds of incense mounting veiled the rood,
> That glimmered like a pine-tree dimly viewed
> Through Alpine vapours . . .

the Anglican Church, which is the *religio loci* corresponding to
the *genius loci* of England, rejects such appalling rites in the hope
that nature, man, and God constitute ultimately "one society":

> the Sun with his first smile
> Shall greet that symbol crowning the low Pile:
> And the fresh air of incense-breathing morn
> Shall wooingly embrace it; and green moss
> Creep round its arms through centuries unborn.

Covenant has replaced, as completely as possible, apocalypse: his
emblem marries nature, time, and the spirit.

The *Ecclesiastical Sonnets*, from which the above extracts are
taken,[18] show Wordsworth is suspicious of everything that could
rouse the apocalyptic passions. This is also an important clue to his
later politics, which seem illiberal, apostate even; a failure of nerve
like his poetry. The evidence against him is indeed black. "That
such a man," cries Shelley, "should be such a poet!" Shelley did not
know Wordsworth personally, but even the faithful Crabb Rob-
inson, who made all the possible allowances, is compelled to ad-
dress Dorothy in 1827: "I assure you it gives me a real pain when
I think that some future commentator may possibly hereafter

write: 'This great poet survived to the fifth decennary of the nine-
teenth century, but he appears to have died in the year 1814, as far
as life consisted in an active sympathy with the temporary [viz.
temporal] welfare of his fellow-creatures.' "[19] Only in matters of
Church doctrine, as distinguished from Church or national poli-
tics, does something of Wordsworth's liberalism remain. His views,
says H. N. Fairchild, praising where he thinks to blame, are "wholly
consistent with modern Christian liberalism . . . very loose and
vague, however, for a nineteenth-century High Churchman."[20]

Wordsworth, it is clear, has passed from the idea that change
(let alone revolutionary change) intends a repossession of the
earth to the idea that it might cause a greater dispossession than
ever. Harper has documented his panic fear of change. It is a
deeply emotional and imaginative thing, and has almost no rela-
tion to his own very small prosperity. The Reform Bill of 1832, for
instance, seems to him to herald a revolt of the masses. He proph-
esies ruin and destruction to England and thinks of having to
leave it. His jeremiads indicate a soul which knows itself too well,
and is still afraid in others of those "blasts of music" and "daring
sympathies with power" to which he had given ear at the time of
the French Revolution.[21]

Dark thoughts—"blind thoughts" as he calls them in "Resolu-
tion and Independence"—certainly continue to impinge on him.
Yet how deep they lie, almost too deep for notice. They come to
the surface only in matters of politics, and in exceptionally self-
conscious verses, like those in memory of Chamonix. The most
famous of the River Duddon sonnets, the "After-thought" of the
series, runs truer to course. The whole series, less conventional
than it seems, participates in the poet's desire to bind together
the powers of his mind and of nature; and to know this illumines
the character of his final sonnet.

The "After-thought" begins very simply:

> I thought of Thee, my partner and my guide,
> As being passed away.

It makes us wonder, this quiet human directness, whom the poet is
addressing, but then Willard Sperry's observation that "his brief
for nature's morality was based upon her openness to our ad-

dress"[22] comes to mind. The more remarkable aspect of the verses
is what Wordsworth can have meant by the river "passing away."

He must have recalled the prophecy of streams shrinking in the
final fire, of "Old Ocean, in his bed left singed and bare."[23] This
must have come to him and threatened the entire basis of his son-
nets, which is the partnership of mind and nature. Or is it his own
death which he foresaw, as in "Tintern Abbey"? But why, in that
case, would he talk of Duddon's death rather than of his own?

I suspect, in any case, that the personal fact of his dying seemed to
him a small matter compared to the river's loss and the foreboded
severing of the loves of man and nature.[24] Duddon is mortal in that
it may die in man or to him as he grows older, but especially in
that it may die to the human imagination, generally, on Words-
worth's death. For if his special mission among poets is to marry
nature to the mind, his death takes on a cosmic meaning. The rest
of the poem, of course, dispels his strange fear concerning Duddon:

> —Vain sympathies!
> For, backward, Duddon! as I cast my eyes,
> I see what was, and is, and will abide;
> Still glides the Stream, and shall for ever glide;
> The Form remains, the Function never dies;
> While we, the brave, the mighty, and the wise,
> We Men, who in our morn of youth defied
> The elements, must vanish;—be it so!
> Enough, if something from our hands have power
> To live, and act, and serve the future hour;
> And if, as toward the silent tomb we go,
> Through love, through hope, and faith's transcendent dower,
> We feel that we are greater than we know.

This is pure consolation and too easy. His sympathies (for the
stream!) are "vain" because nature outlives man and will continue
to inspire him; and because man, too, has the promise, through
religion, of an immortality that hopefully does not exclude the
tie of nature.

Yet the distance between "Tintern Abbey" and the River Dud-
don "After-thought" is not great. The primary experience is one of

nature, of the Wye or the Duddon or other great presences. In the earlier poems we are told directly of how the cataracts haunted the boy or how the objects of nature "lay upon his mind like substances" and "perplexed the bodily sense." The same kind of perplexity is produced by the appearance of the white doe. The mystery in nature is that of our relation to it, which is darkly sympathetic, so that Goethe calls it "das offenbare Geheimniss," an incumbent natural mystery. But this experience of relationship, open to all, is followed by the further mystery of its diminution, also shared by all. The poet who returns to Tintern Abbey knows his loss; he sees it in the glass of the landscape, darkly; and a prophetic fear, despite nature's continuing importance, leads him to envisage severance and even death. The conclusion that his death may mean the passing away of nature from the human mind is not yet drawn, for he prays that his sister may continue a relationship to which he is dying. But in the "after-thought" his fear touches that furthest point. It does so fleetingly, yet still bespeaks either a delusion of grandeur or a remarkable conviction that man and nature are growing irremediably apart, and that the gap between them, whether a historical error or a providential test, already verges on apocalypse. "The sun strengthens us no more, neither does the moon."[25]

The burden of this secret consciousness in Wordsworth should not be underestimated. It is he who stands between us and the death of nature; and this is also the truest justification for the "egotistical sublime" in his poetry. He values his own lightest feeling for the sufficiencies of mother earth—

> The night that calms, the day that cheers;
> The common growth of mother-earth
> Suffices me—her tears, her mirth
> Her humblest mirth and tears[26]

—because her call to him, unregarded, augurs a loss in our capacity to respond to nature, and hence the virtual opposite of that "great consummation" of which he sings in the verses that preface the 1814 *Excursion*. He feels that he must personally fasten or new-create the links between nature and the human mind. The "Adonais" Shelley laments is strangely like his own conception of himself.

I may seem to exaggerate Wordsworth's sense of mission; but no one has yet explained the heart-sickness and melancholia of the aging poet. These are prompted, of course, by political fears (which are really imaginative fears) and by personal grief, yet do they differ, except in persistence, from earlier dejections? Is his "fixed despondency, uncorrected"[27] human weakness merely, and the effect of old age, or may it not accord with his own younger picture of himself as a "meditative, oft a suffering man"?[28] What his meditations were, and why linked intimately to a certain kind of suffering, may now be clear. The selfhood Wordsworth knew, and which is always related to a fear of the death of nature, is at first alleviated by his sense of special mission, then cruelly confirmed by what he takes to be his growing isolation.[29] At the time of "Michael," he is still thinking "Of youthful Poets, who among these hills / Will be my second self when I am gone"; it is in hope of these that he spins his homely ballads. But he never recognizes Shelley or Keats or any of the following generation as his second self. He is a stubborn, old, opinionated man—perhaps; the fact remains that Shelley and Keats, though concerned with the humanizing of imagination, have greater affinities with the Renaissance poets and that these have greater affinities with one another than Wordsworth has with any of them. Milton, whose sense of mission is as strong as his, could turn to Spenser and even to Virgil; Blake, though almost unknown in his time, thought of himself as continuing or correcting Milton and the Bible; but Wordsworth, despite his love for the older writers, and especially for Milton, can turn to no one in his desire to save nature for the human imagination. He is the most isolated figure among the great English poets.

IV. CRITICAL BIBLIOGRAPHIES AND NOTES

# Abbreviations

JEGP:   Journal of English and Germanic Philology
MLN:    Modern Language Notes
MLQ:    Modern Language Quarterly
PQ:     Philological Quarterly
RES:    Review of English Studies
SP:     Studies in Philology
SR:     Studies in Romanticism

Bateson, Wordsworth: F. W. Bateson, Wordsworth: A Re-Interpretation (2d ed. London, 1956).
Early Letters: The Early Letters of William and Dorothy Wordsworth, ed. E. de Selincourt (Oxford, 1935).
Fink, Milieu: Zera S. Fink, The Early Wordsworthian Milieu: A Notebook of Christopher Wordsworth with a Few Entries by William Wordsworth (New York, 1958).
Garrod, Wordsworth: H. W. Garrod, Wordsworth (Oxford, 1923 and 1927).
Griggs, Collected Letters, 1, 2: Collected Letters of Samuel Taylor Coleridge, ed. E. L. Griggs (2 vols. Oxford, 1956).
Grosart, 1, 2, 3: The Prose Works of William Wordsworth, ed. A. B. Grosart (3 vols. London, 1876).
Legouis, The Early Life: Emile Legouis, The Early Life of William Wordsworth, 1770–1798 (London, 1897).
Meyer, Formative Years: G. W. Meyer, Wordsworth's Formative Years, University of Michigan Publications in Language and Literature, 20 (Ann Arbor, 1943).
Middle Years: The Letters of William and Dorothy Wordsworth: The Middle Years, ed. E. de Selincourt (2 vols. Oxford, 1937).
Moorman, Wordsworth: Mary Moorman, William Wordsworth: A Biography: The Early Years, 1770–1803 (Oxford, 1957).
Potts, Prelude: Abbie F. Potts, Wordsworth's Prelude: A Study of Its Literary Form (Ithaca, N.Y., 1953).

*Prelude²: William Wordsworth, The Prelude,* ed. E. de Selincourt, 2d ed. revised by H. Darbishire (Oxford, 1959).

*PW, 1, 2* (etc.): *The Poetical Works of William Wordsworth,* ed. E. de Selincourt and H. Darbishire (5 vols. Oxford, 1940–49).

NOTE: Years in parentheses usually are dates of publication; without the parentheses, they are dates of composition.

## List of Bibliographies

The bibliographies precede the notes to each chapter, and are found on the following pages:

# I. Thesis: The Halted Traveler

CRITICAL BIBLIOGRAPHY

The best pages on Wordsworth's "subjectivity" and "self-consciousness" are still those of Willard Sperry, *Wordsworth's Anti-Climax* (Cambridge, Mass., 1935), pp. 23–28. Noting that "the imagination itself rather than the objects upon which it is employed becomes . . . the subject of the work," Sperry stresses Wordsworth's modernity and wonders whether the "objectification of self-consciousness and the esthetic transcript of the workings of the imagination" may not demand a mental subtlety beyond our power (a thought which reflects the theologian in Sperry; cf. T. S. Eliot's reservation on the introspectionist emphasis that leads "From Poe to Valéry," *Hudson Review*, 2, 1949, 327–42). Sperry does not develop his insights by close reading or specific illustration, but he refers us to Charles Lamb's remark that in "The Old Cumberland Beggar," when Wordsworth desires the Beggar to have about him the melody of birds (although he cannot hear them), "the mind knowingly passes a fiction upon herself, first substituting her own feeling for the 'Beggar' and in the same breath, detecting the fallacy, will not part with her wish." This kind of fiction, closely related to surmise, is among the subtlest and least appreciated characteristics of Romantic poetry. Mme. de Staël had remarked of the lyric poet, and of the Romantic lyricist especially, that "il est ébranlé par ses conceptions comme par un événement de sa vie" (*De l'Allemagne*, Pt. 2, ch. 10), and Erich Heller has recently said that Rilke's emotions not only interpret an object but also respond to their own interpretation (*The Disinherited Mind*, New York, 1957, pp. 171–72). There is, one might say, a "Romantic" conceit that should be compared in degree and quality of self-consciousness to the "Metaphysical" conceit: Keats' mind, addressing the nightingale as "immortal bird" in the seventh stanza of his Ode, is also quite clearly "passing a fiction upon itself"—which, by the way, it passes *through*, for the sense of alienation returns via the associated image of Ruth's "forlorn" self. Wordsworth's conceits are usually subtler or harder to detect. W. K. Wimsatt in *The Verbal Icon* (Lexington, Kentucky, 1954), pp. 114 ff., and J. Danby in *The Simple Wordsworth* (New York, 1961) have brought some of his covert and as it were organic "transferences" to our attention (cf. my *The Unmediated Vision*, New Haven, 1954, pp. 21–23, on the opening of "Tintern Abbey"). Wordsworth's mind does not always react on itself in an explicit way, but some reaction, especially under the pressure of "emotion recollected in tranquillity" is rarely absent.

While there have been numerous and interesting interpretations of Wordsworth's egotism, there have been relatively few descriptions of it, and no real analysis or even affirmation of the link in him between self-consciousness and imagination. This is partially due to the fact that these terms are usually given a different meaning by students of the English Romantic movement. Imagination stands for the "sympathetic imagination," and when it is linked to apocalyptic feelings or visions, as in the case of Blake, it clearly betokens the opposite of self-consciousness, the very annihilation of selfhood. This is the place to signal the difficulty rather than to argue the terms, and to add that while Wordsworth does not himself use "self-consciousness," he talks freely of consciousness, underconsciousness, etc. The term seems to have been popularized by German Romantic philosophy, and is imported by Coleridge, for whom the words spirit, self, self-consciousness, and the divine I AM, are synonyms (see *Biographia Literaria*, ch. 12, thesis 6).

On the individual poems, the following discussions (other than those mentioned in the notes) are especially relevant: Danby, *The Simple Wordsworth*, pp. 122–27, on "The Solitary Reaper"; also pp. 111–14, on the Boy of Winander; David Ferry, *The Limits of Mortality* (Middletown, Conn., 1959), pp. 88–89, on the Boy of Winander; Bateson, *Wordsworth*, pp. 21–29, on the Boy of Winander; Harold Bloom, *The Visionary Company* (New York, 1961), pp. 127–36, on "Tintern Abbey." Also, on "The Solitary Reaper," A. A. Mendilow, in *Scripta Hierosolymita, 10* (1962).

NOTES

"The Solitary Reaper"

1. *Biographia Literaria* (1818), ch. 22.
2. Preface (1800) to *Lyrical Ballads*.
3. *Biographia Literaria*, ch. 22.
4. *Letters of Anna Seward, Written between the Years 1784 and 1807* (6 vols. Edinburgh, 1811), *6*, 366–67. On "Anna Seward and the Romantic Poets," see Samuel H. Monk, in *Wordsworth and Coleridge: Studies in Honor of George McLean Harper*, ed. E. L. Griggs (Princeton, 1939), pp. 118–34.
5. A. C. Bradley, "Wordsworth," *Oxford Lectures on Poetry* (London, 1909), p. 104; Pottle, "The Eye and the Object," in *Wordsworth: Centenary Studies*, ed. G. Dunklin (Princeton, 1951), pp. 23–42. For other comments on the 'battle' of the Daffodils, see *Middle Years, 1*, 129, 149, 170.
6. Keats, letter to Richard Woodhouse, October 27, 1818; and letter to John Hamilton Reynolds, February 3, 1818.
7. Jeffrey, review of Crabbe's *Poems* in the *Edinburgh Review* of April 1808; cf. the many remarks by Hazlitt, as in a lecture of 1818 that might have influenced Keats. Members of the modern school of poetry, said Hazlitt, "surround the meanest objects with the morbid feelings and devouring egotism of the writers' own minds. Milton and Shakespeare did not so understand poetry. They gave a more liberal interpretation both to nature and art. They did not do all they could to get rid of the one and the other, to fill up the dreary void with the Moods of their own Minds [the title of a section of Wordsworth's *Poems in Two Volumes*]." See also G. Steiner, " 'Egoism and Egotism' . . .," in *Essays in Criticism*, 2 (1952), 444–52; A. Gérard, *L'Idée romantique de la poésie en Angleterre* (Paris, 1955), pp. 252–56; W. J. Bate, *From Classic to Romantic* (1946), passim.
8. Anna Seward, while by no means without reservations concerning Bloomfield (author of *The Farmer's Boy*), gives the "fidelity" of his "pictures" warm praise (*Letters, 5*, 383), and Jeffrey, while censuring Burns' "rusticity," still contrasts his "authentic rustics" with Wordsworth's (On the *Reliques* of Robert Burns, *Edinburgh Review*, January 1809). Robert Mayo in "The Contemporaneity of the Lyrical Ballads," *PMLA, 69* (1954), 486–522, has shown the degree to which the subjects, themes, and attitudes of Wordsworth's poetry conformed to popular taste.
9. "Surely the Heathens knew better how to joyn and read these mystical Letters than we Christians, who cast a more careless Eye on these common Hieroglyphics, and disdain to suck Divinity from the flowers of Nature," *Religio Medici* (1643), Pt. I, sec. 16.
10. Jeffrey again and again praises an author for his "force, and truth of description," for the "selection and condensation of expression," which are the

great and simple standards of picturesque poetry. His comparison of Crabbe with Wordsworth expresses this pointedly: "He [Crabbe] delights us by the truth, and vivid and picturesque beauty of his representations, and by the force and pathos of the sensations with which we feel that they are connected. Mr. Wordsworth and his associates, on the other hand, introduce us to beings whose existence was not previously suspected by the acutest observers of nature; and excite an interest for them—where they do excite any interest—more by an eloquent and refined analysis of their own capricious feelings, than by any obvious or intelligible ground of sympathy in their situation" (*Edinburgh Review*, April 1808). On the importance of "energetic" picture-making, see J. H. Hagstrum, *The Sister Arts* (Chicago, 1958), passim.

11. Helen Darbishire's introduction and notes to her edition of the *Poems in Two Volumes* (Oxford, 1914 and 1952) set forth Wordsworth's debt to seventeenth-century poetry. His particular relation to Puritanism, or "left-wing" Protestant currents, has not, I believe, been fully considered. There is an interesting note on his relation to Methodism (in the broad sense of the word) in Arthur Beatty, *Representative Poems* (Garden City, New York, 1937), introd. p. xxxi. Wordsworth knew such works as Richard Baxter's "Self-Review," to which he refers in a note to the (1814) *Excursion* IV.131–32; but he may not have read it till reprinted in Christopher (later Bishop) Wordsworth's *Ecclesiastical Biography* (London, 1810). Jeffrey, who had a keen nose for "Methodist" enthusiasm, easily makes a connection in his review of *The Excursion* ("the mystical verbiage of the Methodist pulpit is repeated, till the speaker entertains no doubt that he is the chosen organ of divine truth and persuasion," *Edinburgh Review*, November 1814). The second volume of H. N. Fairchild's *Religious Trends in English Poetry* (New York, 1939–57), esp. pp. 149 ff., remains the best account of the religious temper of the times into which Wordsworth was born; Erich Thurmann, *Der Niederschlag der evangelischen Bewegung in der englischen Literatur* (Emsdetten, 1936), though not concerned with Wordsworth, has interesting sidelights on the vitality of the movement and the reactions to it (including that of the *Edinburgh Review*). Cf. also J. Crofts, *Wordsworth and the Seventeenth Century* (London, 1940), a Warton Lecture which is still the best evocation of Wordsworth's latter-day Puritanism.

12. *PW, 3,* 444–45. Cf. "The Waggoner," lines 209–15, *PW, 2,* 204.

13. On *Prelude* VI.592 ff. see below, Part II of this book.

14. "Les anciens avaient, pour ainsi dire, une âme corporelle, dont tous les mouvements étaient forts, directs, et conséquents; il n'en est pas de même du coeur humain développé par le christianisme: les modernes ont puisé dans le repentir chrétien l'habitude de se replier continuellement sur eux-mêmes." *De l'Allemagne,* Pt. 2, ch. 11.

15. The subdued pathos of the situation emerges more strongly when we consider the poem's genesis. Wordsworth has been *waylaid* by an image (either out of his past or out of his imagination), and now exhorts himself to attend it.

The poem itself, of course, gives practically no hint that a mental traveler is speaking: this kind of consideration is a bonus of biographical study.

16. Cf. Pottle, "The Eye and the Object," passim.

17. Its classical radix is probably the "Fallor? an ..." construction (cf. Keats' "Do I wake or sleep?"), which Milton uses in *Elegy* V.5, and in *Comus*, lines 221–23. Merritt Hughes has pointed out its frequency in Latin poetry (e.g. Ovid, *Amores* 3.1.34, and Horace, passim).

18. Cf. my "Milton's Counterplot," *ELH*, 25 (1958), 1–12.

19. J. M. Murry discusses Keats' use of "speculation," which is close in meaning to "surmise" (*Keats*, 4th ed. New York, 1955, ch. 8). Keats joins the two words in a letter to Benjamin Bailey of November 22, 1817: "have you never by being surprised with an old Melody—in a delicious place—by a delicious voice, felt over again your very speculations and surmises at the time it first operated on your soul." (Louis Martz, in the last chapter of *The Poetry of Meditation*, New Haven, 1954, suggests there may be an intrinsic link between lyric poetry and the "meditative style," pointing out, at the same time, that poetry like Wordsworth's is different from that patterned more deliberately on religious techniques of meditation.)

20. In the "Ode on a Grecian Urn," similarly, only stanza 4 is free of the "overwrought" tempo of speculation: the poet almost comes to rest within his surmise.

21. E. M. Sickels' *The Gloomy Egoist* (New York, 1932) is a valuable compendium of the melancholia of the Romantics. On the "sentimental" (i.e. reflective-sad) character of modern poetry, cf. Schiller's "Über naive und sentimentalische Poesie" (1790).

22. *The Greek Bucolic Poets*, tr. J. M. Edmonds (London and New York, 1928), 364 ff. Theocritus' "epigrams" or "inscriptions" were translated into English for Robert Anderson's edition of *The Works of the British Poets*, (London, 1795), *13*, 157–60.

23. See below, chapter on the *Lyrical Ballads*, pp. 151 f. and notes, for further details concerning the influence of inscriptions on Wordsworth's poetry. Also my "Wordsworth, Inscriptions, and Romantic Nature Poetry," in *From Sensibility to Romanticism*, eds. F. Hilles and H. Bloom (Oxford University Press, 1965).

24. *Wordsworth's Anti-Climax*, p. 27.

25. See "Poems written during a Tour in Scotland," Vol. 2 of *Poems in Two Volumes* (1807), and *PW, 3*, 64–96.

26. "The Nightingale, a Conversational Poem" (1798).

27. See "Resolution and Independence" (1807).

28. "Resolution and Independence," sts. VI and VII.

29. See G. Wilson Knight's "The Wordsworthian Profundity" in *The Starlit Dome* (New York, 1941).

30. A. C. Bradley, *Oxford Lectures on Poetry*, p. 104.

31. *Prelude* VII.643–44.

32. *Prelude* VI.592 ff. Unless I state otherwise, the 1850 *Prelude* is used.

33. Letter to Robert Southey, prefatory to *Peter Bell, PW,* 2, 331.

### The Boy of Winander

1. Comment published in 1815, see *Prelude²,* p. 547.

2. My italics; MS. JJ, *Prelude²,* pp. 639–40.

3. The MSS lead me to think that the second paragraph of "There was a Boy" is a later addition, although there is insufficient evidence for any very firm judgment. The letter in which Wordsworth sent the original lines to Coleridge (probably in November 1798) is lost, and what is left of Coleridge's answering letter of December 10, 1798 (Griggs, *Collected Letters, 1,* 452–53), at least does not indicate that the boy was said to die. In MS JJ the second paragraph is not found, and the first paragraph, as I have indicated, is explicitly autobiographical; but in MS 18a, a notebook of the same time, the paragraph is found, and the episode given a more impersonal setting.

4. "The sports of childhood, and the untimely death of promising youth, is . . . a common topic of poetry. Mr. Wordsworth has made some blank verse about it; but, instead of the delightful and picturesque sketches with which so many authors of moderate talents have presented us on this inviting subject, all that he is pleased to communicate of *his* rustic child, is, that he used to amuse himself with shouting to the owls, and hearing them answer. . . . This is all we hear of him; and for the sake of this one accomplishment, we are told, that the author has frequently stood mute, and gazed on his grave for half an hour together!" ("On Crabbe's Poems," *Edinburgh Review,* April 1808). I have quoted most of the passage to indicate again the dominantly "picturesque" aesthetic of Jeffrey.

5. I quote from the version found in *Prelude* V.391 ff.

### "Strange Fits of Passion . . ."

1. "Hart-Leap Well" (1800).

2. The poem is quoted throughout this section in the revised (not the 1800) version.

3. From his *A Defense of Poetry,* 1821.

4. "She dwelt among the untrodden ways" (1800).

### "Tintern Abbey"

1. *Prelude* (1805) XIII.188 ff.

2. Cf. with "Tintern Abbey" a contemporary analogue printed by *Gentleman's Magazine* in 1808, but identified as lines "written at the place [Finchale Abbey], by a stranger, in the year 1784." The lines hearken back to "those awful days, / When stern Religion with her iron rod / And frown terrific, humaniz'd the soul" (*Gentleman's Magazine, 78,* 924). This kind of reluctant

protestant shudder at the older and sterner religion is quite different from Wordworth's consciousness of "The still, sad music of humanity."

## II. Synopsis: The Via Naturaliter Negativa

CRITICAL BIBLIOGRAPHY

John Jones, in his comprehensive attempt to trace the "History of Wordsworth's Imagination" (*The Egotistical Sublime*, London, 1954) combatted the "large and lazy assumption that the Romantic poets were all striving to express unity." By showing that Wordsworth's best poetry expresses solitude-in-relationship, he recovers the poet's own explicit statement in the "Essay, Supplementary to the Preface [of 1815]" that "in nature everything is distinct, yet nothing defined into absolute independent singleness." Jones does for Wordsworth what Earl Wasserman has done for Keats (*The Finer Tone*, Baltimore, 1953) and Harold Bloom for Shelley (*Shelley's Mythmaking*, New Haven, 1959), except that his schema, like that of E. D. Hirsch (*Wordsworth and Schelling*, New Haven, 1960), is of the both-and rather than dialectical form. Yet despite Jones, G. Wilson Knight's *The Starlit Dome* (New York, 1941), essential pages in L. Abercrombie's *The Art of Wordsworth* (New York, 1952, pp. 129–31), and Bradley's essay in the *Oxford Lectures* (London, 1909), the "solitary" or "sublime" or "apocalyptic" Wordsworth has been neglected for the poet of natural blendings and healing interchanges. The reason is an inability to link the two Wordsworths in a genuinely dialectical manner, and a confusion (from which even Jones is not free) as to Wordsworth's own concept of imagination. It is quite true, as an early commentator saw, that there was a "wonderful interchange" that went on between the poet and all the things about him, "they flowing into him, he going out into them. His soul attracted them to itself, as a mountain-top draws the clouds, and at their touch woke up to feel its kinship with the mysterious life that is in all nature, and in each separate object of nature" (J. C. Shairp, *Studies in Poetry and Philosophy*, Edinburgh, 1868). Shairp, as a professing Christian, is sensitive to Wordsworth's distance from sentimental pantheism, and therefore stresses, like Jones, the "distinct but related" structures of the poet's world. Yet when he goes on to affirm that it is "the cardinal work of the imagination, to possess itself of the life of whatever thing it deals with," he completely disregards the precarious separateness of Wordsworth's imagination, and the fact that true reciprocity—mind meeting world with equal flame—was realized at only two periods in Wordsworth's life, and is mainly a hope, and faith, and desire. Something too strong in the imagination, or too weak in nature, or vice versa, frustrates the "consummation" for which his poetry is a "spousal verse." My own interpretation of Wordsworth's understanding of the relations of mind and nature may not be acceptable to everyone, but it is certain that he is not a mystic or even a materialist (see, for the materialist hypothesis, H. W. Piper, *The Active Universe: Pantheism and the Concept of Imagination in the English Romantic Poets*, London, 1962). If Wordsworth must be labeled, it would be better to call him a radical Protestant whose mind is in love with works ("Working but in alliance with the works / Which it beholds," *Prelude* II.259–60) yet cannot subdue or bind itself to natural objects. "I am principally concerned," says Piper, "with the Wordsworthian notion of the Imagination as the power to communicate with the life in natural objects"—this may possibly be the Coleridgean notion, but it certainly is not Wordsworth's. The strongly neutral or "it" aspect of much Wordsworthian landscape reveals an imagination in man or in nature which is strangely "unnatural," dehumanized: "The Book of Job ends by confronting us with 'rain on the earth, where no man is; on the wilderness wherein there is no man.' There is not the slightest concession to any humanism . . . Much of the Wordsworthian scene is of this order. There are waste places, winds, elemental transactions taking place in indifference to man. . . . Wordsworth, except for rare moments of semi-mystical fulfilment, is always careful to observe the distinction between the objects he contemplates and himself as thinking subject. There is a gulf between. And man was for him an incident in the scene unfolded on the far side of the gulf" (Sperry, *Wordsworth's Anti-Climax*, Cambridge, Mass., 1935, pp. 170–77). Harold Bloom in

*The Visionary Company* (New York, 1961), our first systematic and eloquent questioning of the idea that the Romantics are fundamentally nature poets, and Paul de Man in his essay on the Romantic image, *Revue internationale de philosophie, 14* (1960), 68–84, have also helped to destroy the "large and lazy assumption" of which Jones complained.

NOTES

1. See *Blake, Coleridge, Wordsworth, Lamb, etc., Being Selections from the Remains of Henry Crabb Robinson,* ed. E. J. Morley (Manchester, 1932), pp. 5 and 15.

2. See the Critical Bibliography for this chapter.

3. Throughout this book, quotations from *The Prelude* (unless otherwise stated) are from the 1850 text as printed by De Selincourt and Darbishire in *William Wordsworth, The Prelude* (Oxford, 1959), short-titled *Prelude²*. Charles Moorman has established that there is a pattern to the opening episode, although I will differ from him in my view of the pattern and its meaning. See "Wordsworth's *Prelude: 1,* 1–269," *MLN,* 72 (1957), 416–20. R. D. Havens, *The Mind of a Poet* (Baltimore, 1941), pp. 290 ff., had failed to see any pattern.

4. Emancipated—but through exile. For the allusions to *Paradise Lost* and Exodus, see *Prelude* I.14 and 16–18.

5. Cf. M. H. Abrams, "The Correspondent Breeze: A Romantic Metaphor," in *English Romantic Poets,* ed. Abrams (Galaxy paperback, New York, 1960), pp. 37–54.

6. That the rising up of imagination occurred as Wordsworth was remembering his disappointment rather than immediately after it (i.e. in 1804, not in 1790) was first pointed out by W. G. Fraser in *TLS* (April 4, 1929), p. 276.

7. Marginalia to Volume I of Wordsworth's *Poems* of 1815. I may venture the opinion that Wordsworth, at the beginning of *The Prelude,* goes back to nature not to increase his chances of sensation but rather to emancipate his mind from immediate external excitements, the "gross and violent stimulants" (1800 Preface to *Lyrical Ballads*) of the city he leaves behind him.

8. *The Unmediated Vision* (New Haven, 1954), pp. 17–20.

9. *Hyperion* III.103–07.

10. Cf. the Intimations Ode; also *Prelude* I.597 ff.

11. Of the four sentences which comprise lines 617–40, the first three alternate the themes of eager and of restrained movement ("melancholy slackening . . . Downwards we hurried fast . . . at a slow pace"); and the fourth sentence, without explicit transition, commencing in mid-verse (line 624), rises very gradually and firmly into a development of sixteen lines. These depend on a single verb, an unemphatic "were," held back till the beginning of line 636; the verb thus acts as a pivot that introduces, without shock or simply as the

other side of the coin, the falling and interpretative movement. This structure, combined with a skillful interchange throughout of asyndetic and conjunctive phrases, always avoids the sentiment of abrupt illumination for that of a majestic swell fed by innumerable sustaining events, and thereby strengthens our feeling that the vision, though climactic, is neither terminal nor discontinuous.

12. Cf. Preface (1802) to *Lyrical Ballads:* "[The poet] has acquired a greater readiness and power in expressing . . . especially those thoughts and feelings which, by his own choice, or from the structure of his own mind, arise in him without immediate external excitement."

13. Cf. *The Unmediated Vision,* pp. 129–32.

14. The "return to nature" is anticipated by the last lines of VI-b (lines 613–16).

15. Letter to Francesco Dionigi de' Roberti, April 26, 1336. The end of the quoted passage is an allusion to Seneca, *Epistles* 8.5.

16. Quoted from *The Sacred Theory of the Earth* (1684–89), in Marjorie Nicolson, *Mountain Gloom and Mountain Glory* (New York, 1959), p. 206. Her chs. 5 and 6 on Burnet are especially relevant to the present theme.

17. *Descriptive Sketches* (1793), lines 692–93; see also below, p. 105 f.

18. "Desultory Stanzas," in *Memorials of a Tour on the Continent, 1820* (published 1822).

19. I Corinthians 15:51–54 and Acts 3:21; cf. *PW, 5,* 337 ("Home at Grasmere," line 743).

20. Letter to John Hamilton Reynolds, May 3, 1818. Yet did not Saint Augustine think into the human heart, at an earlier time?

21. Cf. also Keats' *Hyperion,* the quest of Apollo in Bk. III, which is directly under the influence of *Paradise Lost* VIII.253 ff. "The Imagination may be compared to Adam's dream," Keats says in a letter (to Benjamin Bailey, November 22, 1817), "he awoke and found it truth." Keats was haunted by that Miltonic sequence which incorporates, of course, a structural principle of repetition.

22. *Paradise Lost* VIII.273–79.

23. Romans 1:20, one of the proof-texts for the "light of nature."

24. *Paradise Lost* VIII.283–88.

25. Ibid. 253–56.

26. Legouis, *The Early Life,* has pointed out that if there were soldiers at the monastery at this time they could only have been paying a domiciliary visit and were not expelling anyone. See also Moorman, *Wordsworth,* pp. 136–37.

27. "This substance by which mortal men have clothed, / Humanly clothed, the ghostliness of things / In silence visible and perpetual calm" (MS A², 1808, *Prelude²* p. 198); "which so long / Had bodied forth the ghostliness of things / In silence visible and perpetual calm" (1850, VI.427–29).

28. Hart Crane, "Praise for an Urn."

29. The question as to whether the Snowdon excursion took place in 1791 or 1793 remains unanswered, though much evidence points to the former date. For most matters of chronology I depend on the information provided by De Selincourt and Darbishire in *Prelude*².

30. See his attempts to achieve a precise understanding in the variant texts, *Prelude*², pp. 482 f. and 622 f.

31. See below, p. 386, n. 65.

32. *Biographia Literaria*, ch. 14.

33. The source of the Nile was one of the riddles of the world, and its annual overflow one of the wonders. Fantastic theories were propounded which that omnigatherer Coleridge knew well, and which may have found their way into "Kubla Khan." In 1770 James Bruce discovered the source of the Nile (in fact only of the Blue Nile) in Abyssinia. A five-volume account of his adventures was published by him in 1790, further versions in 1805 and 1813. The book or reports of it were probably known to Wordsworth (fond of travelogues)—Bruce, moreover, was himself following up a tradition which placed the Nile's source in Abyssinia. See J. L. Lowes, *The Road to Xanadu* (Boston and New York, 1927), and below, pp. 196 ff.

34. Cf. *The Unmediated Vision*, pp. 29 ff.

35. The appearance in relatively close sequence of abyss (VI.594), Abyssinian (VI.615), and "a depth / of Abyssinian privacy" (VI.661 f.) makes one suspect a perhaps unconscious association of ideas. The earthly Paradise was sometimes placed in Abyssinia, near the hidden source of the Nile (see Dr. Johnson's *Rasselas*).

# III. The Chronological Pattern

## "The Vale of Esthwaite"

### CRITICAL BIBLIOGRAPHY

Bateson, *Wordsworth,* pp. 68–70; Fink, *Milieu,* pp. 19–23; Moorman, *Wordsworth,* pp. 61–63; Potts, *Prelude,* pp. 63 ff. There has been little consideration of "The Vale of Esthwaite": the text was not published till 1940 in *PW, 1.* A recent book by P. M. Spacks, *The Insistence of Horror: Aspects of the Supernatural in Eighteenth-Century Poetry* (Cambridge, Mass., 1962) has important remarks on the "fear-fancy combination" in Collins, Blake, and Coleridge, as well as a host of minor poets, though Wordsworth enters only marginally. Bateson, prompted by his thesis about Wordsworth's guilty conscience, is the only one to ascribe a more than conventional significance to the "flesh-creeping supernatural 'horrors' " of the poem. "Although there was literary precedent enough for such Gothic terrors, Wordsworth's supernatural seems to me to have a nightmare quality that is not literary at all."

NOTES

1. "In truth he was a strange and wayward wight, / Fond of each gentle, and each dreadful scene," Beattie, *The Minstrel*, I.xxii. Dorothy applies these lines to the Wordsworth of 1787 in a letter to Jane Pollard in 1793 (Moorman, *Wordsworth*, p. 61).

2. *PW, 1,* 319 and 368. The quotations and their numbering are from the text printed in *PW, 1,* 270–83.

3. The verbal echoes continue in *An Evening Walk* and *Descriptive Sketches;* most (along with those from Collins and Gray) have been listed by De Selincourt and others. The Progress Poem flourished in the Enlightenment; Potts has relevant remarks about it, limited to Gray and Beattie. The profoundest general (though not genre) treatment I know is in E. L. Tuveson, *Millennium and Utopia* (Berkeley and Los Angeles, 1949), ch. 4, "Nature's Simple Plot: The Credo of Progress," and ch. 5, "Progress as Redemption." Wordsworth's first poem, the "Lines written as a school exercise at Hawkshead," when the poet was fourteen (*PW, 1,* 259–61) is a Progress, and shows how rooted the genre was toward the end of the century. It is probable that Keats' *Hyperion* was meant to sketch the origin and progress of poetry: see E. B. Hungerford, *Shores of Darkness* (New York, 1941), pp. 137–62.

4. *PW, 1,* 369. The "Extracts" are found in MS B, whose date is early although the extract headings ("Pity," "Hope," "Sentiments of Affection for Inanimate Nature," "Evening Sounds," etc. point forward to *An Evening Walk.* For the Farewell, cf. Collins' "The Manners. An Ode," in which the poet turns from the "dim-discovered Tracts of Mind" to observance of nature and social man (manners = mores = ἦθος). The relation between Collins and Milton and, in turn, between Wordsworth and both, is too complex to be broached here. However, in addition to the Farewell which corresponds to Milton's exorcism there is the Welcome, as in the "Ode to Fear" (lines 66 ff.), a poem which Wordsworth, vacillating between visionary and social verse, echoes. "Fancy" and the "Social Sense" are aptly contrasted, with reference to *The Prelude,* in Coleridge's "To William Wordsworth, Composed on the night after his recitation of a poem on the growth of an individual mind," lines 27 f.

5. *PW, 5,* 3–4. The lines, though not published till 1814, may have been written at Alfoxden in 1798.

6. It is hard to determine what adjective is the most appropriate: the choice

lies between socializing, humanizing, and naturalizing. At certain points in *The Prelude* the terms should be distinguished but here it is immaterial which is used. The principle is that of the "dark / Inscrutable workmanship that reconciles / Discordant elements, makes them cling together / *In one society*" (my italics, *Prelude* I.341–44).

7. *The Minstrel,* II.xlvi–lv, and Beattie's note to st. xlvi.

8. *The Minstrel,* II.xlviii.

9. Variant in MS B. Cf. Milton's "parting Genius," in the "Hymn on the Morning of Christ's Nativity," line 186. On Wordsworth and the concept of *genius loci,* see below, pp. 212 ff.

10. "O fortunatos nimium, sua si bona norint, Agricolas," *Georgics* II.458. Cf. "Resolution and Independence," st. iv; also Keats' "too happy" state and his fall into the contrary.

11. *PW, 1,* 259–61. For "Superstition," lines 29 ff. Protestantism and Enlightenment philosophy are here conveniently (and conventionally) equated.

12. See *Guilt and Sorrow* ("Salisbury Plain"), *PW, 1,* 100; *Prelude* XIII.312–35.

13. The eighteenth-century writer would have talked of "vicissitude" rather than alternation: "Even sad vicissitude amused his soul," Beattie, *Minstrel,* I.xxii; and Gray, "Ode on the Pleasures arising from Vicissitude" (1748), published by Mason in 1775. The topos of "grateful vicissitude" goes back at least to Milton, *Paradise Lost* VI.8.

14. *Prelude* XIV.245–46.

15. The pronoun may refer to the individual tree being burnt in the pile. In that case the passage intensifies the thought of a homeless spirit (the dryad) lingering near its former home.

16. What follows seems to be a demonic caricature of the eolian harp theme.

17. De Selincourt remarks in *The Early Wordsworth* (Oxford, 1936): "The most noticeable stylistic trick of Wordsworth's early poems is the continued use of repetition, partly, perhaps, caught from Spenser, partly due to a tentative feeling after his subjects as he writes" (p. 27). See also below, the chapter on *Lyrical Ballads,* pp. 150 f.

18. See lines 498–514 (*PW, 1,* 281), a formal vow celebrated in print no less than four times after this. De Selincourt opens his edition with the poem made from this vow (*PW, 1,* 1) and gives other versions of it in *Prelude²,* pp. 528 ff.

19. This kind of alienation falls under Blake's doctrine of the Spectre. The single most beautiful depiction of that Spectre is, however, John Clare's poem beginning "I hid my love when young till I / Couldn't bear the buzzing of a fly," in which the repressed or displaced love rises up in the forms of nature against the lover.

20. *Prelude* I.398–99.

21. An intriguing image, if it substitutes the effect (what the eyes did) for the cause (the eyes themselves). Vision withers Nature.

22. The "spot" theme is related to a psychical process Jung calls centro-

version, and the poet's descent into the earth to the Night Journey. Concerning the relevance of Jungian or archetypal analysis, see below, the section on "Salisbury Plain," pp. 123 ff.

23. The last two verses, and those quoted above rhyming identically with them, are a direct echo of the opening of Collins' "Ode to Fear": "Thou, to whom the World unknown / With all its shadowy Shapes is shown." Collins is asking whether great poetry can still be written (and, in particular, great drama) if it means a participation by the poet in natural or supernatural terror and if the milder or correcter spirit of his age makes this almost impossible. Wordsworth's use of Collins shows he understood the nexus of imagination and terror, and that, like Collins, he was deeply uneasy about it.

## An Evening Walk

### CRITICAL BIBLIOGRAPHY

Bateson, *Wordsworth,* pp. 72–81; Fink, *Milieu,* pp. 23–42; Legouis, *Early Life,* Bk. 1 ch. 5, esp. pp. 133–47; Meyer, *Formative Years,* pp. 37–62; Moorman, *Wordsworth,* pp. 114–20. Legouis enumerates the literary borrowings and extensions, and destroys the myth that Wordsworth worked exclusively from nature. Beatty has excellent notes of the same kind in his edition of Wordsworth's *Representative Poems* (Garden City, New York, 1937). But he is less cautious than Legouis, and claims there is no sign of the essential Wordsworth in those earliest poems. Meyer reacts against an approach which might empty the early poetry of all personal directness or significance. By juxtaposing *An Evening Walk* and the poet's early letters, he once more relates the poem to Wordsworth's personal (but also extra-literary) dilemmas. His modest, psychologistic conclusion is that the poem is the result (!) not so much of Wordsworth's acquaintance with eighteenth-century poetic tradition as of "the unhappiness felt by William and Dorothy . . . at having no normal domestic existence." His emphasis on personal sincerity is as one-sided as that on artifice, which it protests. F. A. Pottle's chapter on "Emergent Idiom" in *The Idiom of Poetry* (rev. ed. New York, 1946), pp. 109–34, restores the balance by viewing the poem as the struggle of a new sensibility with an old literary diction, and he incidentally (and rightly) insists that there is no such thing as pure nature poetry. F. W. Bateson's recent emphasis on the Augustan "objectivity" of the early Wordsworth yields appreciative pages on the poem's literary density despite the final, ominous comment that "In France Wordsworth stepped out of the Picturesque into Passion, and . . . into the whirlpools of Romanticism." But that *An Evening Walk* is a poem issuing from the mind of someone interested in the mind, and especially the mind of a poet, has not received direct consideration.

NOTES

1. The Isabella Fenwick note quoted in *PW, 1,* 318–19 says that it was composed "at school, and during my two first College vacations." "At school" means, according to De Selincourt, that some of its subject-matter and imagery were borrowed from "The Vale of Esthwaite."

2. See Legouis and Beatty. De Selincourt adds that despite many debts to poets of the eighteenth century, the greatest debt is to Milton. Bateson, *Wordsworth,* has pointed to the widespread Augustan practice of poetry that quotes poetry; the whole question of "quotation" in poetry has been reopened by G. Tillotson and others.

3. *Prelude* (1805) II.138–42.

4. The zeugma, the alliteration joining shades and shines, and the assonance joining rays and shades, not only help the *energeia* of the verse but also carry the theme of alternation into sound.

5. See below, pp. 104 f.

6. Isabella Fenwick note, *PW, 1,* 318–19. It will be noticed that this purely "natural" observation is still mediated by an idea of compensation.

7. *PW, 1,* 12–13, app. crit. The revision has an interesting Thomsonian continuation praising in addition the scientist-visionary, and attempting by various means (including metaphor) to reconcile the eye of the poet, made watchful by the power of love, and the eye of the scientist, darting through earth and heaven.

8. R. A. Aubin, in his *Topographical Poetry in XVIII-Century England* (New York, 1936), uses the term "genre sketches" and "genre pictures" for certain of these frames. He gives an exhilaratingly exhaustive list of the kinds of journey poem that derive from Horace's trip to Brundisium (*Satires* I, v) and Ausonius' *Mosella,* as well as all their *topoi* (the local pride theme, the mountain ecstasy, the mountain horror, the praise of district wines or women, the ruin-piece, etc.). Yet, as he remarks, "It is doubtful if Wordsworth labored under the handicap of extensive reading in topographical poetry" (p. 105). D. L. Durling's *Georgic Tradition in English Poetry* (New York, 1935) is the most sophisticated and relevant study I know of the tradition involving the descriptive poem as Wordsworth practiced it. His conclusion (pp. 207 ff.) touches on most points of importance. He is absolutely right in looking for-

ward to Wordsworth's later poetry and saying that "it is impossible to think of Wordsworth apart from his character as a poet of place."

9. *Prelude* II.115–29.

10. How close Milton and supernatural poetry in general are to Wordsworth can be epitomized by his temptation to add to lines 151–53, descriptive of the setting sun ("A long blue bar its aegis orb divides, / And breaks the spreading of its golden tides"): "Such the dark spear that crossed the sunbroad shield / Of Satan striding o'er the empyreal field," *PW, 1,* 18. This would have reversed the Miltonic technique of comparing a supernatural action to a natural. (The reader may like to compare my analysis of this passage with that of Legouis, *Early Life,* pp. 129–30.)

11. See the verbs in lines 109, 113, 115, 122; and compare below p. 112 and notes.

12. See *The Minstrel* I.xxxviii. Beattie's catalogue and its prefatory verse, "But who the melodies of morn call tell?" put one in mind of the last stanza of Keats' "To Autumn." Cf. Goldsmith's *The Deserted Village,* ll. 113–24.

13. A Miltonic kind of prolepsis. Cf. "to force resistless way," *Paradise Lost* II.62. I mention this only to strengthen the case for Milton's presence here.

14. Revision of 1794, *PW, 1,* 35. The "dangerous night" may be primarily a reference to political dangers (*Paradise Lost* VII.27 ff.) but the idea of blindness and compensation is not excluded.

15. J. M. Murry, *Keats and Shakespeare* (London, 1925).

16. G. Wilson Knight in *The Starlit Dome* (New York, 1941) thinks Wordsworth's faults are related to a "failure in face [sic] of erotic powers."

17. See *Prelude²,* p. xlii, for Dr. Johnson on the distortion of language necessary to blank verse, a passage copied by Wordsworth into the Alfoxden Notebook. I have found similar comments as early as Addison's *Remarks on Several Parts of Italy* (1705). There were those, like Nathaniel Weekes (*Barbados: a poem;* see Aubin, *Topographical Poetry,* p. 70), who saw the potentialities of blank verse for narrative clarity or "the easier facilitating the relation of particulars," but the consensus of opinion, before Wordsworth, stressed the possible obscurity.

18. *Prelude* XII.25–28.

## Descriptive Sketches

### CRITICAL BIBLIOGRAPHY

Fink, *Milieu,* pp. 42–48; Garrod, *Wordsworth,* pp. 40–56; Legouis, *Early Life,* Bk. I, ch. 5; Meyer, *Formative Years,* pp. 62–87; Moorman, *Wordsworth,* pp. 197–99; Potts, *Prelude,* pp. 132–36 (on Goldsmith and Wordsworth). Though by no means a great or even very exciting work of art, *Descriptive Sketches,* in its relation to Wordsworth's growth as man and poet, has been neglected. One reason for this is Legouis' account of its derivative nature: the many borrowings in it from eighteenth-century writers and the extensions of their technique. Legouis is controvertible only on the ground of method: by atomizing the poem he shows convincingly that a great proportion of phrases have a direct or exaggerated relationship to that "gaudiness and inane phraseology" Wordsworth was later to condemn. His view of *Descriptive Sketches* as mainly patchwork, though sincere and alive to nature, has prevailed almost continuously. The few notable attempts to go beyond Legouis should, however, be mentioned. M. L. Barstow, an exact reader, discriminates Wordsworth's "faults" from those of the eighteenth-century landscape school, and states against Legouis that what we find in *Descriptive Sketches* is not "the remnant of an old style; it is the crude but vigorous beginning of the new" (*Wordsworth's Theory of Poetic Diction*, New Haven, 1917, p. 94). But because of her specific approach, the study of poetic diction, she does not, except in a general way, correlate Wordsworth's stylistic struggle with a particular phase in his personal development. De Selincourt, on the other hand, writing almost forty years after Legouis, tried to combine the study of the poet's style with that of his mind. "The early crudities," he declared, "of a great and original poet have a value irrespective of their instrinsic merit in the light they throw upon that fascinating . . . study, the growth of a poet's mind and art" (lecture first given in 1936, reprinted in *Wordsworthian and Other Studies*, Oxford, 1947, pp. 1–33). He applied his principle vigorously to "The Vale of Esthwaite" and other juvenilia, but *An Evening Walk* and *Descriptive Sketches* proved too discouraging. After briefly summarizing the flaws of the former, he passes over its companion with: "The faults of *An Evening Walk* were exaggerated in *Descriptive Sketches*," and we hear no more of that juvenile disaster. Arthur Beatty, at about the same time, gives the fullest and most suggestive account we have of the poem, yet also hedges on its language, said to be, in parts, "almost all borrowed" from two earlier travelers to Switzerland, Cox and Ramond (*Representative Poems*, Garden City, New York, 1937, introd., xxxvii–xliii, and pp. 30–35). Meyer's study of the early poems harmonizes, as has been indicated, the poet's correspondence with the sentiments expressed in his poems, and does not consider their style. Florence Marsh, *Wordsworth's Imagery* (New Haven, 1952), does consider it, but her general thesis that Wordsworth's poetic decline begins when light and dark and other "blendings" disappear from his landscapes is open to the objection that she sees blendings where there is primarily contrast and that she has no means to value contrast. F. A. Pottle (*The Idiom of Poetry*) has not dealt with the poem, but his remark that in *An Evening Walk* "a powerful and original genius [is] grappling with the problem of poetic diction" takes us back to the point at which serious interpretation of the early poems begins (and from which it has not advanced), to Coleridge's comment in the fourth chapter of *Biographia Literaria*. The language of *Descriptive Sketches*, he says, "is not only peculiar and strong, but at times knotty and contorted, as by its own impatient strength."

### NOTES

1. Lines 702–813. It is an attempt to identify the idea of Nature and the idea of Freedom even though the actual descriptions of Nature previously given evoke Powers that are not purely on the side of Freedom—they sometimes show man stunned and superstitious. Lines 774 ff. modulate into an apocalyptic mood which reveals the suppressed tenor of the entire poem.

2. In his *A Guide through the District of the Lakes in the North of England,* etc. (1835; first separate edition, 1822), comparing the countryside of the Lakes with that of the Alps, Wordsworth remarks: "only during late spring and early autumn is realized here the assemblage of the imagery of different seasons, which is exhibited through the whole summer among the Alps"; and also, "We have then for the colouring of Switzerland, *principally* a vivid green herbage, black woods, and dazzling snows, presented in masses with a grandeur to which no one can be insensible; but not often graduated by Nature into soothing harmony." Grosart, 2, 293–94. I would like to say again that though the following pages study the ideal (in the old and neutral sense of the word) character of Wordsworth's landscapes, this will by no means exclude their basis in nature.

3. *PW, 1,* 42–91.

4. Blake's phrase (in *Milton*) which I adapt to my purpose.

5. "The Ruined Cottage," line 148; *PW, 5,* 382.

6. The lines beginning "The brook and road" were first written, according to Wordsworth, in 1799, first published in 1845, and appear as *Prelude* VI.621–

40. It has been suggested that the "three hours of our walk among the Alps [which] will never be effaced" of Wordsworth's long letter to his sister in September 1790 (*Early Letters, 1, 32*) refer to the experience of crossing the Alps via the Simplon Pass (Max Wildi, "Wordsworth and the Simplon Pass," *English Studies, 40,* 1959, 226 ff.). If so, the mystery of the omission of this episode in *Descriptive Sketches* deepens. In the September letter the mood is so cheerful that several hypotheses have been offered to explain the difference between it and the melancholy of *DS.* Yet the letter contains in germ the themes of rapid succession and strong contrast emphasized by *DS,* which is composed at almost two years' distance from the event and already begins to deepen, through memory, its interpretation, a process that will take many years to complete (see below).

7. *Prelude,* VI.592 ff. See above, Part II.

8. Coleridge's theory of Imagination was based in part on this later talent of Wordsworth's. He was first fully convinced of his friend's powers on hearing an early version of *Guilt and Sorrow,* and what impressed him was "the union of deep feeling with profound thought; the fine balance of truth in observing, with the imaginative faculty in modifying, the objects observed; and above all the original gift of spreading the tone, the atmosphere, and with it the depth and height of the ideal world around forms, incidents, and situations, of which, for the common view, custom had bedimmed all the lustre, had dried up the sparkle and the dew drops" (*Biographia Literaria,* ch. 4). For the best description of Wordsworth's later techniques, see F. A. Pottle's "The Eye and the Object," *Wordsworth: Centenary Studies,* ed. G. T. Dunklin (Princeton, 1951), pp. 23–42. In a letter to Landor, January 21, 1824, Wordsworth admits his liking for a poetry "where things are lost in each other, and limits vanish, and aspirations are raised."

9. See *Prelude* I.301–02, 351–56; and VI.746 ff.

10. "The Ruined Cottage," line 150 f. (*PW, 5,* 382–83).

11. I.e., from the beginning to the end of time (proleptic phrasing). The experiential order of the two sights is reversed in *Prelude* VI.

12. Names of rivers at the Chartreuse (Wordsworth's note). Cf. *Prelude* VI.439: "the sister streams of Life and Death."

13. Cf. Barstow, *Poetic Diction,* pp. 98 ff.

14. *Prelude* III.157 ff. shows that the poet became aware of the despotism of the eye as early as his Cambridge years, i.e. from the age of 17 on.

15. *PW, 5,* 4.

16. Cf. *Prelude* XII.131 ff.

17. "Mont Blanc" (1816).

18. *Prelude* VI.624–40. The fused or composite nature of this vision is suggested by the appearance in it of two details attributed in *DS* to different parts of the Alps: the "torrents shooting from the clear-blue sky" (*DS,* 130) belong to Lake Como, and "Black drizzling craggs" (*DS,* 249–50) to the region of the

River Reuss. Como came immediately after the Simplon Pass, and it is possible, of course, that these features were transferred from the gloomy strait to the localities mentioned by *DS*. What matters is that *poetically* Wordsworth achieves in one sketch what all of *DS* failed to achieve. On a similar *transference*, see below, p. 123.

19. *Prelude* XII.142 ff.

20. See Shelley's "Mont Blanc," esp. lines 12–48.

21. Having already discussed imagery, I deal with it here only insofar as it bears on syntax and verse form.

22. *Early Life*, p. 128. But cf. Pottle, *The Idiom of Poetry* (rev. ed. New York, 1946), pp. 129–30 and pp. 223–25.

23.        A heart that vibrates evermore, awake
           To feeling for all forms that Life can take,
           That wider still its sympathy extends
           And sees not any line where being ends.

Verses added to *An Evening Walk* in the revision of 1794 (*PW, I,* 10).

24. The octosyllabic form of the couplet, on the other hand, does not have room for such tension between closed and open. It trots along too efficiently.

25. Cf. Pottle on Wordsworth's maturer technique in "The Eye and the Object," in *Wordsworth: Centenary Studies,* ed. G. Dunklin (Princeton, 1951).

26. See the examples collected by Legouis in *Early Life,* Bk. I, ch. 5, and cf. Barstow, *Poetic Diction.*

27. Three other features of Wordsworth's earliest style may be linked to this pattern: (1) the placing of a transitive verb in an intransitive site: "Where rocks and groves and power of waters shakes / In cataracts"; (2) the pluralizing, also illustrated by the above; and (3) the abuse of the possessive pronoun to effect quick personifications ("Behind her hill the Moon, all crimson, rides"). The last, in particular, helps the poet to spread the sense of life through a multiplication of bounded or quasi-visual entities, the possessive pronoun both linking two objects and giving them separate status through the implied personification.

28. *Prelude* XII. 121–47. It is interesting that the dominance of the eye coincides, at one point, with that of the analytic intellect, a fact supported by the present study. From both the explicit and stylistic evidence here given it is difficult to agree with scholars who have dated the period of the eye's dominance as late as 1793 (De Selincourt) or even 1795 (R. D. Havens). The poet himself calls it something "almost . . . inherent in the creature," and such depictions as "The Ruined Cottage," lines 85–108 (*PW, 5,* 381–82), suggest that this dominance was always potentially present. The confusion may be resolved by remembering that Wordsworth in the above quoted passage distinguishes between an almost *inherent* and an *accidental* tyranny of the eye: the latter is directly associated with the crisis of circa 1793, and was aggravated

by "picturesque" habits of thought, but the former predisposes to the latter and is more relevant to *Descriptive Sketches* and the growth of the poet's mind. Among interesting interpreters of Wordsworth's "eye" are (1) the physiologists, or those relatively without thesis: M. Mead, *PMLA, 34* (1919), 202–24; Garrod, *Wordsworth*, pp. 73–81; W. G. Fraser, *RES, 9* (1933); Gerhard Hensel, *Das Optische bei Wordsworth* (Marburg, 1930); (2) those who place the matter in the context of the history of ideas and of sensibility: e.g. "It was necessary for him to break the tyranny of the bodily eye before he could 'see into the heart of things.' This is the key to the difference between the 'romantic' and the 'picturesque' approach to nature." Samuel Monk, *The Sublime: A Study of Critical Theories in XVIII-Century England* (Ann Arbor Paperbacks, 1960), pp. 204–05; A. Beatty, *William Wordsworth: His Doctrine and Art in Their Historical Relations* (3d ed. Madison, 1960), pp. 57–63 (an interesting discussion of the relation of poetic diction and eye-writing); M. H. Abrams, "The Correspondent Breeze," *English Romantic Poets*, ed. Abrams (Galaxy paperback, New York, 1960), esp. pp. 51–52; E. L. Tuveson, *The Imagination as a Means of Grace* (Berkeley and Los Angeles, 1960), passim. The distinction of possibly influencing Wordsworth's attitude toward things visual has been variously attributed to Gilpin, Hartley, Joseph Priestley, Alison, Erasmus Darwin (interludes to *The Botanic Garden* and the poem itself). I can only suggest, here, the (probably later) influence of Edmund Burke, to whom, if to anyone, Wordsworth's revolt against purely descriptive or ocular poetry should be attached. Like Lessing, Burke made an important distinction in terms of the difference between poetry and painting: "In reality poetry and rhetoric do not succeed in exact description so well as painting does; their business is, to affect rather by sympathy than imitation; to display rather the effect of things on the mind of the speaker, or of others, than to present a clear idea of the things themselves." *A Philosophical Enquiry into the Origin of Our Ideas of the Sublime and Beautiful* (1756), Pt. V sect. 5. Cf. Tuveson, *The Imagination as a Means of Grace*, pp. 173–74.

29. Of the two interpretations here given, the first (see my previous paragraph) is implicit in *DS* and culminates poetically in *Prelude* (1805) VI.553–72; and the second (see this paragraph) is not fully realized until the moment of composition that produces *Prelude* (1805) VI.525–48. The poet allows both passages to stand side by side, so that the later intuition (1804) forestalls, without negating, the viewpoint of the lines composed some five years earlier (1799).

30. *Prelude* XIII.290 ff. Cf. Coleridge's "we receive but what we give, / And in our life alone does Nature live" "Dejection: An Ode" (1802).

31. *PW, 5,* 5. The Prospectus is taken from the end of "The Recluse" but may have been written as early as 1798: see *PW, 5,* 372. For "blendings," see below, pp. 175–76.

32. *PW, 5,* 340–45 (appendix B), and below, ch. 6.

33. The anagogical function of contrast may recall Plato, *Republic* 523 ff., and 532 ff., where the dialectic is conceived as at once initiating thought and emancipating the student from a "despotism of the eye" (the phrase is Coleridge's, *Biographia Literaria,* ch. 6). Yet for Wordsworth, nature itself is propaedeutic and participates providentially in the dialectic ascent from visible to invisible. Perhaps the "abstruser argument," never entered into, yet promised as "matter for another Song" ("The Recluse"? Wordsworth's philosophical epic? See *Prelude,* 1805, XI.176–85, cited above) would have clarified the relation between Wordsworth's thought and Plato's. According to Christopher Wordsworth, the poem's title, "The Prelude," was fixed on, after the poet's death, by Mary, so that no clear evidence exists linking it to the προοίμιον of *Republic* 532 (see *Memoirs of William Wordsworth,* London, 1851; but also an interesting speculation by Potts, *Prelude,* pp. 366–72). My suspicion is that in the later Wordsworth a strange new linkage of Plato and Paul was in the making, "Nature" being understood as the *res factae* of Romans 1:20. That the contrasts in the scene of storm studied above are anagogical rather than "picturesque," i.e. essentially different from those of the "Pleasures of the Imagination" poem, is indicated by the poet's own (not unambiguous) comment: *PW, 1,* 62. The finest example, however, of anagogical contrast is found in the vision from Snowdon that brings *The Prelude* to a close.

34. See Wordsworth's note on "There was a Boy." *Prelude*[2], p. 547.

## From "Salisbury Plain" to "The Ruined Cottage"

### CRITICAL BIBLIOGRAPHY

Garrod, who labels one of his chapters "1793," has given explicit recognition to this year as an epoch in Wordsworth's life (*Wordsworth,* ch. 4). While G. M. Harper (*William Wordsworth,* 3d ed. London, 1929) questions *The Prelude*'s chronological reliability, since the letters of 1790–97 betray no sign of a crisis, Garrod thinks "Salisbury Plain" and *The Borderers* corroborate *The Prelude,* and show the poet in the grip of emotional turmoil and the "strong disease" of Godwinism. His view of Wordsworth's development during this period is the most specific yet offered. According to Garrod, Wordsworth's tendency toward Freedom and Nature (the two being identified through Rousseau) was disturbed by the shock of 1793, which, together with the tyrannous course of the Revolution, undermined his belief that nature, and government according to the "general will," would produce a new and freer type of man. There follows a stage of flirtatious or "semi"

Godwinism, lasting from 1793–95, then a stage of complete God-winism (revealed by *The Borderers*) in which Wordsworth rejects every form of social contract and gives himself totally to the prop-osition that there is no reason save that of the individual (*Words-worth*, pp. 57–94). There is, finally, as the *Lyrical Ballads* testify, a sudden re-surrender to natural influences. Garrod's thesis, which cannot be criticized here in detail, respects fully the drama of 1793–97, but also involves him in the hypothesis of an equally dramatic yet less explicable recovery. Because his emphasis is so strongly on the ideological component (Rousseau, Godwin), he sees neither the existential preparation for the shock of 1793 nor the possible interaction of crisis and cure. He allows for confusion but not for dialectic. His interpretation of "Salisbury Plain" and *The Borderers* is, moreover, only as probable as his theory, for the two works are candidly used to approve a point of view taken from *The Prelude* rather than studied in their own right or in sequence with other poems. My own thesis, though it also corroborates (or seeks corroboration from) *The Prelude,* does not depend on this poem, being part of a view covering all of Wordsworth's produc-tions. Against the 'negative' evidence of the letters, it places "Salis-bury Plain" and *The Borderers* rather than the retrospective *Prelude.* Besides Garrod, there is an important consideration of the poems of 1793–97 by Meyer, *Formative Years,* chs. 4 and 5 (Bate-son, *Wordsworth,* ch. 4, skimps them, and is implicitly in agree-ment with Meyer). In his careful and substantive study, Meyer accepts Harper's view that there was no crisis, and again takes the letters as a more reliable source than the few, though affecting and reiterated, passages of *The Prelude.* Having no sudden recovery to account for, Meyer links "Salisbury Plain" and *The Borderers* to "the self-same progress" which leads Wordsworth to "Ruined Cot-tage" and *LB.* His view is that the Wordsworth of 1793 was an angry young man whose "Letter to the Bishop of Llandaff" and the almost contemporaneous "Salisbury Plain" were documents of revo-lutionary propaganda inflaming readers against a corrupt and hyp-ocritical society. In *The Borderers,* however, Wordsworth is said to change his tactics, and to take from Godwinism not its negative attitude toward constituted government (as Garrod thought) but rather a positive faith in the natural goodness and benevolence of man. *The Borderers* is seen as an optimistic play, which, like "The Ruined Cottage" and *LB*, calls our attention to the inexhaustible chances for reform in human life instead of to existing evils. Meyer's thesis, I fear, gravely simplifies *The Borderers*,\* slights *The Prelude*, and neglects the fact that "Salisbury Plain," though without a doubt politically inspired, holds us mainly by its strange psychology, and only occasionally by its political virulence. I accept his view of "The Ruined Cottage" and *LB*, but not his equation of their spirit with that of *The Borderers*. One need only read D. G. James on the play (*Scepticism and Poetry*, London, 1937, pp. 153–55) or the brilliant bodings of G. Wilson Knight (*The Starlit Dome*, New York, 1941, pp. 24–35) or John Jones (*The Egotistical Sublime*, London, 1954, pp. 54–61) to realize in full the disjunction of *The Borderers* and the later poetry. The best reconstruction of the vital transition of 1790–98 in terms of ideas that Wordsworth *lived* is found in Basil Willey, *The Eighteenth Century Background* (London, 1940), ch. 12, " 'Nature' in Wordsworth," pp. 253–70. Concerning the striking changes of style between 1793 and 1798 there are hints only: in Bateson (*Wordsworth*, pp. 126–27), and in F. R. Leavis' appreciation of "The Ruined Cottage," *Revaluation* (London, 1936).

NOTES

1. *Excursion* VI.553–55.
2. *Prelude* X.266 ff. and cf. XI.173 ff.
3. Having chosen to describe Wordsworth's "consciousness about consciousness," I am approaching the subject phenomenologically, and leave aside the question of what consciousness actually is, though I am aware of the (Heideggerian) attack on the idea that consciousness involves alienation. The whole matter is difficult, and requires a terminological as well as notional study, so that it seems best not to engage in it here. Only the following statements can

\* That *The Borderers* is a "problem play" does not mean that Wordsworth must have given signs of troublement in his letters or social life, no more than that Shakespeare need have been as visibly disturbed as his Hamlet. The assumption of a necessary correspondence between the "life and letters" of the man and his poetry has been a stumbling block in this and many other inquiries.

be made with some certainty: (1) the radical sense of betrayal from which Wordsworth suffered has been felt by the greatest men (cf. Charles Williams, *The English Poetic Mind,* Oxford, 1932); (2) only a history of the sense of betrayal would reveal the inordinate number of different causes blamed; (3) the blame, however, is laid in each individual case on one cause or event. An earlier shock of Wordsworth's, for instance, is also called a "first," and described in terms of a schism, yet Wordsworth passes it over for the later climax (see *Prelude* VII.382 ff.).

4. For the text of "Salisbury Plain," see *PW, 1,* 94–127, and notes, 334 ff. To get the earliest *complete* text, I have made my own collations on the basis of the manuscripts reprinted by De Selincourt and checked these as far as possible against the xerox copies at the Cornell University Library. This involves some artifice and the possibility of occasional error (but not, I hope, misrepresentation). For these two stanzas see *PW, 1,* 95–96, and notes, 335–36.

5. *PW, 1,* 98–99.

6. The word is defined below, p. 123.

7. *PW, 1,* 100. This stanza from MS 1 is addressed to the traveler by "a voice as from a tomb." In the version finally published as *Guilt and Sorrow* (1842) the powerful circle is implicitly linked to the image (and worship) of the setting sun: "The weary eye—which, wheresoe'er it strays, / Marks nothing but the red sun's setting round, / Or on the earth strange lines, in former days / Left by gigantic arms."

8. *The Borderers* I.389 (*PW, 1,* 143).

9. See Mircea Eliade, *Patterns in Comparative Religion* (New York, 1958), sects. 81 and 140–45. A vital assemblage of materials with a minimal intrusion of thesis.

10. The sexual or birth-channel implications, should they be present, do not obtrude: if the history of the individual repeats that of the race, archetypes will have this kind of synthesizing energy.

11. See *Lyrical Ballads,* "The Female Vagrant," line 163.

12. The idea of a flood or ocean is present, but it is *of stone;* cf. the stanza quoted above beginning "It was a spectacle . . ." and the description of the desert in MS 1 as "dark and void as ocean's barren deep" (*PW, 1,* 101).

13. The whirlwind is present in MS 1 but is directly associated with Stonehenge only in MS 2 ("Beneath that fabric scarce of earthly form / More dreadful was the whirlwind's rage extreme," *PW, 1,* 101); and we do not know exactly when the final version of "Winds [that] met in conflict, each by turns supreme," so reminiscent of *Prelude* VI, and published in 1842, was composed.

14. See especially his "The Stages of Life," in *Modern Man in Search of a Soul* (New York, 1933); also Gerhard Adler, *The Living Symbol* (New York, 1961); and Erich Neumann, "Centroversion and the Stages of Life," in *The Origins and History of Consciousness* (New York, 1954), 2, D.

15. See *PW, 1,* 103–04, MS 1 version, especially lines 6–14 of the long pas-

sage quoted by De Selincourt. On the Night Journey: Adler, *Living Symbol*, pp. 210 ff.

16. For Wordsworth's comments on "The Thorn," *PW*, 2, 511. The Isabella Fenwick note on *Guilt and Sorrow* quoted in *PW*, *1*, 330, reads: "I have assigned this poem to the dates 1793 and 1794; but in fact much of the 'Female Vagrant's' story was composed at least two years before."

17. *Biographia Literaria*, ch. 4, but see Legouis' comment on its residual artifice in Griggs, ed., *Wordsworth and Coleridge* (Princeton, 1939), pp. 6–7.

18. Legouis comes close to observing this but does not entirely comprehend the importance of the "post-revolutionary Iago . . . armed with logic and philosophy." See *The Early Life*, pp. 270–76. Cf. G. Wilson Knight on Oswald: "He is a deliberate embodiment in self-conscious action of certain dramatic tendencies that forecast Emily Bronte, Herman Melville, and Dostoievsky" (*Starlit Dome*, p. 29), and L. Abercrombie, *The Art of Wordsworth* (New York, 1952), pp. 71 ff. On the relation of revolutionary activity and "crimes of the intellect" there is no stronger and more clairvoyant statement than the opening lines of Camus' *L'Homme revolté* (Paris, 1951).

19. All quotations are from the text of *The Borderers* in *PW*, *1*, 128–25. I have used the published (1842) text, which De Selincourt prints in extenso, as my base. The notation, MS B, refers to an earlier version given in the *apparatus criticus* and representing the play as it stood circa 1797. The first numeral after citations refers to the act, the second to the initial line as De Selincourt numbers it.

20. While Othello also discovers that what he thought an act of justice is a crime, his agony before the murder is not due, as in Marmaduke's case, to the possibility that he may be deceived or that he has not the right to kill. It is a weakness of Wordsworth's play that Marmaduke's "passion" is divided into two parts: what he suffers before the murder, and what after, and that his prior suffering is stronger or more deeply meditated. When Marmaduke realizes his essential solitude in III.1466 ff., the spiritual action of the play is concluded: the remainder merely seals the action, makes it irreversible, and for this purpose is too long. See also below, n. 28.

21. If Malraux and Dostoevsky go back at this point to the Romantic movement, it is by way of Byron (*Cain, Manfred*) and not Wordsworth.

22. See "The Function of Criticism at the Present Time," *Essays in Criticism* (First Series), 1865.

23. It is, however, directly preceded by Schiller's *The Robbers*, which Wordsworth knew, if only through Coleridge.

24. Although the *word* "Nature" is used very diversely in *The Borderers* (cf. I.148, II.1123, III.1575 f., and IV.1819), and Oswald, like a Shakespearean villain, calls on Nature when it suits his purpose (IV.1875), the *thing* that Oswald questions is always the same, namely, positive law, which in the eight-

eenth century is increasingly justified as having its base in "natural law." For him there is no Nature that is not established or manipulated by man.

25. MS B, corresponding to IV.1854; see *PW, 1,* 201.

26. This transition is studied exhaustively in Hegel's *The Phenomenology of Mind* (1807). Wordsworth's play is concerned with issues Hegel analyzes in his section on self-consciousness (especially the chapters on lordship and bondage, and stoicism, skepticism, and the unhappy consciousness); it also has affinities with sections Hegel wrote with the cataclysm of the French Revolution in mind, such as "Reason as Lawgiver" and "Reason as a Test of Laws."

27. I prefer not to reduce this "crime" to a specific historical event. It is analogous to, but not identical with, original sin; it also reflects Wordsworth's experience of the French Revolution: the revolutionary discovering once again that a New Order cannot escape a founding crime.

28. Campbell and Mueschke take a different view of the importance of remorse in *Modern Philology, 23* (1926), 465–82. They remark that "Marmaduke's tragedy lies not so much in the hideous nature of the attempted remedy [i.e. Godwinian philosophy], as in the persistence of the remorse. In other words, all of the emotion in the poem gathers around an individual's struggle with 'remorseless remorse' " (p. 472). They say also that "Marmaduke is thrown back upon complete acquiescence in suffering and the poem upon the familiar aesthetic of sentimentalism" (p. 482). This is open to various objections. It (1) puts too exclusive an emphasis on Act V, (2) exaggerates the "struggle" and the "remorselessness" of the remorse. Marmaduke makes it clear that he *chooses* exile and suffering, and his statement "A wanderer *must* I go" (V.2312) expresses a moral rather than an emotional compulsion. MS B puts this beyond doubt. There his decision to "endure" comes after he has confessed to Idonea's face that he is the murderer of her father, and his strength in so confessing and the future memory that he has been that strong (cf. "Michael," lines 448–50, and *Prelude* XII.269–71) lead him to say that he can either become an Oswald ("there doth not lie / Within the compass of a mortal thought / A deed that I would shrink from") or the opposite ("—and I can endure"). This is intellectual and self-conscious resolve, not sentimental acquiescence; and it is curious that Marmaduke raises himself to it by "enlightening" Idonea as he had been "enlightened" by Oswald. In both cases the revelation has a murdering or adamantine effect: " 'Tis done, and so done too / That I have cased her heart in adamant." (*PW, 1,* 216–17).

29. *Miscellanies* (1886), p. 118, quoted by Legouis. It is Oswald, by the way, who gives strongest expression in the play to the spot syndrome, reflecting both his compulsiveness and the unresolved agony of individuation. See especially his fascinated and beautiful description of the naked spot on which he maroons the Captain, IV.1721 ff. In the play as a whole, moreover, two solitaries stand in contrast like antipodal centers: the captain on that isle, under a burning

sun and in a southerly calm, and Herbert deserted among the moony dark-
ness, storm, and roaring water of a northern border region.

30. MS B, corresponding to V.2318 ff; see *PW, 1,* 224.

31. Idonea is also a curious figure. Her father's blindness comes from saving
her from the flames of Antioch, where her mother perished, and Wordsworth
introduces this information to emphasize her indebtedness to her father. By
the same fact, however, she enters the category of the "twice-born." To be
born a second time, especially to be born of the father, is, according to arche-
typal theory, a symbol for the consciousness that is liberated from the ma-
triarchal (natural) realm. Thus, while her father's archetype stands under the
sign of a consciousness founded beyond nature, Idonea's is under the sign of
a violent separation from nature, even though her predominant virtue is pity.

32. *Hints towards the Formation of a More Comprehensive Theory of Life,
The Complete Works of Coleridge,* ed. W. G. T. Shedd (New York, 1853), *1,*
412.

33. Isabella Fenwick note to "We Are Seven," *PW, 1,* 361.

34. Text in *PW, 1,* 287–92. De Selincourt entitles it "Fragment of a 'Gothic'
Tale."

35. Cf. C. G. Jung, *Psychology and Alchemy* (New York, 1953). The relation
of alchemical thought to Romantic poetry has been broached with respect
to Blake and some French poets. It remains fascinating and relatively virgin
ground for exploration.

36. Unpublished prefatory essay to *The Borderers, PW, 1,* 345. The original
has "He goes . . ."

37. I readily admit, in other words, that "betraying" Annette, or "be-
ing betrayed" into that course of events, might have triggered the crisis and
probably did lead up to it. But we must respect (1) how it *appeared* to Words-
worth, and (2) the reverberations, which cannot be reduced to an affair.

38. The fragments quoted above are found in *PW, 1,* 314–15. Related ones
are given in *PW, 5,* 377. They date probably from toward the end of Words-
worth's Racedown sojourn (from spring 1797 rather than from 1795) as Thomas
Raysor has recently argued in "Wordsworth's Early Drafts of *The Ruined
Cottage* in 1797–1798," *JEGP,* 55 (1956), 1–7.

39. Genesis 28:10 ff.

40. I quote from the earliest complete manuscript of "The Ruined Cottage,"
*PW, 5,* 379 ff.

41. *PW, 5,* 399. See Isabella Fenwick note, ibid., 373, for date of composi-
tion, and Raysor, *JEGP,* 55 (1956), 1–7.

42. The emphasis of which I speak is, in one sense, as old as Chaucer, yet,
in the following sense, distinctly modern: the tale not only reflects the teller,
it reacts on him (or the auditor), and this reaction is as important to Words-
worth, or as organic to the tale, as the "incidents."

43. *PW, 5,* 393.

44. *PW, 5,* 403, line 113.
45. *PW, 5,* 401, line 36. One of the drafts for what Darbishire and De Selincourt aptly call a "reconciling passage" to conclude the poem.

## Lyrical Ballads

### CRITICAL BIBLIOGRAPHY

The years 1797–1800 were so rich for Wordsworth that a further chapter is needed to do them justice. This one stresses significant continuities; the next deals more fully with the poet's "conversion," and secondary sources discussing his experiences at Alfoxden are considered there. The following notes take up in sequence the major topics of the present chapter. *Curse Poems:* A significant grouping of *LB* was suggested by Thomas Hutchinson in his distinguished edition of the poems. He described "The Three Graves," "Cain," and "The Ancient Mariner," on which Wordsworth and Coleridge had directly collaborated, as studies in mental pathology, and associated with them *Peter Bell* and "Goody Blake." Adopting a phrase from Coleridge's advertisement to the publication of parts 3 and 4 of "The Three Graves" (*The Friend,* September 21, 1809), he identifies their common subject as "a painful idea vividly and suddenly impressed upon the mind. The *idea* is the same in all five cases—that of a *curse*" (*Lyrical Ballads,* London, 1898, p. 255). Charles J. Smith and W. Strunk, Jr. enrich this group by adding "The Thorn" and two poems from the 1800 *LB,* "Hart-Leap Well" and "The Danish Boy" (Smith, "Wordsworth and Coleridge: The Growth of a Theme," *SP, 54,* 1957, 53–64; Strunk, "Some Related Poems of Wordsworth and Coleridge," *MLN, 29,* 1914, 201–05). In the 1800 poems, however, as Stephen Parrish points out, the curse is implanted only on a spot in nature and not on the mind, and he relates this externalization to a change in dramatic technique, Wordsworth apparently abandoning his attempt to focus interest on the speaker's psychology—or "unconscious self-revelation"—rather than on the incidents ("Dramatic Technique in *Lyrical Ballads,*" *PMLA, 74,* 1959, 85–98). In a previous article of importance, Parrish had noted that the emphasis in Wordsworth's experimental poems, and particularly

"The Thorn," was on teller rather than on tale, on what Words-
worth himself called "character" as contrasted with "incident," so
that these lyrics anticipate the modern dramatic monologue (" 'The
Thorn': Wordsworth's Dramatic Monologue," *ELH, 24,* 1957, 153–
63; cf. Robert Langbaum, *The Poetry of Experience,* London and
New York, 1957, ch. 1). My own view links the curse poems to
the spot syndrome and to a generic stage in the development of
the individual mind; and it harmonizes, I believe, with Parrish's
except that "Hart-Leap Well" does not seem to me to diminish
significantly the interest in psychology, at least not in the psy-
chology of the imagination. Its structure is that of a split situation,
the incidents recounted first, the peasant's and the poet's reaction
later. In this it resembles "The Thorn" as much as it diverges from
it, for the first seven stanzas of the latter give a queer but factual
account that could stand by itself; and only after the introduction
of the questioning voice, and through the repetitive circling of
the narrator, is our interest fully transferred from plot to narrator.
A comparison of the split situation in these two poems and a con-
sideration of a similar structure in "The White Doe of Rylstone"
(Wordsworth's last and most ambitious ballad) would be useful. I
raise the matter to indicate that Wordsworth's concern in 1798, as
in 1800 and 1807, is less with character or psychology than with the
psychology of the imagination or the relation of the primitive and
sophisticated imaginations. While the narrator of "The Thorn"
is chosen to display the way "crude Nature work[s] in untaught
minds" (*Prelude* VII.275), in "Hart-Leap Well" the ˌimagination
of the foil character (the shepherd) and that of the poet are ex-
plicitly identified ("Small difference," says the poet to the shepherd,
"lies between thy creed and mine"). Wordsworth, in fact, main-
tains the essential identity of the rustic and the poetic imagina-
tions in the 1800 Preface to *LB:* what contrast there is lies now be-
tween hunter and shepherd, as if Wordsworth had converted
'martial' and 'pastoral' into distinct modalities of the imagination.

    *Realism:* Little new has been added to a definition of Words-
worth's realism since Legouis' sensible essay in *The Early Life,* Bk.
4, ch. 3. An analysis in the manner of Erich Auerbach, using the
concepts of decorum and social level of style, is still needed. Even

the poet's relation to the 'plain style' (Puritan or secular) has not been studied. See, however, Donald Davie, *Purity of Diction in English Verse* (London, 1953), and René Wellek, *The History of Modern Criticism* (New Haven, 1955), 2, 130–37.* It is also worth considering, under the heading of realism, that Coleridge's assigned duty in *LB*, to naturalize the supernatural, carries on the Romance tradition in lyrical form, whereas no clear prototype for Wordsworth's attempt has been found. The gothic novel, though, does more than give a naturalistic explanation for the supernatural phenomena it exploits: like the German *Novelle*, of which Schiller's *Der Geisterseher* (known to have had an influence on Coleridge's *Osorio*) is an early example, it may also display natural things in a supernatural light, sometimes for a magical and sometimes for an ironic purpose, and with the two not always canceling out. A similar magical realism and ironic supernaturalism is found in Goethe's *Wilhelm Meister*. I suspect that by comparing German and English literature of this sort we will understand better the quality of Wordsworth's realism. Bateson's version of the "two voices" theory, typing Wordsworth's realistic element as the Augustan manner—essentially objective, evincing a strong sense of social responsibility, yet crude, naive and often bathetic—and his magical or supernatural element as the Romantic manner—essentially subjective, egocentric, sentimental, and escapist, yet often charming—seems to me provincial as well as falsely dichotomous (Bateson, *Wordsworth*, ch. 1). It is not so much the Augustan manner which pre-exists (and against which the Romantic manner must affirm itself), but rather a Romance manner censored or suppressed during the Enlightenment; and the question now is how (if at all) a modern mind can reassume that heritage.

"We Are Seven": The interpretation here advanced should be read against the background of the difference of opinion between A. C. Bradley, *Oxford Lectures on Poetry* (London, 1909), pp. 146–48, and Arthur Beatty, *William Wordsworth: His Doctrine and Art* (3d ed. Madison, 1960), pp. 208–10. I must admit my in-

* Since this was written, M. H. Abrams has begun to explore the religious and social bases of Wordsworth's plain style in *Romanticism Reconsidered*, ed. N. Frye (New York, 1963), pp. 60–72.

ability to follow the latter's refutation of Bradley (Beatty thinks
the child's insensibility to death is accounted for by the life in her
limbs) but I agree that the poem's first stanza does seem to point
in Beatty's direction and to contradict the rest of the poem. Could
one consider the narrative proper a refutation of the sentiment
expressed in that first stanza? I have no authority for this; but the
Fenwick note, in any case, reveals that the first stanza was an after-
thought, contributed and considered lightly (*PW*, *1*, 361–62).

*Character versus Incidents in LB:* It is the merit of Klaus Dock-
horn to have recovered the rhetorical significance of "character"
and "incident" as important antithetical terms in Wordsworth
related to the older antithesis of "ethos" and "pathos." ("Words-
worth und die rhetorische Tradition in England," *Nachrichten
der Akademie der Wissenschaften, Göttingen:* Philologisch-His-
torische Klasse, 1944, 255–92.) Dockhorn is not a practical critic,
and does not draw his evidence from the experimental poems but
rather from the letters, the critical prose, and some discursive pas-
sages of poetry, yet it is clear that many ballads are concerned with
the distinctions he recovers. Thus "The Thorn" and "Hart-Leap
Well" differ *technically* from Bürger's "The Parson's Daughter"
and "The Chase" on two counts (1) the greater presence of "char-
acter" in the personages, and (2) a downgrading of the "incidents"
(see Coleridge's letter to William Taylor of Norwich, which quotes
Wordsworth on Bürger: Griggs, *Collected Letters, 1,* 565–66, and
cf. Wordsworth's criticism of Coleridge's Mariner having "no
distinct character"). Since both Dockhorn and Parrish ("Dramatic
Technique," *PMLA, 74,* 1959, 85–98) have discussed at length
Wordsworth's attitude toward Bürger, I would only add that there
are three fundamental issues which should be kept separate: the
relevance to *LB* of the older rhetorical terms (and this has been
established); the different kind of relevance these terms may have
when we compare a 1798 poem like "The Thorn" with a later
poem like "Hart-Leap Well"; and the insufficiency of the older
terms when we look at *LB* in the light of such modern develop-
ments as the dramatic monologue or the speculative stream of nar-
rative issuing from a Henry James or Robbe-Grillet "character."
Issues two and three are, I feel, despite Parrish's valiant work, still

in a state of rich confusion. For further significant comment on "The Thorn" consult the edition of *Lyrical Ballads* (Oxford, 1911) by H. Littledale, who already suggests that the poem is "a psychological study of a self-revealed character" yet asks whether, without Wordsworth's advertisement of 1798, "we should have suspected the existence of this garrulous intermediary between us and the story; and if not, whether he is to be regarded as relevant and necessary." "We do not think of the speaker," he continues, "but of the story . . . No one can get the ring of that terrible moan out of his ears, or fail to see in thought that form of misery beside the wind-swept thorn" (p. 219). Littledale wants it both ways; Roger Sharrock, "Wordsworth's Revolt against Literature," *Essays in Criticism, 3* (1953), 396–412, also insists on the reality of the things seen and their social significance; and J. F. Danby in *The Simple Wordsworth* (New York, 1961), pp. 57–72, brings out the complexity of Wordsworth's persona: the latter is (1) a particular speaker, a captain, and (2) representative, unsophisticated man, a medium for the elemental in the human situation. Danby's account of how the poem's repetitions progressively strip away the irrelevant, fanciful, idly curious, idly compassionate, and literary responses to the absolutely naked (Heart of Darkness) situation, is brilliant, and I agree with his conclusion: "The woman and the Thorn at the end are both seen under the shadow of that quelled or unrealized existence which the Babe stands for . . . Wordsworth's eye travels back from the woman to the three things and the mountain top. Man's inhumanity to man is part of a larger context of anti-vital and elemental forces."

*The Contemporaneity of the LB:* Robert Mayo's article of that title (*PMLA, 69,* 1954, 486–522) reopened effectively the question of Wordsworth's originality by showing that his themes, subjects, and titles were fashionable in the poetry of the 1790s. Mayo's aim is purely critical: he does not offer a new definition of the original element in Wordsworth's ballads but destroys the terms in which the older claims for it were cast. On Wordsworth's debt to tradition (rather than to fashion) in the matter of meter and stanza form, there are excellent remarks in W. P. Ker, *Form and Style in Poetry* (London, 1928) pp. 227–33. But the relation of the tradi-

376 BIBLIOGRAPHY: LYRICAL BALLADS

tional genres to these poems and the quality of that relation are neglected fields of inquiry.

*Wordsworth's Creed:* It is well to let the charges against Wordsworth's "private religion" die a natural death, but they should at least be signaled (Irving Babbitt, *Rousseau and Romanticism,* Boston and New York, 1919; H. N. Fairchild, *Religious Trends in English Poetry, 3,* 1949, esp. 160–77). A cooler-headed study of the function of devotional terms and religious patterns in Romantic poetry has now begun (F. A. Pottle's defense of Shelley, and M. H. Abrams on "The Correspondent Breeze," both in *English Romantic Poets,* ed. Abrams, Galaxy paperback, New York, 1960, pp. 289–306 and 37–54 respectively; Harold Bloom's heuristic use of Martin Buber in *Shelley's Mythmaking,* New Haven, 1959). On two aspects of Wordsworth's creed as expressed in *LB,* its benevolism and its necessitarianism, consult (1) Coleridge's Bristol Address of 1795 on "philosophical" necessity, printed in *The Friend* (1809), Section I, essay 16; (2) a review of contemporary theories of benevolence (and Hazlitt's relation to them) in Herschel Baker's *William Hazlitt* (Cambridge, Mass., 1962), pp. 142–52; and (3) Meyer, *Formative Years,* pp. 237–49, who suggests that if Hartley influenced Wordsworth, it was less through his "vibratiuncles" or the epistemological aspects of the principle of association than through the moral and socializing consequences drawn from it, which include an emphasis on benevolence and the pleasures of sympathy. Coleridge at Nether Stowey, in the company of Wordsworth, understood perfectly, and probably helped to inspire, Wordsworth's counter-revolutionary blend of benevolence and necessitarianism (see below, note 21).

*The Lucy Poems:* Whether correct or not, Cleanth Brooks' interpretation of "A slumber did my spirit seal" brings into relief most of the essential features of that poem ("Irony as a Principle of Structure" in *Literary Opinion in America,* ed. M. D. Zabel, New York, 1951, pp. 735–37). Brooks and Bateson (*Wordsworth,* pp. 30–35) comment on "She dwelt among the untrodden ways," and understand that Lucy, as Bateson puts it, occupies the whole interval between the two terminal images of violet and star. But being primarily interested in rhetorical procedure they do not connect that "interval" with what I have called an "elision of the purely human" found also in "A slumber." Bateson later raises two cruxes, Lucy's early and unexplained death and the curious sexlessness of the poems (pp. 153 ff.). He explains both by the theory that the poems are symbolical and purgative killings of Wordsworth's incestuous love for Dorothy. Even if this were probable, it could still be argued that the truth of these poems is universal and generic rather than local and individual. Concerning "Three years she grew," I am acquainted with the interesting studies by H. W. Garrod, *The Profession of Poetry and Other Lectures* (Oxford, 1929), pp. 81 ff.; and David Ferry, *The Limits of Mortality* (Middletown, 1959), pp. 73–76. F. R. Leavis considers "Strange fits of Passion" in *Revaluation* (London, 1936), pp. 199–202.

*German Sublimity and English Pathos:* When Southey, in 1798, calls "The Ancient Mariner" a "Dutch attempt at German sublimity," *Critical Review, 24* (1798), he is signaling a difference between English and German ballad style. Though Samuel Monk points out that the terrible sublime is as English as it is German (*The Sublime: A Study of Critical Theories in XVIII–Century England*, Ann Arbor Paperbacks, 1960, p. 138), by 1798 it was clearly associated with "The harsh coarse horror of a German Muse" (Joseph Fawcett, *The Art of Poetry*, 1798), while the vein of "true simplicity and genuine pathos" (Wordsworth, "Essay Supplementary to the Preface" of 1815) was felt to be the special property of the original Percy ballads. The migration of the Percy ballads to Germany, and their differing redemption by Wordsworth, Coleridge, William Taylor of Norwich, and others, is studied in O. F. Emerson "The Earliest Translations of Bürger's Lenore," *Western Reserve University Bulletin, 17*, no. 3 (May 1915); and A. B. Friedman, *The Ballad Revival* (Chicago, 1961), ch. 9. For the destiny of the ballads in Germany, see esp. Heinrich Lohre, "Von Percy zum Wunderhorn. Beiträge zur Geschichte der Volksliedforschung in Deutschland," *Palaestra XX* (Berlin and Leipzig, 1902).

### NOTES

1. *PW*, 2, 253. Quotations from *Lyrical Ballads* are always from the earliest published version unless otherwise indicated. All the poems considered in this section were composed or published not later than 1800.

2. *PW*, 2, 514–15, and 5, 319–20 (appendix A). The desolateness of the spot, or rather, that desolateness working on the peasant's mind, elicits the thought of a sympathetic nature, and raises Wordsworth to an intimation of the time when men will be guided by "The vision of humanity, and of God / The Mourner, God the Sufferer."

3. From a note to "The Thorn" appended to the editions of 1800–1805, *PW*, 2, 512.

4. Legouis, *Early Life*, pp. 310–12.

5. De Selincourt, *Early Letters*, p. 446.

6. Intimations Ode, line 144.

7. *Prelude* II.171 ff.

8. A sophisticated version of this is found in "The Brothers," lines 178–83. The Priest speaks to Leonard:

> We have no need of names and epitaphs;
> We talk about the dead by our fire-sides.
> And then, for our immortal part! *we* want
> No symbols, Sir, to tell us that plain tale:
> The thought of death sits easy on the man
> Who has been born and dies among the mountains.

9. *Prelude* III.180–83.

10. G. Wilson Knight, with habitual intuitiveness, strikes at the heart of the matter when he says, commenting in general on Wordsworth: "We all but reach the equation: Death = individual personality." *The Starlit Dome* (New York, 1941), p. 13.

11. *PW*, *1*, 188.

12. *Book of Job* 7:17–18.

13. Cf. the last stanza of "Hart-Leap Well": "One lesson, Shepherd, let us two divide, / Taught both by what she [Nature] shows, and what conceals."

14. *Lyrical Ballads* (1798), Advertisement: "The poem of The Thorn, as the reader will soon discover, is not supposed to be spoken in the author's own person; the character of the loquacious narrator will sufficiently show itself in the course of the story." Cf. note added to editions 1800–1805, *PW*, 2, 512.

15. "Hart-Leap Well" Pt. II, line 1. See also Critical Bibliography under *Character versus Incidents in LB.*

16. Another, less patent, reason, is that by removing our attention from the incidents he centers it inevitably on *one* incident (real or imaginary), which is a further reflection of the spot syndrome.

17. "the co-presence of something regular, something to which the mind has been accustomed when in an unexcited or a less excited state, cannot but have great efficacy in tempering and restraining the passion . . . from the tendency of metre to divest language in a certain degree of its reality, and thus throw a sort of half-consciousness of unsubstantial existence over the whole composition." Preface (1802) to *Lyrical Ballads.*

18. The relation of Wordsworth's lyrics to inscription poetry, touched on in Chapter 1 is considered in a separate essay (see below, note 40). For the genre see Akenside's "Inscriptions" (1772) and Southey's "Inscriptions" (1797); also two juvenile poems of Wordsworth's, *PW, 1,* 300–01.

19. Southey: "a good story for a ballad, because it is a well-known tale," *Critical Review, 24* (1798), in his notice of *LB.*

20. "Lines written at a small distance from my house . . ." The "than fifty years of reason" is later changed to "years of toiling reason."

21. Coleridge always excepted. A passage (later omitted) from "The Ruined Cottage" is quoted in his letter of March 10, 1798, and prefaced with: "I have snapped my squeaking baby-trumpet of Sedition . . . I love fields & woods & mounta[ins] with almost a visionary fondness—and because I have found benevolence & quietness growing within me as that fondness [has] increased, therefore I should wish to be the means of implanting it in others—& to destroy the bad passions not by combating them, but by keeping them in inaction" (Griggs, *Collected Letters, 1,* 397; cf. "that evenness of benevolent feeling which I wish to cultivate," ibid., 401).

22. See above, pp. 50 ff. There is no study of the survival or transformation of the concept of the Light of Nature during the Romantic period.

23. "Prophet and Poet, well understood, have much kindred of meaning. Fundamentally they are still the same; in the most important respect, especially, that they have penetrated both of them into the sacred mystery of the Universe; what Goethe calls 'the open secret.' " Carlyle, "The Hero as Poet" in *On Heroes and Hero-Worship* (1840). Cf. his essay on "The Death of Goethe" (1832) and see *Goethes Werke* (Hamburg, 1953), *12,* "Maximen und Reflexionen," nos. 2, 3, 7, 20. The idea of nature as an open mystery, i.e. as a mystery-religion paradoxically open to all mankind (just as St. Paul had opened the Old Dispensation and transformed Judaism into Christianity) is linked to a persistent concept in the history of ideas, that of the Book of Nature, "that universal and publick Manuscript that lies expans'd unto the Eyes of all" (Sir Thomas Browne, *Religio Medici,* 1643, Part 1, section 16). See also C. F. Harrold, *Carlyle and German Thought: 1819–1834* (New Haven, 1934), pp. 76 ff. and 116 ff.

24. *The Simpliciad* refers to a phrase in one of Wordsworth's poems, "To a Daisy," in the 1807 volumes. Apostolical daisies, however, continued to flourish in the nineteenth century: "that daisy under the heel of a clown has a lesson, if sought for. Yes, and a lesson 'Apostolical' for the clown, though he never heard of the master." *A Note on William Wordsworth with a Statement of Her Views on Spiritualism,* by E. B. Browning (London, 1919), p. 6.

25. "Lines Written in Early Spring."

26. "Expostulation and Reply." The explanation given in this chapter should be complemented by pp. 181 f. below.

27. *PW, 5,* 286–88. The original version of the passage was composed at Alfoxden.

28. *Prelude* XIII.290–91.

29. " 'Throw aside your books of Chemistry,' said Wordsworth to a young man, a student in the Temple, 'and read Godwin on Necessity,' " Hazlitt, *The Spirit of the Age* (1825). The remark attributed to Wordsworth is puzzling. When would it have been made? Why books of chemistry, and not books on natural or moral philosophy? It is possible that Wordsworth was impressed by Godwin's assertion that the spirit of man is *liberated* by recognizing that "in the life of every human being there is a chain of causes, generated in that eternity which preceded his birth [cf. *Prelude* II.228 ff.], and going on in regular procession through the whole period of his existence, in consequence of which it was impossible for him to act in any instance otherwise than he has acted": *An Inquiry concerning Political Justice* (1793). Such paradoxial and methodical necessitarianism, however, can be used for many different ends: as a philosophy of detachment, or to limit moral-metaphysical speculation, or to urge the revision of the penal system and emphasize the power for good or evil of government and education. Wordsworth was attracted, at one time or another, by each of these practical applications of the doctrine of Necessity. But by 1797–98, as "The Convict" of *LB* and the addendum to MS B of "The Ruined Cottage" suggest (*PW, 5,* 400–04), he was interested solely in contrasting the kindly, gradual, but resistless suasion of nature (based on an infinity of expedients) with the brutal monisms of law or reason. Cf. the strange story of the Wedgwood scheme: Moorman, *Wordsworth,* pp. 333–37.

30. Its subtitle: "Being an Argument in favour of the natural Disinterested-ness of the Human Mind. To which are added, some remarks on the systems of Hartley and Helvétius."

31. "A Poet's Epitaph" (1800).

32. *Excursion* IV.991–92.

33. Mill, for example, says in the *Autobiography* (ch. 5) that the 1815 edition of Wordsworth's poems gave him not merely beautiful pictures of natural scenery but "states of feeling, and of thought coloured by feeling, under the excitement of beauty," and that the poems proved to him "with culture of this sort, there was nothing to dread from the most confirmed habit of analysis."

34. "Anecdote for Fathers."

35. For an account of these rituals see A. Van Gennep, *The Rites of Passage* (1908; English tr., Chicago, 1960); also Frazer, *Taboo and the Perils of the Soul* (1911; Part 2 of *The Golden Bough*). The ritual here is the poem itself, and the passage the transition between states of consciousness.

36. Herrick's poems are influenced by similar "brief elegies" in *The Greek Anthology* and it may be that the latter is a common source for both Herrick and Wordsworth.

37. For the concept of boundary beings, see the following chapter.

38. Ondine is representative of this category of spirits who find a home in the German *Märchen* and who are transmitted via German Romanticism to Matthew Arnold as well as to the modern novella.

39. Intimations Ode, lines 82–83.

40. "The Two April Mornings," *LB* (1800). There are more than two Matthew poems, of course; the whole cycle should be studied. I deal elsewhere with the relation of some of them to Inscription poetry and Wordsworth's peculiar elegiac sense (see "Wordsworth, Inscriptions, and Romantic Nature Poetry," in *From Sensibility to Romanticism*, eds. F. Hilles and H. Bloom, Oxford University Press, 1965).

## Toward *The Prelude*

### CRITICAL BIBLIOGRAPHY

Legouis, in *The Early Wordsworth*, Bk. 3, ch. 3, agrees that it is the poet's sense of self-identity which was restored at Alfoxden, but he remains eloquently general about the means by which this was effected. "The link which was to connect his early years with those of his maturity was happiness; happiness formerly spontaneous, but now the result of conscious reflection." Garrod sees Wordsworth's progress as one from a naive sensationalism, to a period of crisis in which his heart was "turned aside" by the rational absolutism of Godwin, to when, at Alfoxden, and with the aid of Coleridge, he placed his sensationalism on a new basis (*Wordsworth*, pp. 102 ff.). But no more than Legouis does he clarify the means by which the restoration came about: Coleridge's help is insisted on rather than explained, and it is even contradicted by the supposition that Wordsworth retreated from Godwinism "not by any logical process, nor by gradations, but suddenly; by a rush of conflicting feeling, by the unpredictable melting of a proud and prodigal temperament. With never a word(!) he lays his head again in the lap of Nature" (p. 104). G. M. Harper gives no special consideration to Alfoxden because he places Wordsworth's crisis in middle life (although this starts, strangely enough, near 1800). *The Prelude* he considers part of that crisis: it is the poem of a philosophical idealist reacting against "the great, positive, naturalistic movement of the preceding century," including his own *Lyrical Ballads!* Harper's position (see *William Wordsworth*, 3d ed. London, 1929, ch. 20) has become less tenable than ever with the publication of MS JJ and the Alfoxden fragments which attach the early history of *The Prelude* to the concerns of "The Ruined Cottage" and "Tintern Abbey." But Bateson, in his *Wordsworth,* salvages something of Harper's thesis by relocating the poet's "lapse into subjectivity" (i.e. his abandonment of the Augustan leaven, of what Harper had described as the "naturalistic movement of the preceding century").* The subjectivist—romantic, idealistic—heresy is now said to have begun in the spring and summer of 1798 and achieved its finest expression in the Goslar poems, which are all connected, directly or indirectly, with childhood (Bateson, ch. 5, "The Egostistical Sublime"). Just as Harper was constrained to see *The Prelude* in many respects antithetical to *Lyrical Ballads,* so Bateson is forced into a curious dichotomy between the "Alfoxden poems," said to be "emotionally impersonal," and the "Goslar poems," which are "intensely personal." The change Bateson views as an instinctive regression to childhood and interprets as either (1) Wordsworth's unconscious attempt to return to a presexual relationship with Dorothy, or (2) a conscious turning away from the disembodied (rational) affections, which had betrayed him into an "ecstatic" intimacy with Dorothy, and toward an emotionally rooted life that would reintegrate his personality. From Bateson we can salvage the obvious fact, overlaid by hypotheses too exclusive of each other to be proposed as alternatives, that Wordsworth is effecting a "psychic continuity" with earlier states of being. But Bateson, and also G. W. Meyer (*Tulane Studies in English, 1,* 1949, 119–56) and Harold Bloom (*The Visionary Company,* New York, 1961, pp. 127–60), are unable to advance us beyond Legouis in determining why Wordsworth's return to the past, or to its memory, is redemptive.

I am not acquainted with any study of the blank verse of this period either in its own terms or for the light it throws on Wordsworth's inner biography. Moorman (cited in note 1) comes nearest.

* The thesis is anticipated, I believe, by Helen Darbishire: "The *Lyrical Ballads* had been the fruits of a supreme effort to escape from personal experience and to enter by a strenuous act of imagination into the 'deep heart of man' and the inner life of Nature. But such an effort of projection could not long be sustained by one of Wordsworth's introspective temper. He retired into himself, revolved once more round the center of his own personal life" *Wordsworth's Poems in Two Volumes* (Oxford, 1914), introd., p. xl.

Potts, *Wordsworth's Prelude,* examines the possible influences of
Beattie, Young, Akenside, etc. on MS JJ and related fragments. Her
study rightly attaches Wordsworth's poem to existing literary con-
cerns but does not follow the thought or style of the early passages
closely enough to determine their own momentum. (My own feel-
ing is that Akenside's revised *Pleasures of the Imagination* did help
to mold Wordsworth's new style and tone.) Her omission of Cole-
ridge has occasioned protest; mine will too; I have not been able
to differentiate, within the limits of this chapter, between his early
blank verse and Wordsworth's, although notice is taken of Cole-
ridge's presence.

NOTES

1. *PW,* 5, 340–47 (appendix B). The only consideration to date is Moorman,
*Wordsworth,* pp. 355–57.
2. "those fleeting moods / Of shadowy exultation." *Prelude* II.312–13.
3. From *The Journals of Emerson,* quoted by Havens, *Mind of a Poet*
(Baltimore, 1941), p. 304.
4. *PW,* 5, 343–44.
5. *PW,* 5, 344.
6. Preface (1800) to *Lyrical Ballads.*
7. *PW,* 5, 341.
8. *PW,* 5, 340.
9. "Home at Grasmere," line 743, *PW,* 5, 337 (appendix A).
10. *PW,* 5, 340–41. The fragment is related to the "Soul of all the Worlds"
passage of MS 18a which is incorporated as the beginning of *Excursion* IX.
11. *Prelude* XI.142–43.
12. *Prelude* II.229–32.
13. *PW,* 5, 340.
14. It would seem to me that the liberated syntax and rhythm of Words-
worth's blank verse is not primarily a recovery of the "language really used by
men" but rather the creation (on that basis) of a *language of thought.* The poet
teaches us to think naturally rather than to speak naturally. We feel a "vivid
pulse of sentiment and thought" (*PW,* 5, 344) because, as personal conscious-
ness increases, perception expands, and vice versa.
15. *PW,* 5, 343.
16. *PW,* 5, 347.
17. *Prelude* I.15.
18. See the beautiful passage in "Home at Grasmere," lines 445–70; *PW,* 5,
328–29.
19. Entry in Thoreau's *Journal* for March 3, 1839, quoted by Perry Miller,

"Thoreau in the Context of International Romanticism," *New England Quarterly, 34* (1961), 150. I am grateful to Alexander Kern for drawing my attention to this article. Cf. *Prelude* XIII.305–12.

20. MS Y, first printed by De Selincourt, see *Prelude²*, pp. 575–76. Lines 169–70 are omitted since they are only partially legible.

21. Blake, *The First Book of Urizen* (1794), plate 4.

22. *PW*, 5, 339.

23. *Prelude* I.47. Cf. H. Lindenberger, *On Wordsworth's Prelude* (Princeton, 1963), pp. 163–66.

24. *PW*, 5, 313–39 (appendix A).

25. *PW*, 5, 348–62 (appendix C).

26. *Prelude* I.37–38.

27. *Prelude* III.132–33.

28. "Home at Grasmere," lines 117–20 (*PW*, 5, 317).

29. " 'Thou art pleased, pleased with thy crags and woody steeps,' said Wordsworth of Grasmere, and he expresses God's own affirmation of the real world." E. D. Hirsch, *Wordsworth and Schelling* (New Haven, 1960), p. 34.

30. "Home at Grasmere," lines 136–49 (*PW*, 5, 317–18).

31. "Home at Grasmere," lines 445–48 (*PW*, 5, 328).

32. *PW*, 5, 5 (line 84 of the verse prospectus to *The Excursion*, cf. *PW*, 5, 339).

33. A very old mystical concept, given scope in our century by Paul Claudel, *L'Art poétique* (Paris, 1907). Cf. Meister Eckhart: "The eye with which I see God is the same with which he sees me" (and I Corinthians 13:12).

34. See Wallace Stevens, "The Noble Rider and the Sound of Words" in *The Necessary Angel* (New York, 1951).

35. Cf. *Prelude* III.278 ff. A line in the 1805 text, "My Surplice, gloried in, and yet despised" (III.318), catches his mood of conflict explicitly.

36. *PW*, 5, 338.

37. MS JJ, *Prelude²*, p. 640.

38. Lines 643 f. (*PW*, 5, 335).

39. I do not think the Hermit is simply a picturesque prop; cf. my *The Unmediated Vision* (New Haven, 1954), pp. 32–34.

40. Coleridge, "The Eolian Harp," 1795.

41. Valéry in *La jeune Parque* of the serpent: "O vifs détours tout courus de caresses." Hart Crane, in *The Bridge,* of the moon reflected in a stream: "I could see / Your hair's keen crescent running."

42. *PW*, 5, 341.

43. Cf. the repetition of the demonstrative at the beginning of "Tintern Abbey."

44. *PW*, 5, 341.

45. The term is coined on the analogy of the "Miltonic turn": see De Selincourt, *Poems of John Keats* (5th ed. London, 1926), pp. 490–92. Cf. *The Early Wordsworth* (Oxford, 1936), p. 27.

46. *PW*, 5, 344 and 343. The manuscript reads "into breathless dream."

47. See Wordsworth's sonnet "A poet!—He hath put his heart to school" (1842). I am adapting the line to my purpose.

48. Griggs, *Collected Letters*, 4, 574.

49. *PW*, 5, 343. A remarkably prosy passage. Was it prose originally? The first line, left incomplete by De Selincourt, is addressed to "Henry," with the name crossed out. The theme of the fragment reminds one of Young's *Night Thoughts* (Night VI), "Our *senses*, as our *reason*, are divine," and Wordsworth acknowledges Young in a note to "Tintern Abbey" appended to "of all this mighty world / Of eye and ear, both what they half-create, / And what perceive." But Young is basing himself specifically on the theory that the secondary qualities of objects are contributed or "created" by the senses.

50. See R. H. Fogle, *The Idea of Coleridge's Criticism* (Berkeley and Los Angeles, 1962).

51. "If the doors of perception . . .": Blake, *Marriage of Heaven and Hell*; "nascent vision . . .": Coleridge, *Biographia Literaria*, ch. 12.

52. This is too well-known to require documentation, but in addition to the overt evidence of the *Biographia Literaria*, see R. F. Brinkley's fine compilation, *Coleridge on the Seventeenth Century* (Durham, 1955).

53. *PW*, 5, 343. Concerning Coleridge's role, see also below, pp. 194 f. I suspect that what in Coleridge was purely speculative, and, from a religious point of view, precariously so, namely the theory of monads ("Infinite myriads of self-conscious minds"), supported Wordsworth's *direct* experience of nature in the Alfoxden period. The difference between them, therefore, was probably even less substantive than I suggest, since Coleridge always encouraged his friend to treat man as a subject of eye and ear.

54. See above, chapter on *Lyrical Ballads*, pp. 154 ff.

55. *PW*, 5, 346.

56. Cf. *The Unmediated Vision*, pp. 21–22 (on the omission of the intermediary of perception).

57. On "anthropomorphitism" see "Essay, Supplementary to the Preface" (1815), *PW*, 2, 439 f.; and M. H. Abrams, *The Mirror and the Lamp* (New York, 1953), pp. 290–97.

58. *PW*, 5, 340. Here again Wordsworth's *experience* parallels Coleridge's *ideas*, for the equation between sound and light had suggested itself to the latter via Boehme's *Aurora* before his trip to Germany in September 1798. See J. B. Beer, *Coleridge the Visionary* (London, 1959), pp. 163–65; *The Unmediated Vision*, pp. 40–43; and below, "Eye and Ear on Snowdon."

59. *Prelude* II.302–11. Like "there would he stand . . . ," to which it is verbally and thematically related, a draft of this is found in the Alfoxden notebook, and is therefore, as De Selincourt points out, among the first parts of *The Prelude* to be written (*Prelude*², pp. 523–24).

60. *Prelude* V.595–96.

61. Early draft for *Prelude* XIV.63 ff. quoted in *Prelude*², p. 622.

62. *Prelude* XIV.88–90.

63. *Prelude* XIII.290–91.

64. MS W, *Prelude²*, p. 624.

65. Wordsworth emphasizes the activity of nature at the expense of tautology, when he adds "by putting forth" to "Exhibited" in *Prelude* (1805) XIII.75. He keeps the phrase, though dangling, in the 1850 version, XIV.79. Unless the phrase is construed as a gerund (shadowed: how? by a putting forth) it takes "That mutual domination" as object and makes it refer to the way in which imagination (the "one function" of line 78) is exhibited, rather than to imagination itself, as the passage seems to require:

> One function, above all, of such a mind
> Had Nature shadowed there . . .
> That mutual domination which she loves
> To exert. . . .

Or is the *function* both the faculty and the mode whereby it is (self-) exhibited?

66. *Prelude* XI.234 ff.

67. With Wordsworth we remain in the phenomenal world, however surprising a particular revelation may be (cf. *Prelude* I.458–60). But reversal is strongly characteristic of apocalyptic experiences, though here it comes to Wordsworth in a purely natural context.

68. My metaphors of "flowing" and "fixity" are justified by the vision (XIV.58 ff.) and the meditation (XIV.73 ff.).

69. *Prelude²*, pp. 484–85. On this matter of transformation or transfer, see also (1) above, pp. 65 f. (2) the living chiasmus depicted in a related episode of MS W, *Prelude²*, p. 624, the picture of a horse which is "A living Statue or a statued Life;" and (3) *Excursion* VII.518 ff., "faculties, which seem / Extinguished, do not, *therefore*, cease to be. / And to the mind among her powers of sense / This transfer is permitted." The reference is to the sensitivity of ear and touch in a blind man.

70. See Wordsworth's critique of Macpherson's *Ossian*, PW, 2, 423: "In nature everything is distinct, yet nothing defined into absolute independent singleness."

71. Genesis 28:12.

72. *Prelude* XII.11.

73. MS Y, *Prelude²*, p. 430.

74. "The Circus Animals' Desertion," *Last Poems*.

75. We read, for example, in the *Corpus Hermeticum*, eds. A. D. Nock and A. F. Festugière, 2 (Paris, 1945), 233–34: "le Démiurge, je veux dire le Soleil, lie ensemble le ciel et la Terre, envoyant en bas la substance, élèvant en haut la matière, tirant près de lui et jusqu'à lui toutes choses, et . . . répand sur tous, libéralement la lumière. Car il est de qui les bonnes énergies pénètrent non seulement dans le ciel et l'air, mais aussi jusqu'au gouffre le

plus profond et à l'abîme." For glimpses of the hinterland of theosophical and cosmological speculation which Milton must have known, see Karl Reinhardt, *Kosmos und Sympathie* (Munich, 1926), pp. 308 ff. Du Bartas condemns certain theories of "sympathetic nature" as fables: *The Complete Works of Joshua Sylvester*, ed. A. B. Grosart *1* (Edinburgh, 1880), 53a.

76. See his "On Mr. Milton's Paradise Lost."

77. Northrop Frye, *Fearful Symmetry* (Princeton, 1947), ch. 6, sects. 3–7, gives an account of this to which I am greatly indebted.

78. The Enthusiasts of the Enlightenment, says Novalis ironically, "waren rastlos beschäftigt, die Natur, den Erdboden, die menschliche Seele und die Wissenschaften von der Poesie zu säubern,—jede Spur des Heiligen zu vertilgen, das Andenken an alle erhebende Vorfälle und Menschen durch Sarkasmen zu verleiden und die Welt alles bunten Schmucks zu entkleiden. Das Licht war wegen seines mathematischen Gehorsams und seiner Frechheit ihr Liebling geworden. Sie freuten dass es sich eher zerbrechen liess, als dass es mit Farben gespielt hätte, und so benannten sie nach ihm ihr grosses Geschäft—Aufklärung" *Die Christenheit oder Europa*, 1799.

79. "Conjectures on Original Composition" (1759). The example of the English *Aeneid* is my own.

80. See his letter to Flaxman of September 12, 1800: Geoffrey Keynes, *The Complete Writings of William Blake* (New York, 1957), p. 799. More than half a century later, in *William Shakespeare* (1864), Victor Hugo adopts the same promiscuous position vis-à-vis secular and sacred authors.

81. *PW, 5,* 286 and app. crit.

82. For these emblems see L. Spitzer, *Classical and Christian Ideas of World Harmony* (Baltimore, 1962); also J. W. Beach, *The Concept of Nature in Nineteenth-Century English Poetry* (New York, 1936), esp. pp. 99–109.

83. See esp. *The First Book of Urizen*, and Harold Bloom, *Blake's Apocalypse* (New York, 1963), passim.

84. *PW, 1,* 13.

85. *Biographia Literaria*, ch. 10.

86. *The Road to Xanadu* (Boston and New York, 1927), ch. 5 and passim.

87. *PW, 1,* 13. But it is hard, here, to distinguish Akenside's influence from Thomson's. See Akenside's description of the forms of genius in Bk. 1 of *Pleasures of the Imagination*, and Potts, *Prelude*, ch. 10.

88. From Coleridge's plan for one of his "Hymns," *The Notebooks of Samuel Taylor Coleridge, 1794–1804*, ed. Kathleen Coburn (2 vols. New York, Bollingen, 1957), *1*, entry 174.

89. *Georgics* IV.475 ff.; for Thomson's translation, see his preface to the second edition of *Winter*. It is given in the *Poetical Works of James Thomson*, ed. J. Logie Robertson (Oxford, 1908), pp. 241–42.

90. *The Poetical Works of Samuel Taylor Coleridge*, ed. E. H. Coleridge (Oxford, 1912), *1*, 133; and cf. an earlier draft, *2*, 1025.

91. I am not aware of any direct study of the subject, but the following

secondary sources may prove useful: Lowes, *The Road to Xanadu* (pp. 385–96); M. H. Nicolson, *Mountain Gloom and Mountain Glory* (Ithaca, 1959), esp. ch. 5 on Burnet's *Sacred Theory*; N. P. Stallknecht, *Strange Seas of Thought* (Bloomington, 1958), ch. 4, "Imagination and the Mind's Abyss." Any modern mythologian, like Mircea Eliade, provides additional materials. It is perhaps enough to remember Aristaeus's water-*nekya* in the fourth book of the *Georgics*, the flood symbolism of the Bible (Genesis 7:11; Psalms 24:2, 29:10, 18:15), and Burnet's *Sacred Theory*, esp. Bk. 1, ch. 11.

92. "Autumn," lines 796–813. The collocation of Atlas, Abyssinia, and the Mountains of the Moon is significant, and points to an area of speculative mythology explored below in note 96 and "Myth without Myth (2)."

93. Beside sources referred to in note 91, consult: James Bruce, *Travels to Discover the Sources of the Nile,* 1790 (Lowes, 370 ff.); any classical or medieval Latin poem, e.g. Claudian's epigram "De Nilo"; any modern gathering of evidence, e.g. Eliade, *Patterns in Comparative Religion,* ch. 6, "The Moon and Its Mystique." Also Erasmus Darwin on the "Central Fires," in note 6 to *The Botanic Garden* (Lowes, pp. 98–99).

94. Northrop Frye, "New Directions from Old," in *Myth and Mythmaking,* ed. H. A. Murray (New York, 1960). Cf. F. A. Pottle, "Wordsworth and Freud, or the Theology of the Unconscious," *Bulletin of the General Theological Seminary, 34* (1948), 18–27.

95. *Jerusalem* III, plate 71.

96. The arcana of this subject being immense, I am content to refer to the section that follows, and to mention these passages or poems that stand in an exoteric relation to Nile mysticism: *Paradise Lost* I.778 ff., *Prelude* VI.613–16; Shelley, "To the Nile." The idea that man is himself a *mesocosm* can be found in Pico della Mirandola, for whom man is the "vinculum et nodus" of celestial and earthly. I have tried to say something about the changed significance of this idea in contemporary literature in *The Novelist as Philosopher,* ed. J. Cruickshank (New York, 1962), pp. 162–64.

97. Keats, "Epistle to John Hamilton Reynolds," esp. lines 67–84. These verses arguing for the "material sublime" were influenced, surely, by Wordsworth's "Recluse" passage prefacing the 1814 *Excursion*. Yet the imagination, for Wordsworth, is originally and perhaps inherently apocalyptic.

98. Joseph Warton, *The Works of Virgil in Latin and English* (4 vols. London, 1753), 2, 297.

99. *Prelude* XII.105–21.

100. In a later passage of the fourth book, Virgil brings Atlas and Aethiopia together: "Oceani finem juxta solemque cadentem, / Ultimus Aethiopum locus est, ubi maximus Atlas / Axem humero torquet stellis ardentibus aptum . . ." IV.480–83.

101. Cf. in Keats' *Hyperion* the relation of the new gods (Apollo; the young God of the Seas) to the old. Keats' initial picture of Saturn, "quiet as a stone, /

Still as the silence round about his lair; / Forest on forest hung about his head / Like cloud on cloud," subsumes the tradition that the Titans became mountains.

102. *Endymion* I.293 f. ("Hymn to Pan"). My italics.

103. *PW*, 2, 438.

104. "A Borderer dwelling betwixt life and death . . ." *Prelude*², p. 624.

105. Cf. *The Unmediated Vision,* pp. 33–34.

106. See *The Borderers* (composed 1796–97). The border region is also the background to the "spot of time" described in *Prelude* XII.225 ff.

107. *Excursion* I.430–31.

108. Dr. Johnson's remark comes in criticism of an irremediable flaw in *The Seasons,* since in this kind of descriptive poetry "no rule can be given why one [appearance] should be mentioned before another; yet the memory wants the help of order, and the curiosity is not excited by suspense or expectation." See his "Life of Thomson."

109. *Prelude*², pp. 174–75 and app. crit.

110. Pliny; and Wordsworth's epigraph for the "Vernal Ode."


*The Prelude*

CRITICAL BIBLIOGRAPHY

A review of all books which have regarded *The Prelude* in its relation to Wordsworth's philosophy of mind would require a small dissertation. The leading issues and controversies are succinctly set forth in James V. Logan, *Wordsworthian Criticism* (Columbus, 1947 and 1961), ch. 6, "Wordsworth's Philosophy." The chapter takes us from Arnold's refusal to see the *value* of Wordsworth's philosophy, through Legouis, Beatty, Rader, Stallknecht, and Havens. My own position lies closer to Rader and Havens than to Beatty; although I do not feel that the "transcendentalist" interpretations of Wordsworth are much truer than the "sensationalist" or "associationist." Two questions are involved: whether Wordsworth was, in any sense, a systematic thinker, and what significant label to give to his system or non-system. These questions, I suspect, will be resolved, if at all, together: Wordsworth's thinking is of the existential or phenomenological kind, which starts with objects not as they *are* but as they *appear* to a mind fruitfully perplexed by their differing modes of appearance, and which does not try to reduce these to a single standard. The poet values the varying types of relations and responses of his mind to objects because they potentially unlock some truth about himself. Wordsworth's thought is also, therefore, of a *basically* religious kind, as Chapter 1 of this book argues; every truth or error in relationship is a source of revelation. Since the time of Havens, A. F. Potts, *Wordsworth's Prelude* (Ithaca, New York, 1953), and Herbert Lindenberger, *On Wordsworth's Prelude* (Princeton, 1963) have brought out forcefully the debt of Wordsworth both to specific eighteenth-century poems and to the "older rhetoric" in general, but there has been no new view of the philosophy of mind—or of nature—contained in *The Prelude,* with the following significant exceptions: (1) a consensus is shaping that what is important in Wordsworth's thought, and to an extent in his poetry, is the "I thinking," the quick of his consciousness; (2) there are attempts, almost abandoned after A. C. Bradley's brilliant studies, and D. G. James' *Scepticism and Poetry* (London, 1937), to remove the stigma of parochialism from Wordsworth, and to see his thought and poetry in the context of European literature, as in E. D. Hirsch's "typological" essay on *Wordsworth and Schelling* (New Haven, 1960); (3) David Ferry in *The Limits of Mortality* (Middletown, 1959), particularly in his chapter on *The Prelude;* David Perkins, via many remarks in the first three chapters of *The Quest for Permanence* (Cambridge, Mass., 1959); John Jones' comments in *The Egotistical Sublime* (London, 1954) on the poetry of solitude and of relationship; and Harold Bloom in the relevant sections of *The Visionary Company* (New York, 1961), have deepened our understanding of the problematical relations between mind and nature in Wordsworth's poetry, and moved away from a too simple (Arnoldian) notion of Wordsworth as healing and reconciling nature poet; (4) a movement is gathering strength, fed by some of the explorations cited above, but especially by W. Empson, *The Structure of Complex Words* (London, 1951), pp. 289–305, and John Jones' "Epilogue," to emphasize the epistemological subtleties in the poetry. What Wimsatt did in "The Structure of Romantic Nature Imagery," *The Verbal Icon* (Lexington, Kentucky, 1954), is being extended to the syntactical and lexical levels, as in Colin

Clarke's *Romantic Paradox* (London, 1963).* My own work, which does attempt to present a new and comprehensive view of Wordsworth's 'consciousness of consciousness' (together, in this chapter, with a view of the structure of *The Prelude* as it centers on this) harmonizes often with the above developments, except that it sees Wordsworth's dialectic as a dialectic of love, his epistemology as a love-epistemology (cf. *The Unmediated Vision*, pp. 13–26). The fundamental relation, as between subject and object, posited by Wordsworth, is not something intrinsic and inalienable, but part of a deeply operative principle of generosity which reaches beyond rememberable time and cannot be understood by epistemic schemas. The proper analogy is, rather, the mystery of creation (God, though self-sufficient, went out of himself to create the world, so the imagination goes out to nature, becomes fertile, and produces a "creation," see *Prelude* III.173 ff., and the verse prospectus to the 1814 *Excursion*, PW 5, 5). When Coleridge says that "of all men I ever knew, Wordsworth has the least femininity in his mind. He is *all* man. He is a man of whom it might have been said, 'It is good for him to be alone' " (*Table Talk and Omniana*, ed. T. Ashe, 1884, p. 339, and a reference to Genesis, 2:18), he recognizes the autonomy and separateness that Wordsworth—for whom relationship is not given, but *the* form of creative action, even the form of Creation—valued in all things.

NOTES

1. *PW*, 5, 347 (appendix B, 1.) and *Prelude*[2], p. 636 (MS JJ).
2. "I was lost" (*Prelude* VI.596); "I am lost" (*Prelude* XII.273).
3. Cf. also Preface to *The Excursion* of 1814: "Several years ago, when the Author retired to his native mountains, with the hope of being enabled to construct a literary Work that might live, it was a reasonable thing that he should take a review of his own mind, and examine how far Nature and Education had qualified him for such employment. As subsidiary to this preparation, he undertook to record, in verse, the origin and progress of his own powers, as far as he was acquainted with them" (*PW*, 5, 1–2).
4. Corroborative evidence for this is found in many letters, and suggests

* On Wordsworth's verbal style in general, I find the pioneering study of Josephine Miles, *Wordsworth and the Vocabulary of Emotion* (Berkeley, 1942), still the most useful. Cf. also her "Wordsworth: The Mind's Excursive Power," *Eras and Modes in English Poetry* (Berkeley, 1957).

that Wordsworth's daemon had to trick him into autobiography. See the letters
to De Quincey, March 6, 1804; Sir George Beaumont, December 25, 1804 and
May 1, 1805; and Richard Sharp, February 1805.

5. Coleridge, *Table Talk* (July 21, 1832), quoted *Prelude²*, p. xxxviii; also
Griggs, *Collected Letters*, 2, 1033–34.

6. See MSS RV, U, V, and MS JJ (the last reprinted in *Prelude²*, pp. 633–
42).

7. MS JJ, *Prelude²*, p. 640.

8. The best consideration of Wordsworth's "animism" is by R. D. Havens,
*Mind of a Poet* (Baltimore, 1941), ch. 5. He recognizes as the simple and even·
archaic origin of Wordsworth's notion "the belief in spiritual beings who, like
the dryads and nymphs of classical mythology, are associated with certain
places" but does not link this specifically to the idea of the *genius loci*. There
were significant eighteenth-century survivals of the idea, some serious, some
purely ornate, in Pope, Gray, Collins, and Burns; and Milton, of course, used
the notion pregnantly in the Nativity Ode (line 186) and "Lycidas" (line 183).
A glance at the Wordsworth Concordance will show the early existence and
late persistence of the idea, as well as further linkages between "genial" and
*genius loci*. When Wordsworth says, in "Tintern Abbey," "Nor perchance, /
If I were not thus taught, should I the more / Suffer my genial spirits to
decay," he is conscious of the fact that those spirits have been linked to spirit
of place.

9. *Prelude²*, p. 42, app. crit.

10. *PW*, 2, 504–06.

11. "Three years she grew in sun and shower" (1800).

12. See above, p. 132. But Coleridge, of course, was himself conversant with
genii, natal daemons, etc. See the strange Neoplatonic passage quoted by J. B.
Beer, *Coleridge the Visionary* (London, 1959), pp. 150–51; and the much more
accessible source for similar beliefs, *The Arabian Nights,* which he mentions
poignantly in his autobiographical letter to Thomas Poole, *Collected Letters,
1,* 347, and cf. *1,* 354 ("my early reading of Faery Tales, and Genii etc etc"),
and *Prelude* V.460–509.

13. *Prelude* XII.219.

14. *Prelude* XII.225 ff.

15. On the destruction of the concept of the Way, see above, pp. 46 ff.

16. Coleridge, "To William Wordsworth, Composed on the Night after His
Recitation of a Poem on the Growth of an Individual Mind" (1807).

17. I purposely do not use an exclusive set of terms to describe, via Words-
worth, the maturing and humanizing of the child: let the psychologist talk of
"fixation" and "integration," or the philosopher of religion of a "daemonic
dread" that must be moralized yet persists as numinous underpresence. Words-
worth touches here the very origin of metaphor, of living metathesis, without
which an individual cannot communicate or receive his life. Cf. his compressed
account of the boy's growing mind in *Excursion* I.118 ff.

18. "Annotations to *The Excursion* . . ." (written 1826).

19. Cf. esp. *Prelude* I.553–58, its mention of "those first-born affinities that fit / Our new existence to existing things," preceded in MS JJ (*Prelude²*, pp. 636 f.) by a direct address to the "Soul of things"; also such passages as II.241 ff., quoted below. The "fitting" is something that is *possible* through the "progressive" life of the individual or the species.

20. The proper counterpoint to this is Shelley's "Triumph of Life" and Blake, passim. Nature as the great betrayer, the *femme fatale* and Whore of Babylon, is the anti-theme of Harold Bloom's *The Visionary Company* (New York, 1961).

21. Keats, not Arthur Beatty, is here the best reader of Wordsworth. "How, then are Souls to be made? How then are these sparks which are God to have identity given them—so as ever to possess a bliss peculiar to each one's individual existence? How but by the medium of a world like this? . . . Do you not see how necessary a World of Pains and troubles is to school an Intelligence and make it a soul?" (letter to George and Georgiana Keats, February 14–May 3, 1819). Yet Wordsworth's view is complicated by the fact that "his" soul is not blank of identity (a kind of neutron) on coming to this world but has an obscure supernatural identity which must be borne or put off or amalgamated. The transcendental strain in Wordsworth is cogently emphasized by Melvin Rader, "Presiding Ideas in Wordsworth's Poetry," *University of Washington Publications in Language and Literature, 8*, no. 2 (Seattle, 1931), 121–216.

22. *Mind of a Poet*, p. 376. Yet see Havens' later comment, "it is possible that in writing V he consciously or unconsciously had the development of the imagination in mind and that the unusual emphasis and striking omissions were due to his preoccupation with the faculty which is, for the poet at least, of supreme importance" (p. 381).

23. The dream of Book V approaches in time of composition the rising up of Imagination at VI.592; it is certainly closer to it than the episodes of the Boy of Winander and of the drowned man both of which originated circa 1798 (see MS JJ), while the dream is first found in MS M, and is *entered* after March 6, 1804. See *Prelude²*, p. xxx.

24. A correspondence with my point of view will be found in W. H. Auden, *The Enchafèd Flood* (New York, 1950) and Robin Skelton, *The Poetic Pattern* (London, 1956), pp. 208–15.

25. "And wedded man to man by purest bond / Of nature, undisturbed by space or time" *Prelude* (1805) V.105 f.; but Wordsworth finding the paradox "nature . . . undisturbed by space or time" difficult, changes the 1850 version to read "purest bond / Of reason."

26. Concerning this "fixing" (and the danger of concentrating on the apparently discrete symbols rather than the action that subsumes them) see my remarks on Snowdon, above, pp. 65 f.

27. A substitution (and displacement) not unusual in dreams, and related to "metonymy."

28. *Excursion* IV.136 f.

29. Or, to keep to his own image, "the cloud / Of infancy," *Excursion* IV.83–84.

30. This picture of Beaupuy gives us a possible reason for the curious mistake Wordsworth makes as to the time and place of his death. According to Wordsworth, he died while fighting on "the borders of the unhappy Loire" (IX.425) during the Vendean Civil War of 1793, whereas he was really killed on the Rhine front in 1796, fighting not against his fellows but against the Austrians. Yet Wordsworth's version of his death, perhaps confused with that of Beaupuy's brother (who did die in the Vendean war), brings his friend closer to being a Lad of the Loire parallel to the Boy of Winander or the other "lovely Boys" whose birth- and death-place are joined.

31. Preface (1800) to *Lyrical Ballads*.

32. Cf. *The Unmediated Vision*, pp. 131–32.

33. Is the natural basis for this metaphor the action of a water mill and/or the latin "(re)volvere" (as in *The Aeneid* I.305)? "Turned round" could suggest the dizziness of a suddenly disoriented mind, or the being turned back to a prior, neglected significance, as in VI.592 ff.

34. I extrapolate freely from Wordsworth's obliquities. Later, perhaps, as Basil Willey suggests, Burke's evaluation that the Revolution was made by man helped to turn Wordsworth away from it, but the idea at first enabled his fuller participation. See *The Eighteenth Century Background* (London, 1940), pp. 240 ff.

35. The main concept to which Wordsworth seems to be referring is that nature eventually destroys anything that gains a power or intent contrary to natural law. The nearest *literary* analogue to Wordsworth's state of mind is perhaps Andrew Marvell's attitude toward Cromwell in the Horatian Ode, for Cromwell is at once the ruin of the "great work of time" and the instrument of nature or "angry heaven." See also Z. S. Fink, "Wordsworth and the English Republican Tradition," *JEGP, 47* (1948), 107–26, esp. 119–24.

36. *Excursion* III.818.

37. *PW, 1,* 316.

38. *The English Poetic Mind* (Oxford, 1932), pp. 153–71.

39. The morning coming "out of the bosom of the night" is hymned at Robespierre's death, *Prelude* X.578–81, and here, *Prelude* XII.31–34, which may contain a reminiscence of *Paradise Lost* III.40–44.

40. Though Snowdon affected him consciously, and contains an element of sterner beauty, it is an earnest of nature's non-apocalyptic regenerative influence.

41. *PW, 1,* 120.

42. Cf. XIV.43, "A hundred hills their dusky backs upheaved," with *Paradise Lost* VII.285–86, "The mountains huge appear / Emergent, and their broad bare backs upheave."

43. *Paradise Lost* XI.836–38.

44. *Prelude²,* pp. 623–26.

45. *Prelude* XIV.232 ff. The 1850 version adds a tribute to Mary (lines 266–75).
46. Both Legouis, *The Early Life*, Bk. 3 chs. 1 and 2, and G. M. Harper, *William Wordsworth* (3d ed. London, 1929), chs. 9 and 10, do them full justice.

## 1801–1807: The Major Lyrics

### CRITICAL BIBLIOGRAPHY

Thomas Hutchinson's *Poems in Two Volumes* (London, 1897), and Helen Darbishire's *Poems in Two Volumes* (Oxford, 1914 and 1952), are both of them excellent editions. Hutchinson's preface has significant details on the reception of the 1807 *Poems,* and he adds a valuable appendix (Vol. 1, 208–26) on the Wordsworthian sonnet. Helen Darbishire's notes excel in indicating literary indebtedness to seventeenth-century authors.

On the period 1801–07 there is very little that is synoptic. Moorman's biography takes us to 1803.* She is so close to a wealth of materials that her theories on Wordsworth's development give occasionally an ad hoc appearance. I often found chs. 5 and 6 of H. M. Margoliouth's *Wordsworth and Coleridge, 1795–1834* (New York, 1953), the only useful account. He is able to link Wordsworth's poetry to his life without vulgarizing the poetry. Yet Wordsworth's sense of realities, whether or not it favored his Muse, remains unexplored. We do not have even the beginnings of a phenomenological description. There used to be much honorific comment on it: Arnold saying that Wordsworth deals with more of *life* than other poets; Walter Raleigh concluding with: "Here was a poet who faced the fact, and against whom the fact did not prevail" (*Wordsworth,* London, 1903). But recently there is only Trilling's insistence that the growth of the sense of reality is the subject of the Intimations Ode, and Leavis' emphasis (*Revaluation,* London, 1936) that Wordsworth's hold on the world of common perceptions is the more notable for reposing on an underconsciousness of vi-

* *William Wordsworth: The Later Years* was published in 1965. I have discussed it in *Book Week* (N.Y. *Herald Tribune*), March 6, 1965, p. 4, and in *Studies in English Literature,* VI (1966), 759–61.

sionary experience. There are also occasional historical studies that illumine the poet's close relation to his time. Kenneth MacLean, in his *Agrarian Age: A Background for Wordsworth* (New Haven, 1950), finds that even between the first and second edition of *Lyrical Ballads* Wordsworth's thought was becoming more concrete, and his description of the poet's increased interest in social subjects ("Wordsworth as Agrarian") should be set against Bateson's thesis on his relapse into 'Romantic' subjectivity during the same years. Arthur Beatty's use of the 'Three Ages of Man' theory (*William Wordsworth,* 3d ed., Madison, 1960) allows at least an abstract respect for Wordsworth's growing awareness of "whole continents of moral sympathy" (Wordsworth's own phrase, in a letter on the Leech-gatherer). If Beatty is abstract, Margaret Sherwood, in the fifth chapter ("Imaginative Will") of *Undercurrents of Influence in English Romantic Poetry* (Cambridge, Mass., 1934), is impressionistic, but she often catches the spirit of the maturer poetry.

On the individual poems the following authors may be consulted:

MICHAEL: E. C. Knowlton, "The Novelty of *Michael* as a Pastoral," *PMLA, 35* (1920), 432–46, esp. 440–46; K. Kroeber, *Romantic Narrative Art* (Madison, 1960), pp. 80–83.

RESOLUTION AND INDEPENDENCE: Coleridge, *Biographia Literaria,* ch. 22; Salvador de Madariaga, *Shelley and Calderón* (London, 1920), pp. 162–65 (part of a remarkable attack on Wordsworth); W. W. Robson, in *Interpretations,* ed. J. Wain (London, 1955), pp. 113–28; Florence G. Marsh, " 'Resolution and Independence,' st. XVIII," *MLN, 70* (1955), 488–90; E. M. Conran, "The Dialectic of Experience: A Study of Wordsworth's *Resolution and Independence*," *PMLA, 75* (1960), 66–74; A. S. Guérard, "*Resolution and Independence:* Wordsworth's Coming of Age," *English Studies in Africa, 3* (1960), 8–20; H. Bloom, *Visionary Company* (New York, 1961), pp. 160–66; S. E. Hyman, *Poetry and Criticism* (New York, 1961), pp. 103–21; Alan Grob, "Process and Permanence in *Resolution and Independence*," *ELH, 28* (1961), 89–100.

INTIMATIONS ODE: G. W. Knight, *Starlit Dome* (New York, 1941), pp. 37–49; C. Brooks, "Wordsworth and the Paradox of the

Imagination," *The Well Wrought Urn* (New York, 1947), ch. 7; L. Trilling, "The Immortality Ode," *The Liberal Imagination* (New York, 1950), pp. 129–60; E. D. Hirsch, "Both-And Logic in the Immortality Ode," *Wordsworth and Schelling* (New Haven, 1960), pp. 147–79; H. Bloom, *Visionary Company*, pp. 166–73. The last essay is valuable in complementing Trilling's naturalistic emphasis without falling into spiritualism. It examines the Ode's "passionate logic of questioning, despairing, and ultimately hoping response . . . derivative . . . from the prophetic portions of the Hebrew Bible." Also, Salvador de Madariago, *Shelley and Calderón*, pp. 143–44, for a negative point of view on the Ode's "forced and self-conscious exaltation."

ODE TO DUTY: M. Sherwood, *Undercurrents of Influence in English Romantic Poetry*, pp. 190–91; Jane Worthington, *Wordsworth's Reading of Roman Prose* (New Haven, 1946), pp. 61–65 (the Stoic sources with which the Ode seems to harmonize); N. P. Stallknecht, *Strange Seas of Thought: Studies in William Wordsworth's Philosophy of Man and Nature* (Bloomington, 1958), pp. 204–22 (a study of the Ode as spiritually intermediate between a doctrine analogous to that of Schiller's "Die schöne Seele" and rigorous stoicism). R. Wellek in his *Kant in England* (Princeton, 1931), already cautioned against attributing to specific philosophic sources an attitude that could easily have developed from Christian commonplaces. The analogies from contemporary German ethical philosophy which Stallknecht brings to bear are interesting, since moral theory tends to raise the same kind of problems, but I do not think them specific or appropriate enough to define a stage in Wordsworth's development. Wordsworth's mind is at once more autonomous than the comparative method leads us to believe, and more dependent on the mediation of national and literary sources.

PEELE CASTLE: E. D. Hirsch, *Wordsworth and Schelling*, pp. 88–97; H. Bloom, *Visionary Company*, pp. 179–82. My view differs from both of these in not taking the poem to be a "palinode on Wordsworth's gospel of Nature" (Bloom) or a radical change in Weltanschauung (Hirsch).

Essays on the *general* structure of Wordsworth's lyrics, or of his "recognitions," are hard to come by. Carlos Baker's introduction to the Rinehart *Wordsworth* contains a relevant generalization on the poet's "double exposure technique": "He often juxtaposes two widely separated periods of time in such a way that we are made dramatically conscious of the degree of growth that has taken place between Stage One and Stage Two." F. A. Pottle's "The Eye and the Object" has been mentioned. There is an illuminating comparison of a Wordsworth sonnet and a Yeats poem in Paul de Man's "Symbolic Landscape in Wordsworth and Yeats," *In Defense of Reading,* eds. R. A. Brower and R. Poirier (New York, 1962). Robert Langbaum's *The Poetry of Experience* (New York, 1957), esp. ch. 1, has important remarks on the structure of recognition in Wordsworth's poetry. K. Kroeber contrasts the "narrative" and "visionary" components of Wordsworth's lyrics in *Romantic Narrative Art* (Madison, 1960), pp. 51–56. E. Wasserman, in *SR* IV (1964), 17–34, gives an interesting epistemological analysis. M. H. Abrams traces the genealogy of the "Greater Romantic Lyric" in *From Sensibility to Romanticism,* eds. F. Hilles and H. Bloom (New York, 1965), pp. 527–60.

### NOTES

1. Coleridge's urgings begin as early as 1799. See Griggs, *Collected Letters, 1,* 527.

2. See fragments printed in *PW, 2,* 479–80, and *PW, 5,* 401.

3. So 1832; the version of 1800 is more crudely emphatic, and reads: "These fields, these hills, / Which were his living Being, even more / Than his own Blood." Unless otherwise stated, in this chapter all extracts from the poems of 1800 are quoted from the version of 1800, and all extracts from the 1807 *Poems* from the version of 1807.

4. See also Wordsworth's letter to Thomas Poole, April 9, 1801: "I have attempted to give a picture of a man, of strong and lively sensibility, agitated by two of the most powerful affections of the human heart; the parental affection, and the love of property, *landed* property." *Early Letters,* p. 266.

5. *PW, 5,* 287 (*Excursion* IX.20 f.), originally in MS 18a.

6. *PW, 2,* 480.

7. *The Letters of Charles Lamb,* ed. Lucas (London, 1935), *1,* 246.

8. *PW, 2,* 439–40.

9. Dorothy and William spent the morning of April 25, 1802, reading the *Prothalamion;* his poem was begun May 3. The stanza form, of course, though not un-Spenserian in mood, is not that of the *Prothalamion:* Chaucer and also Chatterton's "Balade of Charitie" may have exerted some influence on it. For

the Chaucerian influence, and the allegorical prototype in general, see E. M. Conran, *PMLA, 75* (1960), 66–74. A. F. Potts suggests Spenserian influences on other poems of the period in *SP, 29* (1932), 607–16.

10. See esp. *PW, 5,* 400, fragment 1. Both *Prelude* VI.592 ff. and *Prelude* XIV.63 ff., which are studied in detail in Part II above, could be considered as after-images, and become "spots of time" insofar as they reach through intermediate tracts of time. The Snowdon vision itself is, moreover, almost a paradigm case of doubling. I leave the question of after-image, mirror-image, and eidetic image to a further essay. Cf. Gerhard Hensel, *Das Optische bei Wordsworth* (Marburg, 1930), and above, pp. 165–68.

11. This means, unless the occasion is an actual revisiting of the scene as in "Tintern Abbey," that the mind is moved more by itself, by its own recollection, than by the original event. Even in "Tintern Abbey" the mind is really comparing two reactions and being moved toward a self-recognition, an omen of its progressive destiny.

12. A similar thing occurs in st. II of the Intimations Ode. The sudden rise in feelings of "Liberty and Power" as Wordsworth comes to the moon indicates also a dissolving of barriers between past and present, or a return of the childhood power to go out and participate in the life of things. "The moon is treated," says Cleanth Brooks, "as if she were the speaker himself in his childhood, seeing the visionary gleam as she looks round her with joy" (*Well Wrought Urn,* ch. 7). But the child's participation in the life of nature is, of course, unself-conscious: cf. st. III of the present poem: "I heard the woods and distant waters roar; / Or heard them not, as happy as a boy."

13. My comment, because of the complexity of the transitions, is only roughly correct. St. VI, for example, is a subtle counter-turn to st. V; so that, in a sense, there is no "stand." (The edition of 1807, by the way, has no stanza numberings.) "The ode was intended for such readers only as had been accustomed to watch the flux and reflux of their inmost nature, to venture at times into the twilight realms of consciousness, and to feel a deep interest in modes of inmost being" (Coleridge, *Biographia Literaria* ch. 22).

14. Coleridge, in his dialogue with the Intimations Ode, uses "joy" to mean the feeling that enables or accompanies a living, regenerative contact with nature (see the Dejection Ode).

15. The supposition that the first two stanzas are the "utterance" mentioned in st. III is strongly supported by Hirsch, *Wordsworth and Schelling,* pp. 150–51. Cf. Margoliouth, *Wordsworth and Coleridge,* p. 101.

16. *PW, 4,* 12. *Evening Voluntaries,* IX (composed 1817).

17. Grosart, *1,* 326. From Wordsworth's "Answer to the Letter of Mathetes" published in *The Friend* in 1809.

18. I use Protesilaus' phrase in Laodamia (st. VIII) to suggest an analogy.

19. Grosart, *1,* 349. From a letter of 1830 to the Rev. Dr. Wordsworth. Earlier proof that this is the sense of duty intended by Wordsworth may be

drawn from his first reasoned classification of his poems, in a letter to Coleridge in May 1809. The "Ode to Duty" is there classed among a group of poems "relating to the social and civic duties, chiefly interesting to the imagination through the understanding, and not to the understanding through the imagination, as the political sonnets" etc. (*Middle Years, 1,* 308–09).

20. There are three poems to the daisy in the 1807 collection. *The Simpliciad* objected to his giving the daisy a "function apostolical," but the last stanza of the opening poem of Vol. 1, "Child of the Year!" etc., is a good example of wantoning high style.

21. "Milton! thou should'st be living at this hour" (composed 1802, published 1807).

22. Grosart, *1,* 318.

23. Grosart, *1,* 326. Coleridge understood perfectly this conception of Duty, after hearing *The Prelude* recited: "Then (last strain) / Of Duty, chosen Laws controlling choice." (1807, "To William Wordsworth").

24. "It is the first mild day of March" (*Lyrical Ballads*).

25. Grosart, *1,* 326.

26. That there is a vagueness in Wordsworth's conception and imagery is argued by Brooks, *Well Wrought Urn,* ch. 7.

27. Preface (1802) to *Lyrical Ballads.*

28. Letter to Lady Beaumont, April 3, 1815 (Harper, *Wordsworth,* p. 528).

29. It did in fact add its light to nature. The conditional tense indicates a potentiality then exercised, but not consciously, and not in the form of an actual painting.

30. It is also tempting to bring in Burke's theory of the sublime ("And this huge Castle, standing here sublime . . .") since the contrast turns on feelings of beauty replaced by feelings of sublimity.

31. The first poem which Coleridge patterns on this structure of separation and vicarious participation is "This Lime-Tree Bower, My Prison," which stems from 1797 and so anticipates "Tintern Abbey." The most pathetic instance of it is his verse letter to Sara Hutchinson, later the Dejection Ode. See Griggs, *Collected Letters, 2,* 790–98.

32. Moreover, by the time of "Peele Castle," Wordsworth has finished *The Prelude* and faced the challenge of the past: "I said unto the life which I had lived / Where art thou? Hear I not a voice from thee / Which 'tis reproach to hear?" (*Prelude* XIV.377–79). His program now is to be haunted no longer by childhood and adolescence. There is no desire to be cut off from them (as in 1793) but also none to enter again that area of trial.

33. *PW, 4,* 265. See also the preceding poem "To the Daisy." Both poems, though composed in 1805, were not published till much later.

34. *Early Letters,* p. 460.

35. "Brook! whose society the Poet seeks" (1815).

36. *PW, 5,* 5–6.

37. A Blakean might object: "No: Blake is prior and of course more radical

—Nature is absolutely other than human, and to know this is to properly grow in Humanity."

38. Cf. E. D. Hirsch on "The Two April Mornings," *Wordsworth and Schelling*, pp. 84–88.

39. Quotations in this paragraph are in order of mention: Job 38:3; Nerval, *Aurélia;* Blake, marginalia to Wordsworth's *Poems;* Goethe, *Maximen und Reflexionen;* Coleridge, *Biographia Literaria,* ch. 10.

40. Wallace Stevens, "Notes toward a Supreme Fiction."

*The Excursion*

CRITICAL BIBLIOGRAPHY

There is no real body of criticism on *The Excursion.* The reviews it received, the opinions of a few poets, and some specialized studies constitute nearly all there is. A single full-length book by J. S. Lyon appeared in 1950 (*The Excursion: A Study,* New Haven, 1950). G. M. Harper's chapter on the poem is full of good though miscellaneous comment; he sees that it grew out of the failure of Wordsworth's revolutionary hopes, and that it urges us to "admit our failure . . . and retrieve our error by building on a broader basis" (*William Wordsworth,* London, 1929, p. 525). *Wordsworth's Anti-Climax* (Cambridge, Mass., 1935) by Willard Sperry, is the justest review of the various reasons offered for the poet's decline. Sperry has a thesis of his own, which is that the decline was a foredoomed matter since Wordsworth had made a theology out of a restricted body of experience which he could not transcend because of the very articles of his faith. Wordsworth's articles or "system" are said to be derived from Associationism (Sperry and Beatty agree in this), so that he could not genuinely write about anything but infancy and boyhood. Sooner or later these were bound to be exhausted, and the poet was left without energy or subject (Sperry, ch. 8, "The System"). Sperry does not see that Associationism, for Wordsworth, is not an exclusive explanation for the growth and operation of the mind. It is only one kind of evidence that the imagination can be "socialized." Wordsworth was committed not to Associationism but to humanizing an originally transcendent imagination. It is just not true that he foresaw himself as fulfilling the "psychological scriptures" of

Hartley and Alison, which included the prophecy that the imagina-
tion must pass away (Sperry, p. 139). Wordsworth wanted to have
the imagination pass into life, and what he foresaw was the pre-
cariousness of this task, both from the point of view of life and of
imagination. Moreover, as J. M. Murry has said, the Romantic
poets were all faced with making religion or system out of their
experience. He approaches the heart of Wordsworth's difficulty in
a chapter on "Keats and Wordsworth" (*Keats*, 1930; 4th ed. New
York, 1955). "What he [Wordsworth] was trying to do was partly
to communicate a profound spiritual experience, partly to expound
a religion based upon this experience; and this religion was in
process of identifying itself with Christianity" (Murry, p. 171).
That identification, in Wordsworth, proved to be at the expense of
the personal and prophetic element; for if it is mysticism, or at least
secular mysticism, to make a religion out of personal experience,
then the Christian theology Wordsworth adopted in later life was
opposed to mysticism. In Keats, where the identification with a
theology never occurred, the sheer burden of prophecy remained;
and only Blake went the way of the older mystics, who successfully
brought together the most discrepant personal and historical ex-
perience with literal scripture.

### NOTES

1. A convenient summary of early reactions is found in J. S. Lyon, *The
Excursion: A Study,* ch. 1 and appendix I.

2. "Milton" (1825), essay contributed to the *Edinburgh Review.*

3. All quotations are from the text of De Selincourt and Darbishire, *PW, 5.*

4. *Excursion* I.231–32.

5. Cf. *Excursion* IV.602, and Preface to the edition of 1815: "The Imagina-
tion is conscious of an indestructible dominion;—the Soul may fall away from
it, not being able to sustain its grandeur; but, if once felt and acknowledged,
by no act of any other faculty of the mind can it be relaxed, impaired, or
diminished." *PW,* 2, 441–42.

6. "Mr. Crashaw's Answer for Hope": "by thee [Hope] / Young Time is
taster to Eternity."

7. See in his "Life of Waller" the animadversions which conclude: "The
ideas of Christian Theology are too simple for eloquence, too sacred for fiction;
and too majestic for ornament; to recommend them by tropes and figures is
to magnify by a concave mirror the sidereal hemisphere."

8. *PW*, *5*, 4.

9. Sources or analogues in Lyon, *The Excursion*, pp. 28–42, but no critical discussion of them; a more synoptic review of the genre and its appeals in D. L. Durling, *Georgic Tradition* in *English Poetry* (New York, 1935).

10. Preface (1800) to *Lyrical Ballads*.

11. *The Prelude* retains, of course, features of the ambulatory poem and travelogue. Yet Wordsworth is always engaged on two journeys, being the mental as well as original traveler. This creates a depth of shifting perspectives, as his mind goes beyond its original insight, or sees new distances between present and past, or is tempted to "pregnant confusions." For the persistence of schemes drawn from the ambulatory poem, see also R. A. Foakes, *The Romantic Assertion* (New Haven, 1958), ch. 4, "The Unfinished Journey."

12. It was commonplace in eighteenth-century criticism to consider Virgil's *Georgics* as a tour de force, and to praise it and didactic poetry for ennobling, invigorating, elevating expressions. My quotation comes from Warton's "Reflections on Didactic Poetry" in *The Works of Virgil in Latin and English* (4 vols. London, 1753), *1*, 403–04.

13. See "The Idiot Boy," line 451, and *PW*, *1*, 316.

14. He traces the footprints (*vestigiae*) of man rather than of God—behind this deeply moving, archaeological quest is a long religious tradition to which Adam is made to refer in his lament: "In yonder nether World where shall I seek / His bright appearances, or footstep trace?" *Paradise Lost* XI.328–29.

15. *PW*, *5*, 401.

16. *PW*, *1*, 281 ("The Vale of Esthwaite," lines 494–97).

17. *Excursion* III.277–80, cf. *Faerie Queene* I.9.40.

18. *Faerie Queene* I.10.52–67; *Excursion* II.834 ff.

19. For the last three quotations, see *Paradise Regained* I.1–17.

20. It is sometimes forgotten that the Neoclassical poets, in their verse essays and verse epistles, and in didactic poetry in general, tried to achieve a "middle flight," not exactly in the sense in which Milton here uses the term, but still related. The somewhat elevated and abstract style of *The Excursion*, though Lyon calls it "nonconversational" (he gives a thorough classification of its elements in chapter 5 of his book) would actually have been the norm of what the eighteenth century considered as the middle or conversational mode: see e.g. Akenside, *The Pleasures of Imagination* (1744), "The Design." Akenside says he had two models: "that ancient and simple one of the first Grecian poets, as it is refined by Virgil in the Georgics, and the familiar epistolary way of Horace. This latter has several advantages. It admits of a greater variety of style; it more readily engages the generality of readers, as partaking more of the air of conversation . . . Add to this the example of the most perfect of modern poets who has so happily applied this manner for the noblest part of philosophy, that the public taste is in a great measure formed to it alone."

21. See his *Dante* (London, 1900), p. 107.

22. "A Poet's Epitaph" (1800).

23. *Excursion* IV.1263.

24. *Paradise Lost* XI.303 f.

25. *PW*, 5, 5.

26. Wallace Stevens, "The Rock."

27. As Shelley does when he talks in the "Hymn to Intellectual Beauty" of "Love, Hope, and Self-Esteem."

28. See, e.g., George Wither, *A Collection of Emblemes, Ancient and Moderne* (London, 1635), Bk. II, illustration 44, p. 106; Spenser, *Faerie Queene* I.10.14 (for the anchor only). The symbol is, in part, a development of Hebrews 6:19.

29. "Lines left on a seat in a Yew Tree . . ." The reply to this Romantic argument will come from another Romantic, Dostoevsky, who argues in *The Brothers Karamazov* that "man is too broad."

30. *PW*, 5, 402. Because another MS has "of pleasure and of power," De Selincourt calls the present reading "clearly a copyist's error." But is it?

31. *PW*, 5, 402.

32. *PW*, 5, 400.

33. Ibid.

34. Cf. *Paradise Lost* III.26 ff.

35. Coleridge, before Ruskin and the others mentioned here, had translated Schiller's complaint on the vanished gods and names: "But still the heart doth need a language, still / Doth the old instinct bring back the old names. . . ." (see his *Piccolomini*, 1799). Hazlitt quoted and praised *Excursion* IV on mythology in his *Examiner* review: *Complete Works*, ed. P. P. Howe (21 vols. London, 1903–05), *4*, 115.

36. "I do entreat you to go on with 'The Recluse,'" Coleridge writes to Wordsworth in the summer of 1799, "and I wish you would write a poem, in blank verse, addressed to those, who, in consequence of the complete failure of the French Revolution, have thrown up all hopes of the amelioration of mankind, and are sinking into an almost epicurean selfishness, disguising the same under the soft titles of domestic attachment and contempt for visionary *philosophes*." Griggs, *Collected Letters, 1*, 527.

37. Wordsworth's essays on epitaphs, two of which appeared in *The Friend* (1809–10), and the first of which was appended as a note to Book V of *The Excursion*, are closely related to what De Selincourt calls his second bout of constructive work on the poem (*PW*, 5, 371 f.).

38. "Prospectus of the Engraving of Chaucer's Canterbury Pilgrims" (written 1809). Keynes, *Complete Writings of W. Blake*, p. 590.

39. An echo of his revolt against Godwinism; see *Prelude* XI.223 ff.

40. There exists, Wordsworth had written in 1805 (*Prelude* X.969 f.), "One great Society alone on earth, / The noble Living and the noble Dead"; and in *The Convention of Cintra* (1809), which together with his work on epitaphs

led into Books V–VIII of *The Excursion,* he reaffirmed the thought: "There is a spiritual community binding together the living and the dead; the good, the brave, and the wise, of all ages. We would not be rejected from this community." Sperry, in *Wordsworth's Anti-Climax,* pp. 66–70, contrasts these extracts with the sentiment expressed in the "Letter to the Bishop of Landaff" (written 1793) that "Mr. Burke roused the indignation of all ranks of men when, by a refinement in cruelty superior to that which in the East yokes the living to the dead he strove to persuade us that we and our posterity to the end of time were riveted to a constitution by the indissoluble compact of—a dead parchment, and were bound to cherish a corpse at the bosom when reason might call aloud that it should be entombed." Sperry suggests, and he is surely right, that (1) at some time between 1793 and 1805 Wordsworth came to accept what Burke called strikingly "the great primeval contract of eternal society . . . connecting the visible and invisible world" (the term, *akedah,* is quite relevant here), and (2) that this is the radical change in political thinking Wordsworth underwent. Wordsworth, however, may equally well be drawing on and secularizing the Augustinian idea that there is a community of the living and the dead predestined for salvation and distinguished from the community of the living who are not all so predestined.

41. From "I hid my love when young." I take "prove" to have approximately the same meaning as in "Come live with me and be my love / And we will all the pleasures prove."

42. *The Marriage of Heaven and Hell* (1793), "Proverbs of Hell."

43. MS 18a, *PW, 5,* 286 f. and app. crit.

44. MS 18a, *PW, 5,* 286 and app. crit.

## Epilogue

### CRITICAL BIBLIOGRAPHY

Valuable comments on *The White Doe of Rylstone* are to be found in the critical edition of the poem by A. P. Comparetti, Cornell Studies in English 29 (Ithaca, New York, 1940); G. M. Harper, *William Wordsworth* (London, 1929), pp. 472–76; Jane Worthington, *Wordsworth's Reading of Roman Prose* (New Haven, 1946), pp. 69–71; Darbishire, *The Poet Wordsworth* (Oxford, Clarendon Press, 1950), pp. 154–58; Florence Marsh, *Wordsworth's Imagery* (New Haven, 1952), pp. 61–63; Donald Davie, *Purity of Diction in English Verse* (New York, 1953), pp. 114–21; John Jones, *The Egotistical Sublime* (London, 1954), pp. 144–57; Martin Price, "Imagination in *The White Doe of Rylstone," PQ, 33*

(1954), 189–99; J. F. Danby, *The Simple Wordsworth* (New York, 1961), pp. 130–45. Martin Price's understanding of the doe's "mode of being" anticipates the view of the present chapter: "The qualities of the Doe which make her mysterious and provocative in the first canto are given a largely natural explanation in the ensuing narrative. The result is not an explaining away but a deepening of the import of the Doe's influence. A natural explanation of the Doe is an occasion for greater wonder than the 'fancies wild' of the naive worshippers." It should be added that Wordsworth's aim, as in *Lyrical Ballads,* is to purify our imaginative responses by turning them from a cruder to a finer, or from a superstitious to a natural nutriment. It is as if the imagination (in Wordsworth's view) had to return to nature in order to achieve the spiritual. Harper notes that Wordsworth had never before accepted so fully the mechanism of Romance, and that the poem is, in that respect, a fresh departure, but he then connects it only with poetry already written. Both John Jones and Donald Davie signal a correlative feature of Wordsworth's new interest in Romance, his novel and vigorous use of emblems, but neither sees that the complexity surrounding their use is due to the poet's attempt to define the progress from a Catholic to a Protestant mode of imaginative participation. Owen Barfield's *Saving the Appearances* (London, 1957), Elizabeth Sewell's *The Orphic Voice* (New Haven, 1960), and Basil Willey's earlier but essential "On Wordsworth and the Locke Tradition" (*The Seventeenth Century Background,* London, 1934, ch. 12) are valuable in illumining the Romantic and modern concern with what Lovejoy calls "immediacy" but which is really a concern with participation. I am inclined to subordinate all the philosophical or topical concepts of vital, plastic, and animate Nature, which Beach examines in *The Concept of Nature in Nineteenth-Century English Poetry* (New York, 1936), to this question. They are attempts to save or refine older notions of a sympathetic cosmos (on the decay of cosmological thinking and the rise of subtler notions of "sympathy," see, inter alia, D. C. Allen, *The Harmonious Vision,* Baltimore, 1954; E. Wasserman, *The Subtler Language: Critical Readings of Neoclassic and Romantic Poems,* Baltimore, 1959; and R. Langbaum, *The Poetry of Experience,* London and

New York, 1957). Wordsworth's mysterious assertion in "The Recluse" that the individual mind, or even the *progressive* powers of the whole species, is fitted to the external world, while that is also fitted to the mind ("Theme . . . little heard of among men"), and his further statement that mind and world, by their blended might, produce something worthy to be called "creation," do not fully make sense unless we hold, with Barfield or Novalis, that "The world is changed with the Advent of Man."* While Wordsworth generally limits himself to the growth of the individual mind, his basic form is the Progress Poem, and his poetry does suggest, however mildly, the possibility of a providential (ecological?) change in human consciousness.

NOTES

1. Isabella Fenwick note, *PW, 3, 543.*
2. *Prelude* III.176–78.
3. She is, in addition, "consecrated" by Francis' prophecy before he leaves with the other Nortons (see end of Canto 2).
4. All quotations are from the text in *PW, 3, 281–340.*
5. See Coleridge's letter quoted in *PW, 3, 545.*
6. Letter to Wrangham, January 18, 1816: *PW, 3, 547.*
7. Francis, a man in conflict with himself, is not reducible to one position: Wordsworth's dramatic power reaches a certain intensity in his case. He is brought, by his conflict, to the pitch of prophecy, and his parting words to Emily contain not only a stoical but also an apocalyptic element: "The young horse must forsake his manger," etc. He foresees, in his "dream of night," a state in which the soul is supported only by the grace of God and by itself, in which all other "sympathies" are destroyed or cast out. The poem, I think, shows him to be morally as well as factually mistaken on this point: he underestimates the bond between nature and man, one that both disturbs the soul, whose sympathies are not allowed to detach themselves, and provides a genuine consolation. He is still perhaps too close to the older faith to understand the *spiritual* role of nature.
8. I cannot develop here what Owen Barfield has said about participation in *Saving the Appearances* (London, 1957). Though he underestimates Words-

* *Hymns to Night,* 1799. The eschatological hopes expressed by Novalis in these hymns are a mixture of humanistic and christological, as well as apocalyptic and millennial imaginings, and should be compared with "The Recluse" passage mentioned above, dating probably from 1798, and Blake's position in, e.g., *The Four Zoas* of 1797 and after.

worth (and Blake) in favor of Goethe, his ch. 19 on "Symptoms of Iconoclasm" is important for the understanding of Romanticism. It is also miraculously brief.

9. "Elegiac Stanzas Suggested by a Picture of Peele Castle." Cf. Wordsworth's dedicatory sts. with T. Warton's ode "Sent to Mr. Upton on His edition of the Faerie Queene."

10. Letter to Lady Beaumont, May 21, 1807, concerning the sonnet "With ships the sea . . ." (*Middle Years, 1,* 128–29).

11. There may be a direct polemical relationship between Shelley's dedication and Wordsworth's, but the younger poet's explicit comments on Wordsworth indicate rather his displeasure with *Peter Bell* and *its* prologue. At the beginning of 1808, when completing *The White Doe,* Wordsworth wrote to Sir George Beaumont that "Every great Poet is a Teacher: I wish either to be considered as a Teacher, or as nothing" (*Middle Years, 1,* 170).

12. "Elegiac Stanzas."

13. *Ecclesiastical Sonnets* (1822), Pt. III, 46.

14. See the suggestion of Charles Williams in *The English Poetic Mind* (Oxford, 1932), pp. 166–67.

15. J. M. Murry, *Keats* (4th ed. New York, 1955), p. 281; Coleridge, letter to Lady Beaumont, April 3, 1815 (Harper, *Wordsworth,* p. 528).

16. Journal for September 16, 1820: *PW, 3,* 484–85.

17. From an addendum to "The Ruined Cottage," *PW, 5,* 402. Cf. Barfield's remarks on "the liberation of images" in *Saving the Appearances,* p. 132 and passim.

18. Pt. III, 49: *PW, 3,* 403–04.

19. The quotations from Shelley and Crabb Robinson are found in two hard-hitting chapters (23–24) of Harper's *Wordsworth.*

20. *Religious Thought, 3,* 260.

21. *Prelude* X.437–63.

22. *Wordsworth's Anti-Climax* (Cambridge, Mass., 1935), p. 184.

23. *Prelude* V.33; cf. II Peter 3:10 and "Lycidas," lines 132–33. In the last of the *Ecclesiastical Sonnets,* the scriptural "there shall be no more sea" (Revelation) is quietly displaced by a reference to the "living waters."

24. Cf. Intimations Ode, st. xi.

25. D. H. Lawrence, *Apocalypse* (London, 1932).

26. *Peter Bell,* Prologue.

27. Edward Quillinan to Crabb Robinson, letter of October 14, 1849 (quoted in Harper, *Wordsworth,* p. 609): "You will find your old and faithful friend, the poet, pretty much as he was on your last visit. The same social cheerfulness—company cheerfulness—the same fixed despondency, uncorrected [an allusion to Bk. IV of *The Excursion,* 'Despondency Corrected']. I esteem him for both; I love him best for the latter."

28. *Prelude* (1805) XIII. 126.

29. This isolation is more the result of a spiritual judgment brought by Wordsworth against his age than an apparent fact. It is true that the *Poems* of 1807 received a more overtly hostile reception than *Lyrical Ballads;* the former, indeed, were comparatively well received (cf. Oswald Doughty, "The Reception of Wordsworth by His Contemporaries," *English Miscellany,* ed. M. Praz, *13,* Rome, 1962, 81–97). But his reputation grows into national fame, even if we discount the acknowledgments he receives from close friends like Coleridge and Lamb, and from the Leigh Hunt circle. Leigh Hunt writes in his *Feast of the Poets* (1814) that Wordsworth is "capable of being at the head of a new and great age of poetry; and in point of fact, I do not deny he is so already, as the greatest poet of the present." Wordsworth's notorious judgment of Keats's Hymn to Pan (*Endymion*) as "a pretty piece of paganism" shows either provincial bigotry or an acute and intransigent awareness of his own difference.

# General Index

The index attempts to respect the dialectical character of certain concepts by pairing them and in the arrangement of their subheads. Authorities and secondary sources are listed in the bibliographies and are not included in the index. The bibliographies and notes are only sparingly indexed in other respects. Works appear under the name of the author, but for the works of Wordsworth, see index p. 416.

# Index to Wordsworth's Poetry and Prose

The notes and bibliographies are only selectively indexed.